D1553657

THE CONTEST FOR THE LEGACY OF KIEVAN RUS'

JAROSLAW PELENSKI

EAST EUROPEAN MONOGRAPHS, BOULDER
DISTRIBUTED BY COLUMBIA UNIVERSITY PRESS, NEW YORK
1998

EAST EUROPEAN MONOGRAPHS, NO. CCCLXXVII

To
CHRISTINA
(as always)

Professor Jaroslaw Pelenski

TABLE OF CONTENTS

Permissions   vii

Abbreviations   ix

List of Maps   xiii

List of Illustrations   xv

Foreword   xix

Chapter 1: The Contest for the Kievan Inheritance in
            Russian-Ukrainian Relations: Origins and
            Early Ramifications   1

Chapter 2: The Contest for the Kievan Succession (1155-1175):
            The Religious-Ecclesiastical Dimension   21

Chapter 3: The Sack of Kiev in 1169: Its Significance
            for the Succession to Kievan Rus'   45

Chapter 4: The Origins of the Muscovite Ecclesiastical
            Claims to the Kievan Inheritance   61

Chapter 5: The Origins of the Official Muscovite Claims
            to the Kievan Inheritance   77

Chapter 6: The Sack of Kiev of 1482 in Contemporary
            Muscovite Chronicle Writing   103

Chapter 7: The Emergence of the Muscovite Claims
            to the Byzantine-Kievan "Imperial Inheritance"   117

Chapter 8: The Contest between Lithuania and the
            Golden Horde in the Fourteenth Century for
            Supremacy over Eastern Europe [Specifically
            for All the Lands of Rus']   131

Chapter 9: The Incorporation of the Ukrainian Lands of
            Kievan Rus' into Crown Poland (1569): Socio-
            Material Interest and Ideology (A Reexamination)   151

Chapter 10: Muscovite Imperial Claims to the Kazan Khanate
[Based on the Muscovite Theory of Succession
to the Lands of Kievan Rus'] 189

Chapter 11: The Ukrainian-Russian Debate over the Legacy
of Kievan Rus', 1840s-1860s 213

Appendix: State and Society in Muscovite Russia and the
Mongol-Turkic System in the Sixteenth Century 228

Maps 245

Illustrations 253

Note on Lists of Rulers and Hierarchs 297

Supplementary Select Bibliography 299

Index 311

About the Author 325

PERMISSIONS

The author wishes to thank the original publishers and editors of the studies listed below for permission to reprint them in this volume.

1. "The Contest for the 'Kievan Inheritance' in Russian-Ukrainian Relations: Origins and Early Ramifications," in Peter J. Potichnyj, Marc Raeff, Jaroslaw Pelenski, Gleb N. Žekulin, eds., *Ukraine and Russia in Their Historical Encounter* (Edmonton, Canadian Institute of Ukrainian Studies Press, University of Alberta, 1992), pp. 3-19.

2. "The Contest for the 'Kievan Succession' (1155-1175): The Religious-Ecclesiastical Dimension," *Harvard Ukrainian Studies*, 12-13 (1988-1989): 761-780.

3. "The Sack of Kiev of 1169: Its Significance for the Succession to Kievan Rus'," *Harvard Ukrainian Studies*, 11, no. 3/4 (1987): 303-316.

4. "The Origins of the Muscovite Ecclesiastical Claims to the 'Kievan Inheritance'," in Boris Gasparov and Olga Raevsky-Hughes, eds., *Christianity and the Eastern Slavs*, vol. 1: *Slavic Cultures in the Middle Ages, California Slavic Studies*, 16 (Berkeley, etc., University of California Press, 1993), pp. 102-115.

5. "The Origins of the Official Muscovite Claims to the 'Kievan Inheritance'," *Harvard Ukrainian Studies*, 1, no. 1 (1977): 29-52.

6. "The Sack of Kiev of 1482 in Contemporary Muscovite Chronicle Writing," *Harvard Ukrainian Studies*, 3/4, part 2 (1979-1980): 638-649.

7. "The Emergence of the Muscovite Claims to the Byzantine-Kievan 'Imperial Inheritance'," *Harvard Ukrainian Studies*, 7 (1983): 520-531.

8. "The Contest between Lithuania-Rus' and the Golden Horde in the Fourteenth Century for Supremacy over Eastern Europe," *Archivum Eurasiae Medii Aevi*, 2 (1982): 303-320.

vii

9. "The Incorporation of the Ukrainian Lands of Old Rus' into Crown Poland (1569): Socio-Material Interest and Ideology — A Reexamination," in Anna Cienciala, ed., *American Contributions to the Seventh International Congress of Slavists, Warsaw, August 21-27, 1973*, vol. 3: *History* (The Hague and Paris, Mouton, 1973), pp. 19-52.

10. "Muscovite Imperial Claims to the Kazan Khanate," *Slavic Review*, 26, no. 4 (1967): 559-576.

11. "State and Society in Muscovite Russia and the Mongol-Turkic System in the Sixteenth Century," *Forschungen zur osteuropäischen Geschichte*, 27 (1980): 156-167. Originally published in Abraham Ascher, Tibor Halasi-Kun, Bela K. Kiraly, eds., *The Mutual Effects of the Islamic and Judeo-Christian Worlds: The East European Pattern* (New York, Brooklyn College Press, 1979), pp. 93-109.

ABBREVIATIONS

AE	*Arkheograficheskii ezhegodnik za 1957 g.*
AI	*Akty istoricheskie, sobrannye i izdannye Arkheograficheskoiu Kommissieiu*
AIuZR	*Akty, otnosiashchiesia k istorii Iuzhnoi i Zapadnoi Rossii*
AIZ	*Arkheologicheskie izvestiia i zametki*
AMV	*Alma Mater Vilnensis*
AU	*Akta Unji Polski z Litwą, 1385-1791*, S. Kutrzeba, W. Semkowicz, eds. (Cracow, 1932)
AW	*Ateneum Wileńskie*
AZR	*Akty, otnosiashchiesia k istorii Zapadnoi Rossii*
ChOLDP	*Chteniia Obshchestva liubitelei drevnei pis'mennosti*
ChOIDR	*Chteniia v Obshchestve istorii i drevnostei rossiiskikh*
DD	*Diariusz Lubelskiego Sejmu Unii. Rok 1569*, A.T. Działyński, ed. (Poznań, 1856).
DK	*Dnevnik Liublinskago Seima 1569 goda, Soedinenie Velikago Kniazhestva Litovskago s Korolevstvom Pol'skim*, M.O. Koialovich, ed. (St. Petersburg, 1869).
DOP	*Dumbarton Oaks Papers*
GBL	Gosudarstvennaia biblioteka im. V.I. Lenina
FOG	*Forschungen zur osteuropäischen Geschichte*
HUS	*Harvard Ukrainian Studies*
IIAN	*Izvestiia Imperatorskoi Akademii nauk*

ix

IL	*Ioasafovskaia letopis'*, A.A. Zimin, ed. (Moscow, 1957).
IORIaS	*Izvestiia Otdeleniia russkogo iazyka i slovesnosti*
IZ	*Istoricheskie Zapiski*
JfGOE	*Jahrbücher für Geschichte Osteuropas*
LL	*L'vovskaia letopis'*
LVR	*Letopisets velikii russkii*
LZAK	*Letopis' zaniatii Arkheograficheskoi kommissii*
NChL	*Novgorodskaia chetvertaia letopis'*
NL	*Nikanorovskaia letopis'*
NPL	*Novgorodskaia pervaia letopis' starshego i mladshego izvodov*, M.N. Tikhomirov, ed. (Moscow and Leningrad, 1950).
OI	*Otechestvennaia istoriia*
PDRV	*Prodolzhenie Drevnei Rossiiskoi Vivliofiki*
PHW	*Przegląd Historyczno-Wojskowy*
PH	*Przegląd Historyczny*
PRSZG	*Pamiatniki russkoi stariny v zapadnykh guberniiakh*
PSRL	*Polnoe sobranie russkikh letopisei*
PVL	*Povest' vremennykh let*, D.S Likhachev, ed. (Moscow and Leningrad, 1950).
RB	*Russkaia beseda*
RIB	*Russkaia istoricheskaia biblioteka*

RL	*Radzivilovskaia letopis'*
RTPNW	*Rozprawy Wydziału III Towarzystwa Przyjaciół Nauk w Wilnie*
RWHFAU	*Rozprawy Wydziału Historyczno-Filozoficznego Akademii Umiejętności*
SEER	*Slavonic and East European Review*
SIRIO	*Sbornik Imperatorskogo russkogo istoricheskogo obshchestva*
SL	*Simeonovskaia letopis'*
SPL	*Sofiiskaia pervaia letopis'*
SSK	*Sobranie sochinenii N.I. Kostomarova* (St. Petersburg, 1903).
SSM	*Sobranie sochinenii M.A. Maksimovicha*, 3 vols. (Kiev, 1876-1880).
SR	*Slavic Review*
Transactions	*Transactions of the Connecticut Academy of Arts and Sciences*
TL	*Troitskaia letopis'. Rekonstruktsia teksta*, M.D. Priselkov, ed. (Moscow and Leningrad, 1950).
TODRL	*Trudy Otdela drevnerusskoi literatury*
VI	*Voprosy istorii*
VID	*Vspomagatel'nye istoricheskie discipliny*
VPL	*Vologodsko-Permskaia letopis'*
VV	*Vizantiiskii vremennik*
ZhMNP	*Zhurnal Ministerstva narodnogo prosveshcheniia*

LIST OF MAPS

Map 1   Kievan Rus'. 11th-12th centuries.

Map 2   Corelands of Kievan Rus'. 12th century.

Map 3   Rostov-Suzdal'-Vladimirian State. 12th-13th centuries.

Map 4   Galician-Volynian State. 12th-13th centuries.

Map 5   Lithuanian-Ruthenian State. End of the 14th century.

Map 6   Polish-Lithuanian Commonwealth. After 1569.

Map 7   Kazan Khanate. End of the 15th — mid-16th centuries.

LIST OF ILLUSTRATIONS

Plate 1   Silver coin of Prince Volodimer Sviatoslavich of Kiev (obv. & rev.). End of the 10th century. State Hermitage Museum, St. Petersburg.

Plate 2   Silver coin of Prince Volodimer Sviatoslavich of Kiev (obv.), c. 1000. State Hermitage Museum, St. Petersburg.

Plate 3   Silver coin of Prince Volodimer Sviatoslavich of Kiev (rev.). End of the 10th century. State Hermitage Museum, St. Petersburg.

Plate 4   Grand Princess Gertruda and her son Iaropolk Petr... venerating Apostle Peter. Miniature from the *Egbert Psalter* (*Codex Gertrudianus*), c. 1078-1086.

Plate 5   Prince Iaropolk Petr and his wife Kunigunda receiving from Christ the crown of life. Miniature from the *Egbert Psalter*, c. 1078-1086.

Plate 6   *Our Lady of Vladimir*. Icon. First half of the 12th century. Tretiakov Gallery, Moscow.

Plate 7   Andrei Bogoliubskii removing the icon of the Blessed Mother of God from Vyshhorod.... Miniature from the *Radziwiłł Chronicle* (*Radzivilovskaia letopis' RL*), end of the 15th century, entry 1155.

Plate 8   Vladimirians expressing their gratitude to the icon of Our Lady of Vladimir.... Miniature from the *RL*, entry 1164.

Plate 9   Capture of Prince Mstislav Iziaslavich's wife, his son, and his retinue...following the sack of Kiev in 1169. Miniature from the *RL*, entry 1169.

Plate 10   Mstislav Andreievich installing his uncle Gleb in Kiev.... Miniature from the *RL*, entry 1169.

Plate 11   Mstislav Andreievich installing his son Gleb in Kiev....
                Miniature from the *RL*, entry 1169.

Plate 12   Andrei Bogoliubskii installing Roman Rostislavich in
                Kiev.... Miniature from the *RL*, entry 1171.

Plate 13   Vsevolod Iur'evich, Iaropolk Rostislavich, and their
                retinues taken prisoner by the Rostislavichi....
                Miniature from the *RL*, entry 1173.

Plate 14   Retreat of Andrei Bogoliubskii's army, following the
                failed second major campaign against the Kievan land
                and the siege of Vyshhorod in 1173. Miniature from
                the *RL*, entry 1173.

Plate 15   Andrei Bogoliubskii's assassins breaking into the en-
                trance hall of his castle. Miniature from the *RL*, entry
                1175.

Plate 16   Assassination of Andrei Bogoliubskii in 1175. Minia-
                ture from the *RL*, entry 1175.

Plate 17   Assassins cutting off Andrei Bogoliubskii's arm....
                Miniature from the *RL*, entry 1175.

Plate 18   Andrei Bogoliubskii laid to rest.... Miniature from the
                RL, entry 1175.

Plate 19   Townspeople and servants of Andrei Bogoliubskii's
                court sacking the houses of his governor and adminis-
                trators, and killing them.... Miniature from the *RL*,
                entry 1175.

Plate 20   Feodul...the clergyman, the servants, and the
                Vladimirians transporting Andrei Bogoliubskii's body
                from Bogoliubovo to Vladimir. Miniature from the
                RL, entry 1175.

Plate 21   Grand Prince Vsevolod Iur'evich witnessing the miraculous appearance of the icon of the Blessed Mother of Vladimir.... Miniature from the *RL*, entry 1177.

Plate 22   Destruction of the city of Vladimir...by the great fire of 1185. Miniature from the *RL*, entry 1185.

Plate 23   Roman Mstyslavych of Halych entering Kiev.... Miniature from the *RL*, entry 1202.

Plate 24   Ingvar Iaroslavych installed in Kiev.... Miniature from the *RL*, entry 1202.

Plate 25   Sack of Kiev in 1203.... Miniature from the *RL*, entry 1203.

Plate 26   Kievans taken into captivity, following the sack of Kiev in 1203. Miniature from the *RL*, entry 1204.

Plate 27   Roman Mstyslavych of Halych advising Riurik Rostislavich.... Miniature from the *RL*, entry 1204.

Plate 28   Roman Mstyslavych of Halych punishing Riurik Rostislavich of Kiev.... Miniature from the *RL*, entry 1205.

Plate 29   Dionisii, *St. Petr* (the Metropolitan of Moscow). Icon (detail). Late 15th century (?). The Cathedral of the Dormition, Moscow.

Plate 30   Dionisii, *St. Aleksei* (the Metropolitan of Moscow). Icon (detail). Late 15th century. Tretiakov Gallery, Moscow.

Plate 31   *St. Iona* (The Metropolitan of Moscow). Sculptural relief on the wooden coffin panel (detail). 17th century. The Church of the Repository of the Robe, Moscow Kremlin.

Plate 32   *Constantine and Helena*. Fresco. 1547-1551. The
             Cathedral of the Annunciation, Moscow Kremlin.

Plate 33   *St. Volodimer and St. Olga*. Fresco. 1547-1551. The
             Cathedral of the Annunciation, Moscow Kremlin.

Plate 34   *Aleksandr Nevskii and Ivan Kalita*. Fresco. 1547-1551.
             The Cathedral of the Annunciation, Moscow Kremlin.

Plate 35   *King Władysław Jagiełło*. Sculptural relief on the
             tombstone (detail). After 1434. The Wawel Cathedral,
             Cracow.

Plate 36   Wit Stwosz, *King Kazimierz Jagiellończyk*. Sculptural
             relief on the tombstone (detail). 1492. The Wawel
             Cathedral, Cracow.

Plate 37   Santi Gacci, *King Zygmunt II August*. Sculptural relief
             on the tombstone (detail). 1574-1575. The Wawel
             Cathedral, Cracow.

Plate 38   The Polish Parliament (*Sejm*). Woodcut from: Jan
             Łaski, *Communes Regni Poloniae privilegium*
             (Cracow, 1506).

Plate 39   The Parliament (*Sejm*). Woodcut from: Jan Herburt,
             Statuta (Cracow, 1570).

Plate 40   *The Church Militant* (*Tserkov voinstvuiushchaia*) (the
             celebration of Russia's conquest of Kazan in 1552).
             Icon. Second half of the 16th century. Tretiakov
             Gallery, Moscow.

Plate 41   *Our Lady of Kazan*. Icon. Mid-17th century. Russian
             State Museum, St. Petersburg.

FOREWORD

Of the twelve studies that comprise this volume, all but one (that contained in the Appendix) pertain mainly to a single theme, namely the contest for the legacy of Kievan Rus'. They are arranged in topical-chronological order. Study one, which provides the general outline of the problem, should be regarded as an introduction to the volume; two and three deal with the Suzdalian-Vladimirian aspect of the contest for the Kievan legacy; four, five, six, and seven are devoted to the Muscovite claims to the Kievan legacy; eight is concerned with the Lithuanian and the Golden Horde's struggle for the legacy of Kiev and all of Rus'; nine analyzes Polish pretensions to Kievan Rus'; ten examines how the Muscovite claims to Kievan Rus' were applied to justify the conquest of the Kazan Khanate; and eleven, which serves as a conclusion to the volume, deals with the first modern Ukrainian-Russian scholarly debate about the legacy of Kievan Rus'. The study contained in the Appendix, which compares the Muscovite and Mongol-Tatar political and social systems, provides explanatory material for the topic in question.

The studies were written and published over a period of approximately twenty-five years; the first (that is, study ten) in 1967, the last (study four) in 1993. Study eleven (previously unpublished) was written in 1989-1991. All were conceived as preparatory material for a comprehensive work on the contest for the legacy of Kievan Rus' that the author ultimately hopes to write.

The contest for the legacy of Kievan Rus' (the core area of which approximately corresponds to the territory of present-day Ukraine) has involved highly controversial historical-cultural and political developments over a period of nine hundred years and is still a matter of contemporary relevance. However, not a single scholarly monograph has been devoted to the subject, and such discussions of it as appear in general histories of Russia and in monographs and articles on Russian and East European historical, cultural, and political developments have been distorted by an uncritical Russian-centered point of view, that exclusively identifies Russia with Kievan Rus'. This uncritical view has been unconditionally accepted not only by Russian scholarship, but also by most specialists of Russia in the Western scholarly community. The only exceptions to this general tendency are the publications of the Ukrainian Research Institute at Harvard University, the Canadian Institute of

Ukrainian Studies at the University of Alberta, some monographs series, the leading example being East European Monographs, and the writings of a few individual scholars.

The concept "Kievan Rus'" was not used literally in original Rus' sources. It has been applied by scholars to denote the period of Rus' history in the age of Kiev's preeminence. At that time, that is, from the early tenth century to 1240, Kievan Rus' was a major European multi-ethnic country with vast territories strategically located at the crossroads between East and West and North and South along the Dnieper River with an access to the Baltic Sea in the North and the Black Sea in the South (see Map 1). Members of her dynasty entered into marital bonds with members of the major dynasties of Europe, including Byzantium. She was also a center of commerce through which ran important trade routes, the famous "route from the Varangians to the Greeks" being one example. Her "golden domed" capital city Kiev — the cradle of East Slavic Christianity, which she accepted from Byzantium — was perceived as "the second Constantinople" and consequently assumed the status and became a symbolic image of the most sacred and venerable religious center of Rus'.

The aim of this volume is to show how various competitors throughout the centuries have attempted to claim succession to Kievan Rus'. It focuses on the origins of these claims, particularly those of Muscovy, who waged the most relentless struggle for the Kievan legacy, as attested both in Muscovite sources and in a Russian scholarly literature permeated with ideological preconceptions, artificially construed paradigms, and even outright falsifications. Because of her political, economic, and religious significance, Kievan Rus' became a target of numerous competitors — Chernihivia, Suzdalia-Vladimiria, Galicia-Volynia, the Golden Horde, Lithuania, Muscovy, and Poland — who succeeded for periods of time in ruling over her. Her legacy particularly became an object of contention among her descendants, first of Chernihivia, Suzdalia-Vladimiria, and Galicia-Volynia, subsequently of Muscovy and the Lithuanian-Ruthenian state, and eventually of the three East Slavic peoples, the Ukrainians, the Russians, and the Belorussians, with the latter conflict continuing to the present day. Initially, Muscovy adopted the policy of her predecessor Suzdalia-Vladimiria, which aimed at separation from and even ruination of Kievan Rus'. But after the mid-fifteenth century, she advanced all-embracing claims to prove her exclusive right to the Kievan Rus' legacy, and this effort, with some adjustments, was continued throughout Imperial Russia's history.

In the Soviet period, the treatment of the Kievan Rus' legacy underwent modification during the celebration of the Tercentenary of the Pereiaslav treaty concluded between Muscovite Russia and Cossack Ukraine in 1654. At that time, that is in the mid-1950s, equal rights to the Kievan Rus' legacy were recognized for the three East Slavic peoples, the Ukrainians, the Russians, and the Belorussians, and these rights were promulgated as official Party and state doctrine that remained binding until the breakup of the Soviet Union in 1991. At least it was theoretically binding; in practice the traditional attitude prevailed.

Most recently, the Russian and Ukrainian scholarly attitudes on the issue of the Kievan Rus' legacy have come to differ almost as much as they did between the 1840s and the 1930s. With the rise of neoslavophilism and state nationalism in contemporary Russia, most Russian scholars have reverted to the traditional, pre-revolutionary conception of Russia's exclusive right to claim the legacy of Kievan Rus'. Scholars in an independent Ukraine, on the other hand, have gone back to the Ukrainian national theory, which holds that Ukraine is the principal descendant from Kievan Rus' by way of Galicia-Volynia and the Hetman state, both of which were Ukrainian states. Belorussian historical scholarship, for its part, has also revived a national theory, according to which the Principality of Polotsk served as the cradle of the Belorussian people and their state and the Lithuanian-Ruthenian state was an important link in the development of the Belorussian historical and national consciousness, with both of these serving as transmitters of the Kievan Rus' cultural legacy.

In this author's judgment, the preponderance of existing evidence shows Ukraine to be the primary, senior, and most legitimate successor to the legacy of Kievan Rus'. This does not mean that Russia has no claim to the Kievan Rus' legacy whatsoever, or, for that matter, that Belarus has none. But the pretensions of the two latter claimants are secondary and can at best be characterized as those of junior cultural successors. If Kiev was the "mother of the Rus' cities," then Moscow was one of its "younger daughters." And accordingly, if one were to distribute objectively the legacy of Kievan Rus' among the three contending successors in approximate quantitative terms, the result would be: Ukraine — sixty-five to seventy-five percent; Russia — fifteen to twenty percent; and Belarus — ten to fifteen percent.

The articles reprinted in this volume are in general reproduced without change, the exceptions being correction of typographical misprints and minor factual errors, some improvement in the translations, and a few minimal revisions. Because they were originally written as separate and independent works and published as such over an extended period of time, some of them repeat material found in others and some contain minor fontological inconsistencies, which should be attributed to the evolution of the author's research.

The articles originally appeared in a variety of scholarly publications that applied different transliteration systems to the East Slavic languages that make use of the Cyrillic alphabet. In this volume the transliteration has been standardized throughout according to a modified Library of Congress system. The only exceptions to this rule are certain commonly used terms and geographic names for which the contemporary Anglicized forms and English transliterations are retained (Kiev, Moscow, Poland, Lithuania, for example). Standardization has also been applied to proper names, geographic locations, titles of sources, and abbreviations. Certain explanatory remarks have been added here and there in the text, usually in parentheses or square brackets.

Since there is no consistent and generally accepted system of citing the titles of the original Slavic sources, they are, for the purpose of simplification, italicized throughout this volume. This is true of the titles that appear in both published and unpublished original sources as well as of those titles used by scholars to designate originally untitled sources. Among the latter are titles using a country, city, or land (the *Kievan Chronicle*, the *Suzdalian-Vladimirian Chronicles*, the *Galician-Volynian Chronicle*, for example), an original location (the *Hypatian Codex*, which was found at the Hypatian Monastery, for example), an original owner (the *Nikon Chronicle*, owned by Patriarch Nikon, or the *Radziwiłł Chronicle*, owned by Prince Radziwiłł), an original editor or copyist (the *Laurentian Codex*, copied by the monk Laurentii, or the *L'vov Chronicle*, edited and published by N.A. L'vov), and so forth. The *Ipat'evskaia letopis'* and the *Lavrent'evskaia letopis'* are translated as the *Hypatian Codex* and the *Laurentian Codex* respectively, because each incorporates a number of chronicles and therefore should be regarded as a chronicle of chronicles.

In the original Slavic sources the names of the Kievan rulers Volodimer I Sviatoslavich and Volodimer Monomakh are spelled as Volodimer and Vladimer interchangeably, with Volodimer predominating. In this volume, the older form, Volodimer, is used throughout. For the purpose of parallelism with Galicia-Volynia, the Suzdal' and Vladimir grand principalities are given the name Suzdalia-Vladimiria wherever this is deemed necessary. However, the term "Vladimiria" should not be confused with the term "Ladimeria," which was derived from Volodymyr-Volyns'kyi to denote Volynia in the Middle Ages. With a few exceptions, the illustrations at the end are ordered according to the chronology of the articles in the volume. The same applies to the maps.

Since the writing of the studies that compose this volume, new literature on the topic under consideration has appeared, both in the West and in the former Soviet Union. The most important and immediately relevant of these works, including a few originally inadvertently overlooked publications, are listed in the Supplementary Select Bibliography.

The author wishes to thank his colleague, Professor Ellis W. Hawley (Department of History, University of Iowa), his former student, Professor Janusz Duzinkiewicz (Division of Social Sciences, Purdue University North Central), his cousin Martha Pelensky, cartographer Nina V. Hrekhova (Institute of History, National Academy of Sciences of Ukraine), Mary E. Strottman and Virginia A. Ockenfels (both of the Department of History office, University of Iowa), and, foremost, his wife Christina Pelenski, all of whom in many different ways helped to bring this volume to fruition. The author also wishes to express his gratitude to Professor Stephen Fischer-Galati for extending the hospitality of the East European Monographs series to this collection of studies, and for his patience.

Iowa City
September 1997

1

THE CONTEST FOR THE KIEVAN INHERITANCE IN RUSSIAN-UKRAINIAN RELATIONS: ORIGINS AND EARLY RAMIFICATIONS*

The contest for the inheritance of Kievan Rus' has represented one of the oldest bones of contention in the history of Russian-Ukrainian cultural and political relations. It began among the Eastern Slavs in the second half of the eleventh century and culminated in the famous controversy between the "Northerners" (*severiany*) and the "Southerners" (*iuzhany*), that is, between Russian and Ukrainian scholars in the nineteenth century.[1] This controversy over the question of who are the legitimate heirs to the Kievan legacy – the Russians or the Ukrainians, which has continued until the present day, has had a profound impact on the development of the cultural perception, historical awareness, modern national consciousness, and the national mythology of the intelligentsias and even common people of the two sides involved.

The three major theories or schools of historical interpretation formulated by modern scholarship about the Kievan inheritance are as follows:

1. The Russian national theory of monolineal and exclusive right to the legacy of Kievan Rus' developed already in the late eighteenth but basically in the nineteenth century in the works of such Russian historians of the national-imperial school as V.N. Tatishchev, M.N. Karamzin, S.M. Solov'ev, and V.O. Kliuchevskii. Resting largely on religious-ecclesiastical and historical-ideological claims and on political-juridical theories formulated in Muscovy between the 1330s and the late 1560s, this theory was founded on the transfer of the Kievan metropolitan see from Kiev, first to Vladimir on the Kliaz'ma

---

* For illustrations pertaining to this chapter, see Plates 1, 2, 3, 4, 5.

River and eventually to Moscow, on the uninterrupted dynastic continuity of the "Riurikides," and on the theory of succession (*translatio* of states) from Kievan Rus' through (Rostovia) through (Rostovia)-Suzdalia-Vladimiria and Muscovy to Russia.[2]

The notion that Muscovy and subsequently Russia have been the only legitimate heirs to Kievan Rus' has influenced the interpretations not only of Russian, but also of Western historiography. Views critical of Muscovite and Russian theories about the Kievan inheritance and of the canons of Russian nineteenth-century national historiography generally, even if expressed by such distinguished Russian scholars and intellectuals as A.N. Pypin, P.N. Miliukov, A.E. Presniakov, and M.K. Liubavskii, have been conveniently disregarded.

2. The Ukrainian national theory of monolineal and exclusive right to the legacy of Kievan Rus' advanced by Ukrainian national historiography between the 1840s and the end of the 1930s. It was summarized most clearly by Mykhailo Hrushevs'kyi in his *Istoriia Ukrainy-Rusy* (the *History of Ukraine-Rus'*) and in his seminal article on the "rational organization" of early East Slavic history.[3] This Ukrainian theory found its own line of continuity, from Kievan Rus' through Galicia-Volynia, Lithuania-Ruthenia and Little Russia – Cossack Ukraine to Ukraine, and utilized mainly territorial, ethno-demographic, social, and institutional arguments.

3. The official Soviet theory, which in ideological terms allotted equal rights to the Kievan inheritance of the three East Slavic peoples – that is, the Russians, the Ukrainians, and the Belorussians – but which in fact was much closer to the traditional Russian theory and its forceful advocacy of Russian national interests than it was to the Ukrainian. This Soviet theory also came coupled with a distinct preference for research on Kievan Rus' conducted in Russia proper and by Russian scholars primarily. Thus, the major studies of the Kievan Rus' history since World War II have been written by Russian scholars such as B.D. Grekov, B.A. Rybakov, M.N. Tikhomirov, M.K. Karger, and D.S. Likhachev. The last of these has been the first to deal specifically with the origins of the Muscovite preoccupation with the Kievan succession, again from an exclusively Russian perspective. It is significant that Soviet Kiev was not the principal center for the study of the history and culture of Kievan Rus'.

The Soviet theory was first articulated in the late 1930s, but was not elevated to the status of an official state doctrine until the Tercentenary of the Pereiaslav Treaty in 1954. Then it was enunciated in a document of extraordinary importance, entitled "The Theses Concerning the Tercentenary of the Reunification of Ukraine with Russia (1654-1954) Approved by the Central Committee of the Communist Party of the Soviet Union."[4] According to it, "the Russian, Ukrainian, and Belorussian peoples stem from one root which is the old Rus' nationality (*narodnost'*) that formed the old Rus' state – Kievan Rus'."[5] The formation of the three East Slavic peoples, or, in Soviet terminology, "nationalities" (*narodnosti*), took place, according to this theory, in the fourteenth and fifteenth centuries, when the Russian (or Great Russian) nationality played the most important role of guarding the Kievan tradition not only during that formative period, but also in the two succeeding centuries.

Although there have been serious differences of opinion among the proponents of each of the three schools of thought, with a few exceptions like M.S. Hrushevs'kyi and A.E. Presniakov, they all have shared several assumptions about the nature of the Kievan Rus' state. One of them has been that Kievan Rus' had been a well integrated polity based upon a unified old Rus' people or nationality of East Slavic ethnic origin inhabiting the "Rus' land," which allegedly nurtured an inherent proclivity for territorial, ethno-national, and political unity.[6] Nineteenth- and early-twentieth century Russian and Ukrainian historians, therefore, stressed the ethnic homogeneity, political unity, and cultural coherence of Kievan Rus', familiar concepts in all modern national ideologies. From this perspective, it was not difficult for them to go a step further and develop coherent and well-integrated continuity theories that linked their own later-day nationalities with ancient Kievan Rus'. To do so they had only to modernize and refine earlier versions and couch them in appropriate academic terminology.

This image of a unified, integrated, and even ethnically defined Kievan Rus', which has been handed down to us by several generations of scholars, however, reflects the ideological concerns of the authors and editors of the *Kievskaia letopis'* (the *Kievan Chronicle*), the *Russkaia pravda* (the *Rus' Law*), Metropolitan Ilarion's *Slovo o zakone i blagodati* (the *Sermon on Law and Grace*), and the *Zhitiia* (the *Vitae*) of the Kievan rulers more than it does the political, cultural, and ethnic realities of Rus'. Kievan Rus' was never really a unified polity. It was a loosely bound, ill-defined, and heterogeneous conglomeration of lands and cities inhabited by tribes and population groups whose loyalties were primarily territorial, *landespatriotisch*, and urban but not national in the modern sense of the term. They were ruled for a time by a dynasty which very soon dissolved into several rival subdynasties which fought each other more fiercely than they battled the much-maligned nomadic "heathens" of the East. Although the decline and dissolution of Kievan Rus' are usually attributed to "bad neighbors," internal factors played a larger part. Among them was the victory of patrimonial-territorial states and city-states over multiterritorial and heterogeneous empires or proto-imperial polities.

Kievan Rus' was a transitional polity which exhibited some of the characteristics of an empire, but it lacked a well-structured imperial framework. Comparing it to the Carolingian Empire or the Holy Roman Empire of the German Nation is, therefore, not quite justified, not only because of differences in ethnic and territorial composition, but also because Kievan Rus' lacked a hierarchy of dynasties and an administrative superstructure. The "Riurikide" dynasty and the ruling elite of Kiev and the Kievan land – the most developed patrimonial-territorial unit and for a time the senior principality within the broader multiterritorial conglomerate of Kievan Rus' – attempted to impose on their highly diverse polity the integrative concept of *russkaia zemlia* ("the Rus' land") and the unifying notion of a "Rus' people." In the long run they failed, however, for both concepts soon took on entirely different meanings. The concept "Rus'" did, however, refer to a relatively integrated cultural entity based on the Orthodox religion, a Slavicized Byzantine culture, and a transplanted *lingua franca* in the form of Church Slavonic. This cultural unity was elevated to an ideal which, in the realm of ideology, was applied to the political and ethnic spheres as well. The city of Kiev and the Kievan land were among the oldest and richest in that part of the world and Kiev had long been the actual or nominal capital of Rus'. This lent prestige to Kiev from the perspective of the new polities that were emerging from the amorphous superstructure known as Kievan Rus'. The new polities could emancipate themselves so easily not because an artificially invented old Rus' nationality had disintegrated into three new nationalities, but because the old cities and lands provided a foundation for transforming ethno-territorial groups into peoples or nationalities. For a variety of reasons their elites then laid claims to what they perceived as their rightful inheritance, and these claims ultimately assumed the status of national myths.

The first phase of the contest between the claimants of the Kievan inheritance, that is, the senior capital city of Kiev and Kievan Rus', lasted from the late eleventh to the late thirteenth century. Until the mid-1260s it was characterized by political and ideological succession struggles between the subdynasties that ruled the four patrimonial states of Chernihivia, Suzdalia-Vladimiria, Smolensk, and Galicia-Volynia. These struggles were followed by the transfer of the Kievan metropolitan see from Kiev, first to Vladimir (between 1250 and 1300) and subsequently to Moscow in 1326, and by the establishment in the first half of the fourteenth century of the Metropolitanate of Halych. This unprecedented division of the Metropolitanate of Kiev marked the beginning of the conflict between Suzdalia-Vladimiria and Galicia-Volynia over the Kievan ecclesiastical legacy.

Of the four contenders, the house of Chernihiv conducted the most protracted struggle, the beginning of which can be traced to the 1070s.[7] From that time until the Mongol invasion of the Rus' states in the 1230s-1240s, several princes of the Chernihivian dynasty managed intermittently to ascend the Kievan throne and to rule with varying degrees of success. Their aim, it appears, was to govern Rus' from Kiev using the practices and customs observed in their own patrimonial-territorial principality. Since the principality of Chernihiv declined after the Mongol invasion, its competition for Kiev had no lasting historical consequences. The Chernihivian dynasty did not die out until the beginning of the fifteenth century, and some of its rulers even retained the title of "Grand Prince" of Chernihiv. But the title no longer carried any real significance at that time, and no evidence suggests that the Chernihivian dynasty perpetuated its claims to be legitimate heirs to Kiev.[8]

Until the end of the 1160s, the contenders for the Kievan inheritance aimed at full control of Kiev and the adjoining land and at reestablishing the traditional relationship with other parts of Rus' that had existed in the reigns of Volodimer I, Iaroslav I, Volodimer II Monomakh, and Mstislav I Harold. Throughout that early period, the takeover of Kiev itself was regarded by the contenders as the primary goal, since Kiev was considered the most prestigious city and the proper capital from which to govern the Rus' polity.

This perception changed dramatically with the sack of Kiev in 1169 by an army acting on the orders of Prince Andrei Iur'evich Bogoliubskii of Suzdal'-Vladimir – the second contender for the Kievan inheritance. That unprecedented event was crucial in shifting the attitude of the Russian ruling elite in the emerging Suzdalian-Vladimirian principality from respect to hostility toward Kiev.[9] This dual approach to Kiev is particularly evident in the formative years (especially during the reigns of such rulers as Andrei Iur'evich Bogoliubskii [ruled 1157-75], Vsevolod III Iur'evich [1176-1212], and Aleksandr Iaroslavich Nevskii [1252-63]) of the Suzdalian-Vladimirian principality, when it was torn between the need to retain dynastic and historical ties with Kievan Rus', on the one hand, and the desire to diminish its status and enhance that of their own rising patrimonial-territorial Grand Principality of Suzdal'-Vladimir, on the other, as reflected both in practice and contemporary ideological writings.[10]

Vladimirian rulers claimed the Kievan inheritance through dynastic connections to the Kievan dynasty. This led them to refer to Kiev as their "patrimony and ancestral property" and to develop a set of ideological justifications to substantiate their "rights" to Kiev, based on the assumption that the Christianization of their land and the founding of the city of Vladimir had been accomplished by Prince Volodimer I. Using this assumption, parallels could then be drawn between Bogoliubskii and Volodimer I, who had been the senior prince of all Rus'. Andrei Bogoliubskii, who aspired to be a senior prince of all Rus', attempted to subordinate the other princes of old Rus' by referring to them as his vassals (*podruchniki*).

On the other hand, the Vladimirian rulers were responsible for two sacks of Kiev – directly for the sack of 1169 ("for three days they plundered the entire city of Kiev, as well as the churches and the monasteries. And they seized icons and books and vestments")[11] and indirectly for the sack of 1203. They also tried to reduce the status of Kiev as the capital and the religious center of Rus' in order to elevate Vladimir to the status of the principal city of that entity. Under Bogoliubskii an attempt was made to establish an independent metropolitanate in order to undermine Kiev's position as the ecclesiastical center of Rus', but it was not successful. In addition, an ideological program was developed to supersede Kiev and replace it by Vladimir. It included such undertakings as the building of new impressive churches, the development of the cult of the Icon of Our

Lady of Vladimir (an icon originally taken from the Kievan land), the celebration of the Feast of the Veneration of the Virgin Mary, as well as of a new Feast of the Savior, and the veneration of the newly discovered relics of Bishop Leontii of Rostov.[12]

Similar dual approach to Kiev is evident in the political program advanced by Aleksandr Nevskii, as reflected in contemporary chronicle writing and in the ideological statement made in his *Zhitie* (*Vita*). Nevskii was credited by some chroniclers with having succeeded in obtaining from the Mongols "Kiev and all the land of Rus'."[13] According to his *Vita*, written from a devotional point of view, he was linked dynastically with the saintly *srodniki* Boris and Gleb and Iaroslav I. These references may be later interpolations in the text. The crucial opening passage of the *Vita* states only that his dynastic lineage reached back to his father Iaroslav III Vsevolodovich and his grandfather Vsevolod III Iur'evich, both of Suzdal'-Vladimir. The same *Vita* refers to a eulogy allegedly delivered by Metropolitan Kirill at Nevskii's funeral in which the metropolitan proclaimed that upon Nevskii's death, "the sun had set in the Suzdalian land."[14] Curiously enough, the *Vita* emphasizes the Suzdalian-Vladimirian dynastic lineage of Aleksandr Nevskii and extols the image of the Suzdalian land, but refrains from mentioning Kiev and the Rus' land.

The Vladimirian claims to Kiev were, therefore, not formulated with the purpose of supporting a Kievan revival or in anticipation of its glorious future. On the contrary, Kiev was to be subordinated to the rising capital city of Vladimir. The Kievan inheritance would provide the Suzdalian-Vladimirian grand principality with a convenient tool for gaining hegemony over the lands of old Rus'. That attitude toward the Kievan inheritance has remained a Russian tradition, regardless of the changing nature of the Russian state or the capital city of the Russian Empire. In 1482, for example, when the Crimean Tatars sacked Kiev at the instigation of Grand Prince Ivan III, the latter committed blasphemy by accepting from Khan Mengli Girei a gift of the sacred vessels plundered from the St. Sophia Church. Significantly, this happened during a gap in the development of the governmental Muscovite theory of continuity from Kievan Rus' through (Rostovia)-Suzdalia-Vladimiria to Muscovy formulated between the mid-1450s and 1504.[15]

The last principal claimant to the Kievan inheritance was the patrimonial-territorial state of Galician-Volynian Rus'.[16] Its dynasty raised claims to the Kievan succession about half a century after the princes of the Grand Principality of Suzdal'-Vladimir. Originally the intentions of the Galician-Volynian dynasty were not even in direct conflict with those entertained by Suzdalia-Vladimiria, but they were more on a collision course with an older contender, the house of Chernihiv.

Similar in several respects to their northern competitors, rulers of Galicia-Volynia such as Roman Mstyslavych (1199-1205) and Danylo Romanovych (1237-1264) succeeded for brief periods in controlling Kiev and, by extension, southwestern Rus'. Their ultimate aim was to claim succession to all of Rus' in order to attain an exalted status for their principality among the lands of old Rus'. Like Andrei Bogoliubskii and Vsevolod III Iur'evich, Roman and Danylo were not interested either in ruling Kiev or in ruling from Kiev according to the old tradition. They preferred to exercise the power of investiture and install minor princes or later, in the case of Danylo, even a governor. Danylo's replacement of a vassal prince by a governor can be interpreted as an additional contributing factor to the decline of Kiev both in the political and judicial spheres.

The Galician-Volynian dynasty devised its own ideological program with regard to Kiev and the all-Rus' inheritance based on the law of investiture, on patrimonial ties with the Kievan dynasty, and on the special relationship to Kiev of certain religious objects. This program is set forth in the *Halyts'ko-Volyns'kyi litopys* (the *Galician-Volynian Chronicle*), the third major component of the *Ipat'evskaia letopis'* (the *Hypatian Codex*).[17] Of particular significance is the special "Introduction" to the *Hypatian Codex*, which explicates the exclusive historical and dynastic rights of the Galician-Volynian house to the Kievan succession:

> These are the names of Kievan princes who ruled in Kiev until the conquest of Batu who was in [the state of] paganism: The first to rule in Kiev were co-princes Dir and Askold. After [them followed] Oleg. And following Oleg [came] Igor'. And following Igor' [came] Sviatoslav. And after Sviatoslav [came] Iaropolk. And following Iaropolk [came] Volodimer, who ruled in Kiev and who enlightened the Rus' land with holy baptism. And following Volodimer, Sviatopolk began to rule. And after Sviatopolk [came] Iaroslav. And following Iaroslav [came] Iziaslav. And Iziaslav [was succeeded] by Sviatopolk. And following Sviatopolk [came] Vsevolod. And

after him [followed] Volodimer Monomakh. And following him [came] Mstislav. And after Mstislav [followed] Iaropolk. And following Iaropolk [came] Vsevolod. And after him [followed] Iziaslav. And following Iziaslav [came] Rostislav. And he [was followed] by Mstislav. And following him [came] Gleb. And he [was followed] by Volodimer. And following him [came] Roman. And after Roman [followed] Sviatoslav. And following him [came] Riurik. And after Riurik [followed] Roman. And after Roman [came] Mstislav. And after him [followed] Iaroslav. And following Iaroslav [came] Volodimer Riurikovich. Danylo installed him in his own place in Kiev. Following Volodimer, [when Kiev was governed by] Danylo's governor Dmytro, Batu conquered Kiev.[18]

This "Introduction" was composed either just after the conquest of Kiev by Batu in 1240, or after Danylo had made his final attempt to reclaim Kiev from the Tatars in the mid-1250s, or just following Danylo's death in 1264. The line of Kievan rulers it provided from its origins to Danylo and his governor Dmytro was intended not only to demonstrate an uninterrupted dynastic line from the Kievan to the Galician-Volynian rulers, but also to show that at the beginning of the thirteenth century the center of power was transferred to southwestern Rus'.[19] According to it, the last legitimate overlord in Kiev before the Mongol-Tatar invasion was none other than Danylo, who invested the last nominal ruler, a vassal prince and ultimately a governor. Therefore, any attempt to lay claim to the Kievan succession on the part of other Rus' rulers, including the Suzdalian-Vladimirian line, which for a brief time between the early 1240s and the early 1260s succeeded with the help of Mongol-Tatars in obtaining the title of Kiev,[20] was illegitimate and invalid. This "Introduction" to the *Hypatian Codex* reflects the contents of many parts of this work, especially its component, the *Galician-Volynian Chronicle*, and provides evidence that both the *Codex* and the *Chronicle* were compiled to justify, among other things, Galician-Volynian claims to the Kievan inheritance.

The ideological programs of the two dynasties differed in several respects. The compilers of the *Galician-Volynian Chronicle*, in contrast to their Suzdalian-Vladimirian counterparts, did not attempt to diminish the image of Kiev in favor of any one of their principal cities (Halych, for example), nor did the Galician-Volynian rulers engage in a sack or plundering of that ancient city. The compilers of the *Galician-Volynian Chronicle* treated Halych as an important center of Galicia-Volynia, but they did not try to substitute Halych for Kiev. Nothing in the *Galician-Volynian Chronicle* suggests that it advocated any idea of Halych as a "second Kiev."[21] Steps were taken to attribute religious significance to the founding and rebuilding of towns such as Kholm and Volodymyr-Volyns'kyi, but never with the aim of undermining the status of Kiev. They were simply meant to show that the Galician and Volynian lands also had towns worthy of note. An attempt was even made to link those cities with Kiev, as attested, for example, in the account of the rebuilding of Kholm following Batu's invasion. When the Church of St. John was erected, it was said that Danylo brought icons and a bell from Kiev and donated them to the new church.[22]

Although the two territorial states observed many of the same religious conventions, including a providential interpretation of history, religion played a much greater role in the Suzdalian-Vladimirian ideological program than it did in the Galician-Volynian counterpart. Religious practices such as the veneration of icons, celebration of religious feasts, and adoration of relics of saints constituted an important part of the Suzdalian-Vladimirian ideological program. The Galician-Volynian elite was more pragmatic, as evidenced by data in the *Kievan Chronicle* pertaining to Galicia-Volynia and in the *Galician-Volynian Chronicle* itself. It did not involve itself in developing a system of religious ideological justifications, and its outlook remained more worldly.

Comparable differences can be seen in the relationship between secular power and ecclesiastical authority in the two states. Almost from the beginning, Vladimirian rulers aggressively interfered in the affairs of the church, first by attempting to organize an anti-Kievan metropolitanate, somewhat later by endeavoring to dominate the Kievan metropolitanate and, finally – just like the later Muscovite rulers – by making every possible effort to regain exclusive control over the Kievan metropolitan see, which was eventually moved to the north. Such a transfer was accomplished easily, because the Metropolitan See of Kiev and all of Rus' was still an ecclesiastical province of the Byzantine patriarchate.

The Galician and Volynian rulers also had their conflicts with ecclesiastical authorities, especially after two of their appointees to the metropolitanate, Kirill and Petr, proved to be "turncoats." Those two metropolitans did not hesitate to accommodate themselves to the political and ecclesiastical designs of the Vladimirian and Muscovite rulers, the Golden Horde, the Patriarchate of Constantinople, and the Byzantine Empire, all of whom were interested in maintaining the unity of the Kievan metropolitan see and its center, first in Vladimir and later in Moscow.[23]

When this new ecclesiastical arrangement proved intolerable, because the metropolitans of Kiev had become tools of the rising Muscovite rulers and the religious needs of southwestern Rus' were completely neglected, the Galician-Volynian rulers simply curtailed their contacts with the Vladimir- and Moscow-based Kievan metropolitanate and negotiated with the Byzantine patriarchate for the establishment of a separate Halych Metropolitanate of "Little Rus'."[24] In contrast to their Vladimirian and Muscovite counterparts, who clung tenaciously to the administrative link with the Kievan church, the Galician-Volynian ruling elite was more inclined to seek pragmatic solutions to religious and ecclesiastical problems and to abandon its ecclesiastical administrative claims to Kiev.

As far as secular claims were concerned, the Galician-Volynian dynasty and elite retained their claims to the Kievan inheritance through historical and legal arguments. In them, the interchangeable use of the concepts *Rus'*, *russkaia zemlia*, and *vsia zemlia russkaia* played a significant role. The term "Rus'" and its variants, "the Rus' land" and "all the land of Rus'," lost their original ambiguity and acquired geographically and politically more clearly defined meanings that pertained from about the mid-twelfth century to the Kievan and Pereiaslav lands and subsequently to southwestern Rus' in general.[25] In the thirteenth century and throughout the first half of the fourteenth, these terms referred to the Kievan, Galician, and Volynian lands, and at approximately the same time they began to converge geographically with the emerging concept *Ukraina* ("Ukraine"), which appeared for the first time in the *Hypatian Codex* under the year 1187.[26]

The concepts *Rus'*, *russkaia zemlia*, and *vsia zemlia russkaia* were also used to denote Suzdalia-Vladimiria, though less frequently than they were applied to Galicia-Volynia. In fact, the preponderance of available evidence suggests that over extended periods the use of these terms began to decline in the northeastern regions in favor of other terms. For example, during the reigns of Andrei Bogoliubskii, Vsevolod III Iur'evich, and Aleksandr Nevskii, the terms "Suzdalian land" and "Vladimir" were more commonly used, whereas following the death of Aleksandr Nevskii and until approximately the mid-fifteenth century, the concepts "Suzdalian land," "Grand Principality of Vladimir," and eventually "Moscow" were employed to denote the territories of northeastern Rus'. The traditional terms *Rus'*, *russkaia zemlia*, and *vsia zemlia russkaia* were revived and applied to Russia proper beginning in the second third of the fifteenth century, but by then they acquired still different connotations.

The Galician-Volynian dynasty and elite, on the other hand, continued to advance claims to "Rus'," "the Rus' land," and "all the land of Rus' " and to adamantly restate their historical and dynastic pretensions to those entities until the very end of the state's existence. Beginning with the reign of Iurii L'vovych (1301-1308) and during the co-reign of his sons Andrii and Lev (c. 1309 - c. 1321-22), and subsequently of Iurii II Boleslav (1324-1340), the application of these concepts and claims to the inheritance in question were recorded in documentary sources, in titles on charters, and even affixed on a seal. The seal used by King Iurii and his successors, for example, portrayed the king *in maiestatis*, crowned and seated on a throne with a scepter in his hand. The inscription in Latin surrounding the central image read: *s(igillu) domini georgi regis rusie*. The reverse side of the seal, which depicted a mounted warrior with a shield in his hand, contained the inscription in Latin: *s. domini georgi ducis ladimerie*.[27]

The use of Latin in these inscriptions and in documents is indicative both of the Westernization of the conduct of business in the ruler's chancery and of the evolution the political thought had taken in Galicia-Volynia. It had already manifested itself in the Galician-Volynian state under Danylo, the first native king of Galicia,[28] whose (and later King Iurii's) royalist conception of rule is unique in the history of the East Slavic world. Iurii's sons Andrii and Lev continued in traditional fashion to claim Rus' in their titles, as attested in their charters: *Dei gracia duces totius terrae Russiae, Galiciae et Ladimeriae*, and *dux ladomiriensis et dominus terrae Russiae*.[29] The same can be said about Iurii II Boleslav, who in 1327 referred to himself as *Dux Terre Russie, Galicie et Ladimere*[30] and who, apparently under Byzantine influence, applied the name of Rus' exclusively to Little Rus' in the Charter of 1335, where for the first time he styled himself *dux totius Russiae Minoris*.[31]

This brief analysis of the early history of the contest to claim the legacy of Kievan Rus' can yield some conclusions concerning its origins and its early ramifications. The role of the Kievan inheritance in Russian-Ukrainian relations defies convenient generalization. The complexity of the problem is compounded by its elusive quality, by its involvement in the socio-cultural conditioning of the two peoples' intelligentsias and other segments of their population, and by its absorption into the scholarly paradigms of linguists, ethnographers, and historians of various backgrounds and methodological approaches. Under such circumstances, historians, instead of asking popular "new" questions, might do well to reopen old ones and offer some "unpopular" tentative answers.

The contest for the Kievan inheritance is neither an invention of the contending Russian and Ukrainian national historiographic schools, nor does it fall into the category of traditional territorial disputes, although certain parallels can be drawn with other historical, religious, and national controversies from the Middle Ages to the present day. The notion that national legitimacy rests in tracing one's heritage back to Kievan roots is deeply imbedded in the historical consciousness of Ukrainians and Russians alike, though originally it had no nationalistic implications in the modern sense. For this reason, projecting contemporary national concerns into the history of Kievan Rus' or speaking of a conflict between "nationalities" in the early medieval period, followed by assumptions about the existence of a unified Rus' state, is erroneous and misleading.

There should be no misunderstanding about the realities of the period under consideration. Both hard and circumstantial evidence suggests that little unity or harmony existed in the Kievan Rus' polity and that the desire of its component parts to go their separate ways manifested itself early in its history and prevailed before the Mongol invasion. Following the reign of Iaroslav I the Wise, the dynasties, the lands, the cities, and the people of Kievan Rus' apparently had no real feeling of unity or need for East Slavic "togetherness." Some of them interacted with the nomads of the southern steppes, some with the Poles and the Hungarians, others with the Meria and the Ugro-Finnic tribes. Early in its history, Kievan Rus' displayed all the features of a multicivilizational and proto-imperial polity. Two of its territorial entities, Suzdalia-Vladimiria and Galicia-Volynia followed separate roads of state-building to form two clearly defined and independent monarchical states. These two states shared a common religious and cultural heritage and even found themselves confronted with some similar socio-political domestic problems, such as the conflict between monarchical power and strong *boiar* groups aspiring to greater political influence, and their elites continued to maintain contact.

However, the two states differed in their relationships with other powers, entered into alliances with different partners, belonged to different civilizational and commercial communities, and were in more intimate contact with neighboring states and societies than with each other. Furthermore, the evolution of their two political systems and their general ideological outlook diverged markedly, and the two states were founded on dissimilar ethnically mixed strata which, in fact, contributed to the definitive internal consolidation of the two separate peoples.

The two states displayed contrasting attitudes in their political responses to Mongol-Tatar supremacy in the *ulus* Rus'. The Suzdalian-Vladimirian rulers were ready to cooperate with the Mongols and to serve in the Horde's administration of Rus'. The southwestern rulers, such as Danylo of Galicia-Volynia and Mikhail of Chernihiv, actively opposed the Mongol domination of their states.[32] When Danylo's anti-Mongol policies suffered defeat, his successors managed to contain Tatar influences, and as a result their lands apparently were not integrated as effectively into the Horde's tax collection system as those of northeastern Rus'. For obvious reasons, the *Rostovian-Suzdalian-Vladimirian Chronicles* (also referred to as the *Suzdalian-Vladimirian Chronicles [Vladimiro-Suzdal'skaia letopis'; Suzdal'skaia letopis'; Vladimiro-Rostovskie letopisi]*) are rather circumspect in their treatment of Mongol-Tatar rule and the active cooperation of the Suzdalian-Vladimirian dynasty with the Golden Horde.

Similarly, opposite approaches were taken by the two states with respect to participation in the anti-Mongol coalition and the related issue of the union of churches, both sponsored by Pope Innocent IV. Danylo of Galicia-Volynia, like Mindaugas of Lithuania, was inclined to join the anti-Mongol coalition and, although he did not actually accept the union, he was involved in negotiations. As a result, both rulers were rewarded, in 1253 and 1251 respectively, by Pope Innocent IV with royal crowns for their support of his initiatives. Aleksandr Nevskii was evidently not interested in joining an anti-Mongol coalition, just as he firmly rejected papal overtures concerning the unification of churches.[33]

When Suzdalia-Vladimiria and Galicia-Volynia departed on their separate courses, they joined two different civilizational communities. Suzdalia-Vladimiria became part of a northeastern community of Russians, surrounded by other Eastern Slavs in the southwest, west, and northwest, Ugro-Finnic tribes in the northeast, and Volga Bulgars in the east. Its rulers were chiefly interested in controlling Novgorodian commerce and the Volga trade route. Following the conquest of the Rus' state by the Mongol-Tatars and their takeover of the Volga commerce, Suzdalia-Vladimiria became their junior partner in the Volga trade. Their geographic location made the Suzdalians and Vladimirians natural partners, first of the Volga Bulgars, and later of the Mongol-Tatars. Thus, their state was incorporated into the imperial structure of the Golden Horde and became part of a new civilizational entity along the banks of the Volga River.

Galicia-Volynia, on the other hand, constituted an integral part of the East Central European civilizational community that included Polish territorial states, Hungary, Bohemia, and even Austria, and belonged to the southern commercial complex which embraced those countries. The borders of this complex were defined by the Dnieper River in the northeast and the Danube in the southwest with access to the Black Sea in the southeast. The famous "route from the Varangians to the Greeks" had ceased to function effectively before the Mongol invasion of Rus' not only because salt routes had been cut off by the nomads, but also, and primarily, because the commercial interest of the territorial states found new avenues and better opportunities outside the old framework.

Just as distinct were the differences in the development of their monarchical models, although at the outset they shared common conceptions of rulership ("prince") and utilized analogous (nominal reverential) titles ("grand prince" and even "tsar"). In Suzdalia-Vladimiria the conception of rulership emphasized the senior grand princely position enjoyed by the rulers of that state, and its authors even made use of the Byzantine author Agapetus to buttress the exalted status of the ruler.[34] That status was based on a combination of East Slavic, Byzantine, and later Mongol-Tatar models. Unlike its northeastern counterpart, Galicia-Volynia derived its notion of rulership from the East Slavic concept of "prince" and the European royal tradition in its Hungarian and Polish manifestations.

Although the two monarchical systems were based on the theory of the divine right of rulers and both elites shared an Orthodox providential world-view, certain ideological differences were obvious already in the formative stages of their development. In the official ideology of the Grand Principality of Suzdal'-Vladimir, for example, the Orthodox religious component played a greater role than it did in Galicia-Volynia which was relatively tolerant of other peoples, even those belonging to the Catholic fold. They displayed an open-minded approach toward the vexing issue of the union of churches under papal auspices.[35] The only villains, according to the Galician-Volynian ideology, were the "heathens," that is, the various nomadic peoples of the steppe who lived in a symbiotic relationship with the people of the Rus' lands. But even this attitude was not rigid, for it was no coincidence that some nomadic folklore (the moving legend of the *ievshan zillia*, for example) found its way into the *Galician-Volynian Chronicle*.[36]

Developments on the territories of Rus' ultimately led to the formation of two separate nationalities, that is, the Suzdalian-Vladimirian Russians and the Ruthenians of the central (the Kievan coreland) and western (Galicia-Volynia) Rus' territories, or, in other words, the proto-Russians and the proto-Ukrainians. Many factors were instrumental in transforming a population into a relatively integrated people in medieval times: territorial integration and continuity, consolidation of a territorial monarchical state, conduct of dynastic politics, participation in a civilizational community, development of a common religious culture and of secular attitudes, social changes and economic interests, intermingling of elites and population groups. The histories of the Suzdalian-Vladimirian and Galician-Volynian states provide good examples of the formative processes of the two medieval territorial states and of two peoples.

Which of them was more justified in claiming the Kievan inheritance? The answer depends on the significance one wants to attribute to normative value and on the weight one wants to ascribe to the various pieces of available evidence. If one were to answer it on the basis of religious evidence exclusively, or on a combination of that and some aspects of dynastic politics, the Grand Principality of Suzdal'-Vladimir would have to be credited with having a serious claim. If, on the other hand, all the other factors, such as territorial continuity, ethnic identity, common social and institutional traditions, dynastic politics and religious or cultural evidence are added in, the

Galician-Volynian competitor emerges as the more legitimate successor. Since it was precisely this contest for the Kievan inheritance that significantly contributed to the splitting off of the Russian and Ukrainian peoples and to their consolidation as two separate entities to begin with, the debate over the Kievan succession that has followed since the nineteenth century can itself be regarded as a further step in the protracted process of nation-building.

NOTES

1. For an introduction to this controversy, see A.N. Pypin, *Istoriia russkoi etnografii*, vol. 3, Etnografiia malorusskaia (St. Petersburg, 1891): 301-38. A Soviet-Ukrainian perspective is to be found in N.K. Gudzii, "Literatura Kievskoi Rusi v istorii bratskikh literatur," *Literatura Kievskoi Rusi i ukrainsko-russkoe literaturnoe edinenie XVII-XVIII vekov* (Kiev, 1989), 13-43. [Also see Chapter 11 of this volume, "The Ukrainian-Russian Debate over the Legacy of Kievan Rus', 1840s-1860s."]

2. On the origins of this theory and the literature on the subject. consult J. Pelenski, "The Origins of the Official Muscovite Claims to the 'Kievan Inheritance'," *Harvard Ukrainian Studies* (hereafter *HUS*) 1, no. 1 (1977): 29-52 [see Chapter 5 of this volume]; *idem.*, "The Emergence of the Muscovite Claims to the Byzantine-Kievan 'Imperial Inheritance'," *HUS*, 7 (1983): 520-531 [see Chapter 7 of this volume]; *idem.*, "The Sack of Kiev of 1482 in Contemporary Muscovite Chronicle Writing," *HUS*, 3-4 (1979-80): 638-649 [see Chapter 6 of this volume]; *idem.*, "The Origins of the Muscovite Ecclesiastical Claims to the Kievan Inheritance," published in *Le origini e lo sviluppo della Cristianità Slavo-Bizantina, Nuovi studi storici*, vol. 17 (S.W. Świerkosz-Lenart, ed.) (Rome, 1992): 213-226 [for a revised version, see Chapter 4 of this volume].

3. M. Hrushevs'kyi, *Istoriia Ukrainy-Rusy*, 10 vols. (3rd rep. ed., New York, 1954-58); *idem.*, "The Traditional Scheme of Russian History and the Problem of a Rational Organization of the History of Eastern Slavs 1909," in *Annals of the Ukrainian Academy of Arts and Sciences in the U.S.*, 2 (1952): 355-364.

4. *Tezy pro 300-richchia vozziednannia Ukrainy z Rosiieiu (1654-1954 rr.) skhvaleni Tsentral'nym Komitetom Komunistychnoi Partii Radians'koho Soiuzu* (Kiev, 1954).

5. *Ibid.*, 16.

6. For an antithetical view, see the study by O. Pritsak, "Origins of Rus'," *Russian Review*, 36, no. 3 (July 1977): 249-274, as well as his *The Origin of Rus'*, vol. 1 (Old Scandinavian Sources other than Sagas), (Cambridge, MA, 1981).

7. The history of the Chernihivian land and dynasty has been treated by P.V. Golubovskii, *Istoriia severskoi zemli do poloviny XIV stoletiia* (Kiev, 1881); D. Bagalei, *Istoriia severskoi zemli do poloviny XIV stoletiia* (Kiev, 1882); R.V. Zotov, "O Chernigovskikh kniaziakh po Liubetskomu sinodiku i o Chernigovskom kniazhestve v Tatarskoe vremia," *Letopis' zaniatii Arkheograficheskoi Kommissii 1882-84 gg.*, vypusk 9 (St. Petersburg, 1893), 1-327, 1-47; "Chernigovskie kniazia," *Russkii biograficheskii slovar'* (St. Petersburg, 1905), 22: 231-267; Hrushevs'kyi, *Istoriia Ukrainy-Rusy*, 2: 312-338; O. Andriiashev, "Narys istorii kolonizatsii

Siverskoi zemli do pochatku XVI viku" *Zapysky istorychno-filolohichnoho viddilu Vseukrains'koi Akademii Nauk u Kyivi*, kn. 20 (1928), 95-128; V.V. Mavrodin, "Chernigovskoe kniazhestvo," *Ocherki istorii SSSR (Period feodalizma IX-XV vv. v dvukh chastiakh)*, part 1 (Moscow, 1953), 393-400; A.K. Zaitsev, "Chernigovskoe kniazhestvo," in L.G. Beskrovnyi, ed., *Drevnerusskie kniazhestva X-XIII vv.* (Moscow, 1975), 57-117; M. Dimnik, *Mikhail, Prince of Chernigov and Grand Prince of Kiev 1224-1246* (Toronto, 1981); B.A. Rybakov, *Kievskaia Rus' i russkie kniazhestva XII-XIII vv.* (Moscow, 1982), 498-508.

8. Hrushevs'kyi, *Istoriia Ukrainy-Rusy*, 3: 175-181. The last document of ideological importance bearing on the activities of the house of Chernihiv was the *Vita* of Mikhail of Chernihiv. A.N. Nasonov advanced a plausible hypothesis that the execution of Mikhail by the Mongols in the Horde was the ultimate act in the struggle between the houses of Chernihiv and Vladimir for seniority in the lands of Rus' (*Mongoly i Rus'* [Moscow-Leningrad, 1940/1969], 24-28). In his political biography of Mikhail, Dimnik advanced the hypothesis that the principality of Chernihiv had definitely won the contest for Kiev and had actually become the principal force in Rus' politics on the eve of the Mongol invasion (*Mikhail, Prince of Chernigov*, 136-139). Dimnik's hypothesis is based on the situation in the years 1235-36, which could easily have changed later even if the Mongols had not invaded Rus'. The fact that the principality of Chernihiv ceased to be a serious factor in Rus' politics after Mikhail's death supports the established view that the principality was internally weak. The title phrase of the *Liubetskii sinodik* refers to the grand prince of Chernihiv and Kiev only in a factual manner, but significantly, gives precedence to Chernihiv (Zotov, *O Chernigovskikh kniaziakh...*, 24).

9. For general accounts of the history of the Suzdalian-Vladimirian principality, see D.A. Korsakov, *Meria i Rostovskoe kniazhestvo; Ocherki iz istorii Rostovo-Suzdal'skoi zemli* (Kazan, 1872); A.E. Presniakov, *Obrazovanie velikorusskago gosudarstva: Ocherki po istorii XIII-XV stoletii* (Petrograd, 1918), 26-47; A.N. Nasonov, *"Russkaia zemlia" i obrazovanie territorii drevnerusskago gosudarstva* (Moscow, 1981), 173-196; *idem.*, "Vladimiro-Suzdal'skoe kniazhestvo," *Ocherki istorii SSSR (Period feodalizma IX-XV vv. v dvukh chastiakh)*, part 1 (Moscow, 1953), 320-334; N.N. Voronin, "Vladimiro-Suzdal'skaia zemlia X-XIII vv.," *idem.*, *Problemy istorii dokapitalisticheskikh obshchestv*, V-VI (1935); *idem.*, *Pamiatniki suzdal'skogo zodchestva XI-XIII vv.* (Moscow and Leningrad, 1945); *idem.*, *Zodchestvo Severo-Vostochnoi Rusi XII-XV vv.*, 2 vols. (Moscow, 1961-62); *idem.*, *Vladimir, Bogoliubovo, Suzdal', Iur'ev-Pol'skii* (3rd ed., Moscow, 1967), and his concise article "Vladimiro-Suzdal'skoe kniazhestvo," in *Sovetskaia istoricheskaia entsiklopediia*, vol. 3, cols. 528-533.

10. Ideological writings pertaining to the age of Andrei Bogoliubskii have been discussed by N.N. Voronin, "Andrei Bogoliubskii i Luka Khrizoverg: Iz istorii russko-vizantiiskikh otnoshenii XII v.," *Vizantiiskii vremennik* (hereafter *VV*), 21 (1962): 29-58; *idem.*, "Zhitie Leontiia Rostovskogo i vizantiisko-russkie otnosheniia vo vtoroi polovine XII veka," *VV*, 23 (1963): 23-46; *idem.*, "Povest' ob ubiistve Andreia Bogoliuskogo i ee avtor," *Istoriia SSSR*, 1963, no. 3: 80-97; *idem.*, "Skazanie o pobede nad Bolgarami 1164 g. i prazdnike Spasa," *Problemy obshchestvenno-politicheskoi istorii Rossii i slavianskikh stran (Sbornik statei k 70-letiiu akademika M.N. Tikhomirova)*, V.I. Shunkov, ed. (Moscow, 1963), 88-92; *idem.*, "Iz istorii russko-vizantiiskoi tserkovnoi bor'by XII veka," *VV*, 24 (1965): 190-218; W. Vodoff, "Un 'parti théocratique' dans la Russie du XIIe siècle?," *Cahiers de civilisation médiévale*, 17, no. 3 (1974): 193-215; Iu.A. Limonov, *Letopisanie*

Vladimiro-Suzdal'skoi Rusi (Leningrad, 1967); E.S. Hurwitz, *Prince Andrej Bogoljubskij: The Man and the Myth* (Studia Historica et Philologica 12, Sectio Slàvica 4) (Florence, 1980); J. Pelenski, "The Contest for the 'Kievan Succession' (1155-1175): The Religious-Ecclesiastical Dimension," Proceedings of the International Congress Commemorating the Millennium of Christianity in Rus'-Ukraine, *HUS*, 12-13 (1988-89): 761-780 [see Chapter 2 of this volume].

11. This statement was made by the compilers of the *Suzdalian-Vladimirian Chronicles (Polnoe sobranie russkikh letopisei* [hereafter *PSRL*], 1, issue 2 [1927]: 354). On the events of 1169, confer J. Pelenski, "The Sack of Kiev of 1169: Its Significance for the Succession to Kievan Rus'," *HUS*, 9, no. 3/4 (1987): 303-316 [see Chapter 3 of this volume].

12. For a discussion of the various aspects of this program, confer the literature enumerated in note 10. E.S. Hurwitz has concluded that "Vladimir on the Kliaz'ma was a second Kiev..." (*Prince Andrej Bogoljubskij...*, 50), but contemporary sources make no such explicit claim.

13. *PSRL*, 1, issue 2 (1927): 472.

14. For a critical edition of the *Zhitie Aleksandra Nevskogo*, see Iu.K. Begunov, *Pamiatnik russkoi literatury XIII veka "Slovo o pogibeli russkoi zemli"* (Moscow and Leningrad, 1965), 159-180, especially 159, 165, and 178.

15. J. Pelenski, "The Sack of Kiev of 1482 in Contemporary Muscovite Chronicle Writing," *HUS*, 3/4 (1979-80): 637-649 [see Chapter 6 of this volume].

16. The most comprehensive modern treatments of the history of Galician-Volynian Rus' and of the literature on the subject have been provided by M. Hrushevs'kyi, *Istoriia Ukrainy-Rusy*, vols. 2 and 3; Józef Pełeński, *Halicz w dziejach sztuki średniowiecznej* (Cracow, 1914); V.T. Pashuto, *Ocherki po istorii Galitsko-Volynskoi Rusi* (Moscow, 1950); K.A. Sofronenko, *Obshchestvenno-politicheskii stroi Galitsko-Volynskoi Rusi XI-XIII vv.* (Moscow, 1955); P. Hrytsak, *Halyts'ko-Volyns'ka Derzhava* (New York, 1958); I.P. Krypiakevych, *Halyts'ko-volyns'ke kniazivstvo* (Kiev, 1984).

17. For a convenient English translation of the *Galician-Volynian Chronicle* and the literature on the *Chronicle*, confer the *Galician-Volynian Chronicle* (The Hypatian Codex, part 2), an annotated translation by G.A. Perfecky, *Harvard Series in Ukrainian Studies*, 16, 2 (Munich, 1973).

18. *PSRL* (2nd rep. ed., 1908), cols. 1, 2. Confer also the *Galician-Volynian Chronicle* under the years 1245/46 for the relevant statement, which reads as follows: "Danylo Romanovych, the great prince who ruled the Rus' land, Kiev, Volodymyr [Volyns'kyi] and Halych..." (58).

19. Pashuto, *Ocherki ...*, 17.

20. Nasonov, *Mongoly i Rus'*, 23-34. Available evidence indicates that Danylo attempted to reconquer Kiev in the mid-1250s (the *Galician-Volynian Chronicle*, 73).

21. A. I. Hens'ors'kyi's hypothesis, as well as his comparison of the alleged theory of Halych, "the second Kiev," with Moscow, "the Third Rome," should be regarded as artificial constructions (*Halyts'ko-Volyns'kyi Litopys* [Kiev, 1958], 86-87).

22. The *Galician-Volynian Chronicle*, 75-76.

23. A partial treatment of Kirill's political adjustments has been provided by J. T. Fuhrmann, "Metropolitan Cyrill II (1242-1281) and the Politics of Accommodation" *Jahrbücher für Geschichte Osteuropas*, 24 (1976): 161-172. For a study of Russian-Byzantine relations in the fourteenth century, especially the ecclesiastical

aspect and the literature on the subject, see J. Meyendorff, *Byzantium and the Rise of Russia* (Cambridge, London and New York, 1981).

24. *Ibid.*, 91-95, including the literature on the subject.

25. For introductory discussions of these concepts, see Nasonov, "Russkaia zemlia...," especially 28-29, and L.V. Cherepnin, "Istoricheskie usloviia formirovaniia russkoi narodnosti do kontsa XV v.," in *Voprosy formirovaniia russkoi narodnosti i natsii (Sbornik statei)* (Moscow, 1958), 61-63 and 81-82. A definitive study of this problem has not yet been written.

26. *PSRL* (2nd rep. ed., 1908), 653.

27. *Boleslav-Iurii II, kniaz' vsei Maloi Rusi (Sbornik materialov i issledovanii)* (St. Petersburg, 1907), 249; Hrushevs'kyi, *Istoriia Ukrainy-Rusy*, 3: 113, 115. The Latin term "Ladimeria" (meaning Volodimyria) was derived from Volodymyr-Volyns'kyi and denoted Volynia.

28. The Hungarian kings, who at certain times advanced claims to Galicia, were the first to use the title *Rex Galaciae* (1189) and *Galiciae Lodomeriaeque rex* (1206 and later) (Hrushevs'kyi, *Istoriia Ukrainy-Rusy*, 2: 449 and 3: 18).

29. *Boleslav-Iurii II, kniaz' vsei Maloi Rusi*, 149-150.

30. *Ibid.*, 4, n. 2.

31. *Ibid.*, 154.

32. Nasonov, *Mongoly i Rus'*, 26. Dimnik argues that Mikhail of Chernihiv was the strongest opponent of the Mongols and was, therefore, executed on orders of Batu (*Mikhail, Prince of Chernigov...*, 130-135).

33. *Novgorodskaia Pervaia Letopis' starshego i mladshego izvodov*, A.N. Nasonov, ed. (Moscow and Leningrad, 1950/1969), 305-306.

34. I. Ševčenko, "A Neglected Byzantine Source of Muscovite Political Ideology," *Harvard Slavic Studies*, 2 (1954): 142-144.

35. The *Galician-Volynian Chronicle*, 67-68.

36. *Ibid.*, 17.

2

THE CONTEST FOR THE KIEVAN SUCCESSION (1155–1175): THE RELIGIOUS-ECCLESIASTICAL DIMENSION*

The origins of the religious-ecclesiastical contest for the Kievan succession were connected in Rus' history with the reign of Andrei Iur'evich Bogoliubskii, specifically with the period from 1155 to 1175.[1] The most notable events and developments that took place during the period of that contest, which will be discussed in this study, were:

1. The removal of the Icon of the Blessed Mother of God from Vyshhorod in the Kievan land and its transfer to the Rostovian-Suzdalian land and subsequently to the city of Vladimir on the Kliaz'ma River.
2. An attempt by Andrei Bogoliubskii to elevate Vladimir to the status of a new religious center in Rus' by an ambitious church-building program.
3. The formulation of the Vladimirian religious-ideological program.
4. An attempt by Andrei Bogoliubskii to establish an independent metropolitanate of Vladimir (1166-1167).
5. The sack of Kiev in 1169.
6. The condemnation and the execution of Feodor (1169).
7. The second Kievan campaign of 1173 and its assessment in the *Kievan Chronicle (Kievskaia letopis')*.
8. The inclusion of the *Tale about the Slaying of Andrei [Bogoliubskii] (Povest' ob ubienii Andreia [Bogoliub-skogo])* in the *Kievan Chronicle.*

---

* For illustrations pertaining to this chapter, see Plates 6, 7, 8, 9, 10, 11, 12, 13, 14, 15, 16, 17, 18, 19, 20, 21, 22, 23.

21

An analysis of these events and developments requires a brief discussion of their historical context. Andrei Bogoliubskii's reign in the Suzdalian-Vladimirian patrimonial territorial state can be divided conveniently into two phases: (1) from 1157 to 1167, when his efforts were concentrated on the development and expansion of that northeastern Rus' patrimonial state (during that time he did not actively interfere in the Kievan affairs); and (2) from 1168 to 1175, when he was actively involved in efforts to control Kiev and to subordinate it to Vladimir. Before his reign in the Suzdalian-Vladimirian land, his earliest involvement in Kievan affairs, as a subordinate of his father, Iurii Dolgorukii (who was waging an active personal struggle for the succession to the Kievan throne), dates back to 1149-1155. However, during that time Andrei did not show any concrete interest in the Kievan throne. Even when, following participation in his father's Kievan campaign of 1154-1155 and takeover of Kiev, he was granted Vyshhorod by his father in 1155, which placed him in line for the Kievan throne, he did not make use of that opportunity, but left Vyshhorod for the Rostovian-Suzdalian land. By making that decision, Andrei Bogoliubskii "had abandoned sacred tradition. Never before had the promise of inheritance of the Kievan throne been so unequivocally rejected."[2]

I

The first major development of a religious-ecclesiastical nature pertaining to the contest for the Kievan succession was connected with Andrei Bogoliubskii's removal in 1155 of the Icon of the Blessed Mother of God from Vyshhorod (in the Kievan area) and its transfer to Suzdal' and subsequently to Vladimir. (That icon, in fact, was to have an extraordinary career in Russian history as the Icon of Our Lady of Vladimir.[3]) Bogoliubskii's act was recorded in two of the earliest known brief accounts incorporated in two chronicles: the *Kievan Chronicle*, which constitutes part of the *Hypatian Codex (Ipat'evskaia letopis')*, and the *Suzdalian-Vladimirian Chronicles (Vladimiro-Suzdal'skaia letopis')*, which are part of the *Laurentian Codex (Lavrent'evskaia letopis')*.

The *Kievan Chronicle*

> The same year [1155] Prince Andrei went from his father from Vyshhorod to Suzdal' *without his father's permission* [my italics - J.P.], and he took from Vyshhorod the Icon of the Blessed Mother of God which was brought from Tsesaria-grad on the same ship with the Pirogoshcha [Icon]. And he had it framed in thirty-*grivny*-weight-of-gold, besides silver, and precious stones, and large pearls, and having thus adorned [the Icon], he placed it in his own church of the Mother of God in Vladimir.[4]

The *Suzdalian-Vladimirian Chronicles*

> The same year [1155] Prince Andrei went from his father to Suzdal', and he brought with him the Icon of the Blessed Mother of God which was brought from Tsesariagrad on the same ship with the Pirogoshcha [Icon]. And he had it framed in thirty-*grivny*-weight of gold, besides silver, and precious stones, and large pearls, and having thus adorned [the Icon], he placed it in his own church in Vladimir.[5]

A comparison of the two accounts reveals obvious similarities, but also crucial differences in their treatment of Bogoliubskii's act. According to the *Kievan Chronicle*, Bogoliubskii acted improperly and even illegally, in leaving Vyshhorod without his father's permission and, by implication, in removing the icon. The account in the *Suzdalian-Vladimirian Chronicles*, on the other hand, eliminated references to Andrei's departure without his father's permission and to the icon's domicile at Vyshhorod, and thereby omitted any impression of improper or illegal behavior on the part of the prince.

The differences between the two accounts, in fact, reflect the different approaches taken by the two chronicles in the treatment of Andrei Bogoliubskii and his policies toward Kiev – approaches not apparent to historians who have utilized the chronicles in an exclusively complementary manner, thus overlooking their significantly different perspectives.[6] Whereas the *Suzdalian-Vladimirian Chronicles*, or that part of them which pertains to Bogoliubskii's reign (referred to by some as the *Bogoliubskii Chronicle of 1177 [Letopisets Bogoliubskogo 1177 goda]*), treated the prince and his policies in a positive and complimentary manner, the *Kievan Chronicle* was ambivalent and even openly critical of him and his conduct with regard to Kiev, with one major exception: it included a glorifying *Tale about the Slaying of Andrei [Bogoliubskii]*, about which more will be said later.

The allegations made in the *Kievan Chronicle* about Andrei Bogoliubskii's illicit removal of the icon from Vyshhorod to the Suzdalian land must have been based on solid foundations, for, apparently in order to justify the prince's act, another account with its own version of the removal and the transfer of the icon was included as an introduction in a special ideological work, The *Narration about the Miracles of the Vladimirian Icon of the Mother of God (Skazanie o chudesakh Vladimirskoi Ikony Bozhiei Materi)*, which was composed already in Bogoliubskii's lifetime or shortly after his death (between 1164 and 1185, according to V.O. Kliuchevskii and N.N. Voronin; I am inclined to date it between 1164 and 1168, before the sack of Kiev in 1169).[7] The account reads as follows:

> Prince Andrei wanted to be prince (*kniazhiti*) in the Rostovian land. He began to inquire about icons. He was told of the Icon of the Most Holy Mother of God in the Nunnery of Vyshhorod – how it departed from its resting place three times. It happened the first time when they [the witnesses] entered the Church and beheld it standing by itself in the middle of the Church; they put it back. The second time they saw it with its face turned toward the altar. They said, "It wishes to stand in the altar space." And they placed it behind the altar table. The third time they saw it standing by itself on the side of the altar table; and then they saw a multitude of miracles. When he heard these tidings the Prince [Andrei] was gladdened and went into the Church. He began to look over the icons. Now the aforesaid Icon excelled over all the others. When he saw it, he fell upon his knees and prayed, saying, "O Most Holy Virgin and Mother of Christ Our Lord, You shall be my protectress (*zastupnitsa*) in the Rostovian land. Come and visit the newly enlightened people so that all this may happen according to Your will." And he took the Icon and went to the Rostovian land. He took some clergymen with him.[8]

This account, which can be regarded as a separate legend, offers a new interpretation of the removal/transfer of the icon. It attributes to the icon a kind of "restlessness"[9] in its Vyshhorod-Kievan land domicile and, by implication, a dissatisfaction with it.

Here the icon is presented as the original initiator of its transfer to the Rostovian land and Andrei Bogoliubskii as merely the executor of its wish. According to this version, the Kievan land not only ceases to be the domicile of the miraculous icon, but loses its sacral charisma, which is now transferred to the Rostovian-Suzdalian land and subsequently to the city of Vladimir. The quoted account, as does, in fact, the entire *Narration* in which it is incorporated, displays an obvious anti-Kievan (however, not anti-Byzantine) bias, reflecting the ideological-political program of Andrei Bogoliubskii.[10]

From the perspective of Andrei Bogoliubskii and his ideologists, Kiev and the Kievan land were becoming irrelevant to the future of Rus', whereas the Rostovian-Suzdalian and later Vladimirian lands were assuming a new role as successors of Kiev. Only at a much later stage in the development of Muscovite claims to the Kievan inheritance, namely, in the sixteenth century, is this period of the icon's Kievan domicile, including the notion of its illegal removal, reintegrated into Muscovite political thought, although in a new interpretation: a separate narration about the transfer of the miraculous Icon of the Blessed Mother of God from the Kievan land to Vladimir, included in the *Book of Degrees (Kniga stepennaia)*, composed in the early 1560s under the auspices of Metropolitan Makarii, states that the icon was originally brought from Constantinople to Kiev at that time. Subsequently it was donated to the Devichii Monastery in Vyshhorod, from which it was taken by Andrei Bogoliubskii without the consent of his father, because of the "cunning counsel of the accursed Kuchkovich[es]," the principal conspirators and perpetrators of Bogoliubskii's slaying.[11]

II

The development of the new capital city of Vladimir, especially the ambitious program of church-building aimed at the city's enhancement, chronologically coincided with the first phase of Andrei Bogoliubskii's reign (1157-1167). It also represented the second stage of the religious-ecclesiastical contest for the Kievan succession. The church-building program, remarkable in its scope and the enormous expenses involved, was begun almost immediately following Andrei's takeover of the Rostovian-Suzdalian land.[12] The city of Vladimir was expanded and new fortifications were added, including the Golden Gate, apparently modeled after the Golden Gate of Kiev or Constantinople, or both.[13] Between 1158 and 1160 Bogoliubskii sponsored the construction of the famous Church of the Mother of God in Vladimir "with five domes, and all the domes decorated with gold," dedicated to the Dormition, and endowed it with considerable properties.[14] Furthermore, he had a church (or a chapel) constructed at the Golden Gate of Vladimir, which was completed and consecrated in 1164.[15] During that time construction of the Church of the Savior, started by his father, Iurii Dolgorukii, was completed and the Church of the Intercession (*Pokrov*) in the close vicinity of Vladimir, on the Nerl' River, was built (1165-1166).[16] Finally, in the early 1160s, he had a new town built, his second residence, with the symbolic name of Bogoliubovo.

The development of the new city of Vladimir, particularly the extraordinary effort invested in the construction of churches, attests to a major endeavor on the part of Bogoliubskii not only to create instantly a leading capital and a religious center of Rus', but also to replace Kiev by Vladimir as the most sacred city of Rus', by replicating the myth of the "golden-domed" Kiev.[17]

III

Equally remarkable and ambitious was Andrei Bogoliubskii's ideological program, formulated to a considerable extent already in the 1160s. It was revealed in a series of thematic-ideological treatises of the so-called Bogoliubskii cycle. The aim of the latter was to enhance Bogoliubskii's own position and also that of Rostov-Suzdal' and especially Vladimir as domiciles of religious cults and their own venerable tradition. The most important of the new cults developed in Vladimir pertained to the special veneration of the Virgin. It found its manifestation in the already mentioned *Narration about the Miracles of the Vladimirian Icon of the Mother of God*,[18] the extant text of which described ten specific miracles, nearly all directly related to Andrei Bogoliubskii and the city of Vladimir. The first pertained to Bogoliubskii himself (the miraculous saving of his guide from the waters of the Vazuza River). Others were performed as intercessions on behalf of Andrei's party against a horse gone wild and a Vladimirian inflicted by a "fiery [feverish] disease." Some occurred in response to Andrei's prayers, like the successful delivery by his wife of one of his children and the rescue of twelve

Vladimirians (a symbolic figure for twelve apostles) from under the collapsed gate of Vladimir. Of the ten miracles, two were connected with other areas of Rus' (Pereiaslav in the south and Tver'), but none specifically with the Kievan area. Also, in the already discussed introductory account of the *Narration*, a reference was made to a "multitude of miracles" performed by the icon, apparently before its transfer from Vyshhorod to the north, but none was specifically described.

The cult of the Vladimirian Virgin was intensified through the inauguration about 1165 of the Feast of the Intercession (*Prazdnik Pokrova*) to be celebrated on October 1.[19] To substantiate the celebration of the new holiday, two additional, closely interrelated works were composed by Vladimirian bookmen under the auspices of Prince Andrei: the *Prologue Narration (Prolozhnoie skazanie)* and the *Service Hymn (Sluzhba)*, both of which glorified the intercessory garment (*Pokrov*) and the respective powers of the Virgin.[20] At the very same time Andrei's Church of the *Pokrov-na-Nerli* was completed (1165-1166). The texts related to the cult of the *Pokrov* contained no references to the Kievan tradition. They were intended to emphasize the protection accorded by the Virgin to Andrei's country and the city of Vladimir. This powerful combination of the two cults, that is, the cult of the Icon and the cult of the *Pokrov*, served also as a device to extol the special position of Vladimir as the city chosen by the Virgin for a special role in history.

The enhancement of Rostovia-Suzdalia-Vladimiria to the status of the new center of Rus' also required the establishment of a cult of local saints. That purpose was accomplished by the composition of another significant ideological work under Andrei Bogoliubskii's auspices, namely, the *Life of Leontii of Rostov (Zhitie Leontiia Rostovskogo)*, completed in the early 1160s, before 1164.[21] The treatise glorified the status of Rostov and the person of Andrei Bogoliubskii by connecting him specifically with the Monomakh branch of the Riurikide dynasty ("son of Grand Prince Iurii [Dolgorukii], the grandson of Volodimer").[22] Thus Andrei's lofty status was proven without any direct reference to Kiev and the Kievan land, that is, the country (patrimony) the dynasty in question had ruled.

The most complex and controversial of the Bogoliubskii cycle of thematic-ideological treatises is the *Narration about the Victory against the Bulgars (Skazanie o pobede nad Bolgarami)*, which is connected with the inauguration of the Feast of the Savior celebrated on August 1.[23] It has been argued that this *Narration* was composed during Andrei's lifetime, sometime between 1164 and 1174.[24] Its text relates the progress of the battle against the Bulgars, resulting in Andrei Bogoliubskii's victory, which is attributed to the miraculous intervention of the Icon of Our Lady of Vladimir; following the battle, the icon, according to the text, was returned to the "golden-domed Church of the Virgin of Vladimir." Some of its factual data was borrowed from the brief annalistic *Narration* (under the same title), contained in the *Laurentian Codex* under the entry for the year 1164.[25] Whereas the brief chronicle *Narration* treats the victory over the Bulgars as an exclusively Vladimirian achievement, the expanded *Narration* is a more ambitious work. Its author(s) introduced in it a parallel fictitious campaign by the Byzantine emperor Manuel I (Comnenus) against the Saracens and emphasized an invented special relationship between Andrei and the Byzantine emperor. Furthermore, it was asserted in the expanded *Narration* that the Feast of the Savior was jointly inaugurated by Andrei Bogoliubskii and Emperor Manuel "by the orders of Patriarch Lukas, Metropolitan Constantine [II] of all of Rus', and Nestor, the bishop of Rostov."[26]

The stress on the Byzantine connection and the anachronistic reference to Nestor has caused considerable confusion in scholarship. In particular, the positive reference to the Kievan metropolitan Constantine, against whose institution Bogoliubskii had waged an ideological and ecclesiastical contest, has puzzled researchers. In my opinion, the inclusion of the names of Metropolitan Constantine II, who arrived in Kiev in 1168, and of Patriarch Lukas Chrysoberges makes perfect sense if it is read in the context of the events that took place at that time. In addition to the patriarch's rejection of Andrei Bogoliubskii's request for the establishment of an independent metropolitanate of Vladimir subordinated to Constantinople but not to Kiev, Metropolitan Constantine decreed the execution in 1169 of Andrei's candidate for metropolitan of Vladimir, Feodor, following Bogoliubskii's sack of Kiev in March of the same year.

It can, therefore, be assumed that the expanded *Narration about the Victory against the Bulgars* was composed in late 1169 or at the beginning of 1170. Although Bogoliubskii became the overlord of Kiev for a brief period of time (1169-1171), he had to adjust himself to the requirements of the Patriarchate of Byzantium and the

Metropolitanate of Kiev, presided over by a Greek ecclesiastical official. N.N. Voronin has completely misread the entire cycle of the Bogoliubskii-sponsored treatises and, in particular, the *Narration about the Victory against the Bulgars* by interpreting them as anti-Byzantine challenges;[27] they were at best manifestations of "status-seeking," as aptly characterized by Ihor Ševčenko.[28] The main purpose of these treatises, therefore, was to enhance the status of Vladimir and to challenge Kiev for leadership in the lands of Rus'.[29]

IV

Andrei Bogoliubskii's attempt to establish a competitive metropolitanate, independent from Kiev and subordinated to the Byzantine patriarchate exclusively, was his most challenging endeavor in the contest for the Kievan succession. This attempt can be reconstructed from the text of the sixteenth-century Church Slavonic-Russian translation of a letter by Patriarch Lukas Chrysoberges to Prince Andrei, which evidently represented a response to Bogoliubskii's lost letter to the patriarch.[30]

Since the patriarch's letter is not dated, several scholars have attempted to establish the chronological and contextual framework for its composition in order to determine the time of Andrei's move to establish his own metropolitanate.[31] According to an expert analysis provided by W. Vodoff, the patriarch's letter was written between 1166 and 1168.[32] I agree with Vodoff. The patriarch must have responded to Andrei's request after the completion of the prince's ambitious church-building program and following the development of a powerful patrimonial state in the Rostovian-Suzdalian-Vladimirian area, which were evidently used by Bogoliubskii as major arguments in his lost letter. This makes 1166 the ante-quem date. I am also convinced that the patriarch's letter must have been composed prior to the sack of Kiev, which took place in early March of 1169, since, in my opinion, the patriarch's negative response apparently triggered Bogoliubskii's decision to embark upon the Kievan campaign, which also must have required considerable time to prepare. Therefore, Bogoliubskii must have received the letter from the patriarch in the summer of 1168 at the latest.

As is evident from the patriarch's letter, Andrei Bogoliubskii's request to establish a new metropolitanate of Vladimir, independent of Kiev — his candidate for metropolitan of Vladimir was an ecclesiastic (*vladyka* [?]) by the name of Feodor — was firmly rejected by the patriarch on the grounds that Vladimir could not ever be removed from the jurisdiction of the Bishopric of Rostov and Suzdal', a justification based on a vague reference to the canonical law of the indivisibility of a bishopric or a metropolitanate.[33] However, the real reason for the rejection of Bogoliubskii's request was most probably the patriarch's strict adherence to the traditional Byzantine doctrine of the unitary and indivisible character of the metropolitanate and the polity of Rus' (*Rossiia*).[34] At that junction of history when Bogoliubskii made his request to the patriarch, the Byzantine doctrine favored the southern branches of the Riurikide dynasty against Andrei Bogoliubskii. Only later, beginning with the period following the Mongol invasion of Rus' and until the fall of the Byzantine Empire, would this doctrine immensely help Vladimir and later Moscow in their contest for succession to the Metropolitanate of Kiev and all of Rus'.[35] The only concrete concession made by the patriarch to Andrei was his tentative consent for a bishop of Rostov and Suzdal' to move to Vladimir to stay in the same city with Andrei which in reality amounted to very little. On the related but secondary issue of Andrei's conflict with Leontii, the bishop of Rostov and Suzdal', the patriarch offered a compromise, according to which the metropolitan of all of Rus' in Kiev was the final authority on matters of theology and ecclesiastical discipline in the realm of Rus', and the Kievan ruler, in the patriarch's definition the grand prince of all Rus', was the highest secular authority before whom important conflicts could be adjudicated. In other words, the lines of ecclesiastical and secular authority were clearly defined by the patriarch to the detriment of Bogoliubskii's interests.

As yet the Byzantine patriarch's rejection of Bogoliubskii's request has not been comprehensively analyzed. According to one popular interpretation, it reflected the former's anti-Vladimirian and anti-Russian hegemonistic imperial position and the latter's anti-Byzantine stance.[36] However, neither the patriarch's letter, nor the circumstantial evidence of the contemporary chronicles give any indication that Andrei's endeavor was anti-Byzantine. On the contrary, by writing a letter to the patriarch, Andrei approached the appropriate Byzantine authority directly, bypassing Kiev. At that time, the chair of the Kievan metropolitanate was temporarily vacant between the terms of Metropolitan John IV (1164-1166) and Metropolitan Constantine II, who arrived in Kiev in 1168.[37]

Bogoliubskii apparently wished to become the patriarch's and the Byzantine emperor's chief partner in Rus'.

Andrei Bogoliubskii's political defeat at the hands of the Byzantine patriarch forced him to adjust his strategy for supremacy in Rus'. As I have pointed it out in my study on the sack of Kiev in 1169, he had two options if he wished to pursue his endeavor: (1) to continue the political tradition to rule Kiev and Rus' from Kiev, as did his father, Iurii Dolgorukii, among others; or (2) to destroy Kiev as the center of power and sacral symbolism, and, by doing so, to subordinate it to Vladimir as the new capital of the Rus' lands. The campaign of 1168, the sack of Kiev in 1169, and the installation of his brother Gleb as a "junior" subordinate prince in Kiev attest to his choice of option two.[38]

V

The sack of Kiev by Andrei Bogoliubskii's armies in 1169 was undertaken not only as a device of power politics, but also as an act of stripping "the mother of the cities of Rus'" of her sacral status. Since I have written a separate study about the sack of Kiev in 1169 (see Chapter 3), I shall not discuss it at length in this study, but only provide a brief summary of its two main points as they apply to the topic at hand.[39]

An analysis of the sources relevant to the religious-ecclesiastical aspect of the sack of Kiev in 1169 reveals that: (1) the destruction of the sacral position of Kiev was carried out by the plunder of the churches and the monasteries and by the forceful removal of icons, holy books, and vestments; (2) the justification for the sack of Kiev, as provided in the *Suzdalian-Vladimirian Chronicles* or the hypothetical *Bogoliubskii Chronicle of 1177*, was formulated in religious-ecclesiastical terms exclusively. According to this chronicle, Kiev and Kievans were allegedly justly punished for Metropolitan Constantine's unlawful interdiction of Polikarp, the abbot of the Monastery of the Caves, in connection with the controversy over fasting on Wednesdays and Fridays whenever these days coincided with major holy days of the Lord, a controversy attested as having taken place in Suzdal' in 1164. The authors/editors of the hypothetical *Bogoliubskii Chronicle of 1177* utilized this controversy in an antiquarian, manipulative manner to justify Andrei Bogoliubskii's unimaginable and unprecedented sack of Kiev (*egozhe ne bylo nikogdazhe*) from the Christian perspective. The unease with the sack of Kiev in 1169 is attested to in another Vladimirian narration, namely, in the account about the sack of Kiev in 1203, undertaken by other Rus' princes at the instigation of Vsevolod III Iur'evich (1176-1212), in which the relevant phrase reads: *I sotvorisia veliko zlo v russtei zemli iakogo zhe zla ne bylo ot kreshcheniia nad Kievom* ("and a great evil befell the Rus' land, such as has not been since the baptism of Kiev").[40] This revealing reference to the baptism of Kiev in connection with the sack of 1203 was apparently made to minimize the impact of the sack of Kiev in 1169.

VI

Andrei Bogoliubskii's temporary takeover of Kiev following its sack by his armies in 1169 did not strengthen his position in the protracted struggle with the Metropolitanate of Kiev for power in ecclesiastical affairs. Having failed in his attempt to establish an independent metropolitanate of Vladimir (1166-1167), he apparently made an effort to come to terms with Constantine II, the new metropolitan of Kiev, by turning over to him *vladyka* (?) Feodor, his candidate for metropolitan of Vladimir. However, this effort resulted in another humiliating defeat, namely, the condemnation and execution of Feodor by order of the Kievan metropolitan in the summer of 1169.

These developments can be reconstructed from two almost identical chronicle narrations about the condemnation and execution of Feodor: one incorporated in the *Laurentian Codex* under the entry for 1169 and editorially connected with the account about the sack of Kiev in the same year, and the other, in the *Kievan Chronicle*, misdated 1172[41] and separated from the account about the sack of Kiev in 1169 by other accounts dealing with Kievan developments; the latter also contains additional detailed information, such as the exact location of Feodor's execution – *pesii ostrov* (the dog's island).[42]

The author(s) of the two narrations portrayed Feodor in the worst possible light, by accusing him of insubordination and conflict not only with the metropolitan of Kiev, but also with his own ruler Andrei Bogoliubskii. They reported extensively on his alleged crimes and brutal excesses against the Christian people of Vladimir:

The people [of Vladimir] suffered much from him [Feodor] in keeping him, and they lost villages, weapons, and horses. [Some] were enslaved, [others] were imprisoned and looted – not only the common people, but also the monks, the abbots, and the priests. And this merciless tormentor [shaved] the heads and cut off the beards [of some], and he burned out the eyes and cut out the tongues [of others], and he crucified [others] on the wall. And he tortured mercilessly, wanting to steal everyone's possessions.[43]

Feodor's ouster from Vladimir and "out of the golden-domed Church of the Holy Mother of God of Vladimir" was interpreted in the narrations as "a new miracle performed...by the Lord and Holy Mother of God in the city of Vladimir." His condemnation and in particular his execution decreed by Metropolitan Constantine II were described in the most graphic and horrifying terms:

Metropolitan Constantine charged him [Feodor] with all his transgressions and ordered him to be taken to the dog's island. And there they maimed him and cut out his tongue, as is fitting for an evil heretic, and they cut off his right hand and gouged out his eyes, because he said abusive [things] about the Holy Mother of God.[44]

To the best of my knowledge, never had Old Rus' sources, at least until the end of the sixteenth century, described an execution of an ecclesiastical figure on orders of a superior ecclesiastical official in such drastic form and detail.

Bogoliubskii's turning over of his protégé Feodor to the metropolitan of Kiev for trial and punishment is indicative of his serious difficulties in the unrestrained quest for ecclesiastical status in the contest for the Kievan succession. However, the Feodor affair not only proved to be detrimental to the prince's endeavors, but also must have had a negative impact on Metropolitan Constantine's position, for after 1169 his name disappeared from historical accounts. In fact, from 1169 to 1182, the date of the nomination of Nicephoros II as the new metropolitan of all of Rus', there are only a very few references to other metropolitans of Kiev in the available sources.[45] This lacuna prevents researchers from drawing conclusions about the relations between Andrei Bogoliubskii, the metropolitan of Kiev Constantine II, and the patriarch of Constantinople in the last years of the prince's reign.

Bogoliubskii's policies toward Kiev and the Kievan Rus' met with disapproval from the ecclesiastical establishment of that polity. For example, Kirill, Bishop of Turov, the most distinguished native intellectual of his time, was highly critical of Feodor. The *Prologue Life of Kirill (Prolozhnoe zhitie Kirilla)* refers explicitly to his condemnation of "Feodorets for his outrageous [behavior]...and his heresy."[46] The *Life* also reports, that

> he [Kirill] wrote many epistles to the beloved Prince Andrei [Bogoliubskii] concerning the writings of the Gospels and the Prophets and commentaries on divine holy days and many other sermons of spiritual nature.[47]

One of Kirill's admonitions is the famous "Sermon on Man's Soul and Body, on the Breaking of the Divine Commandment, on the Resurrection of the Human Body, on the Future Judgment, and on Penance,"[48] in which he utilized the legend about the lame and blind man. Although Kirill never specifically mentioned Andrei or Feodor by name, a number of commentators of the sermon have correlated it with the relationship between the prince and the metropolitan-to-be and have interpreted it as an indirect criticism of their ecclesiastical activities. But even if that particular sermon by Kirill is excluded from the body of the anti-Bogoliubskii evidence, the reference in his *Life* suffices to place Kirill among Feodor's and Andrei's critical opponents; the sack of sacred Kiev must have represented to Kirill a highly heretical and sacrilegious act.

VII

In addition to having suffered two major defeats in the struggle for an enhanced status in relations with the Kievan metropolitanate (namely, an attempt to establish a separate metropolitanate in Vladimir and the execution of Feodor, his candidate for metropolitan of Vladimir), Andrei Bogoliubskii faced another problem. Following the death of Gleb, his brother and appointee to the Kievan throne, on 20 January 1171,[49] he failed to maintain his position as the supreme patrimonial overlord of Kiev, which he had assumed following the sack of Kiev in 1169. The ensuing contest for the Kievan throne, which lasted for over two years, led to the Kievan campaign of 1173, Andrei's second attempt to conquer and subordinate Kiev, which this time ended in a humiliating military defeat. Both the contest and the campaign of 1173 were described in three interrelated narrations incorporated in the *Kievan Chronicle*: (1) *The Beginning of the Princely Reign of Volodimer in Kiev*;[50] (2) *The Beginning of the Princely Reign of Roman Rostislavich in Kiev*;[51] (3) the untitled narration about the Kievan campaign of 1173, the most extensive of the three.[52]

The contest for the Kievan throne began when the Rostislavichi of Smolensk challenged Andrei Bogoliubskii's overlordship in Kiev by installing on its throne Volodimer III Mstislavich, who died following a brief reign of four months. The *Kievan Chronicle* reported that

> Andrei was displeased with his [Volodimer Mstislavich's] enthronement in Kiev and he sent [messages] ordering him to leave Kiev and Roman Rostislavich to go to Kiev.[53]

The installation of Roman Rostislavich in Kiev in July of 1171[54] and the tentative subordination of the Rostislavichi proved to be, from Andrei's perspective, only a temporary solution, for soon, under the pretext of patrimonial insubordination, he ordered the Rostislavichi to abandon Kiev and appointed his brother Mikhail Iur'evich as ruler of Kiev.[55] A coalition of the deposed Rostislavichi and Mstislav of Volynia opposed Andrei's plans for Kiev and his new candidate for the Kievan throne. They succeeded in recapturing Kiev and turned over the city to Riurik Rostislavich, who was enthroned on 1 April 1172.[56] The *Kievan Chronicle* commented approvingly that Riurik "entered Kiev with great fame and honor and sat on the throne of his father and grandfather."[57] Andrei responded to this challenge by organizing a major coalition of princes (as in 1168). The Olgovichi of Chernihiv temporarily sided with him. By 1173, he again managed to assemble a major army, including twenty princes, which, according to the apparently inflated information of the *Kievan Chronicle*, amounted to 50,000 men.[58] The huge army conducted operations in Southern Rus' and the Kievan area during the summer and fall of 1173, but, due to internal disagreements in Andrei's army and particularly following the defection of Sviatoslav of Chernihiv, it was decisively defeated.

Whereas the facts of the contest for the Kievan throne and the Kievan campaign of 1173 have been tentatively reconstructed from the narrations in the *Kievan Chronicle* by Mykhailo Hrushevs'kyi,[59] among others, these narrations and particularly the untitled narration about the Kievan campaign of 1173 have not been analyzed in scholarly literature for their ideological content. Hrushevs'kyi merely observed that the treatment of the 1173 campaign in the narration acquired "an epic tone and a pompous, rhetorical style."[60] What makes this narration exceptionally significant for the understanding of the contest for the Kievan succession is not its literary devices, but rather its content, namely, the most stinging criticism, couched primarily in religious-ideological terms, ever to be leveled at Andrei Bogoliubskii in any known contemporary historical or ideological work of Kievan Rus'.

> [The prince is accused of having become] filled with haughtiness and great pride, [of having] placed his hope in martial force, [of having] surrounded himself with a multitude of warriors, and [of having become filled with] burning anger...[61] [of having failed to escape] from the web of the much-deceitful devil, who engages in war against the Christians. Prince Andrei, being such a wise man and so valiant in all his deeds, lost his senses, and lacking restraint, burned with anger. He spoke with such boastful words, which were shameful and vile to God. Boasting and pride come from the devil who plants boastfulness and pride in our hearts. Just as [the Apostle] Paul had said: "God is against those who are proud, but He grants grace to those who are humble." And the word of the Apostle Paul came to pass, as we shall relate later.[62]

After having provided an extensive account of the Kievan campaign and the circumstances which led to the defeat of Andrei's army, the author(s) of the narration concluded:

> Thus the word of the Apostle Paul came to pass, who had said as we wrote before: "He who exalts himself shall be humbled and he who is humble shall be exalted." And all the forces of Prince Andrei of Suzdal' returned. He gathered [his forces] from all the lands and of the multitude of his warriors there was no count. They came in pride and departed to their homes humbled.[63]

The prince was accused of having committed under the influence of the devil the greatest moral sins, namely, those of pride, haughtiness, and boasting. The gravity of the condemnation can hardly be overestimated, in particular if one compares the afore-cited commentary with the simple explanation of the sack of Kiev in 1169 provided by the same *Kievan Chronicle* in its narration about that sack, in which Andrei is not criticized directly and the misfortune which befell Kiev and its people is interpreted as deserved punishment in the spirit of Christian humility (*grekh radi nashikh* ["because of our sins"]).[64]

The author(s) of the narration about the reign of Roman Rostislavich in Kiev, as well as of the untitled narration about the Kievan campaign of 1173, justified their criticism of Andrei Bogoliubskii with the right of resistance, based on moral-religious and legal grounds and opposing unlawful, immoral princely actions and behavior.[65] In the former narration they utilized alleged exchanges between Andrei and the Rostislavichi, in which the former asserted his right to act as he pleased (a prerogative of unlimited patrimonial power) and the latter responded with charges that Andrei broke agreements confirmed by the kissing of the cross and invoked God's judgment in their conflict with him. Andrei's accusation of the Rostislavichi reads:

> You [Roman Rostislavich] and your brothers do not act according to my will. You will leave Kiev, David [must leave] Vyshhorod, and Mstislav – Bilhorod, and you [Rostislavichi] have Smolensk, divide it among yourselves.[66]

The Rostislavichi, who were very unhappy about being deprived of the Rus' land by Andrei Bogoliubskii and by his giving Kiev to his brother Mikhail Iur'evich, countered Andrei's claim to unlimited patrimonial power with a justification of their own:

> Brother, we have called you a father, according to law, and we kissed the cross to you, and by adhering to the kissing of the cross we wished you well. And now you have driven out our brother Roman from Kiev and ordered us to leave the Rus' land, though we have done no wrong. Let God and the power of the cross [be our judges].[67]

A similar exchange of political statements between Andrei and the Rostislavichi was recorded in the narration about the Kievan campaign of 1173. Andrei's emissary to the Rostislavichi was instructed to convey the prince's request:

> You do not act in accordance with my will. You, Riurik, go to Smolensk to your brother, to your own patrimony. Then tell David: "And you go to Berlad', for I do not command you to be in the land of Rus'." Say to Mstislav: "You are the cause of everything, and I do not command you to be in the land of Rus'."[68]

Prince Mstislav responded with a statement based on the right of resistance:

> Until now we have loved you like a father. [But now], since you have sent [us] such a message [speaking to us] not as to a prince, but as to a subject and a common man, do what you have intended to do. Let God be [our] judge.[69]

God's judgment resulted in Andrei Bogoliubskii's defeat, thus settling the moral and legal issues. The use of moral and judicial arguments in the narration about the campaign of 1173 represented the most powerful indictment of Bogoliubskii's policies toward Kiev. It was also one of the infrequent cases in which the authors/editors of the *Kievan Chronicle* relied extensively on religious justifications.

VIII

A discussion of Andrei Bogoliubskii's ecclesiastical policies in the contest for the Kievan succession should include an explanation of the inclusion in the *Kievan Chronicle* of the *Tale about the Slaying of Andrei [Bogoliubskii]* (*Povest' ob ubienii Andreia [Bogoliubskogo]*), written following his death.[70] Paradoxically, the most extensive version of the *Tale*, which actually is a eulogy and a political-ideological treatise glorifying Bogoliubskii and his achievements, was included in the *Kievan Chronicle* that otherwise, with a few minor exceptions, was critical of his policies and in particular of his role and behavior in the Kievan campaign of 1173.[71] By juxtaposing Kiev to Vladimir and Vyshhorod to Bogoliubovo ("and as far as Vyshhorod was from Kiev, so far was

Bogoliubovo from Vladimir"),[72] the Golden Gates of the two capital cities and the martyrdom of Andrei to that of Boris and Gleb,[73] the authors of the *Tale* in the *Kievan Chronicle* not only glorified Bogoliubskii, but also enhanced the image of Vladimir at the expense of Kiev, by elevating its status to that of the ancient capital of Rus'. Why, then, was this *Tale*, so favorably predisposed to Bogoliubskii and his political designs, included in the *Kievan Chronicle* ?

As I have already pointed it out in my study on the sack of Kiev in 1169, the authors/editors of the *Kievan Chronicle* must have incorporated the *Tale* on account of its relevance to Kievan history in a broad sense.[74] Evidently, their general attitude must have been to integrate in the chronicle all Kiev-related materials, regardless of their content. They did not hesitate to accept the entire Kievan inheritance, because they considered themselves its rightful heirs. By comparison, the authors/editors of the *Suzdalian-Vladimirian Chronicles* utilized Kievan materials selectively and adapted them to their political and ideological needs.

Since most, if not all, of the authors/editors of the *Kievan Chronicle* were ecclesiastics,[75] they shared a Christian world-view. They apparently interpreted from that perspective Bogoliubskii's campaign of 1173, on which he embarked having committed the greatest sin of pride. He had been justly punished by defeat and humiliation. In addition to the moral punishment, he had been brutally slain, which could be interpreted as an ultimate punishment. Apparently the time had come to forgive the sinner. The inclusion in the *Kievan Chronicle* of the eulogizing *Tale* about his slaying may have been regarded as the final act of forgiveness.

On the other hand, the *Tale* account of the slaying of Andrei Bogoliubskii could have been included in the *Kievan Chronicle* for didactic reasons. It could have been interpreted from the perspective of the medieval right of resistance, according to which a ruler who violates agreements confirmed by the kissing of the cross, who misuses his power, and who behaves like a tyrant can justly be killed.

NOTES

1. For a treatment of Andrei Bogoliubskii's career and some aspects of his ecclesiastical policies, as well as the literature on the subject, see E.S. Hurwitz, *Prince Andrej Bogoljubskij: The Man and the Myth* (Florence, 1980); W. Vodoff, "Un 'parti thèocratique' dans la Russie du XIIe siècle?," *Cahiers de civilization médiévale*, 17, no. 3 (1974): 193-215.

2. Hurwitz, *Prince Andrej Bogoljubskij*, 12.

3. For a study of the career of this icon and the literature on the subject, see D.B. Miller, "Legends of the Icon of Our Lady of Vladimir: A Study of the Development of Muscovite National Consciousness," *Speculum*, 43, no. 4 (1968): 657-670, and A. Ebbinghaus, "Andrej Bogoljubskij und die 'Gottesmutter von Vladimir'," *Russia Mediaevalis*, 6. no. 1 (1987): 157-183.

4. Concerning the text of the account in the *Kievan Chronicle*, see *Ipat'evskaia letopis'* published in *Polnoe sobranie russkikh letopisei* (hereafter *PSRL*), vol. 2 (1908/1962), col. 482. For a concise description of the *Hypatian Codex* and the literature on the subject, see O.P. Likhacheva, "Letopis' Ipat'evskaia" in "Issledovatel'skie materialy dlia 'Slovaria knizhnikov i knizhnosti drevnei Rusi' (Drevnerusskie letopisi i khroniki)," *Trudy Otdela drevnerusskoi literatury* (hereafter *TODRL*), 39 (1985): 123-128.

5. The text of the account in the *Suzdalian-Vladimirian Chronicles* is contained in the *Laurentian Codex*, *PSRL*, vol. 1 (1926/1962), col. 346. Concerning a discussion of the *Rostovian-Suzdalian-Vladimirian Chronicles* and the literature on the subject, consult Iu.A. Limonov, *Letopisanie Vladimiro-Suzdal'skoi Rusi* (Leningrad, 1967), and Ia.S. Lur'e, "Letopis' Lavrent'evskaia" in "Issledovatel'skie materialy," *TODRL*, 39 (1985): 128-131.

6. For an introductory discussion of the *Kievan Chronicle* and the *Suzdalian-Vladimirian Chronicles* and the differences between the two, see J. Pelenski, "The Sack of Kiev of 1169: Its Significance for the Succession to Kievan Rus'," *Harvard Ukrainian Studies* (hereafter *HUS*), 11, no. 3/4 (December 1987): 303-316 [see Chapter 3 of this volume].

7. The text of the *Skazanie o chudesakh Vladimirskoi Ikony Bozhiei Materi*, edited and with introduction by V.O. Kliuchevskii was published in *Chteniia Obshchestva liubitelei drevnei pis'mennosti* (hereafter *ChOLDP*), 30 (1878): 1-43, for the dating, see 10-14; N.N. Voronin, "Iz istorii russko-vizantiiskoi tserkovnoi bor'by XII v.," *Vizantiiskii vremennik* (hereafter *VV*), 26 (1965): 190-218, especially 198. For a discussion of the text, consult Hurwitz, *Prince Andrej Bogoljubskij*, 54-59.

8. English translation of this passage is provided in Hurwitz, *Prince Andrej Bogoljubskij*, 56.

9. Hurwitz, *Prince Andrej Bogoljubskij*, 56.

10. For N.N. Voronin's hypothesis of the anti-Byzantine orientation of the *Skazanie o chudesakh*, as well as some of the other ideological enterprises of Andrei Bogoliubskii, see his "Iz istorii russko-vizantiiskoi tserkovnoi bor'by XII v.," *VV*, 26 (1965): 190-218, especially 218.

11. *PSRL*, 21, 1 (1908): 230-232. An account about the transfer of the Icon of the Blessed Mother of God from the Kievan land to Vladimir, which includes references to the icon's illegal removal from its original Vyshhorod-Kievan land domicile, the "Bogoliubovo miracle," and the "cunning" advice of the "accursed Kuchkovich(es)," can be found in a brief narration about the life and activities of Andrei Bogoliubskii, contained in a separate treatise, entitled *A se kniazi rus'tii*. The latter treatise was included in the *Manuscript of the Archeographic Commission* (no. 240), preceding the manuscript of the *Novgorodian First Chronicle* (A.N. Nasonov, ed., *Novgorodskaia Pervaia Letopis' starshego i mladshego izvodov* [Moscow and Leningrad, 1950], 467). The text of the treatise *A se kniazi rus'tii* was most probably composed in the middle of the fifteenth century.

12. The most significant contributions to the study of the architecture and art of Suzdal'-Vladimir have been made by N.N. Voronin in his works, *Zodchestvo*

severovostochnoi Rusi XII-XV vekov, 2 vols. (Moscow, 1961), especially vol. 1, and *Vladimir, Bogoliubovo, Suzdal', Iur'ev-Polskii: Sputnik po gorodam Vladimirskoi oblasti*, 2nd ed. (Moscow, 1965). Cf. also his "Vladimiro-Suzdal'skaia zemlia v X-XII v.," *Problemy istorii dokapitalisticheskikh obshchestv*, 5-6 (1935).

13. *PSRL*, 1 (1926/1962), col. 348; *PSRL*, 2 (1908/1962), col. 491. Cf. also N.N. Voronin, *Zodchestvo*, 1: 128-148.

14. *PSRL*, 1 (1926/1962), col. 348; *PSRL*, 2 (1908/1962), col. 491. Cf. also N.N. Voronin, *Zodchestvo*, 1: 128-148.

15. *PSRL*, 1 (1926/1962), col. 351.

16. Hurwitz, *Prince Andrej Bogoljubskij*, 14.

17. The mystique of the "golden-domed" Kiev has survived in Ukrainian culture and political ideology into the twentieth century (O. Pritsak, "Kiev and All of Rus': The Fate of a Sacral Idea," *HUS*, 10, no. 3/4 [December 1986]: 279-300, especially 279).

18. See fns. 7 and 3, above, for the text edition and the literature on the subject.

19. Hurwitz, *Prince Andrej Bogoljubskij*, 59.

20. For a discussion of the texts of the *Prolozhnoe skazanie* and the *pokrov* cult, see Hurwitz, *Prince Andrej Bogoljubskij*, 69-78. The text of the *Prolozhnoe skazanie* was reprinted in Hurwitz, *ibid.*, 93. Consult also the analysis of the *pokrov* cult (including the obvious "anti-Byzantine" bias) in N.N. Voronin, "Iz istorii russko-vizantiiskoi tserkovnoi bor'by XII v.," *VV*, 26 (1965): 208-218.

21. The literature on the *Life of Leontii of Rostov* and its dating is quite extensive. The first major analysis was provided by V.O. Kliuchevskii in *Drevnerusskiia zhitiia sviatykh kak istoricheskii istochnik* (Moscow, 1871/1968), 3-22. N.N. Voronin significantly expanded the research on the work in question and offered a new dating, namely, the early 1160s, which I accept ("Zhitie Leontiia Rostovskogo i vizantiisko-russkie otnosheniia vtoroi poloviny XII v.," *VV*, 23 [1963]: 23-46). For a discussion of the *Life of Leontii of Rostov* and the reprint of its text, see Hurwitz, *Prince Andrej Bogoljubskij*, 79-84 and 94-95.

22. Hurwitz, *Prince Andrej Bogoljubskij*, 95.

23. The text of the *Narration about the Victory against the Bulgars* (1164) was initially published as an integral part of the *Narration About the Miracles of the Vladimirian Icon of the Mother of God* from Miliutin's *Chetii minei* of the mid-seventeenth century by V.O. Kliuchevskii, *Skazanie o chudesakh*, ChOLDP, 30 (1878): 10, 21-25. A more complete and a better text of the same narration, a text which coincides with another version of the identical story to be found in a sixteenth-century *Sbornik* of the Iaroslav Museum, entitled "Narration About God's Grace by Grand Prince Andrei," was made available by I.E. Zabelin, "Sledy literaturnogo truda Andreia Bogoliubskogo," *Arkheologicheskie izvestiia i zametki* (hereafter *AIZ*), 2-3 (1895): 37-49, especially 46-47.

24. For a discussion of the *Narration* and its dating, see above, fn. 23; N.N. Voronin, "Skazanie o pobede nad Bolgarami 1164 g. i prazdnike Spasa," *Problemy obshchestvenno-politicheskoi istorii Rossii i slavianskikh stran* (Moscow, 1963), 88-92; J. Pelenski, *Russia and Kazan: Conquest and Imperial Ideology (1438-1560s)* (The Hague and Paris, 1974), 144-149; Hurwitz, *Prince Andrej Bogoljubskij*, 60-68 (reprint of the text, 90-91).

25. *PSRL*, 1 (1926/1962), cols. 352-353.

26. Cf. my translation of the relevant fragment of the *Narration* (Pelenski, *Russia and Kazan*, 146).

27. Cf. N.N. Voronin's writings referred to in fns. 7, 21, and 24, above.

28. I. Ševčenko, "Russo-Byzantine Relations after the Eleventh Century," *Proceedings of the XIIIth International Congress of Byzantine Studies (Oxford, 5-10 September 1966)*, J. M. Hussey, D. Obolensky, and S. Runciman, eds. (London, 1967/1978), 95-96.

29. In my analysis I have excluded from consideration the statement in the *Narration* that the Feast of the Savior was inaugurated by Prince Andrei, "son of Iurii [Dolgorukii], the grandson of Volodimer Monomakh, tsar and prince of all Russia" (Hurwitz, *Prince Andrej Bogoljubskij*, 91), because, in my opinion, it represents an obvious sixteenth-century interpolation. The *Life of Leontii of Rostov* utilized the same reference to lineage, but in a contemporary formulation: "son of Grand Prince Iurii [Dolgorukii], the grandson of Volodimer" (Hurwitz, *Prince Andrej Bogoljubskij*, 95).

30. The text of the Church Slavonic-Russian translation of the Lukas Chrysoberges letter to Andrei Bogoliubskii was published by Metropolitan Makarii in *Istoriia russkoi tserkvi*, vol. 3 (1888/1968), 298-300; and A.S. Pavlov in *Russkaia istoricheskaia biblioteka* (hereafter *RIB*), 6, 2nd ed. (1908), cols. 63-68, with "additions" from the *Nikon Chronicle* (cols. 68-76) that must be treated with caution because they are representative of sixteenth-century Russian political thought.

31. Traditionally, the letter has been dated to the early 1160s (Pavlov, *RIB*, 6, 2nd ed. [1908], cols. 63-64). N.N. Voronin redated it to 1168 ("Andrei Bogoliubskii i Luka Khrizoverg: Iz istorii russko-vizantiiskikh otnoshenii XII v.," *VV*, 21 [1962]: 29-50, especially 38-41).

32. Vodoff, "Un 'parti thèocratique' dans la Russie du XIIᵉ siècle?," 193-215, especially 197-199.

33. Hurwitz suggests that Patriarch Lukas was probably relying on the twelfth Canon of the Council of Chalcedon (*Prince Andrej Bogoljubskij*, 31).

34. An informative discussion of that Byzantine doctrine as applied to Byzantine-Russian relations in the fourteenth century has been provided by J. Meyendorff, *Byzantium and the Rise of Russia* (Cambridge, 1981), 73-96. Cf. also D. Obolensky, "Byzantium, Kiev, and Moscow: A Study in Ecclesiastical Relations," *Dumbarton Oaks Papers*, 11 (1957): 21-78.

35. For an excellent exposition of the Byzantine doctrine of the unitary character of "Rossiia," see the formulation provided by Patriarch Anthony and his Synod in 1389, conveniently translated into English by Meyendorff, *Byzantium*, 75-76.

36. For a restatement of this interpretation, cf. Voronin, "Andrei Bogoliubskii i Luka Khrizoverg," 29-50, especially 48-50.

37. Ševčenko, "Russo-Byzantine Relations after the Eleventh Century," 95-96.

38. Pelenski, "The Sack of Kiev of 1169: Its Significance for the Succession to Kievan Rus'" includes an analysis of the two chronicles' *skazaniia* (narrations) and related historiographic problems [see Chapter 3 of this volume].

39. Pelenski, "The Sack of Kiev of 1169: Its Significance for the Succession to Kievan Rus'."

40. *PSRL*, 1 (1926/1962), col. 418.

41. *PSRL*, 1 (1926/1962), cols. 355-357; *PSRL*, 2 (1908/1962), cols. 551-554.

42. *PSRL*, 2 (1908/1962), col. 552.

43. *PSRL*, 1 (1926/1962), cols. 355-356; *PSRL*, 2 (1908/1962), col. 552.

44. *PSRL*, 2 (1908/1962), cols. 552-553.

45. Vodoff, "Un 'parti thèocratique' dans la Russie du XIIe siècle?," 208.

46. For the text of Kirill's *Life*, see N.K. Nikol'skii, *Materialy dlia istorii drevnerusskoi dukhovnoi pis'mennosti* in *Sbornik otdeleniia russkogo iazyka i slovesnosti*, vol. 82, no. 4 (6) (1907): 62-64, especially 63.

47. See *ibid.*, 63.

48. For an edition of the text and a Russian translation by V.V. Kolesova, see *Pamiatniki literatury drevnei Rusi: XII vek* (Moscow, 1980), 290-309.

49. *PSRL*, 2 (1908/1962), cols. 563-564.

50. *PSRL*, 2 (1908/1962), cols. 566-568.

51. *PSRL*, 2 (I908/1962), cols. 568-572.

52. *PSRL*, 2 (1908/1962), cols. 572-578.

53. *PSRL*, 2 (1908/1962), col. 566.

54. *PSRL*, 2 (1908/1962), col. 568.

55. *PSRL*, 2 (1908/1962), cols. 569-570.

56. M. Hrushevs'kyi, *Istoriia Ukrainy-Rusy*, vol. 2 (1905/1954), 200, fn. 2.

57. *PSRL*, 2 (1908/1962), cols. 570-571.

58. *PSRL*, 2 (1908/1962), col. 573.

59. Hrushevs'kyi, *Istoriia Ukrainy-Rusy*, 2: 200-202.

60. Hrushevs'kyi, *Istoriia Ukrainy-Rusy*, 2: 201.

61. *PSRL*, 2 (1908/1962), col. 572.

62. *PSRL*, 2 (1908/1962), col. 574.

63. *PSRL*, 2 (1908/1962), cols. 577-578.

64. *PSRL*, 2 (1908/1962), col. 545.

65. For an exposition of the medieval Germanic right of resistance, see the fundamental work by F. Kern, *Gottesgnadentum und Widerstandsrecht im frühen Mittelalter* (Darmstadt, 1963), 138-178.

66. *PSRL*, 2 (1908/1962), cols. 569-570.

67. *PSRL*, 2 (1908/1962), col. 570.

68. *PSRL*, 2 (1908/1962), cols. 572-573.

69. *PSRL*, 2 (1908/1962), col. 573.

70. *PSRL*, 2 (1908/1962), cols. 580-595. The text of the short version, included in the *Suzdalian-Vladimirian Chronicles* (*PSRL*, 1 [1926/1962], cols. 367-369), amounts to one and a half columns, therefore a ratio of nearly 10:1. For a discussion of the *Tale* and the literature on the subject, see N.N. Voronin, "Povest' ob ubiistve Andreia Bogoliubskogo i ee avtor," *Istoriia SSSR* (1963), 3: 90-97; and Hurwitz, *Prince Andrej Bogoljubskij*, 48-53 and 107-108.

71. See above.

72. *PSRL*, 2 (1908/1962), col. 580.

73. *PSRL*, 2 (1908/1962), col. 593.

74. Pelenski, "The Sack of Kiev of 1169: Its Significance for the Succession to Kievan Rus'," 314-315 [see Chapter 3 of this volume].

75. B.A. Rybakov's hypothesis about the participation of the "boiar-chronicler" Petr Borislavich in the composition of various materials of the *Kievan Chronicle* is in need of further study ("Boiarin-letopisets XII veka," *Istoriia SSSR* [1959], 5: 56-79; idem., *Russkie letopistsy i avtor "Slova o polku Igoreve"* [Moscow, 1972], 277-392).

3

THE SACK OF KIEV IN 1169:
ITS SIGNIFICANCE FOR THE
SUCCESSION TO KIEVAN RUS'*

The sack of Kiev in 1169, conducted under the auspices of
Andrei Iur'evich Bogoliubskii (1157-1175), has received relatively
little attention in historical scholarship. In particular, its significance
in the contest for the inheritance of and the succession to Kievan Rus'
has remained essentially unexplored. For most Russian historians and
those who have followed the tradition of Russian national
historiography, it has remained a difficult and inconvenient topic
which does not fit into the framework of the Russian national theory
of continuity from Kievan Rus'; through (Rostovia)-Suzdalia-
Vladimiria and Muscovy to Russia.[1] And even those who, like
Mykhailo Hrushevs'kyi (1866-1934), for example, vehemently
opposed this particular paradigm of Russian national history and
countered it with one of their own theories, that is the line of
succession (*translatio*) from Kievan Rus' through Galicia-Volynia,
Lithuania-Ruthenia, and Little Russia – Cossack Ukraine to Ukraine,
and who regarded the Rostov-Suzdal'-Vladimirian area as the
embryo of the Russian national state and Andrei Bogoliubskii as the
first truly "Russian" ruler, reconstructed the sack of Kiev in 1169
from the chronicles as primarily a historical event.[2]

The two crucial accounts (narrations) about the sack of Kiev in
1169 are contained in two principal sources, namely, the *Kievan
Chronicle (Kievskaia letopis')* (1118-1198[1200])[3] and the *Suzdalian-Vladimirian Chronicles (Vladimiro-Suzdal'skaia letopis')*.[4] To
the best of my knowledge, the two accounts, which can best be
described as two narrations about the taking of Kiev, have not been
analyzed insofar as their ideological significance for the topic under
consideration and for the history of political thought of Rus' is
concerned. Characterized by a number of factual similarities, the two

---

* For illustrations pertaining to this chapter, see Plates 10, 11, 12, 13, 24, 25, 26, 27,
28.

45

accounts also contain considerable political and ideological divergencies. A comparison of the two texts makes these points apparent.

The *Kievan Chronicle*

The same winter [1168/1169] Andrei sent from Suzdal' against the Kievan prince Mstislav [Iziaslavich] his son Mstislav [Andreievich], together with his host and the Rostovians, and the Vladimirians, and the Suzdalians, and Boris Zhidislavich, and eleven other princes: Gleb Iur'evich of Pereiaslav, Roman of Smolensk, Volodimer Andreievich of Dorohobuzh, Riurik of Ovruch, David of Vyshhorod, his brother Mstislav, Oleg Sviatoslavich and his brother Igor', Vsevolod Iur'evich, Mstislav, grandson of Iurii....

In the year [1169], the brothers gathered [their forces] in Vyshhorod. And [as they approached Kiev] they encamped at Dorohozhych near the Church of Saint Kyrill on Sunday, the Feast of Saint Feodor. And in the second week, they surrounded the city of Kiev. Mstislav [Iziaslavich] fortified himself in Kiev, and fought for the city. And everywhere the battle was fierce. Mstislav was losing strength in the city and the Berendeis and the Torks were deceiving him.

And they [the princes and their retinues] stayed for three days at the city. And then [advancing] they came down the Serkhovytsia [hill], and thus charging Mstislav's forces in the city from the hill, they began to shoot [arrows] at their backs. And his retinue said to Mstislav [Iziaslavich]: "Why do you stay here, prince? Abandon the city. We cannot overcome them."

And God helped Mstislav Andreievich and his brothers, and they took Kiev. And Mstislav Iziaslavich fled from Kiev to Vasyliv. And Bastei's tribe, having overtaken him, began to shoot [arrows] at his back. And they took captive many [warriors] of his retinue: Dmytr the Brave, Oleksa Dvorskyi, Sbyslav Zhiroslavich, Ivanko Tvorimirich and his steward, Rod, and many others. And [Mstislav Iziaslavich] and his brother Iaroslav met beyond the Unova [River] and together they departed to Volodymyr[-Volyns'kyi].

And so Kiev was taken on March 8th [12th] in the second week of Lent, on Wednesday. And for two days they plundered the entire city, both the *Podol* and the Hill, as well as the monasteries, and the [churches of] St. Sophia and the Mother of God [namely] the Tithe [Church]. And there was no mercy to anyone from nowhere: the churches were burning, the Christians were being put to death, others were captured, the women, separated by force from their men, were taken into captivity, the children, seeing their mothers taken away, were crying. And much property was plundered; they stripped the churches of icons, books, and vestments, and they, namely, the Smolenians, the Suzdalians, and the Chernihivians, as well as Oleg's retinue, removed the [church] bells, and all the Holy [objects] were taken. And the Monastery of the Caves of the Holy Mother of God was set on fire by the pagans, but it was saved by God from disaster, because of the prayers of the Blessed Mother of God. And moaning and grief and unconsoled sorrow and unending tears befell all the people of Kiev. And all this happened because of our sins.

The Beginnings of the Princely Rule of Gleb in Kiev

Mstislav Andreievich installed his uncle Gleb in Kiev on March 8th [12th]. Gleb gave Pereiaslav to his son Volodimer, and Mstislav Andreievich went to Suzdal' to his father Andrei with great honor and fame.

The *Suzdalian-Vladimirian Chronicles*

The same winter [1168/1169] Prince Andrei sent from Suzdal' against the Kievan Prince Mstislav [Iziaslavich] his son Mstislav [Andreievich] with the Rostovians and the Vladimirians, and the Suzdalians, and eleven other princes: Gleb of Pereiaslav, Roman of Smolensk, David of Vyshhorod, Volodimer Andreievich, Dmitr, and Iurii, Mstislav and Riurik with his brother Mstislav, Oleg Sviatoslavich with his brother Igor'. Mstislav Iziaslavich fortified himself in Kiev and fought hard for the city. And they stayed at the city for three days. And God and the Holy Mother of God, and his father's and grandfather's prayers helped Prince Mstislav Andreievich. And with his brothers he took Kiev, which had never happened before. And Mstislav Iziaslavich, together with his brother and a small retinue, fled from Kiev to Volodymyr[-Volyns'kyi]. And they captured the prince's wife and his son, and his retinue. And for three days they plundered the entire city of Kiev, as well as the churches and the monasteries. And they seized icons and books, and vestments. And that happened because of their sins, and, moreover, because of the unlawfulness of the metropolitan, who at that time interdicted Polikarp, the abbot of the Monastery of the Caves, on account of our Lord's holy

days. He forbade him to eat butter and [drink] milk on the
holy days of our Lord, falling on Wednesdays and Fridays.
And Antonii, the bishop of Chernihiv, stood by the
[metropolitan] and repeatedly prohibited the prince of
Chernihiv to eat meats on the holy days of our Lord. But
Prince Sviatoslav, ill-disposed to him, removed him from the
bishopric. So, we must note, everyone of us, that no one may
oppose God's law. Now let us return to the aforesaid.
Mstislav Andreievich installed his uncle Gleb in Kiev, and returned to Vladimir, together with his retinue. In the year 1169,
Mstislav Andreievich installed his uncle Gleb in Kiev, and he
himself returned to Vladimir. And Gleb gave Pereiaslav to his
son.

The two accounts display similarities in providing factual
descriptions of the military campaign undertaken at the order of
Andrei Bogoliubskii against Kiev and its lawful ruler, Prince
Mstislav Iziaslavich. They both talk of the forces involved in the
campaign, mentioning the names of most of the eleven princes
participating in it, of some aspects of the battle for the city of Kiev,
of its conquest, of the capture of Mstislav Iziaslavich's wife and his
son, of the sack of the city itself and its plundering, specifically of
the churches and the monasteries, and of the removal of icons, books
and vestments, and, finally, of the installation of Gleb in Kiev by
Mstislav Andreievich who himself returned to Vladimir in the north.
Of the two accounts, the narration in the *Kievan Chronicle* is
much more elaborate and detailed in describing the facts surrounding
the battle for Kiev and its ultimate sack. For example, its
author/editor provided the exact date (Wednesday, March 8th [12th])
for the sack of Kiev, specifically named the plundered churches (the
St. Sophia and the Tithe Church), and indicated that the Monastery of
the Caves was spared. He also designated the lands from which the
perpetrators of the sack came (Smolensk, Suzdal', and Chernihiv),
mentioned the taking of the shrines, and reported on the "deceitful"
role and performance of the steppe peoples (the Berendeis and the
Torks) in the Kievan campaign. The account in the *Suzdalian-
Vladimirian Chronicles* simply omitted all references to the steppe
peoples.
The ideological differences between the two accounts are
striking. The author/editor of the Kievan account clearly identified
with the city of Kiev, the fate of its inhabitants, and with their
suffering. As far as the ideological explanation of the sack is

concerned, he, in accordance with the Christian tradition, accepted the sack of Kiev as a just punishment inflicted upon its people for unspecified transgressions (*grekh radi nashikh*). This explanation is reinforced in the Kievan account by the device of lamentation, artfully and appropriately couched in biblical terms. In this context, the notion of the throne of Kiev is also utilized in the Kievan version, whereas it is excluded from the Suzdalian-Vladimirian account. There is only one reference in the account of the *Kievan Chronicle* that deviates from its general line of interpretation empathetic to Kiev and its ruling dynasty of Mstislavichi, namely, that Mstislav Andreievich returned to Suzdal' and to his father Andrei Iur'evich "with great honor and fame."

The Suzdalian-Vladimirian account, on the other hand, treats Kiev as a hostile city which is deservedly sacked and punished for the sins of its inhabitants. At the same time, its author/editor remarked that the sack of Kiev was an event that had never occurred before (*egozhe ne bylo nikogdazhe*). The author's expression of amazement at the sack of Kiev is articulated even more emphatically in another Suzdalian-Vladimirian narration, namely, the account about the sack of Kiev in 1203, undertaken by other Rus' princes at the instigation of Vsevolod III Iur'evich (1176-1212). There the relevant phrase reads: *i sotvorishia veliko zlo v russtei zemli iakogo zhe zla ne bylo ot kreshchenia nad Kievom* (and a great evil befell the Rus' land, such as has not been since the baptism of Kiev).[5] This revealing reference to the time of the baptism of Kiev in connection with the sack of 1203 could have been made to minimize the impact of the commentary on the sack of Kiev in 1169. The most important justification for the sack of Kiev in 1169 in the Suzdalian-Vladimirian account, however, is offered in conjunction with the controversy over fasting on major holy days of the Lord. By blending the materials about the controversy and the interdiction of Polikarp, the abbot of the Monastery of the Caves, by the metropolitan of Kiev Constantine, the author/editor of the Suzdalian-Vladimirian account succeeded in advancing an interpretation which fitted well into the framework of Andrei Bogoliubskii's political and ideological design. In fact, the information on the controversy in the Suzdalian-Vladimirian narration could have been only a projection of an earlier controversy concerning fasting on Wednesdays and Fridays whenever these days coincided with the major holy days of the Lord, which is attested as having taken place in Suzdal' in 1164.[6] The

Suzdalian-Vladimirian account, which was designed to substantiate the position of the Suzdalian-Vladimirian branch of the dynasty in the struggle for control over Kiev, displays an obvious anti-Kievan bias.

The differences between the two accounts reflect the divergencies between the *Kievan Chronicle* and the *Suzdalian-Vladimirian Chronicles*. For the history of Kievan Rus' in the period from 1118 to 1198 (1200), that is, the period encompassing the sack of Kiev in 1169 and the time of Andrei Bogoliubskii's policies toward Kiev, the *Kievan Chronicle*, which constitutes the second major component of the *Hypatian Codex* (columns 284-715 of vol. 2 of *PSRL* – a total of 431 columns), is in both quantitative and qualitative terms superior to the *Suzdalian-Vladimirian Chronicles* – the second major component of the *Laurentian Codex*. However, contrary to the well-researched *Primary Chronicle* (*Povest' vremennykh let*), for example, which constitutes the first major component of both the *Laurentian Codex* and the *Hypatian Codex*, and which amounts to 283 columns in each of the printed editions and embraces the period from the year 852 to 1110 (a total of 258 years), the *Kievan Chronicle*, comprising 431 columns and covering a period of about 80 years, has received inadequate attention in scholarship.[7] It deserves to be noted here, that a text of the *Kievan Chronicle*, prepared and translated into English over a prolonged period of time by the late Tatiana Chyzhevska, will soon be published.[8] Whereas some of the components of the *Kievan Chronicle* have been identified by scholars over the last 120 years, many important problems of its difficult and complex text remain unresolved. Like any other chronicle or codex of this magnitude, the *Kievan Chronicle* provides, in addition to factual historical material, a multitude of source materials with diverse political and ideological orientations. Its principal ideological tenets with respect to Kievan Rus' are the following:

1. The capital city of Kiev, the Kievan land, and what we perceive as "Kievan Rus' "[9] are at the center of attention.
2. The authors/editors were committed to the preeminence of Kiev in Rus', regardless of the fact that various branches and subbranches of the dynasty were competing for the succession to the Kievan throne.
3. They adhered to the notion of continuity from the origins of Rus' to post-Monomakh Rus'.

4. They advocated a concept ideologists have defined as "the Rus' land." This attitude explains their selective, but nonetheless all-embracing incorporation and integration into the *Kievan Chronicle* of materials from various parts of Rus', which at times were even in conflict with and hostile to the concept of the unity of the Rus' lands under Kiev.

5. The concepts of the historical continuity of Kievan Rus' and the inheritance of and succession to that entity were so evidently perpetuated by the authors/editors of the *Hypatian Codex* in its third major component – the *Galician-Volynian Chronicle* – that at least one historian has hypothesized that the *Kievan Chronicle* (the second major component of the *Hypatian Codex*) was continued to the year 1238 and that its last part (embracing the years 1200-1238) was integrated into the *Galician-Volynian Chronicle*.[10] Even if one questions this hypothesis, there is no doubt that the main objective of the authors/editors of the *Hypatian Codex* was to present a very complete account of Kievan Rus' history, embracing a period of approximately eighty years (1118-1198 [1200]), and to emphasize their concept of historical and political continuity from Kievan to Galician Rus', as evidenced by their prefacing the entire *Hypatian Codex* with a special "Introduction," which deserves to be quoted here in full:

> These are the names of Kievan princes who ruled in Kiev until the conquest of Batu who was in [the state of] paganism: The first to rule in Kiev were co-princes Dir and Askold. After [them followed] Oleg. And following Oleg [came] Igor'. And following Igor' [came] Sviatoslav. And after Sviatoslav [came] Iaropolk. And following Iaropolk [came] Volodimer, who ruled in Kiev and who enlightened the Rus' land with holy baptism. And following Volodimer, Sviatopolk began to rule. And after Sviatopolk [came] Iaroslav. And following Iaroslav [came] Iziaslav. And Iziaslav [was succeeded] by Sviatopolk. And following Sviatopolk, [came] Vsevolod. And after him [followed] Volodimer Monomakh. And following him [came] Mstislav. And after Mstislav [followed] Iaropolk. And following Iaropolk [came] Vsevolod. And after him [followed] Iziaslav. And following Iziaslav [came] Rostislav. And he [was followed] by

Mstislav. And following him [came] Gleb. And he [was fol-
lowed] by Volodimer. And following him [came] Roman. And
after Roman [followed] Sviatoslav. And following him [came]
Riurik. And after Riurik [followed] Roman. And after Roman
[came] Mstislav. And after him [followed] Iaroslav. And
following Iaroslav [came] Volodimer Riurikovych. Danylo
installed him in his own place in Kiev. Following Volodimer,
[when Kiev was governed by] Danylo's governor Dmytro,
Batu conquered Kiev.[11]

The *Suzdalian-Vladimirian Chronicles*, which constitute the
second major component of the *Laurentian Codex* (columns 289-437
of vol. 1 of *PSRL*), deal with a period of approximately 100 years,
that is, from 1111 to 1212. They, therefore, cover twenty more
years of history than the *Kievan Chronicle*, but occupy a total of
only 148 printed columns,[12] in comparison with 431 printed
columns of the *Kievan Chronicle*. Whereas the *Suzdalian-
Vladimirian Chronicles* have received considerable coverage in
historical literature, the relationship between the various original
chronicles and codices that have been integrated in their text has not
been clearly established. The same can be said about the relevant
material (up to the year 1203) in the *Radziwiłł Chronicle
(Radzivilovskaia letopis')* and the *Suzdal'-Pereiaslav Chronicle
(Letopisets Pereiaslavlia Suzdal'skogo)*, the text of which for the
years 1138-1214 coincides with that for the same period of the
Radziwiłł Chronicle.[13] In particular, the interconnection between the
hypothetical *Chronicle of Iurii Dolgorukii*, the hypothetical
Bogoliubskii Chronicle of 1177, the hypothetical *Vladimirian Codex
of 1177 (1178?)*, and the hypothetical *Vladimirian Codex of 1189*,
which presumably were used by the authors/editors of the *Laurentian
Codex*, the *Hypatian Codex*, and the hypothetical *Chronicle of 1212*,
have not been sufficiently investigated.[14]

The political and ideological orientation of the *Suzdalian-
Vladimirian Chronicles* with regard to the problem of the Kievan
inheritance (as reflected in the text of the *Laurentian Codex*) is as
follows:

1. The capital city of Kiev, the Kievan land, and "Kievan Rus'"
    are treated from the Suzdalian-Vladimirian perspective.
2. The authors/editors devoted relatively limited space to the
    discussion of the protracted struggle for Kiev in 1146-1162,
    particularly the one conducted by Iurii Dolgorukii until 1157

for the Kievan throne and supremacy over Rus' from Kiev.[15]

3. They advocated the preeminence of the Suzdalian-Vladimirian branch of the dynasty over other branches of the dynasty and of the northern centers over the city of Kiev and the Kievan coreland.
4. They advanced justifications for downgrading and even subordinating Kiev outright to Vladimir on the Kliaz'ma River.
5. They promulgated policies and ideological justifications beneficial to the Suzdalian-Vladimirian branch of the dynasty and disadvantageous to Kievan interests.

In order to better understand the historical context in which the sack of Kiev in 1169 took place and its significance for the contest for the inheritance of and the succession to Kievan Rus', one has to look at the policies and some relevant ideological undertakings sponsored by Andrei Bogoliubskii and his protagonists with regard to Kiev prior to the sack and following it.

Andrei Bogoliubskii's initial involvement in Kievan affairs dates back to the years 1149-1155. During that time he appeared in Kiev in connection with Iurii Dolgorukii's quest for the Kievan throne and its takeover, following the defeat of Iziaslav Mstislavich of Volynia in 1149.[16] He participated in the successful battle of Lutsk, but, apparently unenthusiastic about the continued military campaign, he attempted to mediate a truce between Iurii and Iziaslav.[17] According to the Suzdalian-Vladimirian version, Andrei intended to return to the Suzdalian land in 1151, but his father evidently "detained him for a while."[18] This is one of the rare instances in the *Suzdalian-Vladimirian Chronicles* where Andrei Iur'evich is criticized. Apparently he had participated in his father's Kievan campaign of 1154-1155,[19] and, following Iurii's takeover of Kiev, received Vyshhorod in 1155.[20] This placed him in line for the Kievan succession.[21] However, uninterested in making use of that opportunity, he left Vyshhorod for the Suzdalian land.[22] By making that decision, "he had abandoned sacred tradition. Never before had the promise of inheritance of the Kievan throne been so unequivocally rejected."[23]

Andrei's break with the Kievan tradition is highlighted in the accounts of the two chronicles. They blend the information about his departure from the Kievan area with a brief narration about the prince's removal of the Icon of the Blessed Mother of God from

Vyshhorod, an icon which was to make an extraordinary ideological career in Russian history as the famous Icon of Our Lady of Vladimir.[24] A comparison of the relevant accounts in the two chronicles will reveal different approaches of their authors/editors:

The *Kievan Chronicle*

> The same year [1155] Prince Andrei went from his father from Vyshhorod to Suzdal' *without his father's permission* [my italics – J.P.], and he took from Vyshhorod the Icon of the Blessed Mother of God which was brought from Tsesariagrad on the same ship with the Pirogoshcha [Icon]. And he had it framed in thirty-*grivny*-weight-of-gold, besides silver, and precious stones, and large pearls, and having thus adorned [the Icon], he placed it in his own church of the Mother of God in Vladimir.[25]

The *Suzdalian-Vladimirian Chronicles*

> The same year [1155] Prince Andrei went from his father to Suzdal', and he brought with him the Icon of the Blessed Mother of God which was brought from Tsesariagrad on the same ship with the Pirogoshcha [Icon]. And he had it framed in thirty-*grivny*-weight-of-gold, besides silver, and precious stones, and large pearls, and having thus adorned [the Icon], he placed it in his own church in Vladimir.[26]

The two accounts are similar, except for several, crucially important differences. According to the *Kievan Chronicle*, Andrei Bogoliubskii acted improperly and even unlawfully, by leaving Vyshhorod without his father's permission and by taking with him the icon of the Blessed Mother of God. The authors/editors of the *Suzdalian-Vladimirian Chronicles*, on the other hand, omitted the phrase "without his father's permission" and eliminated mention of Vyshhorod, the original domicile of the icon in Rus'. The authors/editors of some sixteenth-century Muscovite chronicles were even more uninhibited, as far as the elimination of Vyshhorod and the Kievan land, that is, the original Rus' domicile of the icon, from their accounts was concerned: they simply stated that "the pious prince Andrei Bogoliubskii brought from Constantinople the miraculous icon, the image of the Blessed Mother of God."[27] A comparison of the relevant accounts supports the conclusion that the removal of the icon from Vyshhorod was viewed from the Kievan perspective as a hostile and even illegal act, and from the Suzdalian-Vladimirian and later Muscovite perspectives as an act of breaking away from Kiev and not of succeeding to it.

Once he departed from the Kievan area, Andrei Iur'evich embarked on the policy of creating a strong patrimonial territorial state in the Rostovian and Suzdalian lands and of elevating Vladimir as its principal center and that of the entire Rus'. That policy extended from 1157, when Andrei was installed in Rostov and Suzdal', to 1167, when he became involved in the contest for Kiev. During that period his interests in and activities with respect to Kiev were limited, and from 1161 to 1167 he practically did not interfere in Kievan affairs.[28] He did, however, conduct ecclesiastical policies during 1157-1169 aimed at establishing direct princely control over the see of Rostov, at separating it from the jurisdiction of the Metropolitanate of Kiev, and at creating a new metropolitan see of Vladimir, completely independent of Kiev and subordinated directly to the Patriarchate of Constantinople.[29]

Andrei Bogoliubskii's ecclesiastical policies have been analyzed in scholarship primarily from the Vladimirian and Byzantine perspectives.[30] They have received limited attention insofar as their significance for the inheritance of and succession to Kiev is concerned. As is well known, Andrei Iur'evich's attempts to create the metropolitan see of Vladimir in direct opposition to the Kievan metropolitanate was firmly rejected by the Byzantine patriarch Lukas Chrysoberges in about 1168 and resulted in Andrei's major political defeat.[31] It can be concluded, therefore, that if he wanted to continue his quest for supremacy over all of Rus', Andrei faced two options: (1) to perpetuate the political tradition to rule Kiev and Rus' from Kiev, as did his father Iurii Dolgorukii, among others; or (2) to destroy Kiev as the center of power and prestige in Rus', and to subordinate it as a dependency in his new system of the Rus' lands, ruled from Vladimir. The campaign of 1168, the sack of Kiev in 1169, and the installation of Gleb in Kiev attest to his choice of option two.

By sacking Kiev in 1169 and installing his brother as prince in the city, Andrei Iur'evich succeeded, at least for a brief time (less than two years), in bringing option two to realization. However, he was unable to keep Kiev in subordinated position following Gleb's death in 1171. A coalition of Rostislavichi of Smolensk and Mstislav of Volynia opposed Andrei's plans for Kiev and his candidate to rule in Kiev, Mikhail Iur'evich. Andrei, on his part, began, as in 1168, to organize a coalition of princes to settle the contest for Kiev. The Olgovichi of Chernihiv temporarily sided with him. By 1173, he again managed to assemble a major army with 20 princes which, according to the apparently inflated information of the *Kievan Chronicle*, amounted to 50,000 men.[32] The huge army conducted operations in Southern Rus' and the Kievan area, but was decisively defeated by the Volynian-Smolenian coalition. The *Kievan Chronicle* commented: "And all the forces of Prince Andrei of Suzdal' returned. He gathered [his forces[from all the lands, and of the multitude of his warriors there was no count. They came in pride, and departed to their homes humbled."[33] Thus, Andrei's second attempt at conquering Kiev failed. However, that defeat did not quell his efforts to take Kiev, because he again made plans to impose his control over that city. Only Andrei's death on 29 June 1175, at the hands of his political opponents, saved Kiev from his further destructive designs.

A discussion of Andrei Bogoliubskii's attitudes toward Kiev would be incomplete without mention of the *Tale about the Slaying of Andrei [Bogoliubskii] (Povest' ob ubienii Andreia [Bogoliub-skogo])*, written following his death. The *Tale* can best be described as a eulogy and a political-ideological treatise glorifying Bogoliub-skii and his achievements. Paradoxically enough, its most extensive version was included in the *Kievan Chronicle*, which, with a few minor exceptions, was critical of and even hostile to him.[34] The author(s) of the *Tale* juxtaposed Kiev to Vladimir, Vyshhorod to Bogoliubovo ("and as far as Vyshhorod was from Kiev, so far was Bogoliubovo from Vladimir"), the Golden Gate of one capital city to the other, the martyrdom of Andrei to that of Saints Boris and Gleb; they also glorified Vladimir. Their purpose was obvious: besides glorifying Bogoliubskii, they intended to enhance the image of Vladimir at the expense of Kiev, by elevating its status at least to that of the latter capital. Why, then, was this *Tale*, so favorably predisposed to Bogoliubskii and his political designs, included in the *Kievan Chronicle*? The editors of the latter apparently incorporated it because it had relevance to Kievan history. Evidently their general attitude was to integrate in the chronicle all the Kiev-related material, regardless of its contents. It follows that the editors of the *Kievan Chronicle*, similarly to those of the *Galician-Volynian Chronicle*, did not hesitate to accept the entire Kievan inheritance, because they considered themselves to be its rightful heirs, whereas

the editors of the *Suzdalian-Vladimirian Chronicles* used materials
selectively and adapted them to their political and ideological needs.

Russian historiography is characterized by two contradictory
approaches to Andrei Bogoliubskii's reign and his policies with
respect to Kiev. On the one hand, Russian historians have tended to
view Bogoliubskii's policies toward Kiev as a break with the history
of Kievan Rus', and his reign and endeavors in the Rostovian-
Suzdalian land and his capital city of Vladimir as the beginning of a
new period in Russian history that laid a foundation for the establishment of a national centralized Russian state in the Muscovite age.
(A.E. Presniakov and N.N. Voronin modified somewhat the thesis
concerning the innovative and "proto-Muscovite" nature of
Bogoliubskii's reign and policies.) At the same time, Russian
historiography, with the exception of Presniakov and a few of his
followers, has continued to adhere to the late medieval/early modern
Russian theory of continuity from Kievan Rus' through (Rostovia)-
Suzdalia-Vladimiria to Muscovy, developed by Muscovite chroniclers, bookmen, and ideologists in the fifteenth and sixteenth
centuries, even though this theory has been qualified by the thesis
concerning the feudal fragmentation of Kievan Rus'. The sack of
Kiev in 1169 and the policies of Andrei Bogoliubskii toward Kiev
serve as primary evidence against the Muscovite Russian continuity
theory.

1.   The sack of Kiev in 1169 was a logical outcome of Andrei
     Bogoliubskii's Kievan policies, aimed not at the
     "neutralization" of the ancient capital of Rus', but at its sub-
     ordination to Vladimir. The fundamental differences between
     Bogoliubskii's attitudes with respect to the contest for the
     Kievan succession and those entertained by other competi-
     tors, as well as those displayed by his father Iurii Dolgorukii,
     were manifested in his decisions (a) not to personally take
     charge of the military campaigns designed to take over Kiev,
     (b) to sponsor the sack of Kiev in 1169, an unprecedented act
     of violence against the mother of the Rus' cities, (c) not to be
     installed on the Kievan throne, (d) to attempt to establish a
     separate metropolitan see in Vladimir, in opposition to the
     metropolitan see of Kiev, (e) to advance claims to reign over
     all Rus' from Vladimir.

2. The sack of Kiev in 1169 fundamentally changed the perception of Kiev and the Rus' polity in the minds of the Suzdalian and later Vladimirian branch of the dynasty, as well as of other branches of the dynasty and their elites. This perception was at first characterized by a dichotomy of approaches, that is, (a) to tentatively retain lineal dynastic connections and selective identification with Kiev, on the one hand, and (b) to downgrade its status and subordinate it completely to Vladimir, on the other. This dual approach to Kiev is reflected in the political programs advanced by Vsevolod III Iur'evich, Iaroslav III Vsevolodovich, and Aleksandr Nevskii, who, independently or with the help of Mongol-Tatars, attempted to obtain the title of Kiev. Aleksandr Nevskii, for example, is credited by the *Suzdalian-Vladimirian Chronicles* with having succeeded in obtaining from the Mongols "Kiev and all the land of Rus'."[35] However, the lineal dynastic connections to Kiev were simply eliminated in the *Vita* of Aleksandr Nevskii, written from a devotional point of view. It provides a dynastic lineage reaching back only to Nevskii's father Iaroslav III Vsevolodovich and his grandfather Vsevolod III Iur'evich, both of Suzdal'-Vladimir, and extols the image of the Suzdalian land, but it refrains from mentioning Kiev and the land of Rus', thus breaking the link with the Kievan tradition.[36]

3. The sack of Kiev in 1169, the ensuing policies of the Suzdalian-Vladimirian branch of the dynasty toward Kiev, and the evolution of its ideological programs undermine the validity of the theory of continuity from Kievan Rus' through (Rostovia)-Suzdalia-Vladimiria to Muscovy. They show that from 1155/1157 the Suzdalian-Vladimirian branch of the dynasty and the influential elements of northeastern Rus' aimed first at breaking away from Kiev, then at subordinating it to Vladimir, and, finally, at eradicating it from historical memory.

NOTES

1. For the background on the Russian national theory of continuity from Kievan Rus' through (Rostovia)-Suzdalia-Vladimiria and Muscovy to Russia and the literature on the subject, see J. Pelenski, "The Origins of the Official Muscovite Claims to the 'Kievan Inheritance'," *Harvard Ukrainian Studies* (hereafter *HUS*), 1, no. 1 (1977): 29-52 [see Chapter 5 of this volume]; *idem.*, "The Emergence of the Muscovite Claims to the Byzantine-Kievan 'Imperial Inheritance'," *HUS*, 7 (1983): 520-531 [see Chapter 7 of this volume].

2. M. Hrushevs'kyi, *Istoriia Ukrainy-Rusy*, vol. 2 (1905/1954), 196-197.

3. Concerning the text of the narration in the *Kievan Chronicle*, see *Ipat'evskaia letopis'* published in *Polnoe sobranie russkikh letopisei* (hereafter *PSRL*), 2 (1908/1962), cols. 543-545.

4. The text of the narration in the *Suzdalian-Vladimirian Chronicles* is contained in the *Laurentian Codex*, *PSRL*, 1 (1926/1962), cols. 354-355.

5. *PSRL*, 1 (1926/1962), col. 418.

6. *PSRL*, 1 (1926/1962), cols. 351-352; *PSRL*, 2 (1908/1962), cols. 520-521.

7. For a concise description of the *Hypatian Codex*, especially its component the *Kievan Chronicle*, and selected literature on the subject, see O. P. Likhacheva, "Letopis' Ipat'evskaia" in "Issledovatel'skie materialy dlia 'Slovaria knizhnikov i knizhnosti drevnei Rusi (Drevnerusskie letopisi i khroniki)'," *Trudy Otdela drevnerusskoi literatury* (hereafter *TODRL*), 39 (1985): 123-128.

8. Information by courtesy of Professor Omelian Pritsak and Dr. Paul A. Hollingsworth. Another English translation of the *Kievan Chronicle* has been provided by Lisa Lynn Heinrich in her unpublished doctoral dissertation, "The Kievan Chronicle: A Translation and Commentary" (Vanderbilt University, 1977).

9. The concept "Kievan Rus' " was not used literally in contemporary Rus' sources. It has been applied by scholars to denote the period of Rus' history in the age of Kiev's preeminence.

10. V.T. Pashuto, *Ocherki po istorii galitsko-volynskoi Rusi* (Moscow, 1950), 21-67.

11. *PSRL*, 2 (1908/1962), cols. 1-2.

12. Concerning a discussion of the *Suzdalian-Vladimirian Chronicles* and the literature on the subject, consult U.A. Limonov, *Letopisanie Vladimiro-Suzdal'skoi Rusi* (Leningrad, 1967) and Ia.S. Lur'e, "Letopis' Lavrent'evskaia" in "Issledovatel'skie materialy," *TODRL*, 39 (1985): 128-131.

13. For a brief description of the *Radziwiłł Chronicle* and the relevant literature, see Ia.S. Lur'e, "Letopis' Radzivilovskaia" in "Issledovatel'skie materialy," *TODRL*, 39 (1985): 141-143. A short bibliographical note on the "Letopisets Pereiaslavlia Suzdal'skogo" was provided by O.V. Tvorogov, *ibid.*, 110.

14. A convenient summary of the discussion of these interconnections, and especially two useful schemata of these hypothetical codices and chronicles, on the basis of research conducted until the mid-1960s, has been provided by Limonov.

15. The discussion of that contest for succession is limited in the *Suzdalian-Vladimirian Chronicles* to 40 columns (cols. 312-351 in *PSRL*, 1 [1926/1962]).

16. *PSRL*, 1 (1926/1962), cols. 323-326; *PSRL*, 2 (1908/1962), cols. 386-392. For a treatment of Andrei Bogoliubskii's career and the relevant literature, see E.S. Hurwitz, *Prince Andrej Bogoljubskij: The Man and the Myth* (Florence, 1980).

17. *PSRL*, 1 (1926/1962), col. 329; *PSRL*, 2 (1908/1962), cols. 404-405.

18. *PSRL*, 1 (1926/1962), col. 335.

19. Indirectly *PSRL*, 2 (1908/1962), col. 480.

20. *PSRL*, 2 (1908/1962), col. 478.

21. Hurwitz, *Prince Andrej Bogoljubskij*, 12.

22. *PSRL*, 2 (1908/1962), col. 482.

23. Hurwitz, *Prince Andrej Bogoljubskij*, 12.

24. For the treatments of the icon's career and the relevant literature, see N.N. Voronin, "Iz istorii russko-vizantiiskoi tserkovnoi bor'by XII v.," *Vizantiiskii vremennik* (hereafter *VV*), 26 (1965): 190-218; D.B. Miller, "Legends of the Icon of Our Lady of Vladimir: A Study of the Development of Muscovite National Consciousness," *Speculum*, 43, 4 (1968): 657-670; Hurwitz, *Prince Andrej Bogoljubskij*, 54-59.

25. *PSRL*, 2 (1908/1962), col. 482.

26. *PSRL*, 1 (1926/1962), col. 346.

27. See the *Voskresensk Chronicle* (*PSRL*, 8, 254) and the *Sofiia Second Chronicle* (*PSRL*, 6, 254). Cf. also I.U. Budovnits, *Obshchestvenno-politicheskaia mysl' drevnei Rusi (XI-XIV vv.)* (Moscow, 1960), 242, fn. 25. Another tradition in sixteenth-century Muscovite political thought, which placed great emphasis on the Kievan domicile of the icon, was represented by the *Povest'* included in the *Kniga stepennaia* (*PSRL*, 21, 2 [1913/1970]), 424-440.

28. Hurwitz, *Prince Andrej Bogoljubskij*, 16.

29. *Ibid.*, p. 23.

30. For the four related treatments and the literature on the subject, see N.N. Voronin, "Andrei Bogoliubskii i Luka Khrizoverg: Iz istorii russko-vizantiiskikh otnoshenii XII v.," *VV*, 21 (1962): 29-50; I. Ševčenko, "Russo-Byzantine Relations after the Eleventh Century," *Proceedings of the XIIIth International Congress of Byzantine Studies*, J.M. Hussey, D. Obolensky, S. Runciman, eds. (London, 1967), 93-104; W. Vodoff, "Un 'parti thèocratique' dans la Russie du XIIe siècle," *Cahiers de civilisation médiévale*, 17, 3 (1974): 193-215; Hurwitz, *Prince Andrej Bogoljubskij*, 23-36.

31. Concerning a Russian translation of Lukas Chrysoberges's letter to Andrei Bogoliubskii, see *Russkaia Istoricheskaia Biblioteka*, 6 (2nd ed., 1908), cols. 63-68. The *Nikon Chronicle*'s "additions" (cols. 68-76) must be treated with caution, because they are representative of sixteenth-century Russian political thought.

32. *PSRL*, 2 (1908/1962), col. 573.

33. *PSRL*, 2 (1908/1962), cols. 577-578.

34. For the text of the extensive *Tale*, see *PSRL*, 2 (1908/1962), cols. 580-595 (nearly 15 columns). The text of the short version, included in the *Suzdalian-Vladimirian Chronicles* (*PSRL*, 1 [1926/1962], cols. 367-369), amounts to one and a half columns.

35. *PSRL*, 1 (1926/1962), col. 472.

36. Concerning a critical edition of the *Zhitie Aleksandra Nevskogo*, see Iu.K. Begunov, *Pamiatnik russkoi literatury XIII veka: "Slovo o pogibeli russkoi zemli"* (Moscow and Leningrad, 1965), 159-180, especially, 159, 165, and 178.

4

THE ORIGINS OF THE MUSCOVITE ECCLESIASTICAL CLAIMS TO THE KIEVAN INHERITANCE*

One of the principal concerns of Muscovite Russia's national and imperial ideology was her preoccupation with the Kievan heritage and the resulting formulation of official claims to Kievan Rus', at first ecclesiastical and later secular. This concern was subsequently transmitted to modern Russian national consciousness and historical thought. Although the ideological and historiographic controversies over the Kievan inheritance date back to the nineteenth century, concrete antiquarian and conceptual inquiries into the origins of Muscovy's preoccupation with the Kievan inheritance did not begin until the post-World War II period. At that time D.S. Likhachev attempted to show that Muscovite chronicle writing and culture were permeated by a new historicism that served as evidence for his hypothesis about the existence of the early Renaissance in Muscovite Russia during the late fourteenth and fifteen centuries.[1] (As a matter of fact, Likhachev's hypothesis has been questioned in scholarship,[2] and the topic has been apparently abandoned by the author.)

Aside from the conceptual differences of opinion, the new literature on the origins of Muscovy's claims to the Kievan inheritance has tended to concentrate on the official secular claims to Kievan Rus'. Likhachev dates these claims to the late fourteenth or early fifteenth century,[3] whereas I suggest the second half of the fifteenth.[4] Still, for a better understanding of the problem, it is necessary to consider the official ecclesiastical claims as well. Therefore, in this study I shall discuss Muscovy's ecclesiastical claims to the Kievan inheritance, concentrating on four major areas in which they were manifested: (1) the transfer of the Metropolitanate of Kiev and all of Rus' to Moscow, and the elevation of the city of Moscow to the status of a new religious center in Rus'; (2) the contest for the heritage of the Metropolitanate of Kiev and all of

---

* For illustrations pertaining to this chapter, see Plates 29, 30, 31.

Rus'; (3) the canonization of three metropolitans; and (4) the rudimentary theory of continuity from Kievan Rus' through (Rostovia)-Suzdalia Vladimiria to Muscovy in early Muscovite metropolitan chronicle writing.

The Transfer of the Metropolitanate of Kiev and All of Rus'

This transfer from Kiev to Moscow was accomplished in two stages. First, a transition from Kiev to Vladimir took place. It occurred following the establishment of a Mongol-Tatar supremacy over the states of Rus', after an accommodation between the Golden Horde (or the Kipchak Horde), Byzantium, and the Grand Principality of Suzdal'-Vladimir in the realm of ecclesiastical policies, and following the implementation of the Western-oriented policies of the Galician-Volynian rulers like Danylo Romanovych (ruled 1238-1264) and Iurii I (1303-1308), both of whom assumed the title of king after the acceptance by Danylo of a royal crown from Pope Innocent IV (1253). Kirill was the first metropolitan of Kiev and all of Rus' (1242-1281) to move from the coreland of Kievan Rus' to the northeastern Grand Principality of Vladimir where he performed his duties as the chief ecclesiastical official of Rus' during the greater part of his tenure and until his death in Pereiaslavl'-Zalesskii in 1281. In Vladimir, among other things, he presided over Grand Prince Aleksandr Nevskii's funeral (1263) and hosted an important council of Russian bishops (1274).

The transfer of the Metropolitanate of Kiev to Vladimir was completed by Kirill's successor, Metropolitan Maksim (1283-1305), who, according to the *Vladimiro-Suzdal'skaia letopis'* (the *Suzdalian-Vladimirian Chronicles*), while keeping his title Metropolitan of Kiev and all of Rus', left the metropolitan see and escaped from Kiev in 1300, allegedly because "he could not endure the Tatar oppression."[5] This explanation of the metropolitan's move by the *Suzdalian-Vladimirian Chronicles* is rather anachronistic and ideologically motivated since the Mongol-Tatars were not oppressing the church and because Vladimir, where Maksim moved, was located much more deeply in their sphere of influence than Kiev.

In the second stage of its transfer, the Metropolitanate of Kiev and all of Rus' was moved from Vladimir to Moscow. This was undertaken under the auspices of Metropolitan Petr (1308-1326) who had opted for the Muscovite side in the struggle between Moscow and Tver' for the Grand Principality of Vladimir.[6]

This move had an extraordinary significance for Moscow's rise, growth, and victory in the struggle for supremacy in northeastern Rus', in particular, and in the lands of all of Rus', in general. An institution like the metropolitanate would serve in the long run as an ideological, cultural, and, at times, administrative center of the Muscovite state. Among immediate consequences of this transfer was the enhancement of the status of the city of Moscow and the Muscovite Grand Principality. This was reflected in the selection of Moscow by Metropolitan Petr in 1322 to be the permanent residence of the Metropolitanate of Kiev and all of Rus', in the attention paid by early Muscovite ideologists to Petr's special concern for Moscow as a chosen city at a time when it was still struggling for recognition as one of the principal centers of northeastern Rus', and in the cult of Petr as a hierarch-saint of Moscow and the Suzdalian land.

Petr's role as a hierarch-saint is acknowledged in the "Praise of Petr," contained in the second recension of the so-called *Pouchenie Petra Mitropolita* (the *Admonition of Metropolitan Petr*). Paraphrasing other admonitions and to some extent the famous "Praise of Volodimer I" by Metropolitan Ilarion, the Muscovite author, writing probably at the end of 1330s, exclaimed:

> O great miracle. Rome prides itself in having the Supreme Apostle Peter, Damascus proudly philosophizes about having the light of the entire universe – Apostle Paul. The city of Thessalonica rejoices in having the Christian martyr Demetrius, Kiev takes pride in having the new Christian martyrs Boris and Gleb, the Rus' princes – the healers. Rejoice o city of Moscow in having the great hierarchy – Petr.[7]

Metropolitan Petr's pivotal role in the enhancement of the status of Moscow was magnified by Kiprian, another metropolitan of Kiev and all of Rus', who wrote an expanded *Vita* (*Zhitie*) of Metropolitan Petr in 1381. In it he inserted the famous prophecy about the future greatness of Moscow, allegedly made by Petr in an exchange with Ivan Danilovich Kalita, the ruler of Moscow[8]:

> And so, my son, take my advice, and build a church in your city of Moscow, and you shall be glorified above all other

princes, and your sons and grandsons for generations to come. And this city will be glorified in all the cities of Rus', and hierarchs will reside in it, and their arms will be raised above the shoulders of their enemies, and God will be glorified in it, and, finally, my bones will be laid to rest in it.[9]

The *Vita* of Metropolitan Petr by Kiprian became one of the most popular biographies in the Old Rus' literature, as attested by its inclusion, both in the *Velikie minei chetii* (the *Great Menology*) and the *Kniga stepennaia* (the *Book of Degrees*). Paradoxically, both Petr, the author of the ideological enhancement of Moscow, and Kiprian, the author of Petr's influential *Vita*, were not even Muscovites by origin. Metropolitan Petr was, in fact, a native of Volynia or Galicia, who originally had made his ecclesiastical career under the auspices of King Iurii of Galicia, but subsequently abandoned the king for an even higher office under the Muscovite ruler. Kiprian, the Bulgarian – who by his own interpretation of Petr's life and deeds, among other things, contributed immensely to the enhancement of Moscow's position and to the creation of the myth of Moscow – is perceived in scholarship as a relatively even-handed individual in the execution of his duties *vis-à-vis* the Orthodox of all of Rus'. It deserves mention that the Muscovite tradition, including the writings of Metropolitan Kiprian, attempted to play down Metropolitan Petr's Galician connection by emphasizing his Volynian origins and by stressing his sponsorship by a Volynian prince. In reality, it was King Iurii of Galicia who championed Petr's promotion to the position of Metropolitan of Halych.

The Contest for the Metropolitanate of Kiev and All of Rus'

The origins of this contest coincided with the emergence of the Muscovite patrimonial state and the struggle on the part of the Muscovite dynasty for the Grand Principality of Vladimir and supremacy over the various lands of Rus'. They also chronologically coincided with the political-ideological revival of Galician-Volynian Rus' under the auspices of King Iurii I and with the transformation of the Lithuanian polity into a dual Lithuanian-Ruthenian state. From 1322 to 1458 the Metropolitanate of Kiev and all of Rus' was based (with some interruptions) in Moscow and contested by various contenders: Galicia-Volynia, Poland, the Lithuanian-Ruthenian state, and the Polish-Lithuanian union state. In 1458/1461, the metropolitanate was

finally divided into the Metropolitanate of Kiev and all of Rus' –
under the auspices of Lithuania and later the Polish-Lithuanian
Commonwealth – and the Moscow-based Metropolitanate of Kiev
and all of Rus'. For almost 150 years, the Muscovite court in collab-
oration with the Metropolitanate of Kiev and all of Rus' had
conducted a protracted struggle for the Kievan ecclesiastical inheritance, as represented by the unity and indivisibility of that
metropolitanate. They had also made all the efforts to prevent its
division and the creation of other metropolitanates with a claim to
the Kievan succession.[10]

One of them was the Metropolitanate of Halych, a separate
ecclesiastical entity, independent of the Metropolitanate of Kiev and
all of Rus' and established in 1303 at the request of King Iurii I with
the Byzantine patriarch's approval. It was suppressed in 1347 by the
Byzantine Empire in a display of open power politics and revived in
1371 by the Byzantine patriarchate under political pressure from
King Kazimierz of Poland. The Metropolitanate of Halych was not a
lasting success. Originally, it had been created to remove Galicia and
Volynia from the jurisdiction of the Metropolitanate of Kiev and all
of Rus', which was under Tatar and Muscovite control, and to
provide the Orthodox faithful of Galicia with the necessary organizational framework, headed by an ecclesiastical leader, independent
of any secular authority outside of the Galician-Volynian state and
later the Polish Kingdom. Unlike the Muscovite dynasty and the
Moscow-based Metropolitanate of Kiev and all of Rus', which were
engaged in the contest for the entire heritage of the Metropolitanate
of Kiev and all of Rus', the Galician-Volynian rulers and their Polish
successors limited their contest to partial inheritance of the
Metropolitanate of Kiev and all of Rus', that is, the lands under their
control.

Another competitor in the contest for the heritage of the
Metropolitanate of Kiev and all of Rus' was the Grand Principality
of Lithuania, eventually the Lithuanian-Ruthenian state. At first, the
Lithuanian dynasty was involved, like Galicia-Volynia, in the contest
for a partial inheritance of the Kievan metropolitanate which
resulted in the establishment of the first Metropolitanate "of the
Lithuanians" (1300, or rather 1315-1319). However, the continuous
expansion of Lithuania into the lands of Rus', particularly the
attempts by Grand Prince Algirdas (1345-1377) to rule over all of
Rus', contributed to an extension of Lithuanian aims. Algirdas and

his successors, grand princes of Lithuania and joint rulers of the Polish-Lithuanian union state, endeavored and intermittently succeeded in establishing under their own auspices a metropolitanate either of "Kiev and all of Rus'," or of "all of Rus'," or of "Rus'" (1352?, 1355-1362, 1376-1380s?, 1415-1421, 1432-1435). Their grand design ("Kiev and all of Rus' ") was in some respects similar to that of the Muscovite dynasty, as they continued to participate in the contest with Muscovy for the lands of Kievan Rus'.[11]

Muscovy's efforts in her contest for the preservation of a unitary status of the Metropolitanate of Kiev and all of Rus' under the exclusive control of the Muscovite dynasty and government were greatly facilitated by the policies and ideological approach of the Byzantine Empire and patriarchate in the framework of which the Metropolitanate of Kiev and all of Rus' had functioned. From the creation of the Metropolitanate of Kiev and all of Rus' and throughout the period of the contest for the Kievan ecclesiastical inheritance, both the empire, as well as the patriarchate consistently adhered to the doctrine of a unitary status of the Metropolitanate of Kiev and all of Rus' (so aptly explicated by John Meyendorff[12]), which they defended against attempts to create competitive metropolitanates in the realm of Rus', such as the one by Andrei Bogoliubskii, for example.[13] Only in exceptional circumstances, as in the case of the titular metropolitanates in the eleventh century,[14] or in situations of strong political pressures, did they consent to the formation of competing and independent Ruthenian metropolitanates, not subject to the political and ideological control of the Moscow-based Metropolitanate of Kiev and all of Rus' and the Muscovite ruler.

Byzantium's insistence on the unity of the Moscow-based Metropolitanate of Kiev and all of Rus' reflected primarily her political and ideological interests and not the religious and organizational-ecclesiastical needs of the Orthodox Christians of the various Rus' polities, except for Muscovy proper. From the Byzantine perspective, Muscovy potentially had a good chance to be victorious in the contest for the supremacy over the other Rus' polities, and Byzantine emperors and patriarchs acted accordingly. Such an approach seemed to be obvious. Another imperial power, the Golden Horde, had previously drawn exactly the same conclusion in the struggle for the hegemony over Rus' and after some vacillations had decided to make the grand prince of Moscow the khan's principal native executive vassal in Rus'.

The Canonization of Three Metropolitans

Muscovy's ecclesiastical claims to the Kievan inheritance were greatly facilitated not only by the institutional *translatio* of the Metropolitanate of Kiev and all of Rus', but also by the politics of canonization in the framework of that institution. Significantly, three metropolitans of Kiev and all of Rus' in the Muscovite period were canonized as saints of the Russian Church prior to the establishment of the Patriarchate of Moscow in 1589: Petr (in office: 1308-1326), Aleksei (1354-1378), and Iona (1448-1461).

Immediately following his death, Petr was canonized by the Council of Vladimir in 1327. That his canonization was confirmed in Constantinople already by 1339[15] attests to his exceptionally good reputation at the court of the Byzantine patriarch. His *Vita* (*Zhitie*), as already mentioned, was authored by Kiprian, another prominent metropolitan of Kiev and all of Rus'.

Aleksei, who served as metropolitan of Kiev and all of Rus' for twenty-four years, who during the period when Grand Prince Dmitrii Ivanovich Donskoi was a minor acted as a regent and *de facto* head of the Muscovite government, and who was one of the leading Muscovite statesmen, was canonized as a saint of the Russian Church by Iona, the last Moscow-based metropolitan of Kiev and all of Rus'.[16] The latter arranged for Aleksei's canonization immediately following his own ascension to the Metropolitanate of Kiev and all of Rus' in 1448. Like Metropolitan Petr, Aleksei came from Ukrainian Rus'. He was an offspring of a Chernihivian boyar family that had voluntarily migrated to the north where his father, Fedor Biakont, entered the service of the Muscovite ruler. Metropolitan Aleksei's life and activities became the subject of a series of hagiographic and ideological works: a *Vita* by Pitirim, the bishop of Perm, written most probably at the time of his canonization; another *Vita* by Pakhomii the Serbian (Logofet), written at the request of Metropolitan Iona in 1459; an expanded version of the latter, written at the request of Metropolitan Makarii and included in the *Book of Degrees*, the most extensive of all the *Vitae* of metropolitans in that work;[17] and still another *Vita*, composed at the end of the seventeenth century by the monk Evfimii, a disciple of Epifanii Slavenets'kyi.

Unlike Petr and Aleksei, Iona was from Riazan'. He was a Great Russian and the first metropolitan of Moscow not confirmed by the Byzantine patriarchate.[18] He was also a prominent Muscovite politician during the age of Vasilii II and a staunch supporter of that Muscovite ruler. During their tenures the division of the Metropolitanate of Kiev and all of Rus' was finalized. Metropolitan Iona was canonized in two stages: the first stage took place in the period 1472-1479; the second coincided with the Church Council of 1547, conducted under the auspices of Metropolitan Makarii. Iona's life and accomplishments were also eulogized in various recensions of his *Vita*.[19]

The three metropolitans distinguished themselves by a devotion to the Muscovite cause, by a service to the Muscovite ruler, and by a deep involvement in the struggles for the supremacy of Moscow, in which they unhesitatingly and decisively used the weapon of excommunication against the enemies of the Muscovite rulers. As far as the problem of Kievan ecclesiastical inheritance was concerned, they fought with determination for the preservation of the unitary status of the Moscow-based Metropolitanate of Kiev and all of Rus' under Muscovite sponsorship and against all efforts on the part of the Ruthenian, Lithuanian, and Polish rulers to create metropolitanates for Kiev and other Rus' lands, independent from the Muscovite state. In other words, they were the co-architects of the all-Russian version of Muscovite ideology and politics. Their canonizations were based on their political and ideological achievements rather than their religious contributions. The similarity of their careers and contributions was clearly recognized by Iov, another Muscovite master politician, the first patriarch of Muscovite Russia (1589-1605), at whose request Prince Semen Ivanovich Shakhovskoi composed a joint *Vita* and *Praise* of the three metropolitans.[20] The integration of their *Vitae* into a single work attests to their being perceived as representing a unity of purpose and achievement.

The Rudimentary Continuity Theory in Early Muscovite Metropolitan Chronicle Writing

The fourth major factor in facilitating Muscovy's struggle for the Kievan inheritance in the ecclesiastical realm (as well as the secular) was the formulation under the sponsorship of the Moscow-based Metropolitanate of Kiev and all of Rus' of the rudimentary theory of continuity from Kievan Rus' through (Rostovia)-Suzdalia-

Vladimiria to Muscovy. The theory was first promulgated in a codex known as the *Troitskaia letopis' (TL)* (the *Trinity Chronicle*) apparently compiled in the metropolitan's chancery mainly under the auspices of Metropolitan Kiprian[21] from the end of the fourteenth to the beginning of the fifteenth century, and concluded in 1406-1408.

The *TL* was an official metropolitan codex. Its only existing copy, used by the Russian historian M.N. Karamzin who quoted extensively from it in his *Istoriia gosudarstva rossiiskogo*, was destroyed in the Moscow fire of 1812. However, the discovery of the *Simeonovskaia letopis'* (the *Simeonov Chronicle*) by A.A. Shakhmatov greatly facilitated the study of the *TL*, particularly his findings that for the years 1177-1393 the two chronicles were virtually identical. These findings, in turn, immensely helped M.D. Priselkov to reconstruct the *TL* text on the basis of Karamzin's quotations, the *Simeonov Chronicle*, and other materials.[22] The *TL* included as its first component the *Povest' vremennykh let (PVL)* (the *Tale of Bygone Years* or the *Primary Chronicle*), according to the *Lavrent'evskaia letopis'* (the *Laurentian Codex*), or a closely related text, covering the period to the year 1110. From about 1110 to about 1204, it incorporated materials of the *Suzdalian-Vladimirian Chronicles*, also based on the *Laurentian Codex* or a closely related compilation, like the prototype of the *Radzivilovskaia letopis'* (the *Radziwiłł Chronicle*). From 1203 to 1205, it continued to follow the Rostovian, Suzdalian and Vladimirian chronicle materials, although in an edited version. From 1206 to 1263, it again very closely followed the *Suzdalian-Vladimirian Chronicles* until the death of Aleksandr Nevskii in 1263. For the period 1263-1305, it used materials similar to those of the *Laurentian Codex*, as well as materials of other chronicles in northeastern Rus'. Its entries for the years 1305-1408 represented a valuable historical source material, including information pertaining to the history of Muscovy, as well as other Russian states such as Tver', Riazan', and Novgorod, and of the Rus' lands under the sovereignty of the Lithuanian grand principality; until its destruction in 1812, the *TL* was the only surviving Muscovite chronicle covering that period.

What is significant about the *TL* is the approach taken by its authors and compilers, especially by Metropolitan Kiprian, to the post-1110 history of Kievan Rus'. First of all, they did not include the *Kievskaia letopis'* (the *Kievan Chronicle*) (1118-1198 [1200]), or any closely related text. On the contrary, they adapted for their purposes the *Suzdalian-Vladimirian Chronicles* which constituted the second major component of the *Laurentian Codex* for the time period 1111-1203/1204 (or parts of the prototype of the *Radziwiłł Chronicle*) and which treated Kiev, the Kievan land, and Kievan Rus' from an exclusively Suzdalian-Vladimirian point of view. For example, the *TL* contains accounts (narrations) of the sacks of Kiev in 1169 and 1203 to be found in the *Suzdalian-Vladimirian Chronicles*.[23] In other words, the *TL* not only verbally accepted the Suzdalian-Vladimirian interpretations of those events, but also treated the entire history of twelfth-century Kievan Rus' from the generally hostile and anti-Kievan point of view of the *Suzdalian-Vladimirian Chronicles*.[24] The *TL*'s treatment of the period between 1206 and the mid-1260s, as well as some later periods with regard to certain lands and polities of Rus', was even more biased. For example, the entire history of Galician and Volynian Rus' from 1205 to 1340 was virtually eliminated from the *TL*. Its account for the period 1206-1263 deals with the history of northeastern Rus', viewed primarily from the Suzdalian-Vladimirian perspective for the benefit of the grand principality of Vladimir. For the period from 1269 to the end of the thirteenth century, the *TL* concentrates on selected developments in northeastern Rus', with emphasis on the Vladimirian Grand Principality, however without a particular preferential treatment of princely competitors for the Grand Principality of Vladimir. Scholars have argued that from 1305 to 1408 the *TL* reflected the "all-Russian" view, not as much the point of view of Moscow, as of the Moscow-based Metropolitanate of Kiev and all of Rus'. This opinion needs qualification. Whereas the compilers of the *TL* did indeed include in it materials pertaining to other Russian states such as Tver' and Novgorod, as well as to the Lithuanian-Ruthenian state, the overall orientation of the *TL* was clearly pro-Muscovite.

As far as the interpretation of the ecclesiastical claims to the Metropolitanate of Kiev and all of Rus' was concerned, the authors and editors of the *TL*'s component pertaining to the period 1300/1305-1408 emphasized that the metropolitanate must be based first in Vladimir and subsequently in Moscow, and that it must remain indivisible and, by implication, under the auspices of the Muscovite ruler. However, they did not advance any secular dynastic claims for Moscow to Kievan Rus'. They simply referred to Muscovite rulers as rulers of Moscow and stressed the Vladimirian connection of the Muscovite dynasty, particularly as reflected in the annalistic necrologs for the Muscovite rulers.[25] Direct dynastic links to Kiev and claims concerning unification with Kiev were to be developed in Muscovite chronicle writing much later[26] and, specifically, in connection with the takeover and annexation of Novgorod in the 1470s.[27]

However, the principal contribution of the authors and editors of the *TL*, as well as its sponsor, Metropolitan Kiprian, was the advancement of the first known in Russian history rudimentary theory of continuity (*translatio* of states) from Kievan Rus' through (Rostovia)-Suzdalia-Vladimiria to Muscovy (although at that time they evidently were not fully aware of it). This hypothesis is based exclusively on the inclusion in the *TL* as its first component of the *PVL* covering the history of Kievan Rus' to the year 1110. (To be sure, most Rus' chronicles included in the *PVL* in their compilations prior to the *TL*, but the *TL* was the first pro-Muscovite chronicle to do so.)

The *TL* under the entry for the year 1392 contains a reference to a certain *Letopisets' velikii russkii (LVR)* (the *Russian Great Chronicle*) that covered historical events "from [the time of] Iaroslav the Great to this present prince [Muscovite Grand Prince Vasilii I Dmitrievich, who began to rule in 1389]."[28] Traditionally, it has been assumed that the reference to "Iaroslav the Great" applied to Iaroslav I Volodimerovich, the Wise (1019-1054). Therefore, D.S. Likhachev has concluded that the lost *LVR* was the first historical work to provide "a full survey of all Russian history" from the Kievan to the Muscovite period.[29] On the basis of this lost work, the *TL*, and some other inconclusive evidence he has dated the origins of the official Muscovite secular claims to Kievan Rus' in the late fourteenth–early fifteenth century, namely the period of the assumed-by-him early Renaissance in Muscovite Russia.[30] If one were to accept the traditional interpretation of the reference to "Iaroslav the Great" in the *TL*, then the lost *LVR*, compiled probably in the 1380s, would be the first work to have advanced the Muscovite theory of continuity from Kievan Rus' through (Rostovia)-Suzdalia-Vladimiria to Muscovy.

However, an analysis of the relevant entry in the *TL* by G.M. Prokhorov, and in particular his identification of "Iaroslav the Great" as Iaroslav II [III] Vsevolodovich of Vladimir (1190-1238/1246),[31] has established that the lost *LVR* began with the Vladimirian and not the Kievan period. In fact, the same applied to the annalistic necrologs for the Muscovite rulers, included in the *TL*.[32] It can, therefore, be concluded that the *TL*, not the *LVR*, is the oldest known work to have advanced a rudimentary, Kievan Rus'—(Rostovia)-Suzdalia-Vladimiria—Muscovy continuity theory in Russian history.

To be sure, at that initial stage of its development this continuity theory in the *TL* was still unsophisticated and unsophisticated. For example, the *TL* did not include the *Kievan Chronicle* for the period 1118-1198 (1200) or any other related texts. Only in the sixteenth century would such Muscovite works as the *Voskresenskaia letopis'* (the *Voskresensk Chronicle*), the *Nikonovskaia letopis'* (the *Nikon Chronicle*), the *Book of Degrees*, and the *Great Menology* provide more accomplished interpretative versions of the continuity theory. Nonetheless, the first continuity theory devised in the *TL* at the turn of the fifteenth century, regardless of its inconsistencies, crudity, and naive simplicity, was to have an extraordinary career not only in Russian historical and political thought, but also in Western historiography until the present time.

This analysis of the origins of Muscovy's ecclesiastical claims to the Kievan inheritance has concentrated on the Metropolitanate of Kiev and all of Rus' and on historical-ideological works composed within its framework and by its members. The development of the official secular claims to the Kievan inheritance came much later.[33] Its major phase falls between the mid-fifteenth century and the beginning of the sixteenth, which means that the beginnings of the formulation of the secular claims to Kiev and all of Rus' coincided with the division of the Metropolitanate of Kiev and all of Rus' in 1458/1461. Thus, the origins of Muscovy's ecclesiastical claims to the Kievan inheritance preceded the origins of her secular claims to Kievan Rus' by about a century and a half. This, indeed, reflects the level of development of Russian culture in that period.

NOTES

1. D.S. Likhachev, *Natsional'noe samosoznanie drevnei Rusi: ocherki iz oblasti russkoi literatury XI-XVII vv.* (Moscow and Leningrad, 1945), 68-81; *Kul'tura Rusi epokhi obrazovaniia russkogo natsional'nogo gosudarstva: Konets XIV–nachalo XVI v.* (Moscow and Leningrad, 1946), 40-41, 57-97, and 103-104; *Russkie letopisi i ikh kul'turno-istoricheskoe znachenie* (Moscow and Leningrad, 1947), 293-305; *Kul'tura vremeni Andreia Rubleva i Epifaniia Premudrogo: Konets XIV–*

nachalo XV v. (Moscow and Leningrad, 1945), 4, 6, 11-12, 17, 19-20, 90-115, 142-146, and 161-170; *Die Kultur Russlands während der osteuropäischen Frührenaissance vom 14. bis zum Beginn des 15. Jahrhunderts* (Dresden, 1962), 6, 8, 13-14, 18-19, 20-21, 90-117, 145-152, and 167-175; "Predvozrozhdenie na Rusi v kontse XIV–pervoi polovine XV veka,," in *Literatura epokhi vozrozhdeniia i problemy vsemirnoi literatury* (Moscow, 1967), 136-182.

2. J. Pelenski, "The Origins of the Official Muscovite Claims to the 'Kievan Inheritance'," *Harvard Ukrainian Studies* (hereafter *HUS*), 1, no. 1 (March 1977): 28-52 [see Chapter 5 of this volume]; Ch.J. Halperin, "Kiev and Moscow: An Aspect of Early Muscovite Thought," *Russian History*, 7, no. 3 (1980): 312-321, especially 313, fn. 8; J. Meyendorff, *Byzantium and the Rise of Russia*, (Cambridge, 1981), 128.

3. See note 1 above.

4. See J. Pelenski, *The Origins*; 29-52; *idem*, "The Emergence of the Muscovite Claims to the Byzantine-Kievan 'Imperial Inheritance'," *HUS*, 7 (1983): 520-531[see Chapter 7 of this volume]; *idem*, "The Sack of Kiev of 1482 in Contemporary Muscovite Chronicle Writing," *HUS*, 3-4 (1979-1980): 638-649 [see Chapter 6 of this volume].

5. *Polnoe sobranie russkikh letopisei* (hereafter *PSRL*), vol. 1, part 1 (1926/1962), col. 485. For a convenient discussion of the circumstances pertaining to the transfer of the metropolitan, see Meyendorff, *Byzantium and the Rise of Russia*, 29-72.

6. For Metropolitan Petr's life and career, as well as the literature on the subject, see "Petr," in N. Barsukov, *Istochniki russkoi agiografii* (St. Petersburg, 1882), cols. 431-453; E. Golubinskii, *Istoriia russkoi tserkvi*, vol. 2, part 1 (1900), 98-144; V.A. Kuchkin, "Skazanie o smerti mitropolita Petra," *Trudy otdela drevnerusskoi literatury* (hereafter *TODRL*), 18 (1962): 59-79; Meyendorff, *Byzantium and the Rise of Russia*, 149-154; G.M. Prokhorov, "Petr," in D.S. Likhachev, ed., *Slovar' knizhnikov i knizhnosti drevnei Rusi*, no. 1 (XI - pervaia polovina XIV v.) (Leningrad, 1987), 325-329.

7. Cited in V.A. Kuchkin, "Skazanie o smerti mitropolita Petra," *TODRL*, 18 (1962): 64.

8. L.A. Dmitriev, "Rol' i znachenie mitropolita Kipriana v istorii drevnerusskoi literatury (K russko-bolgarskim literaturnym sviaziam XIV-XV vv.)," *TODRL*, 19 (1963): 215-254, especially 236-254. For a text edition of Kiprian's *Zhitie mitropolita Petra*, see G.M. Prokhorov, *Povest' o Mitiae* (Leningrad, 1978), 204-215. See also G.M. Prokhorov, "Drevneishaia rukopis' s proizvedeniiami mitropolita Kipriana," in *Pamiatniki kul'tury. Novye otkrytiia. Ezhegodnik za 1978* (Leningrad, 1979), 17-30. For the text in the *Kniga stepennaia*, see *PSRL*, vol. 21, part 1 (1908), 321-332. Two works, related to the themes of this article have erroneously characterized Metropolitan Kiprian's attitudes as unfriendly toward Moscow and have failed to appreciate the significance of the *Vita* in question, as well as the insertion of the prophecy about Moscow in it (N.S. Borisov, *Russkaia tserkov' v politicheskoi bor'be XIV-XV vekov* [Moscow 1986], 106-111, 113-118, and 132-139; A.S. Khoroshev, *Politicheskaia istoriia russkoi kanonizatsii [XI-XVI vv.]* [Moscow, 1986], 101-104).

9. G.M. Prokhorov, *Povest' o Mitiae*, 211-212; *PSRL*, vol. 21, part 1 (1908), 328.

10. The titles "Metropolitan of all of Rus'," or "Metropolitanate of all of Rus'," or "Metropolitan of Kiev and all of Rus'" were used interchangeably (Meyendorff, *Byzantium and the Rise of Russia*, 73-95). The concept "Metropolitan

of Kiev and all of Rus'" was applied more consistently since 1347, and especially since the early 1390's, when in the course of the contest for the Metropolitanate of Kiev and Rus' the concepts "Metropolitan of all of Rus'" and "Metropolitan of Kiev and all of Rus'" acquired more specific meanings (for a discussion of the use of the titles in sources, see A. Pliguzov, "On the Title 'Metropolitan of Kiev and All Rus'," *HUS*, 15, no. 3/4 (December 1991): 340-353.

11. For a discussion of the history of various contending metropolitanates and the relevant literature, see A.S. Pavlov, "O nachale Galitskoi i Litovskoi mitropolii i o pervykh tamoshnikh mitropolitakh po dokumental'nym istochnikam XIV-go veka," *Russkoe Obozrenie*, 3 (May 1948): 214-251; N.D. Tikhomirov, *Galitskaia Mitropoliia, Tserkovno-istoricheskoe issledovanie* (St. Petersburg, 1985); K. Chodynicki, *Kościół prawosławny a Rzeczpospolita Polska, 1370-1632* (Warsaw, 1934), 3-74; I. Nazarko, "Halyts'ka Metropoliia," *Analecta Ordinis S. Basilii Magni*, ser. 2, sec. 11, vol. 3 (1-2): 145-225; M. Giedroyć, "The Arrival of Christianity in Lithuania: Between Rome and Byzantium (1281-1341)," *Oxford Slavonic Papers*, n.s., 20 (1987): 14-20; *idem*, "The Influence of Ruthenian-Lithuanian Metropolitanates on the Progress of Christianization (1300-1458)," in S.W. Swierkosz-Lenard, ed., *Le origini e lo sviluppo della Cristianità Slavo-Bizantina, Nuovi studi storici*, vol. 17 (Rome, 1992): 315-342.

12. Meyendorff, *Byzantium and the Rise of Russia*, 73-79. See also D. Obolensky, "Byzantium, Kiev, and Moscow: A Study in Ecclesiastical Relations," *Dumbarton Oaks Papers* (hereafter *DOP*), 11 (1957): 21-78.

13. For a discussion of Andrei Bogoliubskii's attempt to create a competitive metropolitanate and the literature on the subject, see J. Pelenski, "The Contest for the 'Kievan Succession' (115-1175): The Religious-Ecclesiastical Dimensions," *Proceedings of the International Congress Commemorating the Millennium of Christianity in Rus'-Ukraine, HUS*, 12-13 (1988-1989): 761-780 [see Chapter 2 of this volume].

14. A. Poppe, "Zur Geschichte der Kirche und des Staates der Rus' im 11. Jh.: Titularmetropolen," *Das heidnische und christliche Slaventum* (Wiesbaden, 1970), 64-75.

15. V.A. Kuchkin, "Skazanie," 71-75; G.M. Prokhorov, "Petr," 327. Contradictory assessments regarding the relationship of church and state and the interconnected problem of canonization politics in Muscovite Russia have been offered in scholarship. Contrary to the preponderance of the available evidence, N.S. Borisov has questioned the established view about the close cooperation between church and state in Muscovite Russia, particularly in the fourteenth century, but also in the fifteenth. Borisov has advanced the hypothesis that the Orthodox Church's support for state policies was "rather modest" and that especially in the fourteenth century the prevailing attitude of the metropolitans of Kiev and all of Rus' toward Moscow was characterized by a "temporizing neutrality" (*Russkaia tserkov'*, 188, and "Moskovskie kniaz'ia i russkie mitropolity XIV veka," *Voprosy istorii*, no. 8 [1986]: 30-43, especially 43). A.S. Khoroshev, however, has maintained that the canonization of Russian saints was a "political institution," that the primary criterion for the canonization of Russian saints was political, and that there existed a most intimate relationship between church and state in Old Rus' (*Politicheskaia istoriia russkoi kanonizatsii*, 189-190. See also *idem, Tserkov'; v sotsial'no-politicheskoi sisteme Novgorodskoi feodal'noi respubliki* (Moscow, 1980).

16. For Metropolitan Aleksei's life and career, as well as the literature on the subject, see N. Barsukov, cols. 27-32; E. Golubinskii, *Istoria russkoi tserkvi*, vol. 2,

part 1 (1900): 171-225; *idem, Istoriia kanonizatsii sviatykh v russkoi tserkvi* (Moscow, 1903), 74-75; A.E. Presniakov, *Obrazovanie velikorusskogo gosudarstva* (Petrograd, 1918), 290-317; G.M. Prokhorov, "Zhitie Alekseia mitropolita," in D.S. Likhachev, ed., *Slovar' knizhnikov i knizhnosti drevnei Rusi*, no. 2 (*vtoraia polovina XIV-XVI vv.*), part 1 (A-K) (Leningrad, 1988), 243-245. N.S. Borisov has treated the symbiotic relationship of church and state during the tenure of Metropolitan Aleksei as an exception in the Muscovite period (*Russkaia tserkov'*, 79-99).

17. *PSRL*, vol. 21, part 2 (1913), 346-386.

18. For Metropolitan Iona's life and career, as well as the literature on the subject, see N. Barsukov, *Istochniki russkoi agiografii*, cols. 266-272; E. Golubinskii, *Istoriia russkoi tserkvi*, vol. 2, part 1 (1900), 469-515; Ia.S. Lur'e, "Iona," in *Slovar' knizhnikov i knizhnosti drevnei Rusi*, vol. 2, part 1 (A-K) (1988), 420-426; Ia.S. Lur'e, "Zhitie Iony," in *Slovar' knizhnikov i knizhnosti drevnei Rusi*, vol. 2, part 1 (A-K) (1988), 270-273. N.S. Borisov's and A.S. Khoroshev's treatments of the activities and the canonization of Metropolitan Iona are rather brief and offer no new insights.

19. N. Barsukov, *Istochniki russkoi agiografii*, cols. 266-272; E. Golubinskii, *Istoriia kanonizatsii sviatykh v Russkoi Tserkvi*, 79-80.

20. N. Barsukov, *Istochniki russkoi agiografii*, cols. 31-32, 271, 449.

21. For Metropolitan Kiprian's life and career and the literature on the subject, see E. Golubinskii, *Istoriia russkoi tserkvi*, vol. 2, part 1 (1900), 297-356; L.A. Dmitriev, "Rol' i znachenie mitropolita Kipriana," *TODRL*, 19 (1963): 215-254; D. Obolensky, "A *Philorhomaios anthropos*: Metropolitan Cyprian of Kiev and all Russia," *DOP*, 32 (1979): 79-98; G.M. Prokhorov, *Povest' o Mitiae*; N.F. Droblenkova, "Bibliografiia," G. M. Prokhorov, "Kiprian," in "Letopistsy i istoriki XI-XVII vv.," *TODRL*, 39 (1985): 53-71; also "Kiprian," in *Slovar' knizhnikov i knizhnosti drevnei Rusi*, vol. 2, part 1 (A-K) (1988), 464-475.

22. For the text of the reconstructed *Troitskaia letopis'*, see M.D. Priselkov, *Troitskaia letopis': Rekonstruktsiia teksta* (Moscow and Leningrad, 1950). The most important scholarly contributions to the study of the *Troitskaia letopis'* are the following: M.D. Priselkov, "Letopisanie XIV veka," in *Sbornik statei po russkoi istorii posviashchennykh S.F. Platonovu* (1922), 24-39; "O rekonstruktsii teksta Troitskoi letopisi 1408 g., sgorevshei v Moskve v 1812 g.," in *Uchenye zapiski Leningradskogo Gosudarstvennogo pedogogicheskogo instituta im. Gertsena*, vol. 19 (1939), 5-42; M.D. Priselkov, *Istoriia russkogo letopisaniia XI-XV vv.* (Leningrad 1940), 113-142; Priselkov, *Troitskaia letopis'*, Introduction, 7-49; S.I. Kochetov, "Troitskii pergamennyi spisok letopisi 1408 g.," *Archeograficheskii ezhegodnik za 1961 god* (1962), 18-27; G.N. Moiseeva, "Otryvok Troitskoi pergamennoi letopisi perepisannyi G.F. Millerom," *TODRL*, 26 (1971): 93-99; Ia.S. Lur'e, *Obshcherusskie letopisi XIV-XV vv.* (Leningrad, 1976), 17-66; G.M. Prokhorov, "Letopisets velikii russkii: Analiz ego upominaniia v Troitskoi letopisi," in *Letopisi i khroniki* (Moscow, 1976), 67-77; C.J. Halperin, "The Russian Land and the Russian Tsar: The Emergence of Muscovite Ideology, 1380-1408," *Forschungen zur osteuropäischen Geschichte*, 23 (1976): 5-103, especially 58-68; Ia.S. Lur'e, "Letopis' Troitskaia," in D.S. Likhachev, ed., *Slovar' knizhnikov i knizhnosti drevnei Rusi*, no. 2 (*vtoraia polovina XIV-XVI vv.*) (1989), part 2 (L-Ia) (Leningrad, 1989), 64-67. Kiprian's role as the sponsor of the *TL* and the latter's significance in the history of Muscovite chronicle writing and ideology has been almost completely overlooked by N.S. Borisov (*Russkaia tserkov'*) and A.S. Khoroshev (*Politicheskaia istoriia*).

23. *PSRL*, vol. 1(1926), cols. 354-355 and 418-419; *Troitskaia letopis'* (hereafter *TL*), 244-245 and 285-286.

24. For a discussion of these interpretations and views, see J. Pelenski, "The Sack of Kiev of 1169; Its Significance for the Succession to
Kievan Rus'," *HUS*, 9, no. 3-4 (December 1987): 303-316 [see Chapter 3 of this volume].

25. J. Pelenski, "The Origins," 36-37 and 41 [see Chapter 5 of this volume].

26. Ia.S. Lur'e, *Obshcherusskie letopisi XIV-XV vv.*, 120-121.

27. J. Pelenski, "The Origins," 46-48.

28. *TL*, 439.

29. Likhachev, *Russkie letopisi*, 295.

30. See note 1, above.

31. Prokhorov, "Letopisets velikii russkii," 67-77, especially 71-74.

32. See J. Pelenski, "The Origins," 36-37 and 41.

33. See J. Pelenski, "The Origins," 29-52; *idem*, "The Emergence of the Muscovite Claims," 520-531 [see Chapter 7 of this volume]; *idem*, "The Sack of Kiev of 1169," 638-649 [see Chapter 3 of this volume].

5

THE ORIGINS OF THE OFFICIAL MUSCOVITE CLAIMS TO THE KIEVAN INHERITANCE*

No other historical-ideological assertion of the Muscovite government and ruling elite has made such a powerful impact on modern Russian historical thought, as well as on Western scholarship dealing with the early history of the Eastern Slavs, as Muscovy's claim to the Kievan inheritance. Its impact has been so strong and so all-pervasive that, until very recently, Muscovite views on Kievan Rus' and her history, and particularly Muscovy's assertions that she succeeded to Kiev by right of inheritance, have been accepted by a large number of historians as matters of fact, beyond the limits of permissible inquiry and critical examination. Some caustic remarks by P.N. Miliukov[1] and by A.E. Presniakov[2] questioning Muscovite perceptions of the Kievan inheritance and bringing up some related problems that seemed to cast doubt upon them have been conveniently overlooked. The profound influence of the historical ideas and ideological propositions of the Muscovite chroniclers and publicists of the fifteenth and sixteenth centuries on Russian historiography has not diminished from the eighteenth and nineteenth centuries up to the present day.

The classical controversy over the Kievan inheritance between the "Northerners" (*severiany*) and the "Southerners" (*iuzhany*), that is, between Russian historians and Ukrainian historians, which began in the nineteenth century (see Chapter 11 of this volume) and culminated in Mykhailo Hrushevs'kyi's "rational organization" of early East Slavic history,[3] has not effectively disturbed traditional patterns of thinking that are always so difficult to revise. National historiographies have devoted a great deal of effort to discussing the influence of the Kievan heritage, or at least its most outstanding features, on subsequent socio-political organizations (for example, the Grand Principality of Suzdal'-Vladimir and Muscovite Russia, in

---

* For illustrations pertaining to this chapter, see Plates 33, 34.

the case of Russian historiography, and the Lithuanian-Ruthenian state and subsequently Cossack Ukraine, in the case of Ukrainian historiography). But the problems of the origins of these claims, their dating, and their promulgators have received only scant attention. Both Miliukov and Presniakov, for example, referred only in very general terms to Muscovite diplomats, bookmen, and "philosophers" of the fifteenth and sixteenth centuries; neither had written explicitly on these problems.

The first attempt to deal more specifically with the origins of the Muscovite preoccupation with the Kievan succession was undertaken by D.S. Likhachev in the process of trying to prove that Russian culture in general, and Muscovite culture and chronicle writing in particular, were permeated by a new historicism – an assumption that also served as the crucial argument for his hypothesis about the existence of an Early Renaissance movement in Russia in the late fourteenth and the first half of the fifteenth century.[4]

The application of the combined concepts of historicism and Early Renaissance to Muscovite culture of this early period not only raises a number of questions of a semantic nature, but also poses serious methodological and theoretical problems concerning Likhachev's understanding of these ideas. Likhachev's use of the concept of historicism is at the same time monogenic and surprisingly sweeping. He reduces historicism to a simple interest in history or participation in a history-related endeavor. His distinction between "real/realistic" historicism and medieval historicism is not very helpful in clarifying his meaning of the term.[5] His thesis about the existence of a "monumental historicism" in the Old Rus' literature and chronicle writing from the eleventh to the thirteenth century is even more ambiguous,[6] mainly because his dating of historicism back to the Middle Ages brings forth additional questions with regard to his methodology and conceptual approach. In the study of modern intellectual history, the origins of historicism – i.e., of a history-oriented mode of thinking and of a general theory of history and culture – have been traced back to the early eighteenth century, that is, to the Enlightenment in France and England, and subsequently to German Classicism and Early Romanticism.[7]

Likhachev has consistently avoided considering the classical discussions of historicism (Ernst Troeltsch, Otto Hintze, Friedrich Meinecke, Karl Popper) in his studies of Russian culture, which may partially explain his surprisingly uninhibited use of this concept. A manifest interest in history or a general preoccupation with history is not necessarily identical with historicism. A historicist approach to history and culture implies an active rethinking and redefining of a historical process, preferably on its own terms, possibly in terms of a superimposed historical perspective. The earliest manifestations of such an approach to history in the West can be detected in Humanism and in the Renaissance, although the revival and the reception of classical antiquity that took place then was formalistic and mechanical, and therefore lacked a genuine historicist quality.

Likhachev's assumption that the historicist mode of thinking was present in Muscovite Russia at the end of the fourteenth and the beginning of the fifteenth century does not stand up to scrutiny. His hypothesis is based primarily on the revival of chronicle writing in Muscovy, as reflected in the compilation of the *Troitskaia letopis'* (*TL*) (the *Trinity Chronicle*) under the auspices of Metropolitan Kiprian during that time.[8]

The *TL* represented an official codex composed in the metropolitan's chancery. It included the *Povest' vremennykh let* (*PVL*) (the *Tale of Bygone Years*) following either the Laurentian recension or a closely related text. For the twelfth and thirteenth centuries, it incorporated Rostovian, Suzdalian and Vladimirian historical materials, also based on the Laurentian version or other closely related sources. Its entries for the years 1305-1408 dealt with materials pertaining to the history of Muscovy, as well as other Russian states like Tver', Riazan', and Novgorod, and of the Rus' lands which were under the sovereignty of the Grand Principality of Lithuania; until its destruction in the Moscow fire of 1812, the *TL* was the only surviving Muscovite chronicle covering that period.[9] However, the discovery of the *Simeonovskaia letopis'* (*SL*) (the *Simeonov Chronicle*) by A.A. Shakhmatov greatly facilitated the study of the *TL*, particularly his findings that for the years 1177-1393 the two chronicles are virtually identical.[10] These findings, in turn, immensely helped M.D. Priselkov to reconstruct the *TL* text on the basis of Karamzin's extensive quotations from it in his *Istoriia gosudarstva rossiiskogo*, of the *SL*, and of other materials.

Likhachev has claimed that the inclusion of the *PVL* in the *TL* by the Muscovite compilers indicates that they were aware of the Kievan tradition and of Moscow's assumed exclusive right to the Kievan inheritance. A different interpretation can be offered in this case. Since most Rus' chronicles contained the *PVL* or an abridged version of it, it can be assumed that it was standard procedure for editors and compilers of Rus' chronicles to begin their compilations with the *PVL* or a synopsis of it, for it was the earliest existing text they had available.

The *Novgordoskaia pervaia letopis'* (*NPL*) (the *Novgorodian First Chronicle*) of the "older" recension (about mid-fourteenth century), as well as of the "younger" recension (about mid-fifteenth century), also included edited Kievan historical materials, as do the Tverian and Pskovian codices, compiled around the middle of the fifteenth century. In fact, the most consistent and historically integrated codices were provided by the editors and compilers of the *Ipat'evskaia letopis'* (the *Hypatian Codex*) and the *Lavrent'evskaia letopis'* (the *Laurentian Codex*), which were completed long before the *TL*. The *TL* reflects the "all-Russian" perspective, however, not so much of the perspective of the Muscovite state as of the Moscow-based Metropolitanate of Kiev and all of Rus'. At the time of Kiprian's tenure, the metropolitanate was attempting to preserve a united ecclesiastical organization for all of Rus', an endeavor supported, for practical and political reasons, by the Patriarchate of Constantinople.[11] Thus, it may be argued that the inclusion of the *PVL* in the *TL* does not represent a reevaluation of the Kievan Rus' history – not even in terms of a hypothetical medieval or providential historicism. The latter variant of historicism cannot be attested in Muscovite historical writing before the sixteenth century; it can be found, for example, in such sixteenth-century works as the *Voskresenskaia letopis'* (the *Voskresensk Chronicle*), the *L'vovskaia letopis'* (the *L'vov Chronicle*), and the *Nikonovskaia letopis'* (the *Nikon Chronicle*). It is particu larly evident in the *Kniga stepennaia* (the *Book of Degrees*), where the new historical and ideological perspective was superimposed on the history of early non-Muscovite Rus'.[12]

The dating of the origins of official Muscovite claims to the Kievan succession is complicated by the appearance of these claims in some texts that traditionally have been regarded as belonging to the so-called Kulikovo cycle. Until the mid-1960s, the majority of scholars who have studied these sources tried to date them soon after the Battle at Kulikovo Field (*Kulikovo pole*) (1380). However, some scholars have begun to question these early attributions, and to revive and refine some of the tentative suggestions made by A.A. Shakhmatov who proposed different dates. Since it is impossible to deal adequately with the cumulative problems of all the texts of the Kulikovo cycle here, I shall concentrate my analysis on those texts that are of an official or semi-official nature, with a few additional remarks about the unofficial *Zadonshchina*. At the same time, I shall present my own chronology of the texts in question and propose a reinterpretation of the crucial Kievan references in them.

It appears that the earliest text that refers to the Kulikovo Battle is the Short Chronicle Tale (1380), entitled *O velikom poboishche, izhe na Donu* of the reconstructed *TL*, the *SL*, and the *Rogozhskii letopisets* (the *Rogozh Chronicle*).[13] This Short Chronicle Tale is the most factual; in its style and composition, it fits perfectly into the general pattern of the Muscovite annalistic tales contained in the *TL* and its control text, the *SL*.[14] It was most probably written for an official Muscovite chronicle, namely, the *Letopisets velikii russkii* (the *Russian Great Chronicle*), which, according to Priselkov, covered events up to the death of Dmitrii Ivanovich Donskoi (1389).[15] It can be assumed that the Short Chronicle Tale about the Kulikovo Battle was composed before the death of Dmitrii Ivanovich, possibly very soon after the battle, that is, in the 1380s. The ideological claims and justifications found in the Tale are limited. According to its author, Dmitrii Ivanovich fought "wishing to defend his patrimony, for the holy churches, and for the true [Orthodox] faith and all the Russian land." The term "all the Russian land" was used in fourteenth-century Russian sources rather loosely, and it usually referred to northeastern Rus' or ethnic Great Russian territory, but seldom to Southern or Kievan Rus'.[16]

The second major text devoted to the Kulikovo Battle is the Expanded Chronicle Tale, entitled *O poboishche izhe na Donu, i o tom, kniaz' velikii kako bilsia s ordoiu* contained in the *Novgorodskaia chetvertaia letopis'* (*NChL*) (the *Novgorodian Fourth Chronicle*),[17] or *Poboishche velikogo kniazia Dmitriia Ivanovicha na Donu s Mamaiem* included in the *Sofiiskaia pervaia letopis'* (*SPL*) (the *Sophia First Chronicle*),[18] the *Nikanorovskaia letopis'* (*NL*) (the *Nikanor Chronicle*),[19] and in other compilations, although with various changes and adjustments. Two views exist in scholarship regarding the dating of the Expanded Chronicle Tale and its relationship to the short version. The first, following the lead of S.K. Shambinago, assumes that the Expanded Chronicle Tale is the earlier version and that the Short Chronicle Tale represents an abridged version of the former.[20] The second school of thought, introduced by A.A. Shakhmatov, holds that the Expanded Chronicle Tale is the more recent. According to M.A. Salmina's analysis, it was composed in the second half of the 1440s, after the Battle of Suzdal' (1445) and before 1448,[21] the year for the compilation of the hypothetical *Codex of 1448*,[22] and it reflected the political atmosphere of the beginning of the last phase of the great Muscovite civil war (1444/46-1453). Salmina's hypothesis may be in need of refinement, but she is certainly on the right track in dating the text after the Battle of Suzdal'.

It can be argued that the account of the Battle of Kulikovo in the Expanded Chronicle Tale represented, among other things, an ideological response to the crushing defeat of the Russian army by the military forces of the emerging Kazan Khanate in the Battle of Suzdal' (7 July 1445), in which Grand Prince Vasilii II was taken prisoner. The dynastic struggle between Vasilii II and Dmitrii Shemiaka made the Tatar problem, then in its Kazanian version, particularly acute, since both contenders sought the support of Ulu Mehmet, the Kazanian khan, in their endeavors to seize the throne of the Grand Principality of Moscow; in addition, Vasilii II was using "service Tatars" in his struggle with Shemiaka. Tatar influence during the final years of the Muscovite civil war is clearly evident in the Pastoral Epistle of five Russian bishops (one of the five was the future Metropolitan Iona), dated 29 December 1447.[23] It appears that the later texts of the Kulikovo cycle have more relevance to the ideological justifications of the Muscovite-Kazanian struggle and the Muscovite relations with the Golden Horde from the time of the invasion of Emir Edigü (1408) to 1480, than to the history of the Kulikovo Battle and its significance for the Muscovite political thought of the late fourteenth and the early fifteenth century. The Expanded Chronicle Tale refers hardly at all to the Kievan inheritance: one perfunctory comparison of Oleg of Riazan' with Sviatopolk Okaiannyi and one vague reference to Boris and Gleb.

Of special significance to the problem of the Kievan succession is the *Vita* (*Zhitie*) of Dmitrii Ivanovich Donskoi, a work thematically connected with the texts of the Kulikovo cycle, although of a different genre and date. The earliest and the most complete of the known texts of this *Vita* are the *Slovo o zhitii i o prestavlenii velikogo kniazia Dmitriia Ivanovicha tsaria rus'skago*, which appears in the *NChL* under the entry for 1389,[24] and the *O zhitii i o prestavlenii velikogo kniazia Dmitriia Ivanovicha, tsaria rus'skago*, included in the *SPL* under the same date.[25] The latter text, with some editorial adjustments and emendations, was incorporated into the official Muscovite chronicles of the 1470s.[26] The earliest Muscovite account of Donskoi's death is found in the *TL* and the *SL* in an annalistic necrolog, entitled *O prestavlenii velikago kniazia Dmitriia Ivanovicha*, composed in a form similar to the necrologs written for the Muscovite rulers before and after him.[27]

The dating of the *Vita* of Dmitrii Ivanovich presents a number of problems. The chronicles into which it was integrated and the contents of the *Vita* itself must be analyzed together in order to obtain a plausible dating. Even A.A. Shakhmatov, the founder of modern critical studies of the Russian chronicles, assumed that it had been composed soon after the death of the prince by someone who had attended the funeral.[28] The first to question this early dating was V.P. Adrianova-Peretts who, because of the stylistic peculiarities of the text – i.e., *pletenie sloves* (the "braiding of words"), came to the conclusion that it could not have been written before 1417-1418, and was probably even later than that.[29] A.V. Solov'ev's attempts to antedate the *Vita* to the 1390s and to attribute it to Epifanii Premudryi do not hold up under scrutiny, and are further examples of his excessively optimistic approach to the study of Old Rus' literature.[30] Furthermore, M.A. Salmina, on the basis of an analysis similar to that used for the Expanded Chronicle Tale of the Kulikovo Battle, has dated the text about 1444-1447, that is, just before the compilation of the hypothetical *Codex of 1448*.[31] Her dating evidently has been based on the assumption that the version of the *Vita* found in the *NChL* was included in the hypothetical *Codex of 1448*, and that it reflected, as did the Expanded Chronicle Tale, the political conditions of Muscovy during the civil war in the later part of the 1440s.

But even if one were to assume the existence of the hypothetical *Codex of 1448*, [32] doubts could be raised about its inclusion of the *Vita* of Dmitrii Ivanovich. In contrast to the Expanded Chronicle Tale about the Kulikovo Battle, which was included, for all practical purposes, in every manuscript copy utilized for the edition of the *NChL*,[33] the *Vita* of Dmitrii Ivanovich was incorporated in only some of them.[34] According to F.P. Pokrovskii and A.A. Shakhmatov, Copies N, G, and T were dated earlier than the other manuscripts utilized for the second edition of the *NChL*.[35]

Salmina is undisturbed by the fact that Copy A ends with the entry for 1447, Copy N with the entry for 1437, and that the final entry for Copy T is unknown. She apparently has assumed that the *Vita* constituted an integral part of the hypothetical *Codex of 1448*, but, particularly in view of Copy N, she evidently has come to the conclusion that all the manuscript copies that included this *Vita* and became the basis for the second edition of *NChL* were taken down at a later time. The textual history of the *NChL* justifies this reasoning; heavy layers of Muscovite political propaganda came to be incorporated into its various manuscripts over time, especially after the events of the 1470s and the final annexation of Novgorod in 1478.

Salmina also believes that the *NChL* version of the *Vita* of Dmitrii Ivanovich is closest to the original work because it is the most complete text. The texts of the *Vita* versions in the *NChL* and the *SPL* are, in fact, virtually identical, except for an extensive and rhetorical middle section of the *Vita*, namely, the "Praise of Dmitrii Ivanovich [Donskoi]," found only in the *NChL*.[36] However, a different conclusion can be drawn from these facts. One is certainly justified in arguing that the middle section of the *Vita*, that is, the "Praise," was lacking in the original work, which was presumably identical to the text in the *SPL*. There seems to be no logical reason why the Novgorodian chroniclers should have included ideologically-imbued Muscovite texts into their own codices. Ia.S. Lur'e, for example, has explained the inclusion of the Expanded Chronicle Tale about the Kulikovo Battle in the *NChL* as a reflection of the formation of a pro-Muscovite faction in Novgorod by the 1440s,[37] but this is rather unlikely. Such a faction could only have emerged in Novgorod a decade or so later, as a result of the Muscovite campaign against that city in 1456[38] and the Treaty of Iazhelbitsy concluded in the same year;[39] consequently, this would be the earliest possible date for the inclusion of pro-Muscovite materials in the *NChL*. However, there is no conclusive evidence it was done even then.

Thus we are left with the text of the *Vita* in the *SPL* as the more reliable of the two earliest versions. This brings us to the question of when it was included in the *SPL*. It was incorporated in all of the known manuscript copies that served as basis for the edition of the *SPL*, with one exception – namely, the Vorontsov manuscript.[40] The *SPL* is a Muscovite chronicle that exists in two recensions: the first was compiled in 1422, and the second ends with an entry for 1456.[41] Whereas Shakhmatov emphasized the similarity between the second recension of the *SPL* (or a hypothetical *Codex of 1456*) with the official *Muscovite Codex of 1479*,[42] Priselkov advanced the hypothesis that the *Codex of 1456* was, in fact, a chronicle written in the metropolitan's chancery.[43] He also suggested that both the metropolitans and the grand princes had chronicles compiled throughout the fifteenth century, and that the hypothetical recensions of 1426 and 1463 of the *Great Russian Chronicle* existed before the compilation of the *Muscovite Codex of 1472*.[44] The view that there were two separate lines of Muscovite chronicle writing (grand princely and metropolitan) during the fifteenth century and that they were perpetuated into the sixteenth century is convincing. There is, therefore, no reason to question Priselkov's hypothesis about the *Codex of 1456*, which reflected the interests both of the grand prince and the metropolitanate. The assumption that such a codex existed is as valid as the notion that the hypothetical *Codex of 1448* existed. It is also much more likely that a pro-Muscovite text such as the *Vita* of Dmitrii Ivanovich was first included in a Muscovite chronicle like the *SPL*, and specifically in its second recension, namely, the hypothetical *Codex of 1456*, thus supporting its dating not in the latter 1440s, but in the mid-1450s.[45] The internal evidence of the *Vita* strongly suggests the political circumstances, the time of writing, and the author of this work.

The *Vita* of Dmitrii Ivanovich Donskoi is an exceptional document loaded with Muscovite ideological content.[46] In it (for the first time, to my knowledge) a direct claim to the Kievan dynastic succession was made for a Muscovite ruler. The opening statement to the *Vita* reads as follows:

> This Grand Prince Dmitrii [Donskoi] was born to his honorable and venerable father, Grand Prince Ivan Ivanovich, and his mother, Grand Princess Aleksandra, and he was a grandson of Grand Prince Ivan Danilovich, the gatherer of the Russian land[s], [and] he was the most fertile branch and the most beautiful flower from the God-planted orchard of Tsar Volodimer, the New Constantine, who baptized the Russian land, and he was [also] a kinsman (*srodnik*) of Boris and Gleb, the miracle-workers.[47]

This statement on the direct and uninterrupted dynastic continuity from the Kievan ruler Volodimer I definitely represented a major departure from the statements on the dynastic lineage that had appeared in the annalistic necrologies of previous Muscovite rulers. Those found in the *TL* and the control text of the *SL* that listed the names of the dynastic ancestors start from the Suzdalian-Vladimirian rulers.[48] For the purpose of genealogical linkage, two rulers were carefully selected. The first, Volodimer I, whose role in the baptism of the Rus' land is emphasized, is elevated to the position of a tsar, a title he never held. The second, Ivan Danilovich Kalita, is given the extraordinary epithet of "gatherer" of Russian lands, apparently alluding to his successful Russian policies. Finally, Dmitrii Ivanovich Donskoi is referred to as a blood relative of the first, martyred saintly princes of Rus'.

The *Vita* abounds with terms designed to strengthen claims to the inheritance of Kievan Rus' and to enhance the position of the Kievan and, even more, of the Muscovite ruler to the highest political rank. Dmitrii Ivanovich is referred to nine times as *tsar* – a title he, like Volodimer, had never dreamed of attaining. Terms such as *tsarstvo, tsarskij, tsarstvovat'* are used quite frequently with regard to his reign and the concept *russkaia zemlia* is employed in the text twenty-two times.[49] Furthermore, the author of the *Vita* twice maintained that the *russkaia zemlia* (the Russian land) is a *votchina* (a patrimony) of the Muscovite ruler.

This last assertion reflects the traditional Muscovite legal theory concerning the relationship between the ruler and the land. Like its Western equivalents, Russian patrimonial theory made no distinction between the private and public spheres in law and political domination (*Herrschaft*).[50] In political terms, the claim was a sweeping extension of the relevant statement in the Testament of Dmitrii Donskoi in which he bequeathed the Grand Principality of Vladimir (in theory, a territory of the grand prince, whoever he might have been) to his son. This step not only was a major departure from the old assumption that Muscovy exclusively had been a patrimony of the Muscovite rulers, but it also signified the merging of the Grand Principality of Vladimir with the Grand Principality of Moscow.[51] The "Praise of Dmitrii Ivanovich [Donskoi]" in the *Vita* concludes with the most extravagant upgrading of Dmitrii Donskoi, placing him above Volodimer I, with a downgrading of the significance of Kievan Rus', and with a glorification of the all-Russian and imperial Muscovite ruler and his country. Paraphrasing the famous Praise of Volodimer I by Metropolitan Ilarion, the author of the *Vita* exclaimed:

The Roman land praises Peter and Paul, the Asian [land] –
John the Evangelist, India [praises] the Apostle Thomas, [the
land of] Jacob – the brother of the Lord; Andrew the Apostle
[is praised] by the Black Sea Coast (*pomor'e*), Tsar
Constantine – by the Greek land, Volodimer [is praised] by
Kiev and the neighboring towns (*Kiev s okrestnymi grady*).
You, Grand Prince Dmitrii [Ivanovich], are praised by all the
Russian land.[52]

A document such as the *Vita* of Dmitrii Ivanovich, in which
the status of the Russian ruler is elevated to that of a *tsar* and his
position in the world is exalted, could hardly have been written
during a Muscovite dynastic civil war, and certainly not at a time
when the Muscovite grand principality, in spite of all its intra-
Russian expansionism, was only an insignificant territorial state. A
text with such exaggerated political claims could only have been
written after the fall of Constantinople (1453), when the Muscovite
ecclesiastical and political establishment had begun to recognize the
religious-political significance of the Council of Florence (1438-
1439) and, in view of the conquest of Constantinople by the Turks,
to offer its ideological interpretation of the two epochal events.[53]
Only in Muscovite texts of the Florentine cycle can one find claims
and assertions analogous to the *Vita* of Dmitrii Ivanovich. The two
texts of relevance to our discussion are the *Tale of Simeon of
Suzdal'*, fully titled *Povest' Simeona Suzdal'tsa, kako rimskii papa
Evgenii sostavlial os'myi sobor so svoimi edinomyshlenniki*,[54] and
the *Selections from the Holy Writings*, fully titled *Slovo izbrano ot
sviatykh pisanii ezhe na latyniu i skazanie o sostavlenii osmago zbora
latynskago i o izverzhenii Sidora prelesnago i o postavlenii v rustei
zemli metropolitov. O sikhzhe pokhvala blagovernomu velikomu
kniaziu Vasil'iu Vasil'evichiu vseia Rusi*.[55]
    In both accounts the title *tsar* is used for the Russian grand
prince Vasilii II Vasil'evich (1425-1462): in the *Tale of Simeon of
Suzdal'* the term *belyi tsar*, meaning "white *tsar*," is applied once,
and in the *Selections from the Holy Writings* the term *tsar* is
employed fourteen times, not to mention a frequent appearance of its
variants in this text. The only other contemporary Russian source
that used the terms *tsar, tsarskii, tsarstvuiushchii* in reference to a
Russian ruler – namely, the Tverian Grand prince boris Aleksandrovich (1425-1461) – was a Tverian ideological treatise, entitled *Slovo
pokhval'noe o blagovernom velikom kniaze Borise Aleksandroviche*

(the *Praise of Grand Prince Boris Alexandrovich*), written, in my opinion, after the fall of Constantinople, most probably in 1454 or 1455.[56]

In all three treatises – that is, the two Florentine texts and the *Vita* of Dmitrii Donskoi – Volodimer I and his role in the baptism of Rus' is prominently acknowledged. The *Tale of Simeon of Suzdal'* was definitely written after the fall of Constantinople, in the late 1450s,[57] and the extensive *Selections from the Holy Writings* in the early 1460s.[58] The *Selections* seem to provide the closest parallel to the *Vita* of Dmitrii Donskoi in their glorification of the Russian ruler (Vasilii II). The praises in the two works are strikingly similar in terms of style (*pletenie sloves*).

In 1878, A. Pavlov advanced a hypothesis that Pakhomii Logofet (the Serbian) was the author of the *Selections from the Holy Writings*, as well as of some works attributed to Simeon of Suzdal'.[59] Pavlov based his arguments on stylistic analysis, on the use of the title *tsar*, and on the presence of political terms stressing the God-given nature of the Muscovite ruler's power. Other Russian scholars have disagreed with Pavlov's hypothesis. F. Delektorskii, for example, claimed, without evidence, that Russian authors had been using the title *tsar* quite frequently by that time.[60] Another author maintained that the *Selections* were "imbued with vital Muscovite patriotism" and that Pakhomii Logofet, who was Serbian and who "worked for money, had no reason to be a Russian patriot" and therefore he could not have written the *Selections*.[61] Conclusive evidence exists, however, that Pakhomii knew Simeon of Suzdal', the author of the *Tale*, and that both lived at the Troitse-Sergiev Monastery until 1458-1459.[62] It is quite possible that Pakhomii Logofet helped Simeon of Suzdal' to compose his *Tale*, or parts of it.

The preponderance of evidence points to Pakhomii Logofet as the most probable author of the *Vita* of Dmitrii Ivanovich. He might have written it at the request of Muscovite authorities during his stay at the Troitse-Sergiev Monastery, following the fall of Constantinople, but before the compilation of the *Codex of 1456* – that is, in 1454 or 1455.[63]

The other two principal texts of the Kulikovo cycle, that is, the *Zadonshchina* (the *Battle beyond the Don River*) and the *Skazanie o Mamaevom poboishche* (the *Narration about Mamai's Battle*), need not concern us here. The *Battle beyond the Don River* never became part of the official Muscovite political ideology and, judging by the limited number of its manuscript copies, it seems not to have been widely distributed.[64] However, several important references to the Kievan succession found in the text of the *Battle beyond the Don River* pose certain problems to the researchers of Muscovite ideology. Their research has been complicated by the tendency to date this text as closely as possible to 1380, although the arguments in favor of this early dating are unconvincing, at least for me. In my judgment, this work was composed after the Expanded Chronicle Tale,[65] and after the *Vita* of Dmitrii Ivanovich Donskoi.[66]

It is also very improbable that the early chronological attributions of the *Narration about Mamai's Battle* will stand up to critical scrutiny.[67] Even if one were to assume that the text of the *Narration* of the London (British Museum) manuscript included in the *Vologodsko-Permskaia letopis'* (*VPL*) (the *Vologda-Perm Chronicle*), which concludes with entries for the year 1499 and dates from the second half of the sixteenth century, is the earliest version of the basic recension of the *Narration*,[68] it cannot be dated earlier than into the late 1480s or early 1490s,[69] although a strong case could be made for dating it later, that is, into the 1520s-1540s.[70] The difficulties involving the dating of the *Narration*, combined with its limited official use (it is found only in one provincial, but official codex, the *VPL*), force us to eliminate it from the present analysis.

The composition of the *Vita* of Dmitrii Ivanovich Donskoi and its inclusion in the hypothetical *Codex of 1456* can be characterized as the first stage in the development of the official Muscovite dynastic claims to Kiev. The significance of this *Vita* for the emergence of Muscovite governmental pretensions to the Kievan dynastic inheritance was further enhanced by its incorporation, albeit with some editorial modifications, into the official Muscovite codices of the 1470s, in which additional dynastic claims were raised. The newly articulated claims represented the second stage in the evolution of Muscovite dynastic claims to the Kievan succession. The editors of the *Muscovite Codex of 1472*, as reflected in the *NL*, for example, not only integrated the *Vita* into their work, but also formulated their own version of the dynastic continuity theory from Kievan Rus' through Suzdalia-Vladimiria to Muscovy.[71] The latter version appears in the annalistic tale under the entry for 1471, entitled *O novgorodtsekh i o vladytse Feofile* (*About the Novgorodians and Vladyka Feofil*). The tale is devoted to the struggle between the Novgorodian irredentist faction, which wished to preserve the

Novgorodian constitutional system and ecclesiastical autonomy, and the pro-Muscovite group, which supported Muscovite attempts to subordinate Novgorod to Muscovy. The leaders of the irredentist faction attempted to realize their objectives by inviting Mikhail Olel'kovych of Kiev, a prince with indisputable Orthodox credentials, who came from the Rus' lands of the Grand Principality of Lithuania, as a prince-protector of the Novgorodian city republic. The tale also dwells on the Muscovite diplomatic preparations aimed at Novgorod's subordination.[72]

Two expositions of the dynastic continuity theory appear in the tale. One was allegedly advanced by the leaders of the pro-Muscovite faction; another, similar statement, was put forward by the Muscovite envoys on behalf of Ivan III Vasil'evich.

Pro-Muscovite Novgorodian Leaders

> From antiquity we [the Novgorodians] have been the patrimony of those grand princes, from Riurik, our first grand prince, who with his two brothers had been willingly invited from the Varangians by our own land. Afterwards, Grand Prince Volodimer, [Riurik's] great-grandson, was baptized and [he] baptized all our lands: the Rus' [land] and our Slavic [land], and the Meria [land], and the Krivichiian [land], and the Ves', called the Beloozero [land], and the Murom [land], and the [land] of the Viatichiians, and [many] other [lands]. And from that grand prince, St. Volodimer, and to our [present] lord, grand prince Ivan Vasil'evich....

Ivan's [III] Envoys

> From antiquity, you, the people of Novgorod, have been my patrimony, from our grandfathers and our ancestors, from Grand Prince Volodimer, the great-grandson of Riurik, the first grand prince in our land who baptized the Rus' land. And from that Riurik and up to this day, you have recognized only one [ruling] gens (*rod*) of those grand princes, first [those] of Kiev, and [then] Grand Prince Vsevolod [III] Iur'evich, [and Grand-Prince] Dmitrii [Ivanovich] of Vladimir. And from that grand prince and until my time, we, their kin, rule over you, and we bestow upon you [our mercy], and we protect you against [all adversaries], and we are free to punish you if you shall not recognize us in accordance with the old tradition (*po starine*).[73]

These pronouncements of the Muscovite court were incorporated into the *Muscovite Codex of 1479* [74] and the *SL*,[75] and this suggests that they were fundamental assumptions of official Muscovite political theory in the last quarter of the fifteenth century.[76]

The Muscovite claims to the Kievan dynastic succession were promulgated at the beginning of the three-and-a-half-century-long contest (1450s-1795) between Muscovy and Poland-Lithuania for the lands of Rus'.[77] Whereas the political and military struggles were conducted to conquer as much territory and as many cities as possible, the ideological contest was waged for all of Rus'. During its first phase (1449-1485), this struggle centered on the important Great Russian, albeit non-Muscovite, territories – namely, Great Novgorod and the Grand Principality of Tver' (1449-1485). Its outcome was the annexation of those two Russian states – a major Muscovite victory. Particularly in the process of annexing Novgorod, Muscovy formulated an ideological program that remained in use until the end of the sixteenth century. However, these claims were also employed in anticipation of the second major phase of this contest (1487-1537), which was conducted for the Great Russian border areas, as well as the Belorussian territories and some Ukrainian lands of Rus'. Five major wars (1487-1494; 1500-1503; 1507-1508; 1512-1522; 1534-1537) were waged and they resulted in Muscovy's annexation of the lands of Chernihiv and Novhorod-Sivers'kyi, Briansk, Homel, and Starodub in 1503, and Smolensk in 1514.[78] In the second phase of the struggle, the annexation of Kiev was also a major goal of the Muscovite ruler.

It was during the second phase of the struggle that the third stage in the development of Muscovy's claims to the Kievan dynastic inheritance took place. Specifically, it occurred over a period of eleven years (1493-1504), when Muscovy formulated her claims to all of Rus' against the Jagiellonian double monarchy. The Muscovite court advanced its pretensions cautiously, step by step. In a radical departure from the traditionally established arrangements between Muscovy and Poland-Lithuania concerning the titles of their respective rulers, the Muscovite court, in a charter of 4 January 1493 that verified the credentials of its envoy Dmitrii Davidovich Zagriazskii, used for the first time the phrase "Sovereign of all of Rus'" as part of the Muscovite ruler's title.[79] The Muscovite envoy was instructed to avoid any confrontation regarding the use of this sweeping term; still, the wording of the title and the note of instruction made it clear that Ivan III was claiming sovereignty over all the lands of Rus'.[80] The Lithuanians were well aware of the significance of this addition, but were unable to negotiate any change in the Muscovite position in the summer of 1493.[81]

The Muscovite court, in addition to adhering to its original claim, refined its wording from the point of view of its own patrimonial theory by maintaining that the Muscovite ruler had included in his title only those lands that he had received "from his grandfathers and ancestors and that from antiquity he had been by law and birth the Sovereign of all of Rus'."[82] In diplomatic terms, Muscovy scored a temporary, but nevertheless important, success by forcing Lithuania to recognize the phrase "Sovereign of all of Rus'" as part of the Muscovite ruler's title in the Peace Treaty of 1494.[83] This triumph reflected the great change that had taken place in the relations between Muscovy and Poland-Lithuania since the treaty of 1449. That treaty had been concluded between Kazimierz Jagiellończyk and Vasilii II with the aim of delineating each ruler's sphere of influence in Rus'. In it, the word *Rus'* did not even appear in the title of the Muscovite ruler, who was referred to simply as *moskovskii*, whereas his Polish-Lithuanian counterpart was designated as *ruskii*.[84]

In addition to the claim implicit in the change of the title, the Muscovite court, at the very outset of the sixteenth century, promulgated a patrimonial justification for its expansionist aims in the lands of Rus'. This justification was simultaneously advanced in diplomatic negotiations with the Hungarian king Władysław Jagiellończyk and the Polish-Lithuanian ruler Aleksander Jagiellończyk in 1503-1504. The two statements of the Muscovite government are almost identical in terminology.

Muscovite Response to the Hungarian King

> And we responded to the Hungarian king's envoy that his [Aleksander Jagiellończyk's] patrimony is the Polish land (*liatskaia zemlia*) and the Lithuanian land (*litovskaia zemlia*), but [that] all the Russian land has been our patrimony from antiquity. And those cities, which, with God's help, we conquered from the Lithuanian [grand prince], are our patrimony and we shall not return them. And whichever Russian cities are still [in the possession] of the Lithuanian [grand prince, namely] Kiev, Smolensk and other cities of the Russian land, with God's help, we would like to obtain all this patrimony which is ours.[85]

Muscovite Responses to the Polish-Lithuanian Ruler

> And not only those cities and provinces which are now in our possession are our patrimony, [but] all the Russian land, according to God's will, has been our patrimony [inherited] from our ancestors and from antiquity.[86]

> It is well known to our son-in-law, the king and grand prince Aleksander, that all the Russian land, according to God's will has been our patrimony [inherited] from our ancestors and from antiquity...and his [Aleksander's] patrimony is the Polish land (*liatskaia zemlia*) and the Lithuanian land (*litovskaia zemlia*).... And not only those cities and provinces that are now in our possession are our patrimony, [but] also all the Russian land, [namely], Kiev and Smolensk and other cities that he possesses in the Lithuanian land, according to God's will, has been our patrimony [inherited] from our ancestors and from antiquity.[87]

These statements reveal some confusion in the delineation of the patrimonies; Kiev and Smolensk are both claimed as part of the Russian patrimony and referred to as being in the Lithuanian land. The constant and often ambiguous use of the terms "land" (*zemlia*) and "patrimony" (*votchina*) is indicative of the fact that the Russian patrimonial law of the Muscovite period lacked a sophisticated theoretical framework, limiting itself to a few general assumptions regarding the focus of territorial possession and political domination.

Russia's as well as Poland's preoccupation with Kiev as a symbolic capital of Rus' lasted throughout the sixteenth century. The Muscovite court culminated its claims to Kiev and all the Rus' lands with the assertion that Moscow was "the second Kiev."[88] Earlier, in 1503, the Polish-Lithuanian side had rejected Muscovy's expansionist claims, as well as the Muscovite ruler's insistence on being addressed as the "Sovereign of all of Rus'," as unjustified, since the larger part of Kievan Rus' was under the sovereignty of the Polish Kingdom, i.e., the Polish-Lithuanian state.[89] Later on, in connection with the annexation of the Ukrainian lands of Kievan Rus' into Crown Poland at the Diet of Lublin (1569), the Polish ruling elite and the Polish king Zygmunt II August formulated their own set of legal and historical pretensions to Kiev and all the Rus' lands.[90]

The three stages of the development of the official Muscovite claims to the Kievan inheritance extended over a period of approximately half a century (1454/55-1504). They originated at the time of Muscovy's ideological awakening that had followed the Council of Florence and the fall of Constantinople, when the Muscovite political and ecclesiastical establishment saw its chance to strengthen its position not only in Russia but also in all of Eastern Europe. These ambitions were reinforced by Muscovy's successes in her expansionist policies, especially in Novgorod, where dynastic claims had been successfully applied, and subsequently in the Russian border areas, a large part of the Belorussian territory, and some Ukrainian lands.

Between the initial implementation of these dynastic pretensions to Novgorod in the early 1470s and the full formulation of the claim to all of Rus' in 1493-1504, there was a period of about two decades, when Muscovy's foreign policy, and especially her relations with the Crimea, underwent a major transformation. In particular, Mengli-Girey's campaign against the Kievan area and the sack of the city of Kiev in 1482, which had resulted from the reversal of alliances in Eastern Europe and a close Muscovite-Crimean cooperation, may have delayed temporarily the development of Muscovite ideology.[91] This slow pace may also be attributed to the static and traditionalist nature of Muscovite legal and political theory. By the beginning of the sixteenth century, however, a fairly coherent set of official Muscovite claims to the Kievan inheritance had been formulated, based on the uninterrupted dynastic continuity of the Riurikides, on the theory of succession (*translatio*) from Kievan Rus' through (Rostovia)-Suzdalia-Vladimiria to Muscovy, and on traditional patrimonial law.

NOTES

1. P.N. Miliukov, *Glavnye techeniia russkoi istoricheskoi mysli*, 3rd ed. (Moscow, 1913), 174-177.

2. A.E. Presniakov, *Obrazovanie velikorusskogo gosudarstva: Ocherki po istorii XIII-XV stoletii* (Petrograd, 1918), 2-3, 7, and 19.

3. For a summary of Hrushevs'kyi's views and a convenient English translation of his seminal article on this subject, see "The Traditional Scheme of Russian History and the Problem of a Rational Organization of the History of Eastern Slavs [1909]," in *The Annals of the Ukrainian Academy of Arts and Sciences in the U.S.*, 2 (1952): 355-364. Hrushevs'kyi's views as stated in this article reflect those found in his *Istoriia Ukrainy-Rusy*, 10 vols., 3rd rep. ed. (New York, 1954-58) [see also Chapter 11 of this volume].

4. D.S. Likhachev, *Natsional'noe samosoznanie drevnei Rusi: Ocherki iz oblasti russkoi literatury XI-XVII vv.* (Moscow and Leningrad, 1945), 68-81; *Kul'tura Rusi epokhi obrazovaniia russkogo natsional'nogo gosudarstva: Konets XIV – nachalo XVI v.* (Moscow and Leningrad, 1946), 40-41, 57-97, and 103-104; *Russkie letopisi i ikh kul'turno-istoricheskoe znachenie* (Moscow and Leningrad, 1947), 293-305; *Kul'tura vremeni Andreia Rubleva i Epifaniia Premudrago: Konets XIV – nachalo XV v.* (Moscow and Leningrad, 1962), 4, 6, 11-12, 17, 19-20, 90-115, 142-146, and 161-170; *Die Kultur Russlands während der osteuropäischen Frührenaissance vom 14. bis zum Beginn des 15. Jahrhunderts* (Dresden, 1962), 6, 8, 13-14, 18-19, 20-21, 90-117, 145-152, and 167-175; "Predvozrozhdenie na Rusi v kontse XIV – pervoi polovine XV veka," in *Literatura epokhi vozrozhdeniia i problemy vsemirnoi literatury* (Moscow, 1967), 136-182. An attempt to substantiate Likhachev's hypothesis with an extravagant antedating of Muscovite texts pertaining to the Kulikovo Battle of 1380 was made in an American dissertation: C.J. Halperin, "The Russian Land and the Russian Tsar: The Emergence of Muscovite Ideology, 1380-1408" (Ph.D. dissertation, Columbia University, 1973), especially 22 and 199.

5. Likhachev, *Kul'tura Rusi*, 57.

6. D.S. Likhachev, *Chelovek v literature drevnei Rusi*, 2nd ed. (Moscow, 1970), 25-62.

7. For the most fundamental study of historicism as a phenomenon of intellectual and cultural history, see Friedrich Meinecke, *Die Entstehung des Historismus*, 3rd ed. (Munich, 1959). The concept of historicism was applied to the history of pictorial art in the nineteenth century: L. Grote, ed., *Historismus und die bildende Kunst* (Munich, 1965). Likhachev's introduction of this idealistic and genetic German concept in the Soviet Union in 1946 coincided with attacks on the works of M. Hrushevs'kyi and his school for having "imported" German theoretical concepts from Hegel and Ranke, which in fact Hrushevs'kyi never utilized in his work (cf. J. Pelenski, "Soviet Ukrainian Historiography after World War II," *Jahrbücher für Geschichte Osteuropas*, 12, no. 3 [1964]: 377-378).

8. Likhachev, *Kul'tura Rusi*, 64-67; Likhachev, *Kul'tura vremeni Andreia Rubleva*, 100-103.

9. For the text of the reconstructed *Troitskaia letopis'*, see M.D. Priselkov, *Troitskaia letopis' : Rekonstruktsiia teksta* (Moscow and Leningrad, 1950). The most important scholarly contributions to the study of the *Troitskaia letopis'* are the following: M.D. Priselkov, "Letopisanie XIV veka," in *Sbornik statei po russkoi istorii posviashchennykh S.F. Platonovu* (1922), 24-39; "O rekonstruktsii teksta Troitskoi letopisi 1408 g., sgorevshei v Moskve v 1812 g.," *Uchenye zapiski Gosudarstvennogo pedagogicheskogo instituta im Gertsena*, 19 (1939): 5-42; M.D. Priselkov, *Istoriia russkogo letopisaniia XI-XV vv.* (Leningrad, 1940), 113-142; Priselkov, *Troitskaia letopis'*, Introduction, 7-49; S.I. Kochetov, "Troitskii pergamennyi spisok letopisi 1408 g.," *Arkheograficheskii ezhegodnik za 1961* (1962), 18-27; G.N. Moiseeva, "Otryvok Troitskoi pergamennoi letopisi perepisannyi G.F. Millerom," *Trudy Otdela drevnerusskoi literatury* (hereafter *TODRL*), 26 (1971): 93-99. [For more detailed information on the *TL*, see Chapter 4 of this volume (pp. 68-72, 75, fn. 22).]

10. The text of the *Simeonov Chronicle* was published in *Polnoe sobranie russkikh letopisei* (hereafter *PSRL*), 18 (1913) under the editorship of A.E. Presniakov.

11. For a discussion of Byzantine policies and attitudes with regard to the Metropolitanate of Kiev and all of Rus' in the fourteenth century and the literature on the subject, see the following studies: D. Obolensky, "Byzantium, Kiev and Moscow: A Study in Ecclesiastical Relations," *Dumbarton Oaks Papers*, 11 (1957): 21-78;

I. Ševčenko,"Russo-Byzantine Relations after the Eleventh Century," in J.M. Hussey, D. Obolensky, and S. Runciman, eds., *Proceedings of the XIIIth International Congress of Byzantine Studies* (London, 1967), 93-104; F. Tinnefeld, "Byzantinisch-russische Kirchenpolitik im 14. Jahrhundert," *Byzantinische Zeitschrift*, 67 (1974): 359-384.

12. I have serious reservations about applying the term Renaissance to cultural developments in Muscovite Russia in the fifteenth and sixteenth centuries. Limited space precludes a fundamental critique of Likhachev's notion of the Russian Early Renaissance in this article. The use of this concept as applied to Muscovite Russia is even more problematic than the assumptions about the presence of historicism in the culture and art of Muscovy.

13. Priselkov, *Troitskaia letopis'*, 419-421; *PSRL*, 18 (1913): 129-131. The *Rogozhskii letopisets* was published in *PSRL*, 2nd ed., 15, no. 1 (1922), under the editorship of N.P. Likhachev (for the text of the Tale, see cols. 139-141). For the best treatment of the Short Chronicle Tale and the literature on the subject, see M.A. Salmina, "Letopisnaia povest' o Kulikovskoi bitve i 'Zadonshchina'," in *Slovo o Polku Igoreve i pamiatniki Kulikovskogo tsikla* (Moscow and Leningrad, 1966), 344-384, especially 344-364.

14. Its similarity to the "Tale about the Battle on the Vozha River" prompted Salmina to suggest that both texts had the same author ("Letopisnaia povest'...," 356-359).

15. Priselkov, *Istoriia russkogo letopisaniia XI-XV vv.*, 121-122.

16. For the various uses of the concept *vsia russkaia zemlia* from the twelfth to the fifteenth century, see L.V. Cherepnin, "Istoricheskie usloviia formirovaniia russkoi narodnosti do kontsa XV v.," in *Voprosy formirovaniia russkoi narodnosti i natsii: Sbornik statei* (Moscow and Leningrad, 1958), 61-63 and 79-88. One example from the *NPL* will suffice to illustrate the northeastern Russian meaning of *vsia russkaia zemlia* in the fourteenth century. The entry about the Mongol-Tatar invasion of Tver', undertaken with Muscovite support in 1327, reads as follows : "Na tu zhe zimu priide rat' tatarskaia mnozhestva mnogo, i vziasha Tfer i Kashin, i Novotor'skuiu volost' i prosto rkushche vsiu zemliu ruskuiu i polozhisha iu pustu, tokmo Novgorod ubliude Bog i sviataia Sofeia," (A.N. Nasonov, ed., *Novgorodskaia pervaia letopis' starshego i mladshego izvodov* [Moscow and Leningrad, 1950], 341).

17. *PSRL*, 2nd ed., 4, part 1, nos. 1-2 (1915-1925): 311-325.

18. *PSRL*, 6 (1853): 90-98.

19. The *Nikanor Chronicle* was published under the editorship of A.N. Nasonov in *PSRL*, 27 (1962). For the text of the Tale, see 71-76.

20. S.K. Shambinago, *Skazanie o Mamaevom poboishche* (1907), 1-2.

21. Salmina, "Letopisnaia povest'," 364-376, including the literature on the subject.

22. A.A. Shakhmatov was the first to suggest the existence of the *Codex of 1448* ("Obshcherusskie letopisnye svody XIV i XV vv.," *Zhurnal Ministerstva narodnogo prosveshcheniia* (hereafter *ZhMNP*), n.s., 1909, no. 9, 98 and 104; *Obozrenie russkikh letopisnykh svodov XIV-XVI vv.* [Moscow and Leningrad, 1938], 151-160). Ia.S. Lur'e revived Shakhmatov's thesis and offered additional evidence to substantiate views that it was an all-Russian codex ("K probleme svoda 1448 g.," *TODRL*, 24 [1969]: 142-146; and "Obshcherusskii svod-protograf Sofiiskoi I i Novgorodskoi letopisei," *TODRL*, 28 [1974]: 114-139).

23. *Akty istoricheskie, sobrannye i izdannye Arkheograficheskoiu kommissieiu* (hereafter *AI*), 1, no. 67 (1841): 75-83. For a discussion of the Russian-Kazanian relations and their ideological ramifications, see J. Pelenski, *Russia and Kazan: Conquest and Imperial Ideology (1438-1560s)* (The Hague and Paris, 1974), 23-26 and 180-182.

24. *PSRL*, 2nd ed., 4, part 1, no. 2 (1925): 351-366.

25. *PSRL*, 6 (1853): 104-111.

26. *PSRL*, 27 (1962): 82-87 (under the year 1387); *PSRL*, 25 (1949): 215-218.

27. "O prestavlenii velikago kniazia Danila Moskovskago" under the entry for 1304, and "V leto 6848 (1340) prestavisia kniaz' velikii moskovskii Ivan Danilovich' " (Priselkov, *Troitskaia letopis'*, 351 and 364; cf. also *PSRL*, 18 [1913]: 85, 93). "O prestavlenii velikogo kniazia Vasiliia Dmitrievicha" under the entry for 1425, and "O prestavlenii velikogo kniazia Vasiliia Vasil'evicha" under the entry for 1462 (*PSRL*, 27 [1962]: 100, 123).

28. A.A. Shakhmatov, *Otzyv o sochinenii S.K. Shambinago "Povesti o Mamaevom poboishche"* (St. Petersburg, 1910) (also a separate offprint from "Otchet o 12-m prisuzhdenii premii mitropolita Makariia), 119.

29. V.P. Adrianova-Peretts, "Slovo o zhitii i o prestavlenii velikogo kniazia Dmitriia Ivanovicha, tsaria Rus'skago," *TODRL*, 5 (1947): 73-96, especially 91-92.

30. A.V. Solov'ev, "Epifanii Premudryi kak avtor 'Slova o zhitii i prestavlenii velikago kniazia Dmitriia Ivanovicha, tsaria rus'skago'," *TODRL*, 17 (1961): 85-106.

31. M.A. Salmina, "Slovo o zhitii i prestavlenii velikogo kniazia Dmitriia Ivanovicha, tsaria Rus'skago," *TODRL*, 25 (1970): 81-104.

32. The date 1448 had been set by A.A. Shakhmatov on the basis of the computation of certain holidays. However, Shakhmatov changed his opinion on this matter ("Kievskii Nachalnyi svod 1095 g.," in *A.A. Shakhmatov, 1864-1920* [Moscow and Leningrad, 1947], 135).

33. The following copies were used by F.P. Pokrovskii, the editor of the second edition of the *NChL* (publication of the edition was supervised by A.A. Shakhmatov):

The Stroev Copy, from the last quarter of the fifteenth century, covering historical materials from 912 to 1477 (St);

The Sinodal' Copy, copied in 1544, beginning with the *PVL* and ending with the entry for 1477 (S);

The Public Library Copy (Frolov), taken down in the late fifteenth or the early sixteenth century, starting with the *PVL* and ending with 1447 (P);

The Academy of Sciences Copy from the first half of the sixteenth century, opening with *PVL* and concluding with the entry 1447, like P (A);

The Golitsyn Copy, from the first half of the sixteenth century and ending with 1516 (G);

The New-Russian Copy, from the last quarter of the fifteenth century, starting with the *PVL* and ending with the entry for 1437 (N);

The [F.P.] Tolstoi Copy, taken down at the end of the fifteenth and the beginning of the sixteenth century, lacks the beginning and the end of the manuscript, and covers only the years from 1382 to 1418 (T).

34. The text of the *Vita* was published from Copy A with variant readings from copies G, N, T. The *Vita* was not included in copies St, S, P.

35. *PSRL*, 2nd ed., 4, part 1, no. 1 (1915): ix.

36. *PSRL*, 2nd ed., 4, part 1, no. 2 (1925): 361-365.

37. Halperin, "The Russian Land and the Russian Tsar," 117, fn. 194.

38. For an analysis of the campaign and the resulting developments, see L.V. Cherepnin, *Obrazovanie russkogo tsentralizovannogo gosudarstva v XIV-XV vekakh* (Moscow, 1960), 817-825.

39. For the texts of the Treaty of Iazhelbitsy, see S.N. Valk, ed., *Gramoty Velikogo Novgoroda i Pskova* (Moscow and Leningrad, 1949), 39-43. For a commentary on this treaty, see L.V. Cherepnin, *Russkie feodal'nye arkhivy XIV-XV vekov*, 2 parts (Moscow and Leningrad, 1948-1951), 1: 356-363.

40. *PSRL*, 5 (1851): 243 fn *. Cf. also Salmina, *TODRL*, 25 (1970): 81, fn. 4.

41. Shakhmatov, *Obozrenie*, 208-221; Priselkov, *Istoriia russkogo letopisaniia XI-XV vv.*, 151-154 and 162-164.
42. Shakhmatov, *Obozrenie*, 217.
43. Priselkov, *Istoriia russkogo letopisaniia XI-XV vv.*, 162-164.
44. Priselkov, *Istoriia russkogo letopisaniia XI-XV vv.*, 164-173.
45. Ia.S. Lur'e has postulated the existence of the *Codex of 1453* on the basis of the manuscript GBL M. 3271, the main entries of which end with the year 1453 ("Nikanorovskaia i Vologodsko-Permskaia letopisi kak otrazhenie velikokniazheskogo svoda nachala 70-kh godov XV v.," *Vspomagatel'nye istoricheskie discipliny* (hereafter *VID*), 5 [1973]: 225, 238, and 249-250). However, the manuscript in question does not contain the crucial text of the *Vita* of Dmitrii Ivanovich and does not include any material of relevance for its dating. For a good outline of the contents of GBL M. 3271, consult the informative study by I.M. Kudriavtsev, "Sbornik poslednei chetverti XV—nachala XVI v. iz Muzeinogo sobraniia," *Zapiski Otdela rukopisei Gosudarstvennoi biblioteki im. Lenina*, 25 (1962): 220-288, especially 225-233.
46. It is surprising that such an astute specialist in the field of Old Russian literature as John Fennell could have written: "Indeed, there are few biographies of laymen in medieval Russian literature that are so strikingly lacking in 'message' or political tendentiousness. As the sharp historical outline of earlier works has faded here [in the *Vita* -- J.P.], as fact has given way to generalities, so has ideology receded into the background. For once we are not expected to learn a political lesson from a text" (J. Fennell and A. Stokes, *Early Russian Literature* [London, 1974], 133).
47. *PSRL*, 6 (1853): 104; *PSRL*, 2nd ed., 4, part 1, no. 2 (1925): 351-352.
48. In the *Troitskaia letopis'* and the *SL*, the relevant phrases read as follows: (1304) "prestavis' kniaz' Danilo Aleksandrovich, vnuk Iaroslava [Vsevolodovicha (1238-1246)], pravnuk velikogo Vsevoloda [Iur'evicha (1176-1212)]...."; (1340) "prestavisia kniz' velikii moskovskii Ivan Danilovich, vnuk velikogo Aleksandra [Iaroslavicha (1252-1263)], pravnuk velikogo Iaroslava [Vsevolodovicha]...."
49. Solov'ev, *TODRL*, 17 (1961): 104, fn. 47.
50. For the classical Western definition of patrimonial theory, see M. Weber, *Economy and Society: An Outline of Interpretative Sociology*, G. Roth and C. Wittich, eds., 3 vols. (New York, 1968), 3: 1013, 1028-1029, and 1085-1086. The best historical discussion of the concept of patrimonialism and the scholarly controversies concerning the actual existence of a patrimonial state in medieval Germany has been provided by O. Brunner, *Land und Herrschaft*, 4th ed. (Vienna, 1959), 146-164. For a discussion of the meaning of the term *votchina* in the Old Russian sources and the literature on the subject, see Pelenski, *Russia and Kazan*, 76-78, fn. 1.
51. For the texts of the Testaments of Dmitrii Donskoi and an English translation, see R. C. Howes, trans. and ed., *The Testaments of the Grand Princes of Moscow* (Ithaca, N.Y., 1967), 126-130 and 208-217, especially 127 and 212 (the relevant phrase reads: "And, lo I bless my son, Prince Vasilii, with my patrimony, the Grand Principality").
52. *PSRL*, 6 (1853): 110; *PSRL*, 2nd ed., 4, part 1, no. 2 (1925): 366.
53. For an informative and perceptive discussion of the theological and political currents at the Council of Florence and its impact on posterity, as well as the literature on the subject, see I. Ševčenko, "Intellectual Repercussions of the Council of Florence," *Church History*, 24, no. 4 (1955): 291-323.
54. For the texts of the *Tale of Simeon of Suzdal'*, see V. Malinin, *Starets Eleazarova monastyria Filofei i ego poslaniia* (Kiev, 1901), appendices 17 and 18, 89-114.
55. For the text of the *Slovo izbrano*, see A.N. Popov, *Istoriko-literaturnyi obzor drevnerusskikh polemicheskikh sochinenii protiv latinian* (Moscow, 1875), 360-395.

56. For the text of the *Slovo pokhval'noe*, see N.P. Likhachev, ed., "Inoka Fomy Slovo pokhval'noe o blagovernom velikom kniaze Borise Aleksandroviche," *Pamiatniki drevnei pis'mennosti i iskusstva*, 168 (1908): 1-55. For a review of Likhachev's publication, consult A.A.. Shakhmatov, *Otzyv ob izdanii N.P. Likhacheva: "Inoka Fomy slovo pokhval'noe o blagovernom velikom kniaze Aleksandroviche"* (St. Petersburg, 1909). An interesting analysis of this work was provided by W. Philipp, "Ein Anonymus der Tverer Publicistik im 15. Jahrhundert" in *Festschrift für Dmytro Čyževs'kyj zum 60. Geburtstag* (Berlin, 1954), 230-237.

57. F. Delektorskii showed that Simeon's *Tale* was written many years after the Council of Florence, but before 1458 ("Kritiko-bibliograficheskii obzor drevnerusskikh skazanii o florentiiskoi unii," *ZhMNP*, 300 [1895]: 131-184, especially 138-144). Cf. *idem*, "Florentiisskaia uniia (po drevnerusskim skazaniiam) i vopros o soedinenii tserkvei v drevnei Rusi," *Strannik* (September-November 1893), 442-458.

58. Popov, *Istoriko-literaturnyi obzor*, 359. A. Pavlov, *Kriticheskie opyty po istorii drevneishei greko-russkoi polemiki protiv latinian* (St. Petersburg, 1878), 106, 108.

59. Pavlov, *Kriticheskie opyty*, 99-102 and 105-108.

60. Delektorskii, *ZhMNP*, 300 (1895): 154. M. Cherniavsky repeated Delektorskii's claim; moreover, he maintained that the title *tsar* had been used in Russian documents (*Akty istoricheskie*, I [1841], nos. 44, 56, 60, 61, 63) ("The Reception of the Council of Florence in Moscow," *Church History*, 24, no. 4 [1955]: 347-359, especially 358, fn. 30). A rechecking of the five quoted documents revealed that the title *tsar* does not appear in any of them.

61. V. Iablonskii, *Pakhomii Serb i ego agiograficheskie pisaniia* (St. Petersburg, 1908), 201-202.

62. Pavlov, *Kriticheskie opyty*, 100. Pakhomii Logofet was an intellectual who worked for different employers (from both Novgorod and Moscow) and for a price could adjust his views according to the wishes of his employers. He could easily assume a more patriotic Muscovite tone than any of his Muscovite contemporaries.

63. The following sentence in the *Vita* fits particularly well into the context of the "Florentine" texts and is definitely premature for the period of Dmitrii Donskoi: "ty zhe stolp nechestia razdrushil esi v ruskoi zemli i ne primesi sebe k bezumnym stranam na krestianskuiu pogibel" (*PSRL*, 6 [1853]: 110). Cf. also Salmina, *TODRL*, 25 (1970): 102-103.

64. For a critical edition of the *Zadonshchina* texts and the extensive literature on the subject up to 1965, see *Slovo o Polku Igoreve i pamiatniki Kulikovskogo tsikla*, 535-556 and 557-583. For a reconstruction of an ideal text and an English translation, see R. Jakobson and D.S. Worth, eds., *Sofonija's Tale of the Russian-Tatar Battle on the Kulikovo Field* (The Hague, 1963).

65. Salmina, "Letopisnaia povest'," 376-383.

66. I shall present my arguments for this dating in another study.

67. For a more recent dating of the *Skazanie* between the middle of the fifteenth and the early sixteenth century and the literature on the subject, see M.A. Salmina, "K voprosu o datirovke 'Skazaniia o Mamaevom poboishche'," *TODRL*, 29 (1974): 98-124.

68. The *VPL* has been published in *PSRL*, 24 (1959) under the editorship of M.N. Tikhomirov. For the text of the *Skazanie* from the London copy, see *ibid.*, 328-344.

69. I hope to offer my hypothesis for the dating of this work elsewhere.

70. V.S. Mingalev, "'Letopisnaia povest'–istochnik 'Skazaniia o Mamaevom poboishche'," *Trudy Moskovskogo istoriko-arkhivnogo instituta*, 24, no. 2, (1966): 55-72; *Skazanie o Mamaevom poboishche i ego istochniki* (Avtoreferat kand. dissertatsii; Moscow and Vilnius, 1971), especially 10-13.

71. For a detailed treatment of the relationship between the Muscovite grand princely codices of the 1470s, the *NL*, the *VPL*, and the literature on the subject, see Ia.S. Lur'e, "Nikanorovskaia i Vologodsko-Permskaia letopisi kak otrazhenie veliko-kniazheskogo svoda nachala 70-kh godov XV v.," *VID*, 5 (1973): 219-250.

72. For the text of the tale, see *PSRL*, 27 (1962): 129-134. The more recent literature on Novgorodian affairs, as well as Muscovite policies aimed at the incorporation of Novgorod, is written from the Muscovite point of view. For the two most prominent examples of the Moscow-centered interpretation of Muscovite-Novgorodian relations in the 1470s and the literature on the subject, see Cherepnin, *Obrazovanie*, 855-874, and V.N. Bernadskii, *Novgorod i Novgorodskaia zemlia v XV veke* (Moscow and Leningrad, 1961), 264-313.

73. *PSRL*, 27 (1962): 130; for some additional remarks on the application of the Muscovite dynastic continuity theory to Novgorod, see A.L. Gol'dberg, "U istokov moskovskikh istoriko-politicheskikh idei XV v.," *TODRL*, 24 (1969): 147-150.

74. *PSRL*, 25(1949): 285.

75. *PSRL*, 18 (1913): 226-227.

76. Most of these fundamental assumptions were used not only for the justification of Muscovite expansionism in Russia proper, but also in conjunction with the annexation of non-Russian ethnic territories, as, for example, the Kazan Khanate in the sixteenth century. Cf. Pelenski, *Russia and Kazan*, especially chaps. 6 and 7.

77. An outline of the major methodological and theoretical problems connected with the study of this contest in the fifteenth and sixteenth centuries is presented in my unpublished study, entitled "The Contest between Muscovite Russia and Poland-Lithuania for the Lands of Old Rus' (1450s-1580s)."

78. For the best factual accounts of these wars, albeit from the Muscovite perspective, see G. Karpov, "Istoriia bor'by Moskovskogo Gosudarstva s Pol'sko-Litovskim," *Chteniia v Imperatorskom Obshchestve istorii i drevnostei rossiiskikh*, part 1, 1866, bk. 3, 1-140, part 2, 1866, bk. 4, 1-154; E.I. Kashprovskii, "Bor'ba Vasiliia III Ivanovicha s Sigizmundom I Kazimirovichem iz-za obladaniia Smolenskom (1507-1522)," *Sbornik Istoriko-filologicheskogo obshchestva pri Institute kniazia Bezborodko v Nezhine*, 2 (1899): 173-344; K.V. Bazilevich, *Vneshniaia politika Russkogo tscentralizovannogo gosudarstva* (Moscow, 1952). F. Papée had touched upon some aspects of the first of these wars in his informative work, *Polska i Litwa na przełomie wieków średnich*, vol. 1 (Cracow, 1904), 132-150.

79. *Sbornik Imperatorskogo russkogo istoricheskogo obshchestva* (hereafter *SIRIO*), 35 (1882): 81.

80. *SIRIO*, 35 (1882): 82.

81. *SIRIO*, 35 (1882): 103-108.

82. *SIRIO*, 35 (1882): 107.

83. *SIRIO*, 35 (1882): 125 and 129.

84. For the text of the Treaty of 1449, see L. V. Cherepnin, ed., *Dukhovnye i dogovornye gramoty velikikh i udel'nykh kniazei XIV-XVI vv.* (Moscow, 1950), 160-163.

85. *SIRIO*, 41 (1884): 457.

86. *SIRIO*, 35 (1882): 380.

87. *SIRIO*, 35 (1882): 460.

88. The claim that Moscow was "the second Kiev" was most explicitly formulated in the *Kazanskaia istoriia*, whose author or authors stated that "the capital and the most famous city of Moscow shines forth as a second Kiev..." (G.I. Moiseeva, ed., *Kazanskaia istoriia* [Moscow and Leningrad, 1954], 57). A parallel to this statement is found in the last sentence of the *Otryvok russkoi letopisi*, which reads: "May we see as ruler in Kiev, the Orthodox Tsar, Grand Prince Ivan Vasil'evich of all of Russia" (*PSRL*, 6 [1853]: 315). For additional comments and the literature on this problem, see Pelenski, *Russia and Kazan*, chpt. 7.

89. "...v korolevstve i pod korolevstvom est' bol'shaia chast' Rusi..." (*Akty, otnosiashchiesia k istorii Zapadnoi Rossii*, 1 [1846]: 347-348).
90. For an extensive discussion of this problem and the literature on the subject, see J. Pelenski, "The Incorporation of the Ukrainian Lands of Old Rus' into Crown Poland (1569): Socio-Material Interest and Ideology – A Reexamination," *American Contributions to the Seventh International Congress of Slavists*, Warsaw, 21-27 August 1973, vol. 3 (The Hague and Paris, 1973), 19-52, especially 38-46 [see Chapter 9 of this volume]; cf. also *idem*, "Inkorporacja ukraińskich ziem dawnej Rusi do Korony w 1569 roku: Ideologia i korzyści—próba nowego spojrzenia," *Przegląd Historyczny*, 65, no. 2 (1974): 243-262, especially 252-256.
91. For factual accounts of the sack of Kiev in 1482, see Papée, *Polska i Litwa*, 83-92; and Bazilevich, *Vneshniaia politika*, 192-199. The actual attitude of Ivan III toward Kiev and Kievan sacred places and ecclesiastical treasures is best reflected in the following statement of the oppositional Muscovite codex: "Kniaz' velikii posla k Mengireiu k Krymskomu, povele voevati korolevu zemliu; Mengirei zhe s siloiu svoeiu vzia Kiev, vsia liudi v polon povede, i derzhatelia Kievskago svede s soboiu i s zhenoiu i s detmi, i mnogo pakosti uchinil, Pecherskuiu tserkov i monastyr' razgrabil, a inii bezhali v pecheru i zadkhoshasia, i sudy sluzhebnye Sofei velikoi, zolotyi potir' da diskos, prislal k velikomu kniaziu" (*PSRL*, 6 [1853]: 234).

6

THE SACK OF KIEV OF 1482 IN CONTEMPORARY MUSCOVITE CHRONICLE WRITING

On 1 September 1482 (St. Simeon's Day), a Tatar army from the Crimea under the command of Khan Mengli Girey (1468-1478, with interruptions; 1478-1514) conquered and sacked the city of Kiev as part of a major campaign against the Podolian and Kievan lands. The principal facts of this campaign have been reconstructed from the sources by East European and Russian historians, who have provided us with a fairly accurate and composite picture of events leading up to the conquest, the sack itself, and the raid which followed.[1]

Mengli Girey's invasion of the Ukrainian lands of Rus' and the sack of Kiev resulted from a reversal of alliances in Eastern Europe which brought about a period of Muscovite-Crimean cooperation against the disintegrating Golden Horde and against Poland-Lithuania. The cooperation lasted, with several interruptions, for a relatively prolonged period, namely, from 1472 to 1511. This reversal of alliances has been viewed by Russian historians as a great diplomatic achievement on the part of Grand Prince Ivan III.[2]

The stage for the invasion and conquest of Kiev in 1482 was set by seven Muscovite diplomatic missions to Khan Mengli Girey in the years from 1472 to 1482.[3] The documentary evidence – i.e., the diplomatic instructions for the preparation of this invasion – remains among the most complete records preserved for that period. These diplomatic instructions and narrative sources, such as the official grand princely chronicles, leave no doubt whatsoever that Ivan III was the principal instigator of the invasion, and that he suggested a specific area for the Crimean attack. The Muscovite envoy Mikhailo Vasil'evich Kutuzov, who was sent to Mengli Girey in May of 1482, was instructed to request urgently an invasion of the territories under Lithuanian rule, specifically, of "the Podolian land or the Kievan localities"[4] by the Crimean Tatars. The account of the official Muscovite chronicles confirms the version of the diplomatic instructions that the invasion was undertaken at the request (*po slovu*) of Ivan

103

III.[5] The latter's appreciation of the Crimean adherence to the alliance and fulfillment of the Crimea's obligations, which obviously included the invasion of the Ukrainian lands of Rus', was conveyed to Mengli Girey by Prince Ivan Volodimirovich Lyko-Obolenskii in the spring of 1483.[6]

The great Tatar raid of 1482 was a complete success from the Crimean point of view. Ivan Khodkevych, the palatine of Kiev, received notice about the Tatar advance only four days prior to the actual attack. He attempted to organize a defense of the city and the castle in which he took refuge along with his family, the abbot and monks of the Monastery of the Caves, and the treasury chest.[7] However, the defenders of Kiev could not withstand the onslaught of the superior Tatar forces, who conquered the city without much difficulty and put it, its suburbs, and neighboring villages to the torch. Most of those who escaped the fire and death at the hands of the invaders, including the palatine, his wife and their two children, were captured by the Tatars. The palatine's wife and their son Aleksander were later released for an appropriate ransom. The palatine himself and his daughter were less fortunate and died in Tatar captivity. Following the sack of the city of Kiev, the Tatar army devastated the Kievan land, took many captives (*polonu bezchisleno vzia*), and, according to the *Pskovian Chronicle*, captured and sacked eleven additional border towns of Rus'.[8] The sack of Kiev was so terrible that forty years following the event it was still remembered as a shattering experience and portrayed as such in contemporary sources.[9]

In the aftermath of the sack, the ancient city of Kiev became desolate. It lapsed into considerable decay at the end of the fifteenth century, and was partially rebuilt only in the mid-seventeenth century. Consequently, Kievan urban life became centered in another part of the city and assumed a somewhat different character.[10] The three sacks of Kiev by Mongol and Tatar armies (that of Khan Batu in 1240, that of Emir Edigü in 1416, and that of Mengli Girey in 1482) not only undermined considerably its political and economic position, but also significantly contributed to its decline as one of the principal centers of Rus'.

The sack of Kiev in 1482 has been viewed in scholarly literature primarily as a significant political and military event in the intricate relationships among Muscovy, Poland-Lithuania, the disintegrating Golden Horde and her Tatar successor states – that is, the

Kazan, Crimean, and Astrakhan Khanates. Another important dimension of this event, which has not received the attention it deserves, is its treatment in Muscovite chronicle writing, especially in conjunction with the origins of the official Muscovite claims to the Kievan inheritance.[11] The sack of Kiev under discussion occurred between the second and third stages of the formulation of Muscovite claims to the Kievan inheritance that extended over a period of approximately half a century (1454-1504). It also happened roughly between the first two phases of a protracted, three-and-a-half-century-long contest between Muscovy and Poland-Lithuania for the lands of Old Rus'. The first phase extended from 1449 to 1485, and resulted in the annexation by Muscovy of two Great Russian states: Great Novgorod and the Grand Principality of Tver'. The second phase covered the years 1487-1537, in the course of which five major wars were waged and Muscovy was able to conquer not only Great Russian border areas, but also Belorussian territories and some lands of Ukrainian Rus'.[12]

The first stage of the articulation of official Muscovite claims to Kiev coincided with the Muscovite ideological awakening of the 1450s and the 1460s, following the Council of Florence (1438-39) and the fall of Constantinople (1453). It was reflected particularly in the *Vita* of Dmitrii Ivanovich Donskoi in which the concept of direct and uninterrupted dynastic continuity from the Kievan ruler Volodimer I to the aforesaid Muscovite grand prince was developed in Muscovite official thought for the first time. During the second stage, which belonged to the early 1470s, the editors of the official *Muscovite Codex of 1472* not only integrated this *Vita* into their work, but also formulated their own version of the dynastic continuity theory from Kievan Rus' through Suzdalia-Vladimiria to Muscovy. The third stage can be dated to the period from 1493 to 1504, when the Muscovite court formulated its claims to all of Rus' and, specifically, to Kiev in its struggle against the Jagiellonian dual monarchy.[13]

Four different versions and interpretations of the sack of Kiev in 1482 can be found in Muscovite chronicles of the last two decades of the fifteenth century, and one of them reappeared in the same or in a slightly edited form in Muscovite chronicle writing of the sixteenth century. The most factual and extensive of the four is an annalistic tale included as a separate account under the year 1483 in some manuscript copies of what is now referred to as the

Vologodsko-Permskaia letopis' (*VPL*) (the *Vologda-Perm Chronicle*).[1]
It reads as follows:

About the Conquest of the City of Kiev by the Crimean Tsar
[Mengli Girey].

> In the year 1483,[15] because of our sins, the Lord did not
> spare his own image[s] [the icons] and the Holy Sacraments
> and let loose the godless Tsar Mengli Girey, the son of
> [Khan] HAči [Ḥāǧǧi] Girey, who, having gathered mighty
> forces, advanced against the Lithuanian land, against the
> famous city of Kiev. Ivan Khodkevych was the viceroy and
> the palatine of the city at that time. He received the message
> about the tsar's advance from Perekop to Kiev only four
> days [before his arrival]. He [then] strengthened the fortifica-
> tions of the city. And many people fled to the city, and the
> abbot with all the monks came from the Monastery of the
> Caves into the city, and he brought with him the treasury
> [chest] and the sacred sacramental vessels to the city. And
> the Tsar reached the city on the day of St. Simeon, who
> changes years [on the First of September], at one o'clock,
> arranged his regiments, and approached the city, surrounding
> it. And because of God's anger, after much struggle, he set
> fire to the city, and all the people perished or were put to
> death. And a small number of those who managed to flee
> from the city were captured, and the suburbs and neighbor-
> ing villages were burned. Following all this, he did not
> disband his troops, but departed to his own Horde.[16]

This version, which apparently has not been critically
analyzed, brings up questions as to its origins and the context in
which it might have been composed. The manuscript copies of the
VPL in which the tale was inserted contained materials similar to
those included in the *Simeonovskaia letopis'* (*SL*) (the *Simeonov
Chronicle*) and other official Muscovite chronicles for the period
from 1425 to 1480. However, for the period from 1480 to 1538 they
contained more original materials of a mixed nature, some of them
praising the policies of the Muscovite court, which was a reflection
of official chronicle writing, and others expressing an independent
point of view.[17]

The detailed description of the event, including such precise
information as the exact time, suggests that the material for the tale
was provided by an eyewitness to the event, or by someone who was

familiar with the circumstances of Mengli Girey's invasion and the response to his advance by Ivan Khodkevych, the palatine of Kiev, and, in particular, with the reaction of the abbot and the monks of the Kiev Monastery of the Caves. The information could have come from someone in Kiev, possibly at the monastery, or from someone in Muscovy who had close contacts with Kiev and the monastery. The tale was most probably composed soon after the event; it was carefully edited and given a separate title. The exclusively religious interpretation of the sack of Kiev ("because of our sins," "because of God's anger"), and the display of an appropriate empathy for "the famous city of Kiev" which had experienced such a great misfortune indicate that the author/editor of this annalistic tale must have been associated with some Great Russian ecclesiastical circles. At the same time, he carefully avoided any allusions to the political framework in which the event took place, or to the broader ideological ramifications it could have set in motion. Whereas the account was disapproving of the sack per se, it did not, significantly enough, mention either the Polish-Lithuanian ruler or the Muscovite grand prince Ivan III, or, specifically, the latter's role in the Crimean campaign. The tale refrained from any indirect criticism of the Muscovite ruler, which suggests that its author/editor did not wish to present him in an unfavorable light or as someone who had instigated an attack on the most venerable city of Rus' and on fellow Orthodox Christians. The author/editor did his utmost to record the event as truthfully as he could and, at the same time, to spare the Muscovite ruler the deserved religious embarrassment.

Curiously enough, the tale in question was included in the copies of the *VPL* among entries closely connected with the Vologda and Perm areas. More specifically, it appeared following the information about the fire in Vologda given under the entry for the year 1481.[18] However, it is unlikely that it was composed at the provincial episcopal chancery of Perm. More probably it was written and edited at a Muscovite monastery which had some connections with Perm. A tale of this sort could not have been included in a chronicle compiled at this bishopric without the permission either of the bishop of Perm himself or of some other appropriate authority. However, the tale was not disseminated widely, and significantly enough, it was not included in its entirety in any of the central Muscovite chronicles.

The remaining three Muscovite versions of the sack of Kiev in 1482 were abbreviated and edited accounts that contained less factual information. Instead, they conveyed a pointed political and ideological interpretation. From among the three the official version of the Muscovite court deserves special attention. It was included in the official continuations of the *Muscovite Codex of 1479*, compiled in the 1480s and the 1490s, with the best and probably the earliest text, preserved in the form of an annalistic tale with a separate title in the *SL*:

About the Great City of Kiev

> In the year 1484,[19] on the first day [of September] at the request of Grand Prince Ivan [III] Vasil'evich of all of Rus', Tsar [Khan] Mengli Girey of the Perekop Horde of the Crimea arrived with all his mighty [forces] and conquered the city of Kiev and set fire to it. And he captured Ivan Khodkevych, the palatine of Kiev, and took a countless multitude of prisoners, and he devastated the Kievan land because of the king's [Kazimierz Jagiellończyk's] transgression who brought Tsar [Khan] Ahmet of the Great [Golden] Horde with all his forces against Grand Prince Ivan Vasil'evich, wishing to destroy the Christian faith.[20]

By carefully selecting the convenient principal points, such as the greatness of Kiev (in the title), the explicit request of Ivan III to attack Kiev, the power of the Crimean khan, and the conquest and the devastation of Kiev and the Kievan land by the Crimean Tatars, the editor of the official account offered his own interpretation. He proposed that the sack of Kiev was undertaken as retaliation for the Polish-Lithuanian ruler's alleged instigation of Ahmet's invasion of Muscovy in 1480, which ended with the famous "Vigil on the Ugra River" ("Stoianie na Ugre" or "Ugorshchina") that led to Ahmet's retreat, his subsequent political failure, and the symbolic end of the Golden Horde's overlordship over Muscovy.[21] The juxtaposition of the two events, separated only by two years' time, was a convenient device used by the editor to place the blame for the Kievan catastrophe and for the intent to harm Christianity on the Polish-Lithuanian ruler. The city of Kiev was treated in the tale as a major city in a foreign country, and no claim to any special relationship of Moscow to that city was intimated in this official account. An obligatory religious interpretation was added at the end of the tale, which charged the Polish-Lithuanian ruler of attempting to destroy Orthodox Christianity without explaining why other Orthodox Christians were selected as victims of the Tatar retaliatory attack.

The second of the three abbreviated accounts of the sack of Kiev by the Crimean Tatars in 1482 is to be found in the so-called *Rostov Codex of 1489*, which was compiled at the Rostov archbishopric during the tenure of Archbishop Tikhon (1489-1505) and later partially included in the *Tipografskaia letopis'*, [22] in the *Codex of 1497*, [23] and in the *Muscovite Codex of 1518*. [24] Its text reads as follows:

> In the year 1483,[25] because of our sins, Kiev was conquered by Tsar [Khan] Mengli Girey of the Crimea, and the son of [Khan] Azi [Ači Ḥāǧǧi] Girey. And he set the city on fire from two sides. And the people were frightened, and those who fled were captured by the Tatars, and all [those] in the city perished in the fire. And they [the Tatars] captured Lord Ivan Khodkevych who had fled from the fire in the city, and they took him into captivity, together with his wife and children and with the archimandrite of the Monastery of the Caves. This act of malice occurred in the month of September.[26]

This carefully edited account was evidently prepared by its author/editor from selected elements of the annalistic tale found in some of the manuscript copies of the *VPL*. In this version the author/editor eliminated all the information pertaining to the military aspects of the campaign and the conquest, and gave the latter a purely religious interpretation. The concluding comment on the sack of Kiev as a malicious act (*zloba*), which was lacking in the extended version, may be interpreted as a device on the part of the author/editor to express greater disapproval of the misfortune experienced by the city of Kiev, and even as an indirect censure of the Muscovite ruler. However, he avoided any direct criticism of the Muscovite grand prince and refrained from mentioning the Polish-Lithuanian ruler, thus maintaining an absolute impartiality toward the secular authorities involved in the political and military conflicts. The indirect criticism of the Muscovite grand prince in the account is probably a reflection of the contemporary state of relations between Metropolitan Gerontii and Grand Prince Ivan III, who in 1483 attempted to remove the former from the metropolitanate.[27] This account, with its obviously official religious character, must have been prepared by someone interested in offering an interpretation of the event different from that advocated by the Muscovite court.

The question of the authorship of this account is closely interconnected with one of the major unresolved problems of Muscovite chronicle writing, namely, whether official metropolitan chronicle writing still existed in the second half of the fifteenth century.[28] On the basis of the available evidence, the argument can be made that official metropolitan chronicle writing did continue during the period in question, particularly in view of the fact that it was perpetuated into the sixteenth century, as exemplified by the chronicle writing under the auspices of the metropolitans Daniil and Ioasaf.[29] It is rather doubtful that the writing and editing of this account were undertaken at a local bishopric. On the contrary, the available circumstantial evidence suggests that it was composed at the metropolitan chancery, which at that time was the second principal center of Muscovite chronicle writing, and then disseminated to local centers and included in various chronicle compilations.

Interestingly enough, the editors of the *Rostov Codex of 1489* and the *Codex of 1497*, besides including in their codices the account coming from the metropolitan chancery, also inserted the account from the official continuations of the *Muscovite Codex of 1479* under the entry for the year 1484.[30] Thus the reader had two versions of the sack of Kiev in 1482, regardless of their obviously conflicting assessments. This device on the part of the editors sheds light on their general attitudes, as well as those of Archbishop Tikhon and his archbishopric chancery, toward the policies of Grand Prince Ivan III. When it came to the evaluation of the Tatar sack of the most venerable city of Rus', they apparently wished to preserve a certain degree of self-respect and to disassociate themselves from such a pernicious act, but at the same time they wanted to give evidence of their loyalty to the Muscovite grand prince Ivan III.

Of all the Muscovite accounts of the sack of Kiev in 1482, the most outspoken in its criticism of the Muscovite grand prince was the version in the oppositional *Codex of the 1480s*, elements of which can be found in the *Sofiiskaia vtoraia letopis'* (*SVL*) (the *Sophia Second Chronicle*) and in the *L'vovskaia letopis'* (*LL*) (the *L'vov Chronicle*). Under the entry for the year 1482, it describes the event in the following terms:

Grand Prince [Ivan III Vasil'evich] sent [his envoy] to [Khan] Mengli Girey of the Crimea, and he ordered him to wage war against the King's [Kazimierz Jagiellończyk's] land. Mengli Girey with his mighty [forces] conquered Kiev, took all the people into captivity, and took along with him the governor of Kiev, together with his wife and children, and he caused many calamities. And he ransacked the Church and the Monastery of the Caves. And many fled to the caves and suffocated [because of the fire]. And he sent the vessels for [the holy] liturgy, the golden chalice and the plate, from the Great Sophia [Church] to the grand prince.[31]

In this account the Muscovite ruler was directly referred to as the principal instigator of the sack of Kiev and of the calamities which befell that city. The pillage of the religious places was especially emphasized, and the Muscovite ruler was spared no embarrassment. The author/editor of the account reported that Khan Mengli Girey sent the holy vessels from the Great St. Sophia Church as war trophies to Ivan III. From this account the conclusion could be drawn that the Muscovite ruler, by accepting the sacred vessels from a "pagan" war lord, had committed a highly un-Christian and even blasphemous transgression.

Who composed an account so damaging to the reputation of the Muscovite ruler, and who sponsored the compilation of the oppositional *Codex of the 1480s* included in the *SVL* and the *LL*? Those historians who have adhered to the notion that the official metropolitan chronicle writing was continued in the second half of the fifteenth century have been inclined to assume that there existed an official *Codex of Metropolitan Gerontii of 1490*, and that parts of this codex which might have constituted the oppositional *Codex of the 1480s* had been included in the *SVL* and the *LL*.[32] More recently it has been argued that the oppositional *Codex of the 1480s* represented the views of oppositional "militant" ecclesiastics.[33] The attribution of the oppositional *Codex of the 1480s*, as well as the problem of the relationship between official grand princely, official metropolitan, and unofficial chronicle writing, cannot be solved in this study and are in need of further examination. For the time being, the account in the oppositional *Codex of the 1480s* must still be attributed to those Muscovite ecclesiastical circles who were strongly opposed to the policies of Ivan III and felt deeply disturbed about his cynical political behavior toward the city of Kiev and the "pagan" Muslims. It deserves to be noted that, in addition to the text most critical of Ivan III, the editors of the oppositional *Codex of the 1480s* incorporated in their work the official metropolitan version about the sack of Kiev in 1482, apparently to reinforce their criticism of the Muscovite ruler.[34]

The various interpretations of the sack of Kiev in 1482 in contemporary Muscovite chronicle writing reflect a serious division of attitudes in Muscovite ideological thought about the Kievan inheritance. The accounts originating from religious circles reveal a basically compassionate attitude on the part of their authors/editors toward Kiev and even a sense of identification with that "famous" city. The authors/editors of these accounts condemned the sack of Kiev in the same manner that they would have castigated an attack on Moscow or on any other city of Muscovite Russia, and some even dared to criticize openly the Muscovite ruler for his involvement in such an infamous deed.

The official account promoted by the grand princely court stressed the political aspects of the sack. Its authors/editors viewed Kiev for all practical purposes as a foreign city, which could be attacked by an ally regardless of his political and religious affiliations. Thus, the sack of Kiev did not quite fit into the evolution of the official Muscovite claims to the Kievan inheritance which had been developing over a period of thirty years prior to the event, and might even have contributed to delaying the formulation of such claims.

The sharp conflict of opinion between the Muscovite court and the ecclesiastical circles concerning the sack of Kiev in 1482 indicates not only that fundamental "ideological struggles" were conducted within the Muscovite establishment at the end of the fifteenth century. The conflict also shows that this establishment was struggling with the problem of the Kievan inheritance, which has never really been resolved.

NOTES

1. For a discussion of Mengli Girey's campaign of 1482 and the sack of Kiev in 1482, see F. Papée, *Polska i Litwa na przełomie wieków średnich*, vol. 1 (Cracow, 1904), 83-92; M. Hrushevs'kyi, *Istoriia Ukrainy-Rusy*, 10 vols. (reprinted, New York, 1954-58), vol. 4 (2nd ed., 1907/1955), 326-327; K.V. Bazilevich, *Vneshniaia politika Russkogo tsentralizovannogo gosudarstva* (Moscow, 1952), 192-199. The best introduction to the history of the Crimean Tatar Khanate, as well as the literature on the subject, has been provided by A. Fisher, *The Crimean Tatars* (Stanford, 1978), 1-47 and 231-255.

2. Concerning an example of such a view, cf. Bazilevich, *Vneshniaia politika*, 169-281.

3. *Sbornik Imperatorskogo russkogo istoricheskogo obshchestva* (hereafter *SIRIO*), 41 (1884): 1-9, 9-13, 14-16, 16-24, 25-28, 28-32, 32-34.

4. *SIRIO*, 41 (1884): 34.

5. For the best version of the account, see the *Simeonovskaia letopis'* (*SL*), published under the editorship of A.E. Presniakov in *Polnoe sobranie russkikh letopisei* (hereafter *PSRL*), 18 (1913): 270.

6. *SIRIO*, 41 (1884): 35.

7. Papée, *Polska i Litwa*, 89-90.

8. A.N. Nasonov, ed., *Pskovskie letopisi*, vols. 1-2 (Moscow, 1941-55), I: 62-63.

9. Papée, *Polska i Litwa*, 91.

10. V. Antonovych, "Kiev, ego sud'ba i znachenie s XIV po XVI stoletie (1362-1569)," *Kievskaia starina*, I (January 1882): 1-48, especially 42. Antonovych's seminal essay was reprinted in his *Monografii po istorii zapadnoi i iugo-zapadnoi Rossii*, vol. 1 (Kiev, 1885), 221-264.

11. For a discussion of the origins of these claims, see J. Pelenski, "The Origins of the Official Muscovite Claims to the 'Kievan Inheritance'," *Harvard Ukrainian Studies*, 1, no. 1 (March, 1977): 29-52 [see Chapter 5 of this volume]. The image of Kiev in Muscovite official and semi-official sources of the 1550s and 1560s has been analyzed by J. Pelenski, *Russia and Kazan: Conquest and Imperial Ideology (1438-1560s)* (The Hague and Paris, 1974), 113-117.

12. An outline of the major methodological and theoretical problems connected with the study of this contest in the fifteenth and sixteenth centuries is presented in my unpublished study, "The Contest between Muscovite Russia and Poland-Lithuania for the Lands of Old Rus' (1450s-1580s)." For a discussion of Polish claims to Kiev and all the land of Rus' in connection with the incorporation of the Ukrainian lands into Crown Poland in 1569, see J. Pelenski, "The Incorporation of the Ukrainian Lands of Old Rus' into Crown Poland (1569): Socio-Material Interest and Ideology – A Reexamination," in *American Contributions to the International Congress of Slavists*, Warsaw, 21-27 August 1973, vol. 3 (The Hague and Paris, 1973), 19-52 [see Chapter 9 of this volume]; and *idem*, "Inkorporacja ukraińskich ziem dawnej Rusi do Korony w 1569 roku: Ideologia i korzyści – próba nowego spojrzenia," *Przegląd Historyczny*, 65, no. 2 (1974): 243-262.

13. Pelenski, "Origins of the Official Muscovite Claims," 45-52 [see Chapter 5 of this volume].

14. The two principal manuscript copies of the *VPL* are the Copy of the Kirillo-Belozerskii Monastery and the Sinodal Copy. The Copy of the Kirillo-

Belozerskii Monastery has been published in a critical edition as the *VPL* in volume 26 of *PSRL* (Moscow, 1959) under the editorship of M.N. Tikhomirov; it includes variants from the Sinodal Copy, as well as other manuscript copies. The Sinodal Copy had already been utilized by N.M. Karamzin in his *Istoriia gosudarstva rossiiskogo*, 12 vols. in 3 bks., 5th ed. (St. Petersburg, 1842-43).

15. The correct date of the conquest, 1 September 1482, was provided by the so-called Short Kievan Chronicle, entitled "The Origins of the Princes of the Rus' Principality" (862-1514), which was incorporated in the chronicle known as the Supras'l' Manuscript, published under the auspices of M.N. Obolenskii *Supras'l'-skaia rukopis', soderzhashchaia Novgorodskuiu i Kievskuiu sokrashchennyia letopisi* (Moscow, 1836), 138 and 147; cf. Hrushevs'kyi, *Istoriia Ukrainy-Rusy*, 4: 326, fn. 2.

16. *PSRL*, 26 (1959): 274-275. Excerpts from this tale had been quoted by Karamzin from the Sinodal Copy (*Istoriia gosudarstva rossiiskogo*, bk. 2 [notes to vol. 6], 43, fn. 268). They correspond to the text of the tale included in the Copy of the Kirillo-Belozerskii Monastery.

17. For a discussion of the materials in the *VPL* up to the year 1480, see A.A. Shakhmatov, *Obozrenie russkikh letopisnykh svodov XIV-XVI vv.* (Moscow and Leningrad, 1938), 346-360; Ia.S. Lur'e, "Nikanorovskaia i Vologodsko-Permskaia letopisi kak otrazhenie velikokniazheskogo svoda nachala 70-kh godov XV v.," *Vspomagatel'nye istoricheskie discipliny*, 5 (1973); 219-250; and the relevant discussion in Ia.S. Lur'e, *Obshcherusskie letopisi XIV-XV vv.* (Leningrad, 1976), chap. 3 (cf. also my review of this important work in the *American Historical Review*, 84, no. 3 [1979]: 805-806). An analysis of the materials in the *VPL* following 1480 was provided by M.N. Tikhomirov, "O Vologodsko-Permskoi letopisi," *Problemy istochnikovedeniia*, 3 (1940): 225-244. Tikhomirov observed that the tale "About the Conquest of the City of Kiev by the Crimean Tsar," included in the *VPL*, was not available in other chronicle compilations. The two accounts of the Short Kievan Chronicle to be found in the Supras'l' Manuscript are brief and lack the information of the account included in *VPL*.

18. *PSRL*, 26 (1959): 274.

19. The correct date was 1482.

20. *PSRL*, 18 (1913): 270. The text of the official version was also included in several Muscovite chronicle compilations of the late fifteenth century, among them, the Uvarov Copy ending with the year 1492 (*PSRL*, 25 [1949] [cf. 330]), the *Abbreviated Codex of 1493* (*PSRL*, 27 [1962] [cf. 286]), and the *Abbreviated Codex of 1495* (*PSRL*, 27 [1962] [cf. 357-358]). This official version was also inserted in the sixteenth-century chronicles, such as the *Ioasaf Chronicle* (A.A. Zimin, ed., *Ioasafovskaia letopis'* [Moscow, 1957], 124), the *Voskresensk Chronicle* (*PSRL*, 8 [1859]: 215, and the *Nikon Chronicle* (*PSRL*, 12 [1901/1965]: 215).

21. For a discussion of the Russian literary and ideological writings dealing with the "Vigil on the Ugra River," consult I.M. Kudriavtsev, " 'Poslanie na Ugru' Vassiiana Rylo' kak pamiatnik publitsistiki XV v.," *Trudy Otdela drevnerusskoi literatury* (hereafter *TODRL*), 8 (1951): 158-186, and *idem*, "'Ugorshchina' v pamiatnikakh drevnerusskoi literatury," in *Issledovaniia i materialy po drevnerusskoi literature* (Moscow, 1961), 23-67.

22. The text of the *Tipografskaia letopis* was published under the editorship of A.A. Shakhmatov and A.E. Presniakov in *PSRL*, 24 (1921).

23. The *Codex of 1497* was published under the editorship of K.N. Serbina in *PSRL*, 28 (1963).

24. The *Muscovite Codex of 1518* was published under the editorship of K.N. Serbina in *PSRL*, 28 (1963).

25. The correct date was 1482.

26. *PSRL*, 24 (1921): 202; *PSRL*, 28 (1963): 151, 316. This text was also included in the form of a supplementary account in the *Sofiiskaia vtoraia letopis'* and the *L'vovskaia letopis'*, as will be shown later.

27. *PSRL*, 24 (1921): 203; *PSRL*, 6 (1853): 236; *PSRL*, 20, part 1 (1910/1971): 351. Cf. also E. Golubinskii, *Istoriia russkoi tserkvi*, vol. 2, part 1 (Moscow, 1900), 557-558.

28. A.N. Nasonov maintained that official metropolitan chronicle writing did continue in the second half of the fifteenth century (*Istoriia russkogo letopisaniia XI — nachala XVIII v.* [Moscow, 1969], 303-308). For similar views, cf. A.A. Zimin, *Russkie letopisi i khronografy kontsa XV-XVI vv.* (Moscow, 1960), 6. Lur'e contends that official metropolitan chronicle writing was discontinued during the period in question (*Obshcherusskie letopisi XIV-XV vv.*, 211-212, 238-240, and 258).

29. For a discussion of sixteenth-century metropolitan chronicle writing, see B.M. Kloss, "Deiatel'nost' mitropolich'ei knigopisnoi masterskoi v 20-30kh godakh XVI veka i proiskhozhdenie Nikonovskoi letopisi," in *Drevnerusskoe iskusstvo: Rukopisnaia kniga* (Moscow, 1972), 318-337; and *idem*, "Mitropolit Daniil i Nikonovskaia letopis'," *TODRL*, 28 (1974): 188-201.

30. *PSRL*, 24 (1921): 204; *PSRL*, 28 (1963): 152.

31. *PSRL*, 6 (1953): 234; *PSRL*, 20, part I (1910/1971): 349.

32. Nasonov, *Istoriia russkogo letopisaniia*, 303-315; Zimin, *Russkie letopisi i khronografy*, 6.

33. Ia.S. Lur'e, "Nezavisimyi letopisnyi svod kontsa XV v. – istochnik Sofiiskoi II i L'vovskoi letopisei," *TODRL*, 27 (1972): 405-419, especially 418-419; *idem*, *Obshcherusskie letopisi XIV-XV vv.*, 238-240. For his references to the sack of Kiev in 1482, see *ibid.*, 220 and 224.

34. *PSRL*, 6 (1853): 235; *PSRL*, 20, part 1 (1910/ 1971): 350.

7

THE EMERGENCE OF THE MUSCOVITE CLAIMS TO THE BYZANTINE-KIEVAN "IMPERIAL INHERITANCE"*

The development of the official Muscovite claims to the Kievan inheritance, based on the uninterrupted dynastic continuity of the Riurikides, on the theory of succession (*translatio*) from Kievan Rus' through (Rostovia)-Suzdalia-Vladimiria to Muscovy, and on traditional patrimonial law (and formulated in three stages), began in the second half of the fifteenth century.[1] These claims acquired broader conceptual meaning and underwent qualitative ideological transformation during the reign of Grand Prince Vasilii III Ivanovich (1505-1533), specifically in the second and third decades of the sixteenth century.

The three stages of the formulation of Muscovite claims to Kievan Rus' coincided with the first two phases of a protracted, three-and-a-half-century-long contest (1450s-1795) between Muscovy and Poland-Lithuania for the lands of Rus'. The first phase extended from 1449 to 1485, and resulted in the annexation by Muscovy of two Great Russian states: Great Novgorov and the Grand Principality of Tver'. The second phase covered the years 1487-1537, in the course of which five major wars were waged (1487-1494; 1500-1503; 1507-1508; 1512-1522; 1534-1537) and Muscovy was able to conquer not only Great Russian border areas, but also Belorussian territories and some lands of Ukrainian Rus'.[2]

The first stage of the development of Muscovy's pretensions to the Kievan inheritance coincided with the Muscovite ideological awakening of the 1450s and the 1460s, following the Council of Florence (1438-1439) and the fall of Constantinople (1453). It was reflected particularly in the *Vita* of Dmitrii Ivanovich Donskoi in which the concept of direct and uninterrupted dynastic continuity from the Kievan ruler Volodimer I to the aforesaid Muscovite grand prince was developed in official Muscovite thought for the first time. During the second stage, which belonged to the early 1470s, the

---

* For illustrations pertaining to this Chapter, see Plates 32, 33, 34.

117

editors of the official *Muscovite Codex of 1472* not only integrated this *Vita* into their work, but also formulated their own version of the dynastic continuity theory from Kievan Rus' through Suzdalia-Vladimiria to Muscovy. The third stage can be dated to the period from 1493 to 1504, when the Muscovite court formulated its claims to all of Rus' and, specifically, to Kiev in its struggle against the Jagiellonian dual monarchy.[3]

It was during the second phase of the struggle that the development of Muscovite claims to the Kievan inheritance acquired broader conceptual meaning and underwent qualitative ideological transformation. This was reflected in the advocacy of new ideological claims concerning the transfer of gifts, insignia, and imperial crown of Monomakh (Constantine IX Monomachus) of Byzantium to Volodimer Vsevolodovich Monomakh of Kievan Rus' and about the elevation of the latter's status to that of an empire. These legendary ideological claims were advanced in two treatises: the earlier, entitled *Poslanie Spiridona-Savvy* (the *Epistle of Spiridon-Savva*), and the subsequent, *Skazanie o velikikh kniazekh vladimerskikh velikia Russiia* (the *Narration about the Grand Princes of Vladimir of Great Russia*).

The *Poslanie* was written by Spiridon-Savva, a Russian cleric of Tver', who had a rather checkered ecclesiastical and publicistic career.[4] He was first mentioned in Russian chronicles in an entry for the year 1476, where it was stated that he had come to Lithuania from Constantinople, where he had been appointed metropolitan of Lithuania. Spiridon-Savva was not well received by King Kazimierz Jagiellończyk, and a Muscovite chronicle under the year 1482 mentioned that he was imprisoned by the Lithuanian authorities as a suspect individual and was referred to as a "devil." The date of his reported arrest coincided with the sack of Kiev in 1482, which was carried out by a Tatar army from the Crimea under the command of Khan Mengli Girey at the instigation of the Muscovite grand prince Ivan III.[5] Following his incarceration Spiridon-Savva apparently made his way to Muscovy, where he was received no better, since Ivan III had his own metropolitan and Spiridon-Savva's claims to the Metropolitanate of Kiev and all of Rus' were obviously inconvenient for the Muscovite political and ecclesiastical authorities. For all these reasons he was confined to the Ferapontov Monastery, apparently sometime in the early 1490s, and lived there in 1503. During his stay at the Ferapontov Monastery he was involved in literary activities.

He referred once to his age in the *Poslanie*, stating that he was ninety-one years old, but the date of his death is unknown.

The *Poslanie* contains a number of legends with loaded ideological content, among others the fictitious genealogical tale about the origins of Russian rulers from the Roman emperor (caesar) Augustus, the above mentioned invented account concerning the transfer of Monomakh's gifts and regalia, and a partially faked and politically humiliating genealogical tale about the origins of the Lithuanian rulers. According to its internal evidence, the *Poslanie* was composed during the reign of Vasilii III – in the opinion of I.N. Zhdanov before 1523, which R.P. Dmitrieva narrowed to the years 1511-1521.[6] The *Poslanie* was apparently written at the request of the Muscovite authorities and then re-edited into the official *Skazanie*, the earliest recension of which was compiled in the late 1520s or the early 1530s, but before 1533.[7]

While there has been no major disagreement in scholarship about the literary history of the *Poslanie* and the *Skazanie* or about the latter's extraordinary career in official Muscovite political thought during the rest of the sixteenth century,[8] differences of opinion have emerged concerning the dating and possible authorship of the individual components of the two texts and, in particular, of the genealogical tale about the Russian rulers as descendants of Caesar Augustus and the related account about Monomakh's gifts and regalia. Dmitrieva, who dated the *Poslanie* in 1511-1521, regarded the tale and the account as integral parts of the *Poslanie* and attributed their authorship to Spiridon-Savva. A.A. Zimin treated them as separate and original works and connected their composition with the coronation of Dmitrii Ivanovich, the grandson of Ivan III, which took place in 1498.[9] More recently A.L. Gol'dberg has redated the interrelated accounts to a later period, the 1510s and the early 1520s, that is, into the same period as did Dmitrieva. He questioned her attribution of authorship, however, and suggested, instead, that the writer was a "secular" individual, a Muscovite diplomat or a court official, someone like Dmitrii Gerasimov, for example.[10] Whereas Gol'dberg has established one case of correlation between the official diplomatic records and the genealogical tale, specifically in the case of the so-called Prussian towns of Gdańsk, Toruń, Malborg, and Chojnice,[11] his attribution of the entire tale remains less convincing than that of Dmitrieva.

The account about the bestowal of Monomakh's gifts and regalia included in the *Poslanie* and the *Skazanie* reads as follows:

The *Poslanie*

> And in the fourth generation from the Grand Prince Riurik was the Grand Prince Volodimer, who enlightened the Russian land with holy baptism, and who was called in holy baptism Vasilii. And in the fourth generation after him was the Grand Prince Volodimer Vsevolodovich. Taking counsel with his princes, dignitaries, and boyars, he said: "I am the most recent of all those who reigned before me and held in their hands the banners of the scepter of Great Russia as Grand Prince Oleg went [forth] and took from Constantinople, the New Rome, tribute from each inhabitant, and came back in good health; and then Grand Prince Sviatoslav Igor'evich, called the Nimble One (*Legky*), went forth in galleys (*v galiakhkh*) with 2700 men, exacted a heavy tribute from the city of Constantine, and returned to his fatherland, the Kievan land, and died. I am the heir of my grandfather and of my father Vsevolod Iaroslavich and the inheritor of the same honor from God. And I seek advice from you, princes of my palace, and boyars, and *voevody*, and all the Christ-loving host under you; the name of the life-giving Trinity may arise with the power of your bravery, by God's will, under our command; what counsel do you give me?" His princes, boyars, and *voevody* answered the Grand Prince Volodimer Vsevolodovich, saying: "The heart of the Tsar is in God's hands [cf. Prov. 21:1], as it is written, and as for us, we are under your will, who is our ruler after God." Grand Prince Volodimer gathered his highly experienced and wise *voevody* and appointed captains over the various forces – chiliarchs, centurions, and *piatdesiatniki* over the various ranks of forces, and having gathered together many thousands of warriors, sent them to Tsar'grad in Thrace; and they captured it to a great extent and returned in great health with many riches. And so much for this. At that time, in the year 1045, Rome apostacized, and Pope Formos fell away from the faith. Tsar Constantine Monomakh was much saddened by such things; a council gathered on the tsar's advice and on the blessing of the most reverend Kir Larius [Michael I Kerularios, Patriarch of Constantinople], and urgent letters were sent to the other patriarchs: Jerusalem, Alexandria, and Antioch. And these envoys soon returned, together with the envoys of those patriarchs, with their letters and with the

advice concerning things spiritual. And the most reverend ecumenical Patriarch Kir Larius and the Christ-loving Tsar Constantine, called Monomakh, deliberated, with the advice of the ecumenical council of the four patriarchs and those metropolitans and bishops under them, and the lower ranks even to the priests, clerks, and sub-clerks, and they removed the pope's name from the registers [iz paralipomena] of the church altars of the four ecumenical patriarchs. And from that time even unto the present day they "rome" about, having fallen away from the Orthodox faith, and [therefore] they acquired the name of "romers," and for this the pope's name is not mentioned in the church prayers from the four ecumenical altars of the patriarchs. From that time this prating Formos is not called pope, but an apostate from our Orthodox faith, which we received from the evangelical message of our Lord Jesus Christ, the son of God, the word of God, and thanks to the holy teachings of his disciples and the tradition of the seven ecumenical councils. This accursed Formos divided the substance of the life-giving Trinity and introduced to the Latin people a fourth person in the Godhead, babbling that the Holy Spirit emanates from the son. But we, the adherents of Orthodoxy, believe in the eternity of the Father and the co-eternity of his Son, his word, and the Holy Spirit who shares the throne emanating from the immaculate bosom of the Father; the Trinity is con-substantial: the Father, the Son, and the Holy Spirit. And so much about this; let us return to the matter at hand. The God-loving Tsar Constantine Monomakh took counsel and sent envoys to Grand Prince Volodimer Vsevolodovich: Neophytos, Metropolitan of Ephesus in Asia, and with him two bishops, of Malatia[?] (militinska) and of Mitylene (mitilinska), and the strategus (stratiga) of Antioch, Augustalius of Alexandria, and a general of Jerusalem, Eustathius. And from around his neck he took a life-giving cross from the same life-giving tree on which the Almighty Christ was crucified. He took from his head the imperial crown and placed it on a golden platter. He ordered that the sardonyx vessel be brought from which Augustus, the Roman Caesar, had rejoiced [drinking], and a stole, which he wore on his own shoulders, and a censer forged of Arabian gold, and myrrh made with many fragrant flowers of the Indian land, and frankincense [ot zlata araviiska troma smeshenie imat], and many other gifts. And he gave them to Metropolitan Neophytos and the bishops and his noble retainers, and sent them to Grand Prince Volodimer Vsevolodovich. "Accept from us, O God-loving, pious prince, these honorable gifts [ot nachatok vechnykh let tvoego *rodstva pokolenia*] for your glory and honor and for the coronation of the free and autocratic empire. And by means of this our envoys will entreat you, and we ask for your grace, peace, and love; may God's churches be without strife, and all the Orthodox remain in peace under the power of our empire and your free autocracy of Great Russia; may you be called from this time onward a God-crowned Tsar, crowned with the imperial crown by the hand of the Most Reverend Metropolitan Neophytos and the bishops." And from that time Grand Prince Volodimer Vsevolodovich was called Monomakh and Tsar of Great Russia. And from that time with the imperial crown which the great tsar of the Greeks Constantine Monomakh sent him, all the grand princes of Vladimir were crowned, when they were established in the Grand Principality of Russia, just as the free autocrat and tsar of Great Russia Vasilii Ivanovich, the twelfth descendant from Grand Prince Volodimer Monomakh, and from Grand Prince Riurik the twentieth descendant, together with his brothers Ivanovich and Andreevich.[12]

The *Skazanie*

In the fourth generation after Grand Prince Riurik came Prince Volodimer, who enlightened the Russian land with holy baptism in the year 6496 [988]. And in the fourth generation after Grand Prince Volodimer came his great-grandson Grand Prince Volodimer Vsevolodovich Monomakh. And when he reigned in the Grand Principality of Kiev, he began to take counsel with his princes, boyars, and dignitaries, and said: "I am the most recent of all those who reigned before me and held in their hands the banners of the scepter of Great Russia, as Grand Prince Oleg went [forth] and exacted from Constantinople heavy tribute for all his host, and came back in good health; and then Grand Prince Sviatoslav Igorevich went [forth] and exacted heavy tribute from Constantinople. And I am by God's grace the heir of my ancestors and of my father Grand Prince Vsevolod Iaroslavich and the inheritor of the same honor from God. Now I seek advice from you, princes of my palace, and boyars and *voevody*, and all the Christ-loving host under you; the name of the life-giving Trinity may arise with the power of your bravery, by God's will, under our command; what counsel do you give me?" His princes, boyars, and *voevody* answered the Grand Prince Volodimer Vsevolodovich: "The heart of the tsar is in God's hands [cf. Prov. 21:1],

as we are under your will." Grand Prince Volodimer gathered
the highly experienced and wise *voevody* and appointed
captains over the various forces – chiliarchs, centurions, and
piatdesiatniki over the various ranks of forces – and
gathered many thousands of warriors, and sent them to
Tsar'grad in the Thracian province; and they captured most
of it and returned with many riches. At that time the pious
Emperor Constantine was in Constantinople, and he waged
war against the Persians and Latins. And he took wise and
imperial counsel and sent his envoys to Grand Prince
Volodimer Vsevolodovich: Neophytos, Metropolitan of
Ephesus, and with him two bishops of Malatia[?] [militin'ska]
and Mitylene[?] [mitilin'ska], and Antipas, strategus [stratiga]
of Antioch, and the general of Jerusalem, Eustathius, and his
other nobles. And from around his neck he took the life-
giving cross made from the same life-giving tree on which the
Almighty Christ was crucified. He took from his head the imperial crown and placed it on a golden platter. He ordered
the sardonyx vessel to be brought, from which Augustus the
Roman Caesar had rejoiced [drinking], and a stole, which he
wore on his shoulders, and a censer forged of Arabian gold,
and many other imperial gifts. And he gave them to Metropolitan Neophytos and the bishops and the noble envoys,
and sent them to Grand Prince Volodimer Vsevolodovich
pleading with him and saying: "Accept from us, O God-
loving, Pious Prince, these honorable gifts [*ot nachatka
vechnykh let tvoego rodstva pokolen'ia tsar'skii zhrebii*][?],
for your glory and honor and for the coronation of your free
and autocratic empire. And by means of this, our envoys will
entreat you, and we ask for your grace, peace, and love; and
may God's churches be without strife, and may all the
Orthodox remain in peace under the power of your empire
and your free autocracy of Great Russia; may you be called
from this time onward a God-crowned Tsar, crowned with
the imperial crown by the hand of the Most Reverend
Metropolitan Neophytos and the bishops." And from that
time Grand Prince Volodimer Vsevolodovich was called
Monomakh and Tsar of Great Russia. And after that for a
long time to come he remained in peace and love with
Emperor Constantine. And from that time on with the
imperial crown, which the great emperor of the Greeks
Constantine Monomakh sent, the grand princes of Vladimir
were crowned when they were established in the Grand
Principality of Russia.[13]

The account about the bestowal of Monomakh's gifts and regalia (as well as the tale concerning the genealogy of the rulers of Rus' from the Roman emperor [Caesar] Augustus), is an obvious historical fabrication, similar to other medieval and early modern historical legends written with the purpose of proving a distinguished lineage for the ruling dynasty and with the aim of elevating the status of a state in the community of other states. There is no evidence of any direct historical relationship between the two Monomakhs, since Volodimer Monomakh of Rus' (Grand Prince of Kiev, 1113-1125) was born in 1053, whereas Constantine Monomakh died in 1055. However, Volodimer Monomakh's father, Vsevolod Iaroslavich (1030-1093), was apparently married to a Greek woman from the Byzantine imperial family, and Volodimer Monomakh was the offspring of this marriage (*ot tsaritse gr'kyne*). Some historians have speculated that the Greek mother of the Kievan Monomakh may have been a daughter of Constantine Monomakh.[14] Furthermore, the inclusion of the imperial dynastic name Monomakh in Volodimer Monomakh's own name represents a problem which has not been satisfactorily resolved and requires further investigation.[15] Evidently, no actual relations or transfer of regalia between the two Monomakhs could have taken place.

With one major exception, the differences between the version in the *Poslanie* and that of the *Skazanie* are rather insignificant. The major exception is the *Poslanie*'s treatment of the first great schism in Christianity in 1054, which resulted in its breakup into the Catholic and Orthodox versions of the Christian faith, a treatment included in the middle section of the *Poslanie* account.[16] Otherwise, the two versions contain the same essential "historical events" and the relevant ideological claims. For instance, both give considerable prominence to the alleged campaign of Sviatoslav Igor'evich against Constantinople and maintain that he exacted a "heavy tribute" from that city, although Sviatoslav never went to Constantinople but waged war against the Bulgarians. His name was known in Byzantium where he may have had some contacts. Both versions also credit Volodimer Monomakh with an alleged victorious campaign against Constantinople and Thrace which supposedly resulted in great booty for Rus'.

The most important elements of the two versions pertain, of course, to the transfer of Constantine Monomakh's gifts and regalia to Volodimer Monomakh of Rus', the latter's attainment of the status

of the "Tsar of Great Russia," and the transformation of Kievan Rus'
into an "empire" and a "free" (supreme and unlimited) autocracy
already in Monomakh's time, and the subsequent transmission of the
Kievan ruler's title and the status of an empire first to the Grand
Principality of Vladimir and then to "Great Russia" of Muscovy.[17]

Since I.N. Zhdanov's first major scholarly treatment of the
Poslanie and the *Skazanie*, various scholars have pointed out that
those who devised the genealogical tale about the rulers of Rus' –
descendants from the Roman emperor Augustus – and the related
account concerning the Byzantine Monomakh's gifts and regalia, as
well as those who used the tale and the account in question for
official ideological purposes, intended to upgrade the status of the
Muscovite state by connecting it with the Roman Empire of the
antiquity and by claiming direct inheritance from the more recent
but equally prestigious Byzantine Empire.[18] Others have emphasized
the national dynastic foundations of the Muscovite Riurikides as the
decisive element in Muscovite state ideology, and rejected the significance of the Byzantine connection particularly as exemplified by the
marriage of Ivan III to Sophia Palaeologue.[19]

Muscovite ideologues and the court, or those performing
services for them, were indeed not interested in stressing the connection with the most recent period of the Byzantine Empire, since
that empire was ideologically tainted by its acquiescence to the
Council and Union of Florence (1438-1439), for which it had appropriately been punished by the conquest of Constantinople (1453) by
the "infidels" which led to its very downfall. Late Byzantium, "the
second Rome," was hardly a convenient ideological reference.
However, the Byzantine Empire of the "middle period" of the distinguished Macedonian dynasty, to which Constantine IX Monomachus
was related, could serve as a much more suitable predecessor from
which historical precedents could be borrowed and with which ideological affiliations could be construed. It was the Byzantium from
whom Kievan Rus' had accepted Christianity, with whose imperial
dynasty famous rulers of Kievan Rus' had entered into marital
bonds, and who was the bulwark of Orthodox religious purity
against the "perverted" Latins. Spiridon-Savva's incorporation in the
Poslanie of the account pertaining to the religious schism of 1054
was not entirely accidental, although Muscovite authorities decided to
exclude it from the later official version in the *Skazanie*. The
Muscovite court preferred to put greater emphasis on military

conquests and exaction of tribute which fitted into its own and the traditional theory of law by conquest.[20] Byzantium was treated both as a highly respected empire of antiquity, from whom Kievan Rus' had inherited imperial regalia, and as an indispensable link in the chain of Muscovite imperial claims. Without Byzantium, Russian imperial claims could hardly have been advanced.

However, the Muscovite court also became convinced that the advocacy of Muscovite imperial claims would be fortified by a native imperial tradition. With the help of Russian, but non-Muscovite, publicists, who readily offered their services to the rising Muscovite ruler, the Muscovite court promulgated the theory of the Kievan "imperial inheritance," for which there was no objective historical evidence, just as there was no substantiation for the assertion that the grand princes of Vladimir were crowned with an imperial crown, or that the Grand Principality of Vladimir, a relatively insignificant territorial state in its own time, held or even aspired to the status of an empire. The evidence for a conscious preoccupation with the Kievan "imperial inheritance" in official circles in Muscovy during the first decades of the sixteenth century can be found in the writings of Filofei of Pskov, who had a very keen sense of what the Muscovite court wanted to hear. In his *Poslanie k velikomu kniaziu Vasiliiu* (the *Epistle to Grand Prince Vasilii [III]*), composed some-time after 1511 and at about the same time as the *Poslanie* of Spiridon-Savva, Filofei referred to the "blessed St. Volodimer and the great Iaroslav, the chosen of God, and other venerable saints, whose lineage has been extended to you, emperor" in the same manner as to "the other ancient Orthodox emperors" such as the great Emperor Constantine, who in one of the copies of Filofei's Epistle was directly named as an "ancestor" of Vasilii III.[21] Signifi-cantly, Filofei's contribution to the formulation of the claim regard-ing the imperial status of the rulers of Kievan Rus' and the idea of the Byzantine-Kievan "imperial inheritance" was included in one publicistic work in which he began to explicate the theory of "Moscow – the third Rome."

The theory of Kievan "imperial inheritance," as well as those of the Roman and Byzantine "imperial inheritances," had inter-national and domestic implications. These theories served the Muscovite court in its struggle for the lands of Rus' against Poland-Lithuania. They were also instrumental in Muscovy's efforts to enhance the hierarchical status of her ruler not only with respect to the ruler of Poland-Lithuania, its principal competitor for the lands of Rus', but also with regard to other rulers both in Europe and the East. It was during that period that Muscovite diplomacy scored its first, albeit temporary, success by receiving the acknowledgement of the title "tsar," the equivalent of the Western "caesar" ("Kaiser"), for its ruler from a real emperor, Maximilian I, in the anti-Polish offensive alliance treaty Muscovy concluded with his empire in 1514.[22]

The theory of Kievan "imperial inheritance" could also serve very conveniently in efforts to strengthen the authority of the Muscovite ruler at home. Since a "free" autocratic empire had already existed in the "Russian" realm in the Kievan antiquity, it was only natural to continue its political traditions in Muscovite Russia and to extol the status of her rulers in relation to their subjects. Finally, the new claim to the Kievan "imperial inheritance" represented the crowning component of the Muscovite theory of continuity from Kievan Rus' through (Rostovia)-Suzdalia-Vladimiria to Muscovy and elevated it to a much more prestigious "imperial" level.

NOTES

1. For a discussion of these claims, see J. Pelenski, "The Origins of the Official Muscovite Claims to the 'Kievan Inheritance'," *Harvard Ukrainian Studies* (hereafter *HUS*), 1, no. 1 (March, 1977): 29-52 [see Chapter 5 of this volume]. The image of Kiev in Muscovite official and semi-official sources of the 1550s and 1560s has been analyzed in J. Pelenski, *Russia and Kazan: Conquest and Imperial Ideology (1438-1560s)* (The Hague and Paris, 1974), 113-117.

2. An analysis of this contest in the fifteenth and sixteenth centuries is presented in my unpublished study, entitled "The Contest between Muscovite Russia and Poland-Lithuania for the Lands of Old Rus' (1450s-1580s)." For a discussion of Polish claims to Kiev and the whole land of Rus' in connection with the incorporation of the Ukrainian lands of Kievan Rus' into Crown Poland in 1569, see J. Pelenski, "The Incorporation of the Ukrainian Lands of Old Rus' into Crown Poland (1569): Socio-Material Interest and Ideology - A Reexamination," in *American Contributions to the Seventh International Congress of Slavists*, Warsaw, 21-27 August 1973, vol. 3 (The Hague and Paris, 1973), 19-52 [see Chapter 9 of this volume]; and *idem*, "Inkorporacja ukraińskich ziem dawnej Rusi do Korony w 1569 roku: Ideologia i korzyści - próba nowego spojrzenia," *Przegląd Historyczny*, 65, no. 2 (1974): 243-262.

3. Pelenski, "The Origins," 45-52.

4. For an account of Spiridon-Savva's life, see R.P. Dmitrieva, *Skazanie o kniaz'iakh vladimirskikh* (Moscow and Leningrad, 1955), 73-81. The latter work also contains the text editions of the *Poslanie* and the *Skazanie* provided by Dmitrieva

(159-170 and 171-178). Two additional studies on the texts in question by Dmitrieva should be mentioned in this context: "O nekotorykh istochnikakh 'Poslaniia' Spiridona-Savvy," *Trudy Otdela drevnerusskoi literatury* (hereafter *TODRL*), 13 (1957): 440-445, and "K istorii sozdaniia 'Skazaniia o kniaz'iakh vladimirskikh" *TODRL*, 17 (1961): 342-347.

    5. For an analysis of Muscovite sources pertaining to this event, confer J. Pelenski, "The Sack of Kiev of 1482 in Contemporary Muscovite Chronicle Writing," *HUS*, 3-4 (1979-1980), part 2: 638-649 [see Chapter 6 of this volume].

    6. I.N. Zhdanov, *Russkii bylevoi epos* (St. Petersburg, 1895), especially the chapter "Povesti o Vavilone i 'Skazanie o kniaz'iakh vladimirskikh'"; Dmitrieva, *Skazanie*, 81-82.

    7. Dmitrieva, *Skazanie*, 91-109; *idem*, "K istorii sozdaniia 'Skazaniia o kniaz'iakh vladimirskikh'," *TODRL*, 17 (961): 342-347.

    8. Dmitrieva, *Skazanie*, 111-151. For a discussion of the influence of the *Skazanie* on the *Kazanskaia istoriia* or the *Kazanskii letopisets*, and the relevant ideological implications, see Pelenski, *Russia and Kazan*, 106-111. The genealogical tale about the ancestry of the Russian rulers going back to Caesar Augustus, as incorporated into the *Poslanie* and the *Skazanie* and used by Muscovite diplomacy in Russo-Polish relations, became a subject of political satire in the writings of Polish Renaissance authors, including Jan Kochanowski ("Czwartynasty potomek rzymskiego cesarza - Augusta; któż wie, gdzie wziął tego kronikarza!" [Jan Kochanowski, *Jezda do Moskwy* (1583) in *Dzieła polskie*, 2 vols., (Warsaw, 1976), 2: 137]).

    9. A.A. Zimin, review of R.P. Dmitrieva, *Skazanie o kniaz'iakh vladimirskikh*, in *Istoricheskii Arkhiv*, 1956, no. 3, 236-237; *idem*, "Antichnye motivy v russkoi publitsistike kontsa XV v.," in *Feodal'naia Rossiia vovsemirno-istoricheskom protsesse* (Moscow, 1972), 129-238.

    10. A.L. Gol'dberg, "K istorii rasskaza o potomkakh Avgusta i o darakh Monomakha," *TODRL*, 30 (1976): 204-216, especially 210-211, and R.P. Dmitrieva's response restating her position, "O tekstologicheskoi zavisimosti mezhdu raznymi vidami rasskaza o potomkakh Avgusta i o darakh Monomakha," *TODRL*, 30 (1976): 217-230.

    11. Gol'dberg, "K istorii rasskaza," 208.

    12. Dmitrieva, *Skazanie*, 162-165.

    13. Dmitrieva, *Skazanie*, 175-178. The English translation of this crucial passage first appeared in my study *Russia and Kazan*, 107-109.

    14. *The Russian Primary Chronicle* (the *Laurentian Text*), trans. and ed. S.H. Cross and O.P. Sherbowitz-Wetzor (Cambridge, Mass., 1953), 142 and 263, fn. 192. Consult also V.G. Briusova, "K voprosu o proiskhozhdenii Vladimira Monomakha," *Vizantiiskii vremennik*, 28 (1968): 127-135.

    15. The name and title Monomakh appears, of course, in the *Pouchenie* [the Testament] of Volodimer Monomakh inserted in the entries for the *Laurentian Codex* among the entries for 1096. The dates of its writing and incorporation into the *Laurentian Codex* have long defied scholarly explanation (the *Russian Primary Chronicle*, Appendix I, Notes to Testament of Volodimer Monomakh 285, fn. 1). For additional Soviet commentaries and the literature on the *Pouchenie*, see D.S. Likhachev, *Velikoe nasledie* (Moscow, 1975), 111-131, and D.S. Likhachev, ed., *Istoriia russkoi literatury X-XVII vekov* (Moscow, 1980), 96-100. Concerning the discussion of a seal attributed to Volodimer Vsevolodovich and including the name

Monomakh, confer V.L. Ianin and G.G. Litavrin, "Novye materialy o proiskhozh-denii Vladimira Monomakha," D.A. Avdusin and V.L. Ianin, eds., *Istoriko-arkheologicheskii sbornik* (Moscow, 1962), 204-221.

16. Spiridon-Savva's discussion of the schism contains a number of obvious mistakes. For example, the schism did not occur in 1045, as Spiridon-Savva maintained, but in 1054, during the tenure of Pope Leo IX (1049 - April 1054) and not that of the alleged Pope Formos, to whom he referred. An abbreviated summary of his treatment of the 1054 schism was incorporated at the end of the first reconstructed recension of the *Skazanie*, but was completely eliminated from the work's second recension (Dmitrieva, *Skazanie*, 178 and 185-191).

17. The notions of supreme sovereignty and unlimited authority were expressed in Russian sources by the term *vol'nyi*, a paradoxical definition for the contemporary reader. Its early usage can be attested, already in the mid-fifteenth century, by none other than Iona, the first autonomous metropolitan of Moscow, in relation to the Kazan Tatar khan, Mahmut (*Akty istoricheskie, sobrannye i izdannye Arkheograficheskoiu kommissieiu* 1 (1841), nos. 67 and 266, 119-120 and 497). Following the assumption of the title of Tsar by Ivan IV, the term was used officially by Muscovite bureaucrats and publicists.

18. Zhdanov, *Russkii bylevoi epos*, 62-63 and 101-112.

19. G. Olshr, "Gli ultimi Rurikidi e le basi ideologiche della sovranità dello Stato Russo," *Orientalia Christiana Periodica*, 12 (1946): 322-373.

20. For an analysis of the Muscovite theory of law by conquest as applied to the Khanate of Kazan, see Pelenski, *Russia and Kazan*, 81-91. On the Polish theory of law by conquest with regard to Kievan Rus', cf. Pelenski, "Incorporation of Ukrainian Lands, 38-44 [see Chapter 9 of this volume].

21. V.N. Malinin, *Starets Eleazarova Monastyria Filofei i ego poslaniia* (Kiev, 1901), Prilozhenie, 9, 51-52. For a rare earlier reference to Volodimer I as emperor ("Tsar") in the *Vita* of Dmitrii Ivanovich Donskoi, consult Pelenski, "The Origins."

22. The best critical edition of the text of this treaty, its German translation, and a commentary were provided by G. Stökl, in L. Santifaller, ed., *1100 Jahre öster-reichische und europäische Geschichte* (Vienna, 1949), 53-55. For a historical background of the treaty and additional documents, cf. J. Fiedler, "Die Allianz zwischen Kaiser Maximilian I und Vasilij Ivanovič, Grossfürsten von Russland, von dem Jahre 1514," *Sitzungsberichte der Kaiserlichen Akademie der Wissenschaften, Philos-ophisch-Historische Classe*, Closse 43, no 2 (1863): 183-289, especially 196, 197-199 and fn. 1.

8

THE CONTEST BETWEEN LITHUANIA AND THE GOLDEN HORDE IN THE FOURTEENTH CENTURY FOR SUPREMACY OVER EASTERN EUROPE [SPECIFICALLY FOR ALL THE LANDS OF RUS']

Traditional scholarship, in its treatment of the struggles for territorial supremacy in Eastern Europe in the fourteenth and early fifteenth centuries and in its assessment of the impact of non-Slavic neighbors on the destinies of Eastern Slavs, has concentrated on three subjects: (1) the relationships among Suzdalian-Vladimirian, Tverian, and Muscovite Rus' (i.e., the Russian core area) and the Golden Horde;[1] (2) the struggle among the Russian competitors, particularly Muscovy and Tver', for hegemony in the Great Russian ethnic territory;[2] and (3) the relationship between Lithuania and the Eastern Slavs. Here Lithuania has been regarded as both an outsider and an insider of the East Slavic world with equal justification, particularly after her transformation into a Lithuanian-Ruthenian state.[3]

In comparison, the relationship between Lithuania and the Golden Horde, in whose system Muscovy was integrated, has received little attention.[4] This comparative neglect appears unjustified since Lithuania and the Golden Horde were the two principal contestants in the struggle for supremacy in Eastern Europe, specifically for all the lands of Rus', in the fourteenth century.

Lithuania was simultaneously competing with Muscovy for the succession to all of Rus'. However, Lithuanian-Muscovite conflicts and confrontations cannot be analyzed outside the larger scope of the relations between Lithuania and the Golden Horde. Muscovy, a vassal state of the Golden Horde, played a significant, albeit secondary, role in this peculiar triangular relationship. Nevertheless, Muscovite bookmen and ideologists of the fifteenth and sixteenth centuries succeeded in magnifying Muscovy's role in the East European contest out of all proportion to real developments, and in creating a myth about her protracted and farsighted "struggle against the Tatar yoke," which has been perpetuated in Russian historiography up to the present day.[5]

Actually three major interrelated conflicts took place, the overall political significance of which roughly corresponded to their chronological sequence:

1. The struggle between Lithuania and the Golden Horde for all the lands of Rus' took place in two phases: the first phase began in the 1320s and ended with the Lithuanian victory in the Battle of the Blue Waters (*na sinei vode*) in 1362; the second phase came in the last years of the fourteenth century and culminated in the great Lithuanian defeat in the Battle on the Vorskla River (1399).

2. The second major confrontation took place between Lithuania and Muscovy, in the course of which Grand Prince Algirdas (Olgierd) attempted to destroy Muscovy's military power in three campaigns (1368, 1370, 1372), to take the city of Moscow, and to impose Lithuanian supremacy over all of Rus', including the Russian core area. Closely connected with this political struggle were the endeavors of the Lithuanian rulers to establish a second Kiev-based metropolitanate for the Orthodox population of Lithuania. The Lithuanian rulers wanted to create their own ideological center, completely independent from the Moscow-based Metropolitanate of Kiev and all Rus'.

3. The third conflict involved the Golden Horde and Muscovy. Muscovy attempted to exploit difficulties in the Horde for her own benefit, and, by doing so, she provoked Mongol-Tatar punitive campaigns. These ended in two victories for Muscovy, one in the Battle on the Vozha River (1378) and the other at Kulikovo Field (*Kulikovo pole*) (1380). The literary and ideological writings about the latter greatly contributed to the emergence of the myth about Muscovy's determined resistance to the "Tatar yoke."

In this study I shall concentrate on the analysis of the first aspect of the Lithuania-Muscovy-Golden Horde triangular relationship, namely the contest between Lithuania (also referred to as the Grand Principality of Lithuania, the Lithuanian-Ruthenian state, and

Lithuania-Ruthenia) and the Golden Horde for the lands of Rus',
specifically for the Belorussian and Ukrainian core areas.

In contrast to Muscovy's cautious and submissive policy
toward the Golden Horde, which prevailed until the later 1370s and
for most of the century after the Kulikovo battle, the Grand
Principality of Lithuania was the first major power to have actively
challenged the Mongol presence and sovereignty in the lands of Rus'
on a large scale prior to that highly publicized and celebrated Battle
at Kulikovo Field. This challenge was the result both of Lithuania's
expansion into the lands of Rus' and of an attempt by the Lithuanian
rulers, beginning with Grand Prince Algirdas, to implement their
political-ideological claims to rule over all of Rus' (1358).[6]

The origins of Lithuanian expansion into the lands of Rus' go
back to the Mongol invasion of that territory.[7] Beginning in the
1240s the Lithuanian ruler Mindaugas (Mendovg) – and later his
successors as well – had been with brief interruptions in control of
large areas of Black Rus', that is, the northwestern Belorussian
territories, located on the Upper Niemen River.[8] Black Rus', similar
to Podlachia, Polissia, and the Belorussian core area, namely, the
Polotsk-Minsk land, as well as ethnic Lithuania, had not originally
been conquered by the Mongols, primarily because large areas of
these territories were covered by forests which were limiting to the
Mongol methods of waging war. These lands were not incorporated
into the state system of the Golden Horde. In fact, Lithuania became
a member of an emerging anti-Mongol coalition which, however,
collapsed after the Mongols subdued Danylo of Galicia and Volynia
(1257). The only concrete results of this anti-Mongol move for
Lithuania were the granting of the royal crown by Pope Innocent IV
to Mindaugas (1251) and the first major Mongol attack on the
Lithuanian lands (1258-1259).[9] This attack, as well as some others,
had no lasting consequences. The Mongols made no all-out effort to
conquer either Lithuania or territories such as Black Rus' which had
come under Lithuanian sovereignty. The Lithuanian rulers, on the
other hand, gradually continued to extend their influence into the
border areas of Rus', which had not been directly incorporated into
the state system of the Golden Horde.

During the reign of Vytenis (Viten) (1293-1316), and particularly that of Gediminas (Gedymin) (1316-1341), the founder of the
great Lithuanian state, Lithuania expanded into most of the Belorussian territory (the Polotsk-Minsk land, the Principality of

Vitebsk), as well as into Podlachia and Polissia; all these became parts of the Grand Principality of Lithuania.[10] During Gediminas' tenure, the formal transformation of the Grand Principality of Lithuania into a dual Lithuanian Ruthenian state was completed.[11] Gediminas was the first Lithuanian ruler to assume the title *Lethewindorum et Ruthenorum rex* in his relations with other countries.[12] The addition of Rus' in his title best reflects contemporary awareness of this political transformation.

In the reign of Gediminas, a major Lithuanian encroachment into the Golden Horde's sphere of sovereignty took place. Even if one were to follow the Antonovych-Hrushevs'kyi hypothesis and completely reject the accounts in several recensions of the *Lithuanian-Ruthenian Chronicles* (*Litovsko-russkie letopisi*) (also referred to as *Zapadno-russkie letopisi* and *Belorussko-litovskie letopisi*) regarding the conquest of the Volodymyr-Volyns'kyi and Lutsk principalities and, most important, of Kiev and all the Kievan land (that is, the Ukrainian core areas) in the early 1320s,[13] the evidence for the existence of a Lithuanian-Mongol (-Tatar) condominium over Kiev and the Kievan land by 1332 can be relatively safely attested. During that time, a prince by the name of Fedor (Hol'shans'kyi?), a relative (brother, half-brother, or cousin) of Gediminas, ruled in Kiev under the supervision of a Tatar *basqaq* and the political sponsorship of the Lithuanian grand prince.[14] The establishment of this condominium suggests that Gediminas, together with Khan Özbeg, was at least for a time interested in a peaceful resolution of the Lithuanian-Mongol (Tatar) competition, and that the two rulers attempted to avoid an immediate political and military conflict over the *ulus* Rus', or *regnum Russiae*. However, the transformation of the Grand Principality of Lithuania into a Lithuanian-Ruthenian state as reflected in Gediminas' title heralded a major change in the policies of the Lithuanian rulers, who, at a propitious moment, intended to upset this carefully established equilibrium in the Kievan coreland of Rus'.

This moment came after the death of Khan Özbeg (1341), and was followed by another after the death of his son Khan Ğambek (1342-1357), when the Golden Horde experienced its first major time of troubles which was to last for two decades.[15] During that time, which coincided with the reign of Grand Prince Algirdas of Lithuania (1345-1377), Lithuania succeeded in gradually expanding into the still unclaimed Belorussian areas and into five major

Ukrainian lands, which had been under Mongol-Tatar sovereignty.
These were:

1. The land of Chernihiv, which was annexed in three phases:
   the middle region in 1345-1348, the northwestern part in
   the Briansk area between 1355 and 1358, and the city of
   Chernihiv and the southern part in the early 1360s and the
   1370s;
2. Siveria (Sivershchyna), including its main city of Novhorod-Sivers'kyi, which must have been in Lithuanian
   control by the early 1360s;
3. Kiev and the Kievan land, conquered by the Grand Principality of Lithuania by 1361-1363;
4. The land of Pereiaslav, which followed the conquest of
   Kiev;
5. Major parts of Podolia, conquered in the first half of the
   1360s.[16]

These extraordinary successes, particularly the takeover of the
city of Kiev, were made possible by a number of factors, including
the previous relatively peaceful penetration of the Lithuanians into
these lands; noninterference with local, traditional, social, and legal
arrangements; relative religious tolerance (a practice that the non-
Christian Lithuanian rulers shared with the Mongols); a concern for
the welfare and organizational structure of the Orthodox Church;
and, finally, the abolition of the *vykhod* [Tatar tribute] from which
the Golden Horde, the local ruler, and, in certain areas under
Muscovite influence, a khan and a Muscovite grand prince had profited. Furthermore, Algirdas' exceptional political and diplomatic
abilities, attested by the author/compiler of the *Rogozhskii letopisets*,
who can be credited with having been one of the most astute
observers of the contemporary political scene, as well as of Algirdas'
expansionist policies, played an important role in the extension of the
Lithuanian sphere of domination.[17]

However, the decisive factor that assured the transfer of the
Ukrainian Rus' territories to Lithuanian sovereignty must have been
the obvious military equality and at times even superiority of
Lithuanian military forces over the Mongol-Tatars, which manifested itself in the Battle of the Blue Waters (1362). This battle has
never received due recognition in historical scholarship on account

of the scarcity of sources, and because the tale about Podolia, entitled *About the Podolian Land* (*O Podol'skoi zemli*) in the *Lithuanian-Ruthenian Chronicles*, which is the chief source, contains misleading information.[18] Individual scholars have placed this battle into Vytautas' (Vitold's) period and confused it with his campaigns of 1397 and 1398 in the southern Ukrainian lands.[19] S.M. Kuczyński, the author of the single specialized study on the Battle of the Blue Waters, raised every possible doubt regarding the veracity of the Supras'l' recension of the *Lithuanian-Ruthenian Chronicles*, but was compelled to concede that Algirdas indeed victoriously campaigned against the Tatars in 1362, most probably in connection with the takeover of the city of Kiev.[20] Kuczyński's error lay in assigning equal value to the testimonies of the Supras'l' and Uvarov versions, as well as of later recensions of the *Lithuanian-Ruthenian Chronicles*.[21] He could have avoided this and other mistakes had he consulted the authoritative textological study of the *Lithuanian-Ruthenian Chronicles* by T. Sushyts'kyi.

The earliest versions of the *Lithuanian-Ruthenian Chronicles* report the following event:

> When Grand Prince Olgerd [Algirdas] [ruled as] the sovereign in the Lithuanian land, he, together with the Lithuanian forces, embarked upon a campaign, and defeated the Tatars at the Blue Water (*na sinei vode*).[22]

Whereas the names of the three Tatar commanders mentioned in the chronicles may not entirely be correct, and the narrative about Podolia may have been edited to support the Lithuanian claims to this Ukrainian land, the fact that such a battle took place has been substantiated by the *Rogozhskii letopisets*, which, under the year 1363, reads as follows: "This fall Olgerd [Algirdas] [successfully] fought at the Blue Waters and on the White Banks."[23] Since several rivers were known as "Blue Waters," scholars have been confronted with the problem of locating the battlefield itself. Two of the rivers referred to as "Blue Waters" in the sixteenth century were the Siniukha, a left-bank tributary of the Buh River, and the Snyvod', a small river located on the border of the Kievan land, Volynia and Podolia (both names *sin/iukha* and *sny/vod'* are apparent derivatives of *sinia voda*). The distance between the two rivers is approximately one hundred miles. M.N. Karamzin and his followers thought that the battle between the Lithuanian and the Tatar forces took place on the Buh tributary; M. Hrushevs'kyi opted for the Snyvod',[24] basing his argument on a reference found in Podolian cadastre documents.

For a variety of reasons, which cannot be dealt with at length in this study, most Slavic historians have tended to minimize the significance of the Battle of the Blue Waters, an attitude difficult to justify. Although the sources on this event are scanty, the circumstances surrounding the conquest of the city of Kiev and the Kievan lands, as well as of the other four Ukrainian lands, indicate that a major Lithuanian victory would have been necessary in order for the Golden Horde to have accepted such a major infringement of its sovereignty over the lands of Old Rus'. It would be difficult to conceive of the Golden Horde, even with its internal difficulties, as accepting the loss of such a significant part of its state system without a struggle. Since the Golden Horde later attempted and, in some cases, intermittently succeeded in reimposing the collection of tribute from territories incorporated by the Lithuanian-Ruthenian state during Algirdas' period, it is safe to assume that the Golden Horde resisted the conquest of these lands by the Lithuanians.

It may be argued that the Battle of the Blue Waters was a Mongol-Tatar response to the Lithuanian penetration of the Kievan land and Podolia. The Golden Horde must have been particularly disturbed by the Lithuanian takeover of Kiev, the capital of Kievan Rus', which still had considerable political and symbolic significance. Apparently, a Tatar army, under three commanders with orders to contain the Lithuanian advance into Ukrainian Rus', was dispatched by the Horde's rulers. Algirdas mounted a counteroffensive and defeated this army decisively. The central Ukrainian lands definitely ceased to be a part of the Golden Horde's East European empire after the Battle of the Blue Waters.

The Lithuania-Ruthenian state was the only major power to have made a serious attempt at militarily subduing and politically subordinating the Golden Horde. This attempt occurred during the reign of Grand Prince Vytautas (1392-1430). Vytautas' offensive move against the Golden Horde was thoroughly prepared both diplomatically and militarily. He undertook major intelligence operations in southern Podolia, the territories around the mouth of the Dnieper River, and in northern Crimea, in 1397 and 1398. Vytautas had his own candidate for the position of khan of the Golden Horde, Tohtamış, a contender for the control over the

Horde, who had earlier failed to gain the throne. Tohtamış was a tool in Vytautas' hands; the latter could extract many concessions from Tohtamış, who, at this time, was merely a political émigré, living off Vytautas' patronage.

In 1397 or 1398, Vytautas concluded an agreement with Tohtamış, according to which the latter would receive the support of the grand prince of Lithuania in his bid for the throne of the Golden Horde. Tohtamış, on his part, issued Vytautas a *yarlik* for all the Rus' lands, and, by doing so, granted him the territories in which the Lithuanian ruler was vitally interested.[25] This agreement can be interpreted in different ways. The partners entering into the agreement had different conceptions of legal arrangements and different state ideologies. From Vytautas' perspective, it could be interpreted as reciprocal investiture, signifying an expression of equality and mutual respect between the two rulers, or even Tohtamış' submission to Vytautas. From Tohtamış' point of view Vytautas was a convenient ally supporting his legitimate political aspirations. For his support, Vytautas received a *yarlik* for the lands of Rus' which meant that Tohtamış was simply replacing the Muscovite client with a Lithuanian one in the Rus' *ulus*. The Muscovite ruler was the khan's client and could be deprived of his status at the khan's pleasure. As the Lithuanian ruler, Vytautas was Tohtamış' equal partner; so far as Rus' and, in particular, Muscovite Rus' were concerned, he could be looked upon only as a client.

Vytautas organized an impressive army for the steppe campaign of 1399 and the conquest of the Golden Horde, and set out from Kiev to destroy the Mongol-Tatar forces in a single great battle. Khan Temir Kutlu and Emir Edigü, the latter the actual ruler of the Golden Horde, advanced against Vytautas' forces, and the two hostile armies clashed in the open steppe on the banks of the Vorskla River (a tributary of the Dnieper) on August 12, 1399. (Another historic confrontation was to take place nearby, in 1709, namely the Battle of Poltava.) Vytautas suffered a crushing defeat in the ensuing battle, and was forced to flee with the remnants of his army. This event represented the greatest political and military setback in his colorful and dramatic career.[26]

The battle on the banks of the Vorskla River terminated Vytautas' campaign and his ambitions to create a powerful East European empire controlling the Black Sea, including all of Rus', and to become the overlord of the Golden Horde. The latter retained its independence; in spite of constant domestic troubles and gradual decay, the Horde was obviously still a power to be reckoned with. In overcoming Vytautas, the Horde decisively defeated one of the most outstanding East European rulers. Vytautas had organized a strong army with the support of many powerful princes of the Rus' lands. Muscovy remained formally neutral, and most probably rejected Vytautas' proposal to participate in the struggle against the Horde.

A number of Rus' princes took advantage of Vytautas' defeat in the Battle on the Vorskla River to weaken his overlordship in the Rus' lands.[27] Vytautas probably appeared to them at that time as a greater threat than the Muscovite ruler. In addition, many of his prominent supporters from the Rus' lands had been killed in the Vorskla battle, thus contributing to the narrowing of his political base in the lands of Rus'. In short, the Battle on the Vorskla River shattered Vytautas' all-Rus' ambitions. His interference into the internal affairs of the Golden Horde and his later successes in the investiture of Tohtamış' sons Ğelǎl-ed-Dīn (1412) and Kerīm Berdi (1412-1414/1417) as khans, as well as his political sponsorship of Khan Ulu Mehmet (1419-1424; 1427-1437/1438), the later khan of Kazan, had no significant consequences for his imperial policies.

Whereas the most important facts about Vytautas ill-fated campaign against the Golden Horde are well known, his political intentions are somewhat obscured by the divergent testimony in the sources. It is necessary to realize that Vytautas', as well as Tohtamış' political plans have to be deduced primarily from East Slavic chronicles. Some details of these accounts are perfectly accurate and can be utilized for the factual reconstruction of the circumstances surrounding the Battle on the Vorskla River.[28]

Actually, one can extract from the sources two political programs attributed to Vytautas with regard to the Golden Horde and the Rus' lands integrated into its system. The sources chronologically closest to the Vorskla battle credit Vytautas with plans for establishing a protectorate over the Golden Horde and with the intention of imposing his rule over "all the Rus' lands."[29] The success of his endeavors would have represented a successful realization of Algirdas' claim to all of Rus'.

However, the Tale devoted to the Vorskla battle in the influential *Nikon Chronicle* (*Nikonovskaia letopis'*), the original version of which was compiled in the late 1520s–early 1530s, attributes to Vytautas more ambitious and grandiose autocratic imperial plans.[30]

Of all the narrative sources, the *Nikon Chronicle* is the most out-spoken in terms of imperial ideology. A great many historians (Hrushevs'kyi being a notable exception) have accepted the untitled Tale about the battle on the Vorskla River in the Nikon compilation without reservation and without the necessary critical evaluation. The Tale represents a miniature of the *Nikon Chronicle* itself. The editors combined materials from several earlier sources to produce this literary and publicistic work. They also made a number of adaptations and included some text of their own; most important were, of course, their ideological conclusions, which they disguised as Vytautas' grand imperial design.

The description of Vytautas' imperial plans in the Tale is detailed and far-reaching. All the future Tatar state organizations are accounted for in this work: Astrakhan, Kazan (the term used for the Bulgar land, as well), the Iaik Horde, and the Crimea. In addition, the Tale maintains that Vytautas wanted to rule over the Germans, Poland, other unidentified territories, and, of course, over all of Rus'. Furthermore, it did not even mention the idea of reciprocal investiture. According to the Tale, Tohtamış, Vytautas' candidate for the khan of the Golden Horde, was to receive the Horde as a grant from the Lithuanian ruler, along with all the other Tatar political organizations. Hence, the Horde, together with its satellite territories and its new ruler Tohtamış, became in this version the direct posses-sion of the Lithuanian ruler. Vytautas was not to be invested by Tohtamış with the principalities of Rus', but he was to rule there by virtue of his own authority. In the context of the East European history, all this was nothing short of a program for world domina-tion (*universale Weltherrschaftspläne*).[31]

In terms of domestic policy, Vytautas was to rule over the Rus' princes (as well as over the Horde) in strictly autocratic fashion ("according to our will"). He made apparent his intention to put the Horde "to the sword" in the event of insubordination. He would collect annual tribute, and his emblem would be struck on the coins of the Horde. One can infer from all these declarations that he intended to centralize the government of the future empire.

Strangely enough, the *Nikon Chronicle*, which otherwise was very pro-Muscovite and would have been rather reluctant to enhance the virtues of a Lithuanian, a Polish, or a non-Muscovite Rus' ruler, extolled a historical figure, whose policies threatened the position of Muscovy. In comparison, the *Lithuanian-Ruthenian Chronicles*, which tended to eulogize Vytautas and his deeds, reported nothing approaching such grandiose plans. The Tale about the Battle on the Vorskla River in the *Nikon Chronicle* is, therefore, one of the most unusual but at the same time revealing literary and ideological documents of Muscovite political thought of the sixteenth century. It formulated Vytautas' domestic and foreign policies in such a way as to make them understandable and acceptable to Russians in the age of Vasilii III and Ivan IV. In fact, Vytautas' domestic and foreign policy programs almost matched those planned and partly carried out by the two Russian tsars. The substitution in the Tale of the modern term "Kazan" for the ancient term "Bulgar" in order to substantiate the Muscovite theory of Bulgar-Kazan continuity[32] is good evidence for the hypothesis that contemporary political considerations were used to buttress Vytautas' grand imperial design. Although Vytautas' designs proved to be a failure, similar expansionist schemes were more successfully carried out by Russian tsars in their struggle against the east. Hence, the editors of the *Nikon Chronicle* used Vytautas' "grand design" to introduce continuity into their own political thinking. The design ascribed to Vytautas was in fact a reflection of contemporary Muscovite ideas. In any case, this particular text of the *Nikon Chronicle* reveals what Muscovite bookmen of the 1520s-1550s thought about *Weltherrschaft*; they utilized this notion for their own ideological purposes.

But why did the Grand Principality of Lithuania contest the Golden Horde's position in Eastern Europe, and why did Vytautas attempt the political subjugation of this Mongol-Tatar empire? The decision arose from the desire of Lithuanian rulers to build a great Lithuanian state that would include all the territories of Rus'. In particular, the claim of the Lithuanian grand princes to "all of Rus'" and their program of "gathering of all the Rus' lands," advanced even before Muscovite Rus' had developed an equivalent program of her own, promoted the Lithuanian grand principality into the role of successor state to Kievan Rus', and this represented a direct challenge to the Golden Horde. Having embarked upon a policy of expansion into Rus', Lithuania also faced Muscovy as a competitor. Both Gediminas and Algirdas tended to support the Grand Principality of Tver' against Muscovy's attempts to subjugate that land. The Lithuanian rulers were aware that in order to reign over all of Rus' they had either to subdue or to conquer Muscovy. Since Muscovy was the most trusted and obedient subject of the Golden Horde, this expansionist policy of Lithuania challenged the *status quo* in Eastern Europe and collided with the interests both of the Horde itself and of its chief Russian client, Muscovy. The Lithuanian grand princes proceeded by attacking the two states separately. They began by attempting to roll back the Golden Horde's sphere of sovereignty and to take over the strategically located Ukrainian lands of Chernihivia and Siveria, which would make possible the encirclement of Muscovy by a Tver'-Lithuania-Riazan'-Suzdal' coalition. Then Algirdas directly attacked Muscovy in three major campaigns (1368, 1370, 1372) at a time when she was distracted by her final struggle with Tver' for domination of the Great Russian territories. In the first two campaigns, the Lithuanian army, together with its Russian allies, the Tverians and the Smolenians, reached and besieged the city of Moscow,[33] the first such threat to the city to come from the West. However, the combined Lithuanian-Ruthenian armies were unable to take Moscow or to destroy the Grand Principality of Muscovy. Vytautas made another attempt at subduing Muscovy and all of northeastern Rus' (i.e., the Russian core area) by defeating the Golden Horde, but he apparently overestimated both his forces and his resources, and thus failed in the attempt.

In their quest for supremacy over all the Rus' lands, the Lithuanian rulers, regardless of their religious beliefs (Algirdas formally adhered to ancient Lithuanian nature worship and was called "the great king of fire adorationists," whereas Vytautas formally acknowledged Roman Catholicism), consistently conducted a policy aimed at establishing an Orthodox metropolitanate, preferably in the city of Kiev, and completely independent from Moscow.[34] Their religious tolerance, however, did not prevent them from recognizing the role of the church hierarchy and the value of religious ideology in the political conflict with Muscovite Russia. The khans of the Golden Horde both before and after their conversion to Islam displayed a relative tolerance toward Orthodox Christianity, as did the Lithuanian grand princes, and their support was very helpful to the Muscovite ecclesiastical establishment, which cooperated closely with the grand prince and was dependent on his political authority. Thus, in ecclesiastical policy matters, Lithuanian rulers were handicapped by the assistance extended by the Byzantine patriarchate to the Muscovite side and by the latter's reliance on the Tatars' benevolent neutrality. This similarity of attitudes toward religious matters placed the conflict between the Lithuanians and the

Tatars squarely on political and economic grounds; it was devoid of that religious passion that was to characterize Muscovy's struggle with the Tatar world later on.

In addition to conquering the Rus' lands, Lithuania was vitally interested in gaining access to the Black Sea. Vytautas partially succeeded in occupying, at least for a time, the northern region of the Black Sea, between the Dniester and Dnieper rivers. The Lithuanian ruler was obviously trying to gain complete control of the trade routes which led from Poland and the Rus' lands to the Black Sea. The most important of these was the so-called "Tatar route," which ran from L'viv to the Crimea by way of southern Podolia. Another led from Poland by way of Lutsk in Volynia and merged with the "Tatar route" on the lower Buh River.[35] Firm control of the territory extending over the areas where the Dniester, Buh and Dnieper discharge into the Black Sea would have amounted to the control of the northern Black Sea trade by the Lithuanian-Ruthenian state, a development that would have endangered vital economic and commercial interests of the Golden Horde and of the emerging Khanate of the Crimea. Had the plans of the Lithuanian rulers for imposing their supremacy over Novgorod succeeded, a secure access to the Black Sea could have contributed to the revival of the Dnieper trade and the re-establishment of the old *put' iz variag v greki* (route from the Varangians to the Greeks), the cutting off of which by steppe peoples had contributed to the decline of Kievan Rus'.

So far as the Eastern Slavs were concerned, the Lithuanian-Tatar contest had a number of lasting consequences:

1. The Lithuanian conquest of the Belorussian and central Ukrainian Rus' territories terminated the Golden Horde's rule in these lands approximately a century prior to Muscovy's emancipation from the Golden Horde's supremacy. After the Battle of the Blue Waters, the Belorussian and Ukrainian Rus' territories became part of the "West," while Muscovy remained "East."

2. Whereas Lithuania's intervention into the Golden Horde's internal affairs had not been crowned by notable success, it did contribute to the Horde's weakening and disintegration and to the latter's transformation into one of many East European states.

3. The struggle between them marked the end of the age of empires built by small, often nomadic, peoples on the basis of military prowess alone.

4. Lithuania was able to expand into the Belorussian and Ukrainian lands, although in the course of this expansion her elite became slavicized; in this respect, the conquerors were overcome by the conquered. Lithuania's resources were too limited to accomplish the conquest of the steppe.

5. Muscovy profited most from the contest between Lithuania-Ruthenia and the Golden Horde at a time when the outcome of her own struggle for supremacy in the Great Russian lands was still in doubt. In contrast to Lithuania's offensive posture toward the Golden Horde, Muscovy refrained from actively resisting Mongol-Tatar domination and carefully avoided challenging the political supremacy of the Golden Horde throughout most of the fourteenth and a good part of the fifteenth century. The Battle at Kulikovo Field had no significant political consequences. The Lithuanian involvement, the diplomatic negotiations preceding the battle, the battle itself, and the military activities immediately following it have not been sufficiently studied, but they also have been too freely interpreted, at least by some scholars. Such scholars have seen in these events an alliance between Jagiełło and Mamai and conclusive evidence for the existence of a deliberate Lithuanian-Tatar effort to encircle Moscow.[36] The Kulikovo battle did not represent the first defeat of a Tatar army by Russians coming from the Vladimirian-Muscovite grand principality – the Battle on the Vozha River in 1378 was not only earlier, but may be regarded as equally important. Two years after the Battle at Kulikovo Field, in 1382, Tohtamış was able to take Moscow, and twenty-seven years later, in 1409, Edigü conducted a devastating invasion of Muscovy. Both of these events indicate that the Battle at Kulikovo Field had only minor effects upon the relations between Muscovy and the Golden Horde. Muscovy remained in the state system of the Golden Horde, paid it tribute, and continued to rely upon its support and that of its successor states in her conflicts with other Russian states. Even after a considerable weakening of the Golden Horde that followed the formation of

its daughter khanates, Muscovy attempted to become the successor, not the challenger, of the gradually disintegrating Golden Horde. It was only after the actual dissolution of the Golden Horde that Muscovy dared to take the offensive by annexing the Horde's successor states. Muscovy's successes, such as the conquests of the khanates of Kazan (1552) and Astrakhan (1556), came, however, at a much later date and had little to do with her alleged struggle against the "Tatar yoke." In more recent decades, interest in Russian-Tatar relations, particularly the "Tatar yoke" as seen from the Russian perspective, has overshadowed the study of all other aspects of East European territorial conflicts. This emphasis on the confrontation between Muscovy and the Golden Horde and on the enhancement of Muscovy's role in the struggle against the "Tatar yoke" can be partially explained by the relative abundance of historical and literary materials dealing with the Battle at Kulikovo Field, although these originate from a much later period, by an impressive literature on these materials written predominantly from a devotional point of view, and by the glorification of this historical event in Russian historical and literary scholarship. All these factors have contributed to the consolidation of the view that Muscovite Russia, beginning in the later part of the fourteenth century, actively resisted the Mongol-Tatar domination, conducted a protracted liberation struggle into the late fifteenth century, and eventually threw off the oppressive "Tatar yoke." This view, which incidentally represents a belated national response to external challenges and resulting self-doubts, certainly does not reflect the realities of the fourteenth and fifteenth centuries, but rather serves as an example of the perpetuation of national mythology in East European history.

NOTES

1. For the best general surveys of these relations, see A.N. Nasonov, *Mongoly i Rus' (Istoriia tatarskoi politiki na Rusi)* (Moscow and Leningrad, 1940); B. Spuler, *Die Goldene Horde (Die Mongolen in Russland, 1223-1502)* (Wiesbaden, 1965); B.D. Grekov and A.Iu. Iakubovskii, *Zolotaia orda i ee padenie* (Moscow and Leningrad, 1950); G. Vernadsky, *The Mongols and Russia* (New Haven and London, 1953); M.G. Safargaliev, *Raspad Zolotoi Ordy (Uchenye Zapiski Mordovskogo gosudarstvennogo universiteta*, vyp. 11) (Saransk, 1960); and I.B. Grekov, *Ocherki po istorii mezhdunarodnykh otnoshenii vostochnoi Evropy XIV-XVI vv.* (Moscow, 1963).

2. For the most important works and the literature on the subject, see A.E. Presniakov, *Obrazovanie velikorusskogo gosudarstva (Ocherki po istorii XIII-XV stoletii)* (Petrograd, 1920); L.V. Cherepnin, *Obrazovanie russkogo tsentralizovannogo gosudarstva* (Moscow, 1960); and J.L.I. Fennell, *The Emergence of Moscow, 1304-1349* (London, 1968).

3. For the most important works and the literature on these relations, see V.B. Antonovych, *Monografii po istorii zapadnoi i iugo-zapadnoi Rossii*, I (Kiev, 1885); M. Hrushevs'kyi, *Istoriia Ukrainy-Rusy* (10 vols., offset rep. ed., New York, 1954-1958), IV *(XIV-XVI viky – Vidnosyny politychni)*; M.K. Liubavskii, *Litovsko russkii seim. Opyt po istorii uchrezhdeniia v sviazi s vnutrennim stroem i vneshneiu zhizn'iu gosudarstva* (Moscow, 1900); *idem, Ocherk po istorii Litovsko-russkogo gosudarstva do Liublinskoi unii vkliuchitel'no* (Moscow, 1910); A.E. Presniakov, *Lektsii po russkoi istorii* (2 vols., Moscow, 1938-1939), especially I, vyp. 1 *(Zapadnaia Rus' i Litovsko-russkoe gosudarstvo)*; P.G. Klepatskii, *Ocherki po istorii Kievskoi zemli (I. Litovskii period)* (Odessa, 1912); S. Kutrzeba, "Unia Polski z Litwą," *Polska i Litwa w dziejowym stosunku* (Cracow, 1914); O. Halecki, *Dzieje Unii Jagiellońskiej* (2 vols., Cracow, 1919-1920); N. Chubatyi, "Derzhavno-pravne stanovyshche ukrains'kykh zemel' Lytovs'koii derzhavy pid kinets' XIV st.," *Zapysky Naukovoho Tovarystva im. Shevchenka*, 134, 135, 144, and 145 (1924-1926) (and separate ed., L'viv, 1926); L. Kolankowski, *Dzieje Wielkiego Księstwa Litewskiego za Jagiellonów (I. 1377-1499)* (Warsaw, 1930); H. Paszkiewicz, *Jagiellonowie a Moskwa (I. Litwa a Moskwa w XIII i XIV wieku)* (Warsaw, 1933); S.M. Kuczyński, *Ziemie czernihowsko-siewierskie pod rządami Litwy (Praci Ukrains'koho Naukovoho Instytutu*, 38) (Warsaw, 1936); H. Jablonowski, *Westrussland zwischen Wilna und Moskau (Die politischen Tendenzen der russischen Bevölkerung des Grossfürstentums Litauen im 15 Jh.)* (Leiden, 1955); O.P. Backus, *Motives of West Russian Nobles in Deserting Lithuania for Moscow, 1377-1514* (Lawrence, Kansas, 1957); V.T. Pashuto, *Obrazovanie litovskogo gosudarstva* (Moscow, 1959); V.I. Picheta, *Belorussiia i Litva XV-XVI vv.* (Moscow, 1961); and J. Bardach, J. Ochmański, and O.P. Backus, *Lithuanie: Introduction bibliographique à l'histoire du droit et à l'ethnologie juridique*, (D/14) (Bruxelles, 1969).

4. A few specialized studies should be mentioned in this connection: M. Żdan, "Stosunki litewsko-tatarskie za czasów Witolda, w. ks. Litwy," *Ateneum Wileńskie* (cited hereafter as *AW*) 7, III-IV (1930), 529-601; S.M. Kuczyński, "Sine Wody," in *Księga ku czci Oskara Haleckiego wydana w XXV-lecie jego pracy naukowej* (Warsaw, 1935), 81-141; J. Puzyna, "W sprawie pierwszych walk litwinów z tatarmi o Rus' w

latach 1238-1243," *Przegląd Historyczno-Wojskowy* (cited hereafter as *PHW*) 9 (1937), 345-400; R. Batura, "Bor'ba Litovskogo velikogo kniazhestva protiv Zolotoi Ordy (Ot nashestviia polchishch Batiia do bitvy u Sinikh Vod)'' (Avtoreferat dissertatsii na soiskanie uchenoi stepeni kandidata istoricheskikh nauk) (Vilnius, 1972).

5. The notion of the "Tatar yoke'' has become an official one in Soviet historiography and in the history of early Russian literature. For a good example in the field of history, cf. the relevant subheadings such as "Bor'ba russkogo naroda protiv tataro-mongol'skogo iga i litovskoi agresii'' and "Osvobozhdenie Rusi ot tataro-mongol'skogo iga" in *Ocherki istorii SSSR (Period feodalizma IX-XV vv.)*, Part II (Moscow, 1953), 210 and 287. See also the title of Map 2 in that volume "Bor'ba severo-vostochnoi Rusi s tatarskim igom s serediny XIV v. do 1462 g." Two examples in the history of literature will suffice: M.N. Tikhomirov, V.F. Rzhiga, and L.A. Dmitriev, eds., *Povesti o Kulikovskoi Bitve* (Moscow, 1959) and the collective work *Slovo o Polku Igoreve i Pamiatniki Kulikovskogo Tsikla* (Moscow, 1966). For a work stressing Muscovy's role in the struggle against the "Tatar yoke," see I.B. Grekov, *Vostochnaia Evropa i upadok Zolotoi Ordy (na rubezhe XIV-XV vv.)* (Moscow, 1975).

6. The passage outlining Algirdas' political claims reads as follows: "Item postulabant, quod ordo locaretur ad solitudines inter Tartaros et Rutenos ad defendendum eos ab impugnacione Tatarorum et quod nihil iuris ordo sibi reservaret apud Rutenos, sed omnis Russia ad Letwinos deberet simpliciter pertinere; et dicebant: "Si postulata consequi poterimus, voluntatem Cesaris faciemus" (T. Hirsch, M. Töppen, and E. Strehlke, eds., *Scriptores Rerum Prussicarum*, II, 1963, 80).

7. Puzyna, *PHW*, 9 (1937), 345-400.

8. Liubavskii, *Ocherk...*, 13; Pashuto, *Obrazovanie...*, 378.

9. "Toi zhe zimy vziasha Tatarove vsiu zemliu litovskuiu, a samekh izbisha" (A.N. Nasonov, ed., *Novgorodskaia pervaia letopis' starshego i mladshego izvodov* (cited hereafter as *NPL*), (Moscow and Leningrad, 1950), 82.

10. Liubavskii, *Ocherk...*, 17-21; and Pashuto, *Obrazovanie...*, 391-393.

11. Liubavskii dated this transformation to coincide with the first annexation of Black Rus' in the 1240s (*Ocherk...*, 15). However, no evidence for an awareness of this political change can be found in the sources.

12. The use of this title begins in 1323. For the various examples, see I. Danilowicz, ed., *Skarbiec diplomatów... do... Dziejów Litwy, Rusi Litewskiej i ościennych im krajów* (2 vols., Wilno, 1860-1862), I, 153, 154, and 155ff., and K.E. Nap'erskii, ed., *Russko-livonskie akty* (St. Petersburg, 1868), 30-32 and 49-50. The statement of the *Bykhovets Chronicle* to the effect that "Grand Prince Viten ruled in the Grand Principality of Lithuania, Samogitia and Rus' " represents an assessment of Lithuanian-Ruthenian relations from the perspective of the mid-sixteenth century, when the *Bykhovets Chronicle* was composed; it cannot be utilized to date the transformation of the Lithuanian grand principality into a Lithuanian-Ruthenian state (*Polnoe sobranie russkikh letopisei* [cited hereafter as *PSRL*], XVII [1907], col. 490).

13. Antonovych, *Monografii...*, 47-58; M. Hrushevs'kyi, *Ocherk istorii Kievskoi zemli ot smerti Iaroslava do kontsa XIV stoletiia* (Kiev, 1891), 470-484; Hrushevs'kyi, *Istoriia Ukrainy-Rusy*, IV, 17-19 and 73-74.

14. The identification of Prince Fedor and his position toward Lithuania and the Horde is derived from two principal sources, the *Novgorodian Chronicles* ("Kievan Prince Fedor with a Tatar *basqaq*," *NPL*, 344; *PSRL*, IV [1848], 52), and from V.N. Beneshevich's "Selections" pertaining to Russian Church history from a Vatican Codex ("Fedor, brother of Gedymin," M. Priselkov and M. Fasmer,

"Otryvki V.N. Beneshevicha po istorii russkoi tserkvi XIV veka," *Izvestiia Otdeleniia russkogo iazyka i slovesnosti Imper. Akademii Nauk*, 21, I, [1916], 58). For additional comments on this problem, see Paszkiewicz, *Jagiellonowie a Moskwa*, 330; Kuczyński, *Ziemie...*, 16-17, n. 4, 6; Pashuto, *Obrazovanie...*, 396; and F.M. Shabul'do, "Vkliuchennia kyivs'koho kniazivstva do skladu lytovs'koi derzhavy u druhii polovyni XIV v.," *Ukrains'kyi istorychnyi zhurnal*, 1973, no. 6, 82.

15. For a discussion of this period of troubles, see Spuler, *Die Goldene Horde*, 109-121; Grekov and Iakubovskii, *Zolotaia orda...*, 261-293; and Safargaliev, *Raspad Zolotoi Ordy*, 101-136.

16. For an analysis of sources pertaining to the Lithuanian conquest of Ukrainian lands, the dating of the takeover of individual lands and the literature on the subject, see Antonovych, *Monografii...*, 74-132; N. Molchanovskii, *Ocherk izvestii o Podol'skoi zemle do 1434 goda* (Kiev, 1885), 169-227; Hrushevs'kyi, *Istoriia Ukrainy-Rusy*, IV, 14-19 and 63-99; Klepatskii, *Ocherki...*, 14-24; O. Andriiashev, "Narys istorii kolonizatsiii Kyivs'koi zemli do kintsia XV viku," in M. Hrushevs'kyi, ed., *Kyiv ta ioho okolytsia v istorii i pam'iatkakh (Zapysky Istorychnoi sektsii Ukrains'koi Akademii Nauk*, 22 (1926), 33-79, especially 62-63; and Kuczyński, *Ziemie...*, 15-28, 103-122, and 172-234.

17. "I tako, voiuia khitrostiu i skradyvaia, Olgerd mnogi zemli i mnogi mesta i grady i strany poplenil; ne tolma siloiu ieliko umenem voievasha" (*PSRL*, XV [1922/1965], col. 88).

18. The basic texts of the Tale, entitled *About the Podolian Land*, were included in the Supras'l' and Uvarov manuscripts of the *Lithuanian-Ruthenian Chronicles* (*PSRL*, XVII [1907], cols. 81-84 and 99-101); see also *PSRL*, 35 (1980): 66, 74. For an analysis of the texts of this Tale, see T. Sushyts'kyi, *Zakhidn'o-rus'ki litopysy iak pamiatky literatury (Zbirnyk Istorychno-Filolohichnoho Viddilu Ukrains'koi Akademii Nauk*, vyp. 2, parts I-II [Kiev, 1921-29], II, 305-317). A new volume of *Polnoe sobranie russkikh letopisei*, containing chronicles pertaining to the history of Belorussian and Ukrainian Rus', has been published (*PSRL*, XXXIII – Khroniki: Litovskaia i Zmoitskaia, i Bykhovtsa; Letopisi: Bakulabovskaia, Averki i Pantsyrnogo, N.N. Ulashchyk, ed., [Moscow, 1975]). These chronicles, however, were compiled at a later date than those which are crucial for and which have been utilized in this study. The materials of these chronicles, therefore, do not influence my findings.

19. For a survey of such views and interpretations, cf. Kuczyński, "Sine Wody," 85-93.

20. *Idem*, 130-133.

21. Kuczyński apparently disregarded the warning of Molchanovskii concerning the use of the testimony in later versions of the *Lithuanian-Ruthenian Chronicles* regarding the Battle of the Blue Water (*Ocherki...*, 178-179).

22. *PSRL*, XVII (1907), cols. 81 and 99.

23. *PSRL*, XV/1 (1922/1965), col. 75.

24. Hrushevs'kyi, *Istoriia Ukrainy-Rusy*, IV, 81-82; Kuczyński's hypothesis about the city of Zvenyhorod ("Blue Water Town") is rather artificial ("Sine Wody," 131).

25. The *yarlik* of Tohtamış is no longer extant. Its contents were deduced from later *yarliks* of the Crimean khans from the years 1481 and 1472; see A. Prochaska, "Z Witoldowych dziejów. Układ Witolda z Tochtamyszem 1397,"

Przegląd historyczny, 15, III (1912), 260. Hrushevs'kyi was the first to advance the hypothesis that Tohtamış issued such a *yarlik* (*Istoriia Ukrainy-Rusy*, IV, 87).

26. A discussion of Vytautas' foreign policy with regard to the Golden Horde can be found in J. Pfitzner, *Grossfürst Witold von Litauen als Staatsmann (Schriften der philosophischen Fakultät der deutschen Universität in Prag*, VI [Prague, 1930], 145-164). A general survey of Tatar-Lithuanian relations was provided by Żdan, *AW*, 7, III-IV (1930), 529-601. For the military aspect of the campaign, see V.G. Liaskoronskii, "Russkie pokhody v stepi udel'no-vechevoe vremia i pokhod kn. Vitovta na Tatar v 1399 g.," *Zhurnal Ministerstva narodnogo prosveshcheniia* (cited hereafter as *ZhMNP*) (1907), IX, 21-45; *idem*, "K voprosu o bitve kn. Vitovta s tatarami na r. Vorskle v 1399-m godu," *ZhMNP* (1908), XVI, 70-77. Liaskoronskii's studies on Vytautas' campaign and the Vorskla battle should be treated with caution because of their speculative character. For an analysis of international relations in Eastern Europe at the end of the fourteenth and in the early fifteenth century, including a discussion of the Battle on the Vorskla River, confer Grekov, *Vostochnaia Evropa...*, chpts. 2 and 3.

27. Presniakov, *Obrazovanie...*, 331ff.; Pfitzner, *Grossfürst Witold...*, 153.

28. The most important Western account of the events leading to the Battle on the Vorskla River and of the battle itself is to be found in the work of the fifteenth-century Polish historian Jan Długosz, *Historia Polonica, X, Opera Omnia*, III (1874), 526-529.

29. The individual Slavic accounts of this battle, both titled and untitled, may be conveniently referred to as the Tale about the Battle on the Vorskla River. This is how the corresponding texts in the *Lithuanian-Ruthenian Chronicles* were named by Sushyts'kyi, who devoted a special chapter to them (*Zakhidn'o-rus'ki litopysy...*, part II, 333-339). The chronologically earliest available accounts are those of the Muscovite chronicles: M.D. Priselkov, ed., the *Troitskaia letopis' (Rekonstruktsiia teksta)* (Moscow, 1950), 450-451; the *Sophia First Chronicle (PSRL*, V [1851], 251); the *Nikanor Chronicle (PSRL*, XXVII [1962], 89-90); the *Muscovite Codex of 1479 (PSRL*, XXV [1949], 229); the *Voskresensk Chronicle (PSRL*, VIII [1859], 72-73). Actually all the Muscovite accounts have as their source the version of the *Sophia First Chronicle*. The text of the *Troitskaia letopis'* represents a reconstruction.

The Lithuanian-Ruthenian version of the events is represented by the Tale in the *Lithuanian-Ruthenian Chronicles* (manuscript of the Supras'l' Monastery) compiled about the middle of the fifteenth century, based upon an "all Rus'" compilation from the early part of that century (Sushyts'kyi, *Zakhidn'o-rus'ki litopysy...*, part I, 55 and 120-121); for an analysis of the *Lithuanian-Ruthenian Chronicles*, see also V.A. Chamiarytski, *Belaruskiia letopisy iak pomniki literatury* (Minsk, 1969). Sushyts'kyi was of the opinion that the Tale about the battle on the Vorskla River contained in the Supras'l' manuscript was written at the end of the fourteenth century, quite possibly in 1399, because the author was well-acquainted with the details of the battle and may have participated in it (*Zakhidn'o-rus'ki litopysy...*, part II, 333-339).

The third group of accounts can be found in the Novgorodian chronicles. The earliest text was included in the *Novgorodian First Chronicle* of a later recension (*NPL*, 394-395) and the later one in the *Novgorodian Fourth Chronicle* based on a manuscript of the last quarter of the fifteenth or the beginning of the sixteenth century (*PSRL*, IV, vyp. 2 [1925], 384-386). Finally, the text of the *Russian Chronograph of 1512* represents an independent Tale (*PSRL*, XXII, 1 [1911], 423).

30. *PSRL*, XI (1897/1965), 172-174. For an English translation and analysis of the Tale in the *Nikon Chronicle* and its dating in scholarship until 1972, see J.

Pelenski, *Russia and Kazan: Conquest and Imperial Ideology (1438-1560s)* (The Hague and Paris, 1974), 139-143, n. 1 and 161-170. For a more recent dating and the identification of the compiler-editor of the original version of the *Nikon Chronicle*, namely the M.A. Obolenskii manuscript (Tsentral'nyi gosudarstvennyi arkhiv drevnikh aktov [Moscow], F. 201, no. 163), see the studies by B.M. Kloss who has established that the Obolenskii manuscript, which concludes with the entry for the events of 1520, had been written and compiled under the editorship of Metropolitan Daniil (1522-1539) in the late 1520s and the early 1530s ("Deiatel'nost' mitropolich'ei knigopisnoi masterskoi v 20-kh–30-kh godakh XVI veka i prois-khozhdenie Nikonovskoi letopisi," in O.I. Podobedova and G.V. Popov, eds., *Drevne-russkoe iskusstvo [Rukopisnaia kniga]* [Moscow, 1972], 318-337;"Mitropolit Daniil i Nikonovskaia letopis'," *Trudy Otdela drevnerusskoi literatury*, 28 [1974], 188-201; *Nikonovskii svod i russkie letopisi XVI-XVII vekov* [Moscow, 1980]). There is need for additional study of the *Nikon Chronicle* and the dating of its component parts. For a thoughtful but debatable assessment of the applicability of the concept "ideology" to the period from the fourteenth to the sixteenth century in connection with Pelenski's *Russia and Kazan...*, and Grekov's *Vostochnaia Evropa...*, confer G. Stökl, "Imperium und imperiale Ideologie – Erfahrungen am Beispiel des vorpetri-ischen Russland," in *Vom Staat des Ancien Régime zum modernen Parteienstaat, Festschrift für Theodor Schieder zu seinem 70. Geburtstag*, H. Berding, K. Düwell, L. Gall, W.J. Mommsen, and H.-U. Wehler, eds. (Munich and Vienna, 1978), 27-39.

31. Pfitzner, *Grossfürst Witold...*, 151-152.

32. For a discussion of the Muscovite theory of Bulgar-Kazan continuity, see Pelenski, *Russia and Kazan...*, 139-170.

33. For an account of the campaigns, see Paszkiewicz, *Jagiellonowie a Moskwa*, 414-433.

34. For a discussion of the political and ecclesiastical ramifications of the creation of a new metropolitanate of Kiev and its competition with Moscow, see K. Chodynicki, *Kościół prawosławny i Rzeczpospolita Polska (1370-1632)* (Warsaw, 1934), 11-49; D. Obolensky, "Byzantium, Kiev, and Moscow: A Study in Ecclesiastical Relations," *Dumbarton Oaks Papers*, 11 (1957), 21-78; I. Ševčenko, "Russo-Byzantine Relations after the Eleventh Century," *Proceedings of the International Congress of Byzantine Studies*, J.M. Hussey, D. Obolensky, and S. Runciman, eds. (London, 1967), 93-104; and F. Tienefeld, "Byzantinisch-russische Kirchenpolitik im 14. Jahrhundert," *Byzantinische Zeitschrift*, 67 (1974), 359-384.

35. Ždan, *AW*, 7, III-IV (1930), 595.

36. For two examples of such interpretations, see Kolankowski, *Dzieje...*, 19-20, and Grekov, *Ocherki...*, 61-62.

9

THE INCORPORATION OF THE UKRAINIAN LANDS OF KIEVAN RUS' INTO CROWN POLAND (1569) SOCIO-MATERIAL INTEREST AND IDEOLOGY (A REEXAMINATION)*

I

In 1569, the Ukrainian lands of Kievan Rus' (Podlachia,[1] Volynia, Bratslav province, and the Kievan land) were separated from the Grand Principality of Lithuania and incorporated into Crown Poland. This was accomplished in the course of the deliberations of the common Polish-Lithuanian Diet (*Sejm*) of Lublin (December 23, 1568/January 10, 1569 – August 12, 1569), which resulted in the conclusion of the Union of Lublin in 1569. These events had a profound impact on the history of the Poles, the Lithuanians, and the Eastern Slavs (primarily the Ukrainians, but also the Belorussians and the Russians). The general political and legal aspects of this incorporation, as well as the whole complex of problems surrounding the Polish-Lithuanian union, which received its definitive form only in the decisions of the Diet of Lublin, have intermittently attracted the attention of Polish, Russian, Ukrainian, and Belorussian historians – especially from the 1860s through the 1930s. Included was the related issue of the broader contest between Muscovite Russia and Poland-Lithuania for the lands of Rus' from the middle of the fifteenth century to the Truce of Iam Zapol'skii of January 1582. However, in spite of the obvious political interest which these problems evoked, the endeavors of historians have been most rewarding primarily in terms of publications of sources; they were seldom paralleled by equal achievements in the utilization and fruitful evaluation of these valuable source materials or other

---

* For illustrations pertaining to this chapter, see Plates 35, 36, 37, 38, 39.

151

theoretical and interpretative works. Not a single substantial monograph dealing with the Union of Lublin has been produced by scholarship, despite the fact that the most important sources pertaining to
this epoch-making event have been available for quite some time.[2]
The only monograph dedicated to the specific topic of this problem –
the incorporation of the Ukrainian lands of Kievan Rus' into Crown
Poland (1569) – by Oskar Halecki, is basically of a descriptive-
factual nature, albeit slightly tainted by its author's peculiar
conception of the "Jagiellonian idea."[3] In contrast, the Act of Krewo
(1385) and the early phase of this Polish-Lithuanian union have
received much more scholarly attention.[4] The evident neglect of the
problem of the relations between the Eastern Slavs, the Poles, and
the Lithuanians from the end of the fourteenth to the end of the
sixteenth century in professional literature after World War II may
be partially explained by the well-known decline of the historians'
preoccupation with traditional political and constitutional history, as
well as by a prevailing anti-historicist intellectual current and a
changing and nervous search for contemporary relevance in
historical events and developments.[5]

The obvious gaps in traditional scholarship and presentist
considerations are certainly insufficient reasons to justify the discriminatory treatment of two centuries of inter-Slavic relations. It is
difficult to conceive of a genuine and comprehensive understanding
of the subsequent relations between these peoples, as well as of their
political, social, and cultural history, without a proper and thorough
scholarly assessment of these two centuries, which represented a
period of very active intercourse between Muscovite Russia and
Poland-Lithuania and, along with the internal policies of the latter
with regard to Rus' territories, deserve to be rescued from the state
of oblivion to which they have been relegated without any serious
intellectual or professional substantiation.

The principal aims of this study are: First, to examine the
social and material motivations of the incorporation of the Ukrainian
lands of Kievan Rus' into Crown Poland, promulgated before the
Diet of Lublin and in the course of its debates and decision-making
process. Second, but of equal concern, are the historical, legal and
ideological justifications which were articulated by advocates as well
as opponents of this incorporation. Such an analysis should contribute to a better and more refined perception of the relationship of
Realpolitik and ideology – the two components in the argumentation

of the leading representatives of the Polish-Lithuanian ruling elite. Further examination should demonstrate which of the two factors, and to what degree, became incorporated into state documents issued in connection with the decisions of the Diet of Lublin and of King Zygmunt II August, and therefore eventually became integral elements of state law and official Jagiellonian ideology.

There seems to exist a basic consensus among historians that the Diet of Lublin transformed the legal relationship between Crown Poland and the Grand Principality of Lithuania, i.e., a Lithuanian-Ruthenian state, from a personal dynastic union (which had lasted from 1447 to 1492, and, after a brief interruption, from 1501 to 1569) to a real feudal-federal union.[6] The Union of Lublin provided the political and legal foundations for the Polish-Lithuanian Commonwealth until the age of partitions and was adjusted in the constitutional sense only in 1791. As a result of these arrangements, Crown Poland and the Grand Principality of Lithuania became a united commonwealth of nations.[7] A joint ruler was elected in common and crowned as Polish King and Grand Prince of Lithuania. A common parliament was instituted, and a common foreign policy was to be conducted henceforth. Poles and Lithuanians received the right of movement into the various territories of the Commonwealth, and a right to legally acquire possessions in Poland and Lithuania. However, considerable dualism still remained a significant feature of this federal union, for Lithuania – like Poland proper – retained a separate central administration, a separate treasury, army, local self-government, and her own legal system.

It is a matter of general knowledge that the Union of Lublin represented a compromise between the maximalist position of the great majority of the Polish ruling elite – who favored a complete incorporation of the Grand Principality of Lithuania into Crown Poland – and the strong independent line of the great Lithuanian magnates – who defended the sovereignty of Lithuania, as well as their socio-political interests against the Lithuanian, the Ukrainian, and the Belorussian nobility. It was a compromise much closer to the general Polish desires than to those of the Lithuanian magnates. The incorporation of the Ukrainian lands during the course of negotiations of the Diet of Lublin was a partial realization of the Polish maximalist position. At the same time, it symbolized the final outcome of a prolonged contest between Poland and Lithuania for the individual lands of Rus', which had its origins in the fourteenth century when Kazimierz the Great annexed Galician Rus' [8] The incorporation of the Rus' lands can also be viewed as a decisive and, in a certain sense, final phase in the protracted political and military struggle between Poland-Lithuania and Muscovite Russia for these lands.

The decisions of the Diet of Lublin and the Polish-Lithuanian ruler, King Zygmunt II August, to integrate the Ukrainian lands of Kievan Rus' into Crown Poland were set in motion after the failure of the first phase of negotiations between Poland and Lithuania regarding the union. During the night of March 1, 1569, the Lithuanian magnates, i.e., the Lithuanian Diet, under the leadership of Mikołaj Radziwiłł, the Red (*Rudy*), departed as a legal body. On the very same day, the Senate and the Chamber of Deputies demanded from the king the incorporation of Podlachia and Volynia into Crown Poland. The king reacted positively, ordering the senators and deputies from Podlachia to take their seats in the Crown Diet, and issuing a restitution privilege (in Latin) for the two lands, antedated March 5, 1569,[9] as well as a special *Uniwersał* of March 12, 1569.[10] A separate and final restitution privilege for Podlachia was the subject of later re-editing in connection with the preparation of similar Volynian and Kievan documents. It came out (in Latin, as well as in Polish) dated March 5, 1569.[11] Although the incorporations of Volynia and Podlachia were, in principle, decided upon and carried out simultaneously, the final wording and the confirmation statement for the Volynian restitution privilege were apparently postponed, since the document was issued (in Polish only) with the date of May 27, 1569.[12] The reasons for this may have been the resistance of the Lithuanian side and the resumption of negotiations. The texts of the Volynian and Kievan Privileges are very similar in formulation, and it may be assumed that the first was re-edited in conjunction with the annexation of the Kievan land and, therefore, also antedated.

Having succeeded in their efforts with regard to Podlachia and Volynia, the Polish side, i.e., the Chamber of Deputies and the majority of the Senate, with active support from the Volynian representatives, demanded the incorporation of the Kievan land. In spite of some opposition in the Polish Senate and protests from the Lithuanian side, the advocates of the absorption of the Rus' territories were fully successful in their endeavors and after several days of negotiations (June 2-5) were able to convince the king that the annexation of the Kievan land was legally justified and politically desirable. The restitution privilege for the Kievan land (issued both in Polish and in Latin) was officially dated June 6, 1569,[13] and appears to have been the concluding act of the last major territorial and power contest between Crown Poland and Lithuania.[14]

II

The relationship of socio-material interest and ideology in the motivations and justifications of the advocates and opponents of the incorporation of the Ukrainian lands of Kievan Rus' into Crown Poland has attracted only casual references in traditional scholarship. With his customary frankness, M. Hrushevs'kyi formulated the case for the exclusive material and social motivations of the Polish, as well as the Lithuanian, ruling establishment as follows:

> The problem of the annexation of Kiev reveals in full light the naked, completely unadorned egoism of the Polish policy. The most important subject of the debate was the question whether the annexation of Kiev would be *profitable for Poland* [italics M.H.]. Polish politicians were not concerned with ideology in spite of the fact that there was a good case on hand – i.e., the nobilities in Ukraine and Lithuania desired a union but were unable to break away from the influence of the lords [magnates]. The Poles of the sixteenth century left it to their descendants of the nineteenth century to glorify and apotheosize this "union" for posterity.
>   Acknowledging all this brutal ruthlessness and unadorned egoism of the Polish policy, I do not wish to idealize the other side – the opponents of the Union at the Diet of Lublin, the autonomists of the Grand Principality of Lithuania. Here too, egoistic class interests and the desire to continuously retain the government of the Grand Principality of Lithuania in the hands of the oligarchy – without having to share it with the Ruthenian magnates, their own nobility, or the Poles – were beginning to develop under the cover of Lithuanian patriotism.[15]

Hrushevs'kyi was not isolated in his emphasis on the concrete realities which guided the Polish, Lithuanian, Ukrainian, and Belorussian upper class representatives. Others expressed a similar view but in a less drastic manner.[16]

From the very beginning of the debates in the Diet regarding the annexation of Podlachia and Volynia, the issues of material interest and social privilege were of paramount importance. The Crown deputies and the Senate enticed the ruling groups in Podlachia and Volynia with exemptions from the execution of royal domains,[17] for which the executionist reform movement was waging an active, albeit only partially successful, struggle. These exemptions, as well as all other existing social privileges, were confirmed in the restitution privileges issued for Volynia, Podlachia, Bratslav province, and the land of Kiev. While utilizing the notion of material interest with regard to the magnates and nobility of the Ukrainian lands, the representatives of the Crown Diet refrained from articulating their own social and personal aims in these lands, and as a matter of fact, in the preliminary exchanges with the Lithuanian Diet, the acquisition of property and possessions in the Polish and Lithuanian territories was not a bone of contention and was resolved by the common Diet without special difficulties.[18] Actually, there was no compelling need for the Polish side to make direct references to this particular question, since the incorporation of any land would have automatically resulted not only in the application of Polish laws but also in the economic expansion of the Polish elite into the fully integrated territories.

The notions of profit and interest were also candidly employed in the major debate concerning the desirability of the incorporation of the city of Kiev, the ancient capital of Rus'.[19] Contrary to the total unanimity of the Polish Chamber of Deputies and the Senate with regard to the question of Podlachia and Volynia, the Kievan problem brought about a difference of opinion in the Polish political establishment. Whereas the Chamber of Deputies and a majority of the Senate favored the absorption of Kiev with its adjoining land, a minority – including some leading politicians such as Filip Padniewski, the archbishop of Cracow, and Stanisław Myszkowski, the palatine of Cracow – opposed the annexation of Kiev, arguing that this city should remain under Lithuanian authority, and that the Lithuanians alone should pay the costs of its defense, as well as the annual tribute to the "Scythians" (in reality the Tatars) for not raiding the Kievan land. The opposition pointed out that Crown Poland should not be subjected to financial obligations which are beyond its means, particularly when there is an obvious scarcity of funds.[20]

Those advocating the incorporation maintained that it is "extremely necessary" to join Kiev to Crown Poland[21]

> since it is evident that it is very important to the Commonwealth that Kiev should be under the power of the Polish Commonwealth inasmuch as Kiev is almost the gate to all the neighboring provinces, i.e., Volynia and Podolia, which holds back hostile incursions and serves those provinces as a watch tower and a fortified gate.[22]

The Polish deputies also contended that the military defense of Kiev would be jeopardized if Kiev were to remain under Lithuanian rule and maintained that "it will be of profit to the Commonwealth to take Kiev away from the Lithuanians, because if they [Lithuanians] [were to] keep it, they could easily rebel later on."[23] The arguments of both sides suggest that the concept of pure *Interessenpolitik* was an integral part of the political thought of the Polish ruling elite. This open advocacy of *Interessenpolitik* attests to the existence of essentially modern elements in the political theory of the Polish Renaissance, and at the same time brings to light the fundamental differences between Polish and Muscovite theoretical substantiations for political decision-making. The latter relied considerably on ideological justifications.

Material interest was also very much on the minds of the local elites of the four territories to be integrated into Crown Poland. Although the attitudes of the representatives of these territories toward incorporation did not vary significantly, the Podlachian nobility was most positively predisposed toward absorption into Crown Poland.[24] The attitudes of the Podlachian and Volynian nobility regarding real material concerns were expressed in their respective petitions at the Diet of Wilno in 1566. The two territories were particularly concerned by the land seizures, the mercenary attacks, and physical violence perpetrated by the inhabitants of Crown Poland and, especially, by the Mazovians in Podlachia and Volynia. The Podlachian delegates openly stated that if union with the Crown were not to materialize soon, Podlachia would become a "frontier land."[25] Similar complaints were advanced by the deputies of Volynia already at the second Diet of Wilno in 1551[26] and in even more explicit terms at the Diet of Grodno in 1568.[27] In order to alleviate these highly unfavorable and improper conditions, Volynians were requesting a common Diet with Poland.[28]

Throughout the common Polish-Lithuanian Diet of Lublin, the magnates and the nobility of the Ukrainian lands affected by the politics of incorporation most vigorously defended their socio-material interests and personal privileges (offices, appointments, grants, etc.). The success of their endeavors is reflected in the extensive and elaborate treatment of these matters in the incorporation documents, as well as in the continuation of all existing privileges and enjoyment of any favors resulting from their new status under the new political arrangements.[29] The extraordinary concern of the representatives of the Kievan and Volynian lands and the Bratslav province for their interests is most vividly attested in an interesting document, i.e., the king's reply of July 8, 1570 to the petition of the representatives of the lands in question to change the wording of the Recess of the Warsaw Diet of 1570 regarding the reconfirmation of the exemption of property owners from the execution of royal domains. Whereas the contested Recess stated quite clearly that the exemption from the execution was legally binding, the representatives of the Ukrainian lands insisted on the inclusion of an additional phrase, i.e., that the execution "will never [and in no way] affect them."[30] In his reply the king expressed no reservations about these demands in principle, but regretted that the Recess of the Diet had already been published and thus the requested change in wording regarding the reaffirmation of the exemption privilege could not be included in it. The king's response was meant to reassure the representatives of the Ukrainian lands that their freedoms and rights were confirmed in full accord with their wishes.

III

Polish representatives and the king at the Diet of Lublin justified the incorporation of the Ukrainian lands of Kievan Rus' into Crown Poland on the basis, among others, of historical claims which were closely correlated with legal theories and ideological assumptions of a secular nature. These historical claims rested primarily on the contention that the lands in question had at one time belonged to Poland and had only been illegally and temporarily separated from her. It was maintained that Polish rulers had exercised full authority over these territories in the past and that the estates of Crown Poland had always insisted on Poland's right to restitution.

The historical justifications formulated by the king in the incorporation documents issued for the Ukrainian lands appear to have been assiduously synchronized by professional lawyers. They reflect the arguments advanced by Polish deputies and senators at the Diet of Lublin, who asserted that "Podlachia and Volynia had been [a part of] the Crown a long time before Jagiełło,"[31] with the understanding that Podlachia represented a segment of Mazovia,[32] and further professed that "Kiev and this whole state had always belonged to the Crown...."[33] Therefore, it was not a coincidence that the marshal of the Chamber of Polish Deputies, Stanisław Czarnkowski, specifically requested that the incorporation documents be designated as restitution privileges, and not simply as decrees.[34] The king responded favorably to this proposal, and the documents were so phrased; this signified an official acceptance and confirmation of the historical restitution theory advocated by Polish representatives. This theory was first formulated quite precisely and in detail for Podlachia and Volynia in the "short" restitution privilege which was approved by the Chamber of Deputies on March 26, 1569, and issued (in Latin only) with the date of March 5, 1569.[35] Contrary to the two individual restitution privileges for Podlachia and Volynia which followed, the "short" document was not included in the contemporary published collections of laws, statutes and constitutions. It states that, at the request of the councilors of the estates of the Kingdom of Poland and the delegates of the Rus' lands, the king decided that

> we should reintegrate and restore the provinces of Volynia and Podlachia, which in times past belonged by full right to the Kingdom of Poland. We, therefore, are mindful of our oath by which we bound ourselves to all the inhabitants of the kingdom to recover and to reintegrate into the aforesaid kingdom to the best of our ability whatever has been alienated and separated from the kingdom. And we have learned both from the ancient documents and from the privilege of Zygmunt [Kiejstutowicz], Grand Prince of Lithuania, our great-uncle, that the land or province of Volynia belonged to the Kingdom of Poland by full, certain and undoubted right; and likewise the land or province of Podlachia which always by full, certain and undoubted right belonged to the kingdom, even before the reign of Władysław Jagiełło, our great-grandfather, and throughout his reign and also in the reign of Władysław, his son, our great-uncle. Afterwards the

> holy King Kazimierz [Jagielloñczyk], our grandfather, willed
> it to be separated from part of the kingdom, that is Mazovia,
> and thus torn away from the body to which it belonged,
> evidently on the pretext that he held undivided rule over
> both nations; although the estates of the kingdom repeatedly
> protested and did not consent. The estates of the kingdom
> have continually requested and sought the return of that
> land, both from our said grandfather and from the kings of
> Poland and grand princes of Lithuania who succeeded him,
> our predecessors, and from us.[36]

This first restitution privilege issued jointly for Podlachia and
Volynia was clear in intent, however hastily prepared. Eventually the
acts of incorporation required a restatement of the justifications and
the privileges issued for the two provinces individually. Matters
became complicated as the Bratslav province was adjoined to Volynia
and the text of the Volynian restitution privilege had to be rephrased
to cover the territorial aggrandizement. Furthermore, the restitution
privilege for Volynia underwent modifications deemed necessary on
account of the annexation of the Kievan land. However, Polish political leaders and lawyers took utmost care to preserve a remarkable
uniformity of definitions and concepts in all restitution privileges.
The individual Podlachian and Volynian restitution privileges were
signed by the king on March 28, 1569.[37] The Volynian document
underwent several re-editings before it received its definitive form
in early June of the same year; it was finally antedated May 27,
1569.[38] A comparison of the crucial passages pertaining to Polish
historical claims in the two documents reveals a process of continuous reformulation of the justifications before they became the law of
the Commonwealth.[39] In the preamble to both documents the king
expressly stated that he acted upon the request of the estates of the
Kingdom of Poland and the representatives of the two lands in
question when he decided to restore and reintegrate the latter under
the sovereignty of the Crown of Poland.

Podlachian Restitution Privilege

> ... that we should restore and reintegrate to the original body
> and unity of the Kingdom of Poland the land of Podlachia,
> which in times past belonged by full and certain right to the
> Polish kingdom. We, therefore, are mindful of our oath by
> which we bound ourselves to all inhabitants of the Crown to

recover and to reintegrate into the aforesaid kingdom to the best of our ability whatever has been separated or alienated from the aforesaid Crown. And we know well that the land of Podlachia always belonged to the Crown of Poland by perfect right [*wiecznie prawem doskonałym*], even before the reign of King Władysław Jagiełło, our great-grandfather, and throughout his reign, and likewise in the reign of Władysław, his son and our great-uncle. Afterwards the holy King Kazimierz [Jagiellończyk] willed it to be separated from part of the kingdom, that is Mazovia, and thus torn away from the body to which it belonged, evidently on the pretext that he held undivided rule over both nations; although the estates of the Crown opposed this and did not consent. The estates of the Crown have continually requested and sought the return of that land to the Crown, both from our said grandfather and from the kings of Poland and grand princes of Lithuania, our predecessors, and from us. We have decided, therefore, that this land of Podlachia, with all its castles, fortresses, cities, towns, villages, lands, and districts and the appurtenances and appendancies of all these, all and singular, by whatever name or names called, belonging and appertaining in ancient times and now in any way by any reason or right to the same province or any part thereof (so that the general terms may not detract from the specific terms, nor the specific from the general), and with all its right and property, should be reintegrated and reduced to its original state and restored to the same Kingdom of Poland, as to its original and true body and community under its rule, and to the property and indivisible unity [of Poland], as the right, portion, and property and title of the Crown.[40]

Volynian Restitution Privilege

... that we should restore and reintegrate to the original body and unity of the Crown, that is, the Kingdom of Poland, the land of Volynia, which in times past belonged by full and certain right to the Polish Kingdom. We, therefore, are mindful of our oath by which we bound ourselves to all inhabitants of the Crown to recover and to reintegrate into the aforesaid kingdom to the best of our ability whatever has been separated or alienated from the aforesaid Crown. And we know well both from many ancient documents and letters and from the privilege of Zygmunt [Kiejstutowicz], Grand Prince of Lithuania, our great-uncle, that the land of Volynia with all its appendancies should belong to the Polish Crown by full, certain and undoubted right (*całym a zupełnym i niewątpliwym prawem*), since this land even before the reign of Władysław Jagiełło, our great-grandfather, and throughout his reign, and likewise in the reign of Władysław, the honorable and memorable Polish and Hungarian king, his son and our great-uncle, belonged to the Crown and was regarded as one and indivisible body with the Polish Crown and enjoyed the rights and the liberties of the Crown. And King Kazimierz [Jagiellończyk], our grandfather, who is honorably remembered, willed it to be separated from the Crown of Poland as from its own body, evidently on the pretext that he held undivided rule over both nations; although the estates of the Crown opposed this and did not legally consent to this. The estates of the Crown have continually requested and sought to restore and adjoin this land to the Crown, both from our said grandfather and from other Polish kings and Lithuanian grand princes, our predecessors, and from us....

And we have decided, [therefore], that this land of Volynia, that is, the Palatinates of Volynia and Bratslav and all the citizens of the aforesaid land, all and singular, be released and freed forever from allegiance to authority, from obligations and from obedience to the Grand Principality of Lithuania and returned to the Polish Kingdom and [be made] equal with equals and a free people [similar to] the free people [of the Kingdom of Poland] with all its castles, fortresses, cities, towns, villages, lands and districts and the appurtenances and appendancies and properties of all these, all and singular, by whatever name or names called, of the aforesaid land of Volynia or any part thereof, belonging to them in ancient times, by whatever custom, law or means (so that the general terms may not detract from the specific terms, nor the specific from the general) with all the rights, dominions and properties of this land of Volynia, that is the Palatinates of Volynia and Bratslav be reintegrated and reduced to its original state and restored to the aforesaid Kingdom of Poland as to its original and true body and community under its rule, and to the property and indivisible unity [of Poland], as the right, portion, and property and title of the Crown.[41]

Polish historical claims to Podlachia and Volynia were based upon selected historical events and previous historical claims, both of which became integrated into the Polish historical-legal restitution theory. In the case of Podlachia, the claims dating before the times of Jagiełło, must have referred to Ruthenian-Polish border rivalries and struggles of the late twelfth and thirteenth centuries when parts of this territory came briefly under the control of Polish princes. For example, the city of Dorohychyn and its adjoining land were occupied by Konrad of Mazovia in the years 1235-1236 and then transferred by him to the sovereignty of the Teutonic Order in early 1237. Danylo of Galicia subsequently drove the Teutonic Knights out of this city and there he received the royal crown from Pope Innocent IV in 1253. In 1391 Jagiełło gave the Dorohychyn land to Janusz of Mazovia as a Lithuanian feudal possession but Vytautas recovered this territory in 1392. Bolesław of Mazovia acquired the Dorohychyn land after the death of Zygmunt Kiejstutowicz and held it for several years (1440-1443), until the financial settlement with Kazimierz Jagiellończyk returned it again to the Grand Principality of Lithuania. These temporary transfers of the Dorohychyn land to the sovereignty of Mazovian princes made it necessary to include a specific statement in the restitution privilege to the effect that the Podlachian land was separated from Mazovia. In addition, the endeavors of the Polish nobility to colonize Podlachia had made considerable inroads that resulted in legal adjustments. Although Podlachia was legally part of the Lithuanian state, the Dorohychyn land began to apply Polish law restrictively after 1444 and, beginning with 1516, without limitations. The other Podlachian territory, i.e., the Bielsk land, accepted some elements of Polish law in 1501 and embraced it completely in 1547. In short, Polish political penetration and objective legal influence in Podlachia made her a natural object of Polish claims and ambitions.[42]

In contrast to Podlachia, Volynia was not as much affected by Polish colonization and law by the middle of the sixteenth century. Polish claims to this Rus' land were rather tenuous and amounted merely to historical antecedents of short-lasting and contested Polish sovereignty over Volynia. The reference in the restitution privilege to the times before Jagiełło probably related to the Polish-Lithuanian competition for Volynia in connection with the Polish expansion into the territories of Galician-Volynian Rus' during the reign of Kazimierz the Great. Poland raised claims to Volynia again after the death of Vytautas (1430). In particular, the struggle between Świdrygiełło and Zygmunt Kiejstutowicz, the contenders to the Lithuanian grand principality, provided ample opportunity for

Polish intervention. The Volynian restitution privilege refers vaguely to the acts of the Union of 1432-1434, when Zygmunt Kiejstutowicz agreed that after his death the Grand Principality of Lithuania would come under the sovereignty of the Polish Crown. Actually the authors of the Volynian restitution privilege interpreted the documents of Zygmunt Kiejstutowicz very broadly. These documents did not specify that Volynia should be treated any differently from other territories of the Grand Principality of Lithuania. The only exception was the land of Podolia, which was conceded to Poland without any reservations.[43] Furthermore, there is enough evidence to attest that in 1436 Świdrygiełło volunteered to turn over Volynia to Poland in exchange for the recognition of his rule in other Rus' lands and for the termination of Polish support for Zygmunt Kiejstutowicz. The murder of the latter in 1440 prevented the Poles from exerting concerted pressure on Kazimierz Jagiellończyk to incorporate Volynia. Polish leaders did not succeed in their Volynian efforts and suffered a great disappointment when Volynia became a part of the Lithuanian grand principality after the death of Świdrygiełło in 1452. The Polish-Lithuanian controversy over Volynia was apparently settled in 1454, when both sides accepted a political compromise according to which Lithuania kept Volynia and the Bratslav province, whereas Poland received western Podolia and parts of the Volynian area.[44] However, the Polish penetration of Podolia was utilized during the Diet of Lublin to raise additional claims to the Bratslav province. Polish representatives not only maintained that Bratslav and Vynnytsia "had always belonged to the Kingdom" and the Crown,[45] but also stated quite specifically that "the Bratslav palatinate...had belonged to Podolia since antiquity...."[46] The compromise of 1454 settled the Polish-Lithuanian contest for Volynia for more than a century, until the Diet of Warsaw in 1563-1564, at which time the Poles resumed their claims to this land, as well as to Podlachia.

The Lithuanian representatives at the Diet of Lublin countered Polish pretensions to the two lands with their own set of legal arguments, declaring the seizure of Volynia and Podlachia as improper and illegal. While conceding that Podlachia had been given at certain periods to the princes of Mazovia as a security, they emphasized that this land was under the sovereignty of Lithuanian princes since time immemorial, and that it had been returned to Lithuania a long time ago.[47] The Lithuanians insisted, quite correctly, upon the invalidation of Polish claims to Podlachia and Volynia because they were not even mentioned during the conclusion of the Union of Mielnik in 1501 (which incidentally was not ratified by the Grand Principality of Lithuania).[48] Moreover, the most interesting argument advanced by the Lithuanians, in defense of their rights to Volynia, was the statement that "the Volynian land is settled by the Lithuanian and Ruthenian nations and the distinguished princes from the dynasties of Olel'ko, Olgerd, Narymunt, and Korybut, and it has been defended by us against our foes to the present time."[49] Whereas the reference to the princely dynasties was a traditional practice, the emphasis on the ethnic origins of the inhabitants – factually correct and justified – attests to the Lithuanian representatives' cognizance of national concepts, as well as the political value of their implementation.

IV

Following the incorporation of Podlachia and Volynia, the Polish ruling elite embarked upon the annexation of the Kievan land. Since there was evidently no legal basis for this step,[50] new legal claims and political-ideological justifications had to be raised. An examination of these claims, which were formulated to some degree on the pattern of those advanced with regard to Podlachia and Volynia, is crucial for the understanding of the entire problem of Poland's eastern policies and ambitions. On May 12, 1569, the first reference was made to certain privileges according to which Kiev had allegedly belonged to the Crown.[51] According to the Diary of the Diet, Czarnkowski, the marshal of the Chamber of Deputies, went further at a meeting between the deputies and the king on May 28, 1569, at which time he presented to the king "old privileges and proofs that Kiev and this whole state always belonged to the Crown and that all their princes were vassals (*omagiales*) of the king and the Crown...."[52] Hrushevs'kyi speculated that Czarnkowski was alluding to a charter of the Kievan prince Volodimer from the year 1388, according to which the latter had taken a vassal's oath to Jagiełło.[53] This, however, seems to be a narrow interpretation of the marshal's statement which was rather sweeping ("old privileges and proofs") and intentionally ambiguous. On June 2, 1569, the king considered executionist demands pertaining to Kiev which were presented by the Senate and a Commission of four deputies appointed to review this matter.[54] The following day the Chamber of Deputies "entreated that the king annex (*attribuat*) Kiev with its appurtenances to the kingdom as being a province which from antiquity has paid tribute to the kingdom and whose princes used to render homage to our kings, which appears readily from the privileges laid before the King's Majesty...."[55] The Senate followed up with the demand to annex (*attribuat*) Kiev, since it had been a member and part of the Polish Kingdom in ancient times.[56] The arguments regarding the homage allegedly rendered by Kievan princes to Polish kings, and the tribute paid to the Polish Kingdom, were obscure and certainly could not be supported by any evidence other than that found in Polish interpretations of certain events in the relations between Rus' and Poland during the Kievan period in Polish historical works, especially the writings of Jan Długosz and Marcin Kromer.

An example involving tribute will suffice to illustrate how Polish parliamentary politicians arrived at most of their claims. In 1018, the Polish king Bolesław the Valiant conducted a campaign against Kievan Rus' and was able to occupy the city of Kiev.[57] Commenting upon this event, Długosz praised Bolesław's generosity and wisdom with regard to the defeated Russes and asserted, without apparent justification, that "he imposed a modest tribute" on Iaroslav, the prince of Kievan Rus'.[58] Later Kromer simply repeated this allegation, quoting Długosz as his source.[59] This, as well as other similar statements about collection of money in Rus', was utilized as an argument to develop the claim about the tribute-paying princes of Kievan Rus'.

Of all the Polish legal claims raised with respect to Kiev, the one based upon the law of conquest is the most intriguing and very significant for the understanding of medieval and early modern political theory in Eastern Europe, as well as in general.[60] This claim rested on the idea that conquest constituted legal grounds for possession, and Polish representatives added it to other juridical claims advanced with regard to Kiev and all of Rus'. The first enunciation of the theory of law by conquest was made on June 3, 1569, by the deputies of the Chamber, who stated that "it is established from ancient chronicles that the city [Kiev] had thrice been taken and laid waste by Polish kings."[61] The senators supporting the annexation of Kiev were even more explicit on June 5, 1569, by citing alleged examples "which proved with what great prowess ancient Polish kings conquered [*expugnavisse*] Kiev.... The prowess and perseverance of our ancestors who for so many years advised their kings to conquer Kiev and to subdue Prussia were recited."[62] This view was spelled out clearly by Czarnkowski in his remarkable opening oration to the king before the Diet on January 10, 1569.[63] Czarnkowski praised the valor of ancient Polish rulers who "acquired by arms the whole of Rus' and many parts of Germany...."[64] Whereas the statement may have been oratorical and platitudinal, it reflected a traditional and current assumption, apparently widely shared. Modern historians expressed astonishment about three conquests of Kiev and attempted to correct Polish parliamentary politicians in factual terms by pointing out that Polish kings had taken Kiev only twice.[65] Hrushevs'kyi even drew attention to the sources expressing such views, namely the historical works of Długosz and Kromer.[66] However, Polish parliamentary politicians knew quite well what they were doing when they were referring to these Kievan conquests. Whereas their statements may have been brief and based upon manipulated evidence, their aim was to establish the legality of the annexation of Kiev on the basis of the law of conquest and to lay foundations for Polish pretensions to the entirety of Rus'. In spite of its being based on an obvious act of violence, the law of conquest was a common legal idea among a variety of peoples and states. It can be traced back to the "nobler peoples" of antiquity (principally the Greeks and the Romans). Conquest-law was also exercised by Western Christian states in the Middle Ages, and it is even evident in early modern Europe. Although this legal theory may have emanated from the assumption that "might makes right," it was viewed by contemporary rulers and jurists as perfectly acceptable, devoid of any negative moral connotations. It is worthwhile to point out that the Muscovite state among others utilized the law of conquest to justify its annexation of the Kazan Khanate.[67]

Since the Kievan problem is of overriding importance for an understanding of official Polish attitudes towards the lands of Rus', as well as for the perception of the Polish legal and ideological position in the contest between Muscovite Russia and Poland-Lithuania for the lands in question, it will be most appropriate at this point to compare the crucial passages from the two texts (Latin and Polish) of the Kievan restitution privilege, issued by the king at the request of the Polish estates and those favoring the annexation of Kiev, and both dated June 6, 1569.

Kievan Restitution Privilege (translation of the Latin text)

... that we should reintegrate and restore the whole province or land of Kiev, together with the castle and the city called Kiev and all the other castles, fortresses, cities and towns and all their appurtenances which in times past by full right belonged to the Kingdom of Poland. We, therefore, are mindful of our oath by which we bound ourselves to all the inhabitants of the kingdom to recover and to reintegrate into the aforesaid kingdom, to the best of our ability, whatever has been alienated and separated from the kingdom. And we have learned also from the most ancient chronicles and written documents that in the time of the happy reign of Kazimierz [Jagiellończyk], the great king of Poland, our predecessor, the land or province of Kiev as the head [*caput*] of the lands of Rus', Podolia and Volynia, together with the aforesaid lands, came to the lands of the kingdom and the Crown of Poland and that it was perpetually united, incorporated and integrated by the aforesaid King Kazimierz; learning also that the illustrious princes of Kiev, as appears from their documents, preserved in the treasury of the kingdom and which we ourselves saw and heard read publicly in the Senate, well preserved and above suspicion, had promised and sworn to the late serene King Władysław, our great-grandfather, and to his successors and the Crown of Poland, that they would be faithful and subject, and that this land of Kiev with all its appurtenances should return after their death to the aforesaid king and Crown. And so from this and other proofs by which this land of Kiev is shown to have belonged to the Kingdom of Poland by full, certain and undoubted right until the reign of the aforesaid holy Władysław Jagiełło, the late king of Poland, our great-grandfather and in the beginning of his rule, and later in the reign of the same king, doubtless because he then ruled over Poles and Lithuanians together, Kiev was separated, negligently as it were, from its proper body, namely the Crown of Poland, and gradually joined to Lithuanian authority; we have decided, [therefore], that this land or province of Kiev with all its ancient appurtenances with the castle and the city of Kiev and with all other castles, fortresses, cities, towns, villages, lands and districts and the appurtenances and appendancies of all these, all and singular, by whatever name or names called, belonging and appertaining in ancient times and now in any way by any reason or right to the same land or province of Kiev or any part thereof (so that the general terms may not detract from the specific terms, nor the specific from the general), and with all its rights and property should be reintegrated and reduced to its original state and restored to the same Kingdom of Poland as to its original and true body and head as the right, portion, and property and the title of the Crown by right and as a hereditary property. We, therefore, of our certain knowledge and spontaneous and special will, by these present letters and henceforth by law and as a hereditary property, restore and reintegrate [these lands and provinces] as the right portion, property and title of the Crown of the Kingdom of Poland, and we restore, join and incorporate [them] into one undivided body forever by virtue and authority of these presents, so that henceforth [these lands] can never be separated, nor ought ever be separated, from their true and lawful and original body and head, namely the Kingdom of Poland, either in whole or any part thereof.[68]

Kievan Restitution Privilege (translation of the Polish text)

... that we should restore and reintegrate to the original body and unity of the Crown, that is the Kingdom of Poland, the land and the principality of Kiev, which in times past belonged by full and certain right to the Polish Crown. We, therefore, are mindful of our oath by which we bound ourselves to all inhabitants of the Crown to recover and to reintegrate into the aforesaid kingdom, to the best of our ability, whatever has been separated or alienated from the aforesaid Crown. And we know well what everyone can obviously ascertain from all ancient chronicles and documents, that Kiev has been and still is the head [*głowa*] and the major city of the land of Rus', and that the whole land of Rus' [*ruska ziemia wszystka*] has been adjoined to the Crown of Poland among her other foremost members since times past by other predecessors, the Polish kings, partially by means of struggle [*iż częścią walkę*] partially on account of voluntary submissions and inheritances from some vassal princes, who had torn it apart among themselves, before it was united with the Crown and returned to its property, as anyone can openly ascertain from the privileges which are preserved in our treasury, and among which there are many which namely attest that the land and principality of Kiev should always belong to the Crown of Poland by perfect right [*wiecznie prawem doskonałym*], as it had always belonged until the reign of King Władysław Jagiełło, our predecessor, who evidently on the pretext that he held undivided rule over Poles and Lithuanians willed the land and principality of Kiev, which were torn from the Crown of Poland, as from their body, to be joined to the Grand Principality of Lithuania, although the estates of the Crown did not consent to this. The estates of the Crown have continually requested and sought to restore and adjoin this land to the Crown, both from our said grandfather and from other Polish kings and Lithuanian grand princes, our predecessors and from us.... And we have decided, therefore, that this land and principality of Kiev and all the citizens of the aforesaid land, all and singular, be released and freed forever from allegiance to authority, from obligations and from obedience to the Grand Principality of Lithuania and returned to the Polish Kingdom and [be made] equal with equals and a free people [similar] to the free people [of the Kingdom of Poland], with all their castles, fortresses, cities, towns, villages, lands and districts and the appurtenances and appendancies and properties of all these, all and singular, by whatever name or names called, of the aforesaid land and principality of Kiev, or any part thereof, belonging to them in ancient times, by whatever custom, law or means (so that the general terms may not detract from the specific terms, nor the specific from the general) with all the rights, dominions and properties of this land and principality of Kiev, be reintegrated and reduced to its original state and restored to the aforesaid Kingdom of Poland as its original and true body and community under its rule, and to the property and indivisible unity [of Poland], as the right, portion and property and title of the Crown.[69]

There are considerable differences between the two cited excerpts and, in fact, between the entire Latin and Polish versions. The Latin text is rather brief and deals only with the general question of the restitution of the Kievan land. The Polish version is much more extensive and includes the enumeration of the confirmed rights and privileges, with all the necessary specifications, which were extended to the magnates and the nobility of the Kievan land. In this respect, it is reminiscent of the Volynian restitution privilege, which was issued in Polish only. Both texts of the Kievan restitution privilege stress that Kiev allegedly belonged to Poland, that the city of Kiev is the capital of the Rus' lands, that it was "unlawfully" separated from the Crown in the reign of Władysław Jagiełło – something that did not, in fact, occur – and, finally, that it is being justly reintegrated and

restored to the Polish Kingdom. However, several significant
elements which are lacking in the Latin text have been incorporated
in the Polish text: (1) the reference to voluntary submissions and inheritances from vassal princes in Rus'; (2) emphasis on the new
status of equality and liberty which the citizens, namely the magnates
and the nobility of the Kievan land, similar to those of Volynia,
acquired by becoming subjects of the Crown; (3) the inclusion of the
claim to Kiev based on the law of conquest; (4) the statement that
Kiev is still the head of all Rus' lands; and finally (5) the claim that
the whole land of Rus' allegedly belonged to the Polish Kingdom.
The combination of these five elements makes the Kievan restitution
privilege an outstanding ideological document of the late Jagiellonian
period, in which the eastern aspect of the "Jagiellonian idea" was
most clearly and concisely defined. Since this document was included
in all contemporary collections of laws and statutes, it not only
became a document of official state ideology but also received the
widest possible circulation among the Polish ruling, as well as the
educated, class.

V

Polish claims to Kiev and all the land of Rus' were formulated
not only for the purpose of justifying the annexation of the
Ukrainian lands of Kievan Rus' to Crown Poland, but also as a response to the Muscovite challenge in the historical conflict between
Muscovite Russia and Poland-Lithuania for the lands of Rus'.[70]
Whereas the political and military struggle was conducted with the
aim of conquering as many individual lands and cities as possible, the
conceptual contest was waged for the heritage of the entirety of Rus'.
Although Poland-Lithuania had competed with Muscovy for Rus'
territories during the reign of Kazimierz Jagiellończyk, the theoretical confrontation dates from the beginning of the sixteenth century
(1503-1504). At that time, Ivan III began to advance claims to all the
lands of Rus', relying on the concept of uninterrupted dynastic
continuity of the Riurikides, on the Muscovite theory of succession
(*translatio*) from Kievan Rus' through (Rostovia)-Suzdalia-
Vladimiria to Muscovy, and on traditional patrimonial law. The
Muscovite ruler maintained that the entire land of Rus' was his
patrimony and that all the lands of Rus' under Polish-Lithuanian
sovereignty, including those of Kiev and Smolensk, were his

patrimonial possessions.[71] Already at that time the Polish side regarded this claim, as well as the Muscovite ruler's insistence to be addressed as "Sovereign of all Rus'," as unjustified, since the larger part of Rus' was then under the sovereignty of the Polish Kingdom, i.e., the Polish-Lithuanian state.[72] The Muscovite court continued to advance its claims to Kiev and all the Rus' lands throughout the sixteenth century until the Diet of Lublin.[73] These claims became integral elements of Muscovite political thought, culminating in the proposition that Moscow was the second Kiev.[74] The Polish representatives at the Diet of Lublin were certainly familiar with Moscow's appreciation of the strategic and ideological significance of Kiev. They, therefore, vigorously argued for its annexation "because the Muscovite anxiously desires to take over Kiev, the former capital of Rus'."[75]

The Muscovite danger not only played a decisive role in the incorporation of the Ukrainian lands, but was also a determining factor in the conclusion of the Union of Lublin. It was utilized to convince Lithuanians that the union would serve to strengthen the common defense of Poland and Lithuania. Stanisław Karnkowski, the bishop of Cuiavia, made this point quite explicit by observing "that our Muscovite foe... has always been afraid of this union and has closely followed [its development]...."[76] In the early 1580s, i.e., in the course of the final stage of the Livonian War and the siege of Pskov, the same Polish politician Karnkowski, by then archbishop of Gniezno, openly acknowledged that "this [war] with the Muscovite... has driven Lithuania into the union...."[77] The Polish-Lithuanian competition for the lands of Rus' acquired a new dimension during the Livonian War. By that time it became quite obvious that Lithuania was unable to offer effective resistance to the Muscovite advance into the Rus' territories, as exemplified by the conquest of Polotsk in 1563. Thus, Poland had to fill the political vacuum, and in order to do so successfully it was necessary for her to formulate new justifications for the annexation of Kiev, as well as for her presence in the realm of Kievan Rus'. There is no doubt that both Muscovy's and the Polish claims to "the whole land of Rus'" represented ideological justifications of the two countries' expansionist drives to the West and East respectively, which were bound to result in major confrontations and collisions.

VI

It appears from the available materials pertaining to the Diet of Lublin that religious and national considerations were of secondary importance in the political statements and decision-making of the Polish supporters of the annexation of the Ukrainian lands of Kievan Rus', as well as of those who were most directly affected by them, namely the members of the local elites. The king and the Polish representatives at the Diet abstained from injecting any preferences with regard to the religious and national issues in the course of the parliamentary debates. They tended to respond positively to requests and demands from the lands in question as long as this served their political goals. However, certain religious and national policies were advocated and implemented by the king and the Polish ruling elite immediately before and after the Diet of Lublin, with the aim of creating a favorable climate for the cause of the Polish-Lithuanian union, as well as for the incorporation of the Ukrainian lands into Crown Poland.

These policies grew out of the traditionally benevolent approach of the Jagiellonian rulers toward the adherents of the Orthodox religion and their Church in the Grand Principality of Lithuania and in Crown Poland. The Jagiellonians and the political elites of Poland and Lithuania respected the property rights of the Orthodox Church and never used secularization as a weapon to undermine the position of that church. This attitude reflected their general predisposition toward private property rights, which they tended to observe more strongly than their Muscovite counterparts.[78] The Jagiellonians were well aware that domestic tranquility in both countries, and the successes of their foreign policy in the East, depended upon a correct treatment of their own Orthodox subjects. Aside from certain discriminatory decisions of the Union of Horodło (1413), which were retained in the privileges of 1547 and 1551 issued by Zygmunt II August, according to which the rights of the Orthodox to obtain certain types of the highest offices (palatine, castellan, membership in the highest secret council) were curtailed,[79] Jagiellonian rulers such as Kazimierz Jagiellończyk, Zygmunt I, and Zygmunt II August attempted to maintain good relations with their upper-class Orthodox subjects. Zygmunt I even circumvented the established legal norms and appointed distinguished Orthodox magnates, among them Prince Konstantyn Ostrozhs'kyi, to the highest offices.[80]

When the problem of the Polish-Lithuanian union became acute at the beginning of the 1560s, Zygmunt II August issued two important privilege charters for the Orthodox secular upper class of the Grand Principality of Lithuania. The first, granted at the Diet of Wilno on June 7, 1563, extended to the Orthodox magnates and nobility of the Lithuanian, Ukrainian, and Belorussian nationality full and equal political rights.[81] The second, issued at the Diet of Grodno on July 1, 1568, reconfirmed the equal political rights of the Orthodox secular elite groups in the most definite and unequivocal manner.[82] This document was designed to influence the attitudes of the Orthodox and to obtain their positive response to the conclusion of the union.[83] The same can be said about the privilege extended by Zygmunt II August to Orthodox Ukrainian burghers of the city of L'viv on May 20, 1572, at the Diet of Warsaw, a privilege abolishing the legal limitations preventing them from being elected to and holding important city offices.[84] The king extended his consent to the respective requests of the Orthodox L'viv burghers, by granting them political rights equal to other citizens on account of the conclusion of the Polish-Lithuanian union (*laudabilis actus unionis Regni Poloniae cum magno ducatu Lituaniae*). It was maintained since approximately the eighteenth century and up to World War I that equal political rights were granted to the Orthodox under the influence of the Reformation, which had made considerable inroads in the Jagiellonian Commonwealth. In his excellent revisionist study, K. Chodynicki established quite convincingly that it was not so much the reformationist impulse as the political goal of the union which proved to be the determining factor in extending full political rights to the Orthodox Ukrainian and Belorussian upper classes.[85] Whereas a complete elimination of the reformationist component is unwarranted, there is no doubt that the prospects for the successful conclusion of the union were of primary importance in the minds of the king and the advocates of unionist politics.

National and religious elements played a limited role in the politics of the local elites of the four Rus' lands affected by the incorporation. The Podlachian nobility, made up of Poles or polonized Eastern Slavs, was the only nobility to display clearly defined preferences for Polish national culture. Already at the Diets of 1565-1566 and 1568, the Podlachian representatives requested from

Zygmunt II August that the correspondence of the grand princely chancery addressed to their province be conducted in Latin or Polish, because they were unable to read the Ruthenian language.[86] It may be that by acting in this manner the Podlachian nobility wished to obtain the political confirmation of its assimilation and acculturation to a superior Polish Renaissance culture. However, no evidence is available which would provide a better insight into the cultural attitudes of other social groups in Podlachia. The request of the cities of Bielsk and Briansk to be incorporated into Crown Poland – a rare example of political initiative on the part of municipalities at the Diet of Lublin – is recorded in one of the Diaries without further explanation for the motives of their action.[87]

The position of the elite groups in the other Ukrainian provinces was, of course, quite different. Ukrainian magnates, such as the princes Aleksandr Chartoryis'kyi, Konstantyn Ostrozhs'kyi, Bohdan Korets'kyi, Konstantyn Vyshnevets'kyi, and Roman Sangushko, not only made strenuous efforts to obtain the confirmation of their socio-political privileges and personal liberties, but also defended their rights as adherents of the Orthodox faith by requesting specific assurances to the effect that they would not be compelled to convert to a different, in this particular case Catholic, denomination.[88] The king and the Diet readily accepted these demands, as is evident from the restitution privileges for Volynia and the Kievan land, which specifically emphasized that all the rights and privileges were being extended to the magnates, nobility, and the clergy of both "the Roman and the Greek law."[89] In addition, the representatives of Volynia and the Kievan land raised the issue of the official usage of the Ruthenian language, an issue which had obvious national implications. The Diet and the king reacted affirmatively to this special demand and assured the population of the Volynian and the Kievan lands that the Ruthenian language would be used as an official language in all matters pertaining to subjects of the same nationality.[90] Thus, those members of the Orthodox Ukrainian elite who remained committed to their religion and nationality were not to be threatened by the incorporation and the transfer of their lands to Polish sovereignty. Nevertheless, there was one subtle restriction implied in the restitution privileges for the two Ukrainian lands in the documents of the Polish-Lithuania union. There is an official recognition of a "Ruthenian nation" (represented, of course, by the nobility), which shared equal standing with the Lithuanian and

Samogitian nations in the Grand Principality of Lithuania;[91] by contrast, the restitution decrees for Volynia and the Kievan land carefully avoided the political concept, "Ruthenian nation," when referring to the elite groups of these two lands, relying instead on the relatively neutral notion of the estates of the lands. This fact partially explains why a trialistic conception of the Jagiellonian union, with the third component – Rus' – did not materialize.[92] It would, however, be incorrect to hold the Polish side responsible for not having implemented this conception. After all, the initiative for a trialistic solution would have had to originate with the elite of the Ukrainian lands, which at that time was apparently satisfied with a minimalist political program.

VII

Ukrainian secular elite groups did not oppose the absorption of their lands into Crown Poland. On the contrary, there is enough evidence to conclude that the nobility was favorably predisposed to the incorporation, being convinced that the Polish socio-political system had more advantages to offer than its Lithuanian counterpart. In fact, the representatives of the Ukrainian lands advocated the annexation of other Rus' territories to the Crown. The attitudes of the Volynian representatives may serve as a case in point. As evidenced by the correspondence of the Lithuanian magnates, the Volynians actively propagated the incorporation of the Kievan land and parts of Polissia, and were regarded by the Lithuanian opponents of the union as the main instigators of the political calamity which befell the grand principality.[93] The same can be said about the great magnates of the Ukrainian lands. Prince Roman Sangushko, the palatine of Bratslav, was opposed to the separation of his province from the Kievan palatinate. The incorporationist attitude of the nobility and the magnates of the Ukrainian lands may have emanated from their desire to keep the lands of Rus' undivided in one state and under one and the same socio-political system. Another reason may have been the expectation on the part of the local magnates that the incorporation could provide them with better political opportunities and still greater social advantages. Having obtained prominent offices and positions in the highest institutions of Crown Poland, they had certainly risen on the ladder of social and political advancement.

Besides, there was little choice in the political situation of the 1560s-1570s, even if they had preferred a different solution. It was the time of obvious decline for the Grand Principality of Lithuania in international affairs and intensified internal difficulties in the Lithuanian-Ruthenian state. The only available political option they had was a choice between Jagiellonian Poland and Muscovite Russia. The former offered a relatively open constitutional system in which the power of the ruler was limited, social privileges, political rights and personal liberties were guaranteed, relative religious tolerance was maintained, and its Polish version of the Renaissance culture was attractive to any elite group. Muscovite Russia, on the other hand, was a country obviously lacking all these socio-political and cultural inducements, having, in addition, a government of tyrannical autocracy personified by Ivan IV and experiencing the terror of the *oprichnina*, of which the Ukrainian magnates were fully aware. Prince Roman Sangushko, the palatine of Bratslav, a committed advocate of an activist and tough foreign policy toward Muscovy – which he regarded as an aggressive and dangerous power on account of her conquests of Kazan and Astrakhan – exploited the *oprichnina* to convince the king and the Polish leaders of the rightness of his political position.[94] All these considerations made the choice easy and prompted the Ukrainian magnates, such as Prince Konstantyn Ostrozhs'kyi, to name one, to seek "a good agreement with the Poles."[95] From the contemporary point of view, the choice was regarded as calculated, realistic, and even wise. The Polish political model appeared to be viable and held out promise that it would remain open and flexible. The subsequent political and ideological deviation from this model and the abandonment of the policy of relative religious tolerance at the end of the sixteenth and the beginning of the seventeenth century brought about well-known consequences which led to a profound crisis of the Polish-Lithuanian state.

NOTES

1. Cf. *Infra*, n. 24.

2. Extant examples of these sources are the official documents of the Union of Lublin, including all the agreements, decrees and privileges published in an excellent critical edition by two outstanding Polish specialists on the problem, S. Kutrzeba and W. Semkowicz, *Akta Unji Polski z Litwą, 1385-1791* (Cracow, 1932) (cited hereafter as *AU*). The official documentation is supplemented by two major unofficial Diaries of the Diet of Lublin, both of which were based on notes of several participants written predominantly in Polish and later edited by anonymous Polish contemporaries apparently interested in the Diet of 1569, but not necessarily written on official governmental request. One of them, made available by Count Leon Rzewuski from the Podhorecki Archive, was published by A.T. Działyński, ed., *Źródłopisma do dziejów Unii Korony Polskiej i W. X. Litewskiego*, III, "Diariusz Lubelskiego Sejmu Unii. Rok 1569" (Poznań, 1856) (cited hereafter as *DD*). The text of the second major and more extensive Diary appeared in print also in the nineteenth century, edited more critically and prefaced with an introduction by M.O. Koialovich, ed., *Dnevnik Liublinskago Seima 1569 goda, Soedinenie Velikago Kniazhestva Litovskago s Korolevstvom Pol'skim* (St. Petersburg, 1869) (cited hereafter as *DK*). It appears that only two contemporary, authored, publicistic works, i.e., occasional political poems, dealt with the Diet of Lublin. The first was written by one of the participants, Jan Ponętowski, *Krótki Rzeczy Polskich Sejmowych, pamięci godnych Commentarz...* (Cracow, 1569), republished by K.J. Turowski in *Biblioteka Polska*, 44 (Cracow, 1858). The second came from the pen of none other than Jan Kochanowski, *Praporzec albo Hold Pruski* (Cracow, 1587), who devoted his occasional poem primarily to the act of homage of Prince Albrecht II Friedrich before the Polish king Zygmunt II August, but touched on the subject of the Polish-Lithuanian union as well. Although the earliest known edition is dated 1587, the poem most probably originated in 1569. References to other source materials will be made in the appropriate context.

3. With the exception of a few studies, the treatment of the Union of Lublin and the incorporation of the lands of Kievan Rus' was generally confined to special chapters included in works covering either the whole scope of the Polish-Lithuanian union, or in works devoted to selected aspects of the latter's constitutional history. The following are the most noteworthy positions on the two closely interrelated problems: M.O. Koialovich, *Liublinskaia uniia ili poslednee soedinenie Litovskago kniazhestva s Pol'skim korolevstvom na Liublinskom seime v 1569 godu* (St. Petersburg, 1863); W. Sarnecki, *Pamiątka Unji Lubelskiej r. 1569* (Cracow, 1869); N. Dashkevich, "Liublinskaia uniia i eia posledstviia," *Universitetskiia Izvestiia*, 1 (Kiev, 1885), 1-28; "Prisoedinenie Podles'ia k Pol'she na Liublinskom seime 1569 goda," *Pamiatniki russkoi stariny v zapadnykh guberniiakh* (cited hereafter as *PRSZG*), VII (1885), 198-216; I.I. Malyshevskii, "Liublinskii s'ezd 1569 g.," *PRSZG*, VIII (1885), 108-197; M.K. Liubavskii, *Litovsko-russkii seim. Opyt po istorii uchrezhdeniia v sviazi s vnutrennim stroem i vneshneiu zhizn'iu gosudarstva* (Moscow, 1900), 815-850; I.I. Lappo, *Velikoe Kniazhestvo Litovskoe za vremia ot zakliucheniia Liublinskoi unii do smerti Stefana Batoriia (1569-1586)* (St. Petersburg, 1901), I, 1-86; M. Hrushevs'kyi, *Istoriia Ukrainy-Rusy*, 10 vols. (offset rep. ed., New York, 1954-1958), IV: XIV-XVI viky – Vidnosyny politychni (2nd ed., 1907/1955), 386-423;

V.I. Picheta, "Litovsko-pol'skie unii i otnoshenie k nim litovsko-russkoi shliakhty," *Sbornik statei, posviashchennykh V. O. Kliuchevskomu*...(Moscow, 1909), 605-631, reprinted in: V.I. Picheta, *Belorussiia i Litva XV-XVI vv.* *(Issledovaniia po istorii sotsial'no-ekonomicheskogo, politicheskogo i kul'turnogo razvitiia)* (Moscow, 1961), 525-550; "Pol'sha na putiakh kolonizatsii Ukrainy i Belorussii. Liublinskaia uniia i ee politicheskie posledstviia," *Istoricheskie Zapiski*, VII (1940), 59-90, reprinted in his *Belorussiia i Litva XV-XVI vv.*, 551-592; S. Kutrzeba, "Unia Polski z Litwą," *Polska i Litwa w dziejowym stosunku* (Cracow, 1914), 447-658, especially 594-657; "Charakter i wartość unji polsko-litewskiej," *Księga pamiątkowa ku uczczeniu czterechsetnej rocznicy wydania pierwszego Statutu litewskiego, Rozprawy Wydziału III Towarzystwa Przyjaciół Nauk w Wilnie* (cited hereafter as *RTPNW*), VIII (1935), 1-14; "Charakter prawny związku Litwy z Polską, 1385-1569," *Pamiętniki VI Powszechnego Zjazdu Historyków Polskich w Wilnie 17-20 września 1935 r.*, 2 vols., I (Referaty) (Lwów, 1935-1936), 165-173; O. Halecki, *Przyłączenie Podlasia, Wołynia i Kijowszczyzny do Korony w roku 1569* (Cracow, 1915); *Unja Lubelska* (Cracow, 1916); *Dzieje Unii Jagiellońskiej* (2 vols.; Cracow, 1919-1920), II (1920), especially part V, Unia Lubelska z r. 1569, 248-353; J. Adamus, "O prawno-państwowym stosunku Litwy do Polski," *Pamiętnik VI...*, I (Referaty), 174-180; L. Kolankowski, "Jagiellonowie i Unja," *Pamiętnik VI...*, II (Protokoly), 265-292; S. Zakrzewski, "Ze studiów nad dziejami unii polsko-litewskiej," *Zagadnienia historyczne*, 2 vols., II (Lwów, 1936), 177-229, especially 205-229; A. Šapoka, *Lietuva ir Lenkija po 1569 metų unijos, jų valstybinių santykių bruožai* (Kaunas, 1938); S. Kościałkowski, "Rzeczypospolita obojga narodów (1569-1795)," *Dzieje ziem Wielkiego Księstwa Litewskiego, Alma Mater Vilnensis* (cited hereafter as *AMV*), III (London, 1953); J. Bardach, "Krewo i Lublin. Z problemów unii polsko-litewskiej," in his *Studia z ustroju i prawa Wielkiego Księstwa Litewskiego XIV-XVII w.* (Warsaw, 1970), 11-67; extended and revised version of the same study published in *Kwartalnik Historyczny*, LXXVI, 3 (1969), 583-616.

4. In addition to the works of Lubavskii, Hrushevs'kyi, Kutrzeba, and Halecki's *Dzieje Unii Jagiellońskiej* (cited in n. 3), all of which cover more extensively the problems of the period before 1569, the following scholarly contributions should also be consulted: A. Mosbach, *Początki unii Lubelskiej* (Poznań, 1872); A. Lewicki, "Powstanie Świdrygiełły. Ustęp z dziejów Unii Korony z Litwą," *Rozprawy Wydziału Historyczno-Filozoficznego Akademii Umiejętności* (cited hereafter as *RWHFAU*), XXIX (1892), 128-516; and a separate reprint; "Über das staatsrechtliche Verhältnis Litauens zu Polen unter Jagiello und Witold," *Altpreussische Monatsschrift*, 1-2 (1894), 1-94; M.V. Dovnar-Zapol'skii, "Pol'sko-litovskaia uniia na seimakh do 1569 g.," *Drevnosti. Trudy Slavianskoi Kommissii pri Moskovskom Arkheologicheskom Obshchestve*, II, (1898), 118-145; N.A. Maksimeiko, *Seimy Litovsko-russkago gosudarstva do Liublinskoi unii 1569 g.* (Kharkov, 1902); A. Prochaska, "Przyczynki krytyczne do dziejów Unii," *RWHFAU*, XXXIII (1896), 55-122; W. Semkowicz, "Braterstwo szlachty polskiej z bojarstwem litewskim w unii horodelskiej 1413 roku," *Polska i Litwa w dziejowym stosunku*, 393-446; O. Halecki, *Ostatnie lata Świdrygiełły i sprawa wołyńska za Kazimierza Jagiellończyka* (Cracow, 1915); O. Halecki, "Sejm obozowy szlachty litewskiej pod Witebskiem 1562 r. i jego petycja o unię z Polską (Przyczynek do dziejów parlamentaryzmu litewskiego i unii lubelskiej)," *Przegląd Historyczny* (cited hereafter as *PH*), XVIII (1914), 320-352; "Wcielenie i wznowienie państwa litewskiego przez Polskę (1386-1401)," *PH*, XXI

180   THE CONTEST FOR THE LEGACY OF KIEVAN RUS'

(1917-1918), 1-77; O. Balzer, "Stosunek Litwy do Polski," *Pisma pośmiertne Oswalda Balzera*, III (Lwów, 1937), 243-318; *Tradycja dziejowa unii polsko-litewskiej* (Lwów and Warszawa, 1919); J. Jakubowski, "Z zagadnień unii polsko-litewskiej," *PH*, XXII (1919-1920), 136-155; K. Piwarski, "Niedoszła wyprawa t. zw. radoszkowicka Zygmunta Augusta na Moskwę (Rok 1567-68)," *Ateneum Wileńskie* (cited hereafter as *AW*), IV (1927), 252-296, V (1928), 95-119; A. Wiskont, "Wielki książę litewski Witold a Unia Horodelska," *AW*, VII (1930), 469-493; J. Adamus, "Państwo Litewskie w latach 1386-1398," *RTPNW*, VIII (1935), 15-79; "Najnowsza literatura o akcie krewskim," *Wiadomości Studium Historii Prawa Litewskiego*, I (Wilno, 1938), 273-316; H. Łowmiański, "Uwagi w sprawie podłoża społecznego i gospodarczego unji jagiellońskiej," *RTPNW*, VIII (1935), 214-325; "Wcielenie Litwy do Polski w 1386 r.," *AW*, XII (1937), 36-145; A. Šapoka, *Lietuva ir Lenkija Jogailos laikais, Atspauda iš rinkinio "Jogaila"* (Kaunas, 1935); H. Paszkiewicz, *O genezie i wartości Krewa* (Warsaw, 1938); *W sprawie inkorporacji Litwy do Polski w 80-ch latach XIV w.* (Warsaw, 1938); "Litwa przedchrześcijańska. Geneza unii polsko-litewskiej," *AMV*, III (1953); W. Wielhorski, *Polska a Litwa. Stosunki wzajemne w biegu dziejów* (London, 1947); "Okres unii personalnej (1386-1569)," *AMV*, III (1953); H. Jablonowski, *Westrussland zwischen Wilna und Moskau (Die politischen Tendenzen der russischen Bevölkerung des Grossfürstentums Litauen im 15 Jh.)* (Leiden, 1955); O.P. Backus, *Motives of West Russian Nobles in Deserting Lithuania for Moscow, 1377-1514* (Lawrence, Kansas, 1957); S. Zajączkowski, "W sprawie badań nad dziejami stosunków polsko-litewskich za Jagiellonów," *Studia Historica (W 35-lecie pracy naukowej Henryka Łowmiańskiego)* (Warsaw, 1958), 199-217; G. Rhode, "Staaten Union und Adelsstaat," *Zeitschrift für Ostforschung*, LX, 2-3 (1960), 185-215; O.P. Backus, O. Halecki and J. Jakstas, "The Problem of Unity in the Polish-Lithuanian State" (Discussion), *Slavic Review*, XXII, 3 (1963), 411-455; S.M. Kuczyński, "O programie pierwszych Jagiellonów, tzw. idei Jagiellońskiej i rzekomej agresji polskiej na wschód w XV w.," *Studia z dziejów Europy Wschodniej* (Warsaw, 1965), 181-188; Shigeto Toriyama, "A Short History of the Polish-Lithuanian Unions (Down to the Union of Mielnik)," *Slavic Studies. Journal of the Slavic Institute of Hokkaido University*, X (Sapporo, 1966), 1-26 (in Japanese); for general surveys in which the aforementioned problems are covered, consult a useful bibliography by J. Bardach, J. Ochmański, and O.P. Backus, *Lituanie (Introduction bibliographique à l'histoire du droit et à l'ethnologie juridique, D/14)* (Bruxelles, 1969).

5. The great majority of the scholarly literature on this subject, published both in the USSR and in Poland, usually concludes with the end of the fourteenth century, or concentrates on the period beginning with the late sixteenth and early seventeenth centuries. The following three works only partially fill the professional needs in the area of immediate concern: K.V. Bazilevich, *Vneshniaia politika russkogo tsentrali-zovannogo gosudarstva (Vtoraia polovina XV veka)* (Moscow, 1952); I.B. Grekov, *Ocherki po istorii mezhdunarodnykh otnoshenii vostochnoi Evropy XIV-XVI vv.* (Moscow, 1963); A.I. Rogov, *Russko-pol'skie kul'turnye sviazi v epokhu vozrozhde-niia (Stryikovskii i ego Khronika)* (Moscow, 1966).

6. The view concerning the change from a personal to a real union had origi-nally been articulated by Kutrzeba, "Unia Polski z Litwą," 653-657; *RTPNW*, VIII (1935), 7-8; *Pamiętnik VI...*, I, Referaty, 172-173, and has been reemphasized in an authoritative survey of Polish law by Z. Kaczmarczyk and B. Leśnodorski, *Historia*

państwa i prawa Polski, II, *Od połowy XV wieku do r. 1795* (Warsaw, 1968), 39.
Beginning with Liubavskii's classical work on the Lithuanian-Ruthenian Diet, the
feudal-representative aspect of the union began to gain currency in scholarship
(*Litovsko-russkii seim*, 847-850), although the author inadvertently modified his view
by stating that the Diet of Lublin brought about an end to the Lithuanian-Ruthenian
state and its "incorporation" into Crown Poland (*Ocherk istorii litovsko-russkago
prava* [Moscow, 1910], 292). Halecki has been the most prominent proponent of the
federalist conception of the Polish-Lithuanian union; in this particular respect he has
been followed, although from a different theoretical position, by Picheta (*Belorussiia i
Litva XV-XVI vv.*, 562) and I.I. Lappo ("Litovsko-russkoe gosudarstvo v sostave
Rechipospolitoi," *Vedeckie Prace Ruské Lidové Universitety v Praze*, II [1929], 63-
76). The incorporationist-unitary interpretation and critique of the Union of Lublin
advocated by Balzer (*Tradycja...*, 16), L. Kolankowski (*Polska Jagiellonów* [Lwów,
1936], 5, 326), and S. Kościałkowski (*AMV*, III [1953], 68) have apparently not been
accepted by contemporary scholarship. In his discussion of the various legal interpretations of the Union of 1569, Bardach has integrated the concept of the real union
with the notion of the feudal-federal character of the Polish-Lithuanian Commonwealth (*Studia...*, 59). A similar position has been taken by J. Ochmański, *Historia
Litwy* (Wrocław-Warsaw-Cracow, 1967), 110.

7. "Iż już Krolestwo polskie i Wielkie Księstwo litewskie jest jedno
nierozdzielne i nierożne ciało, a także nierożna ale jedna spolna Rzeczpospolita, ktora
się ze dwu państw i narodów w jeden lud zniosła i spoiła" (*AU*, 343, 358).

8. For the most thorough discussion of the sources and the problems
involved, albeit with some controversial interpretations, see H. Paszkiewicz, *Polityka
ruska Kazimierza Wielkiego* (Warsaw, 1925).

9. *AU*, 193-196.

10. *DK*, 189-191.

11. *AU*, 196-207.

12. *AU*, 300-308.

13. *AU*, 308-319.

14. The major events and the day-to-day political negotiations dealing with
the incorporation of the Rus' lands have been extensively related and commented
upon by Halecki in his monograph *Przyłączenie....* For the best chronology of the
parliamentary debates and decision-making, as well as the dating of the crucial documents, see Kutrzeba, "Unia Polski z Litwą," 605-612.

15. Hrushevs'kyi, *Istoriia Ukrainy-Rusy*, IV, 415-416.

16. Halecki, among others, also maintained that the attested antagonism
between the Lithuanian and Ukrainian magnates had no religious overtones, but had
been rooted in familial and social rivalries (*Przyłączenie...*, 43-44).

17. Article 5. "Jż czy Podlassanie y Wolinianie, ktorzy decret krolia jego
moszci przyjmą dobrowolnie, już parebunt koronnie, mają bicz wolni czy od
exequciej dobr stolu krolia jego moszci, wedlye postępku dobr xięstwa
Mazowieczkiego, a ktorziby niechcieli przystacz, abi jem to beneficium nie slo" (*DK*,
128). The whole problem of material incentives and pressures exerted, as well as the
attitudes displayed by the Podlachian representatives, is well attested in the unpublished *Nowiny Lubelskie*, authored, according to Halecki, by Maciej Sawicki, the
general clerk of Lithuania and prefect of Mielnik, describing the events of March 4-5
and dispatched to the departed Lithuanian magnates (*Przyłączenie...*, 6). "Bo były

słowa, przytym obiecanie łaski, urzędy, i niepodleiszenie w exekucyą i wzięcie poborów i szlachty, i z miast to obwarowywali sobie, żeby to im i w poczciwości nie wadziło, i aby byli bezpieczni zdrowia i majętności swych,..." (*Teki Naruszewicza*, LXXVII, 1569, 89-106, especially 90, Cracow, Biblioteka Czartoryskich).

18. The projects of the union promulgated by the Polish and Lithuanian representatives before the latter's departure agree upon the principle of mutual right to acquire possessions in Poland and Lithuania. The wording in the Polish project reads as follows: "aby wolno było zawżdy tak Polakowi w Litwie jako Litwinowi w Polsce każdym słusznym obyczajem dostawać imienia" (*DD*, 24; cf. *DK*, 72). The Lithuanian statement corresponded on this issue ("Wolno też ma bycz, tak Polskiemu narodowi w Litwie, jako Litwie w Polscze, wseliakiem slusnem obyczajem wedlie prawa pospolitego nabywacz ossiadlosczi y wsselakiej maiętnosczi lyczączey,..." [*DK*, 85]) but differed from the Polish on the question of appointments to offices. Cf. paragraph 14 of the union acts of July 1 and July 4, 1569 (*AU*, 345, 360, 369).

19. The entire discussion of the Kievan problem at the Diet of Lublin had been recorded in Latin exclusively by a certain Borkowski, who is the only identified person among several participants taking notes on the proceedings of the Diet (*DK*, 399-406). The inclusion of this Latin text in the Diary, and the absence of a Polish version, was explained by the contemporary editors as due to the illness of the person responsible for recording the proceedings in Polish, and by the desire of the editors to retain the most correct version of what went on at the Diet ("abi sie nie odmienialo") (*DK*, 407).

20. *DK*, 402-403. In his report of February 1570 about the conclusion of the Polish-Lithuanian union, the Muscovite agent Visloi Bulgakov referred to the problem of money ("Liakhom Litve posobliat', a Litve Liakhom posobliati, bez penezei") (*Akty, otnosiashchiesia k istorii Zapadnoi Rossii* [cited hereafter as *AZR*], III [1848], 150).

21. "...Kiioviam regno adiiciendam iudicarent, cum quod sit vehementer regno necessaria,..."(*DK*, 402).

22. *DK*, 403. The view that Kiev was a gate to the Jagiellonian state had been articulated more than three decades earlier. In 1526 the representatives of Lithuania conveyed to King Zygmunt that Kiev was a gate to his entire state ("...Kiev, kotoryi est' kak vorota vsego panstva vashoe milosti...") (*AZR*, II [1848], 173).

23. *DK*, 401.

24. On the eve of its incorporation the Podlachian land comprised the provinces of Dorohychyn, Mielnik, and Bielsk. In ethnic terms the Podlachian land was populated predominantly by inhabitants of Eastern Slavic stock (the majority of them were people akin to the inhabitants of the Ukrainian lands, a minority to those of the Belorussian lands). As far as the social stratification was concerned the majority of the rank-and-file nobility were Poles or polonized Eastern Slavs. Ukrainians and Belorussians constituted the majority of the city population, and the peasants were in overwhelming numbers Eastern Slavs. For an informative review of the socio-economic conditions of the Podlachian land before its incorporation, see I.T. Baranowski, "Podlasie w przededniu Unii Lubelskiej. Trzy studya z dziejów społeczno-ekonomicznych," *PH*, VII (1908), 48-72, 183-203, and 299-321. Cf. also his "Z dziejów feudalizmu na Podlasiu. Rajgorodzko-goniadzke 'państwo' Radziwiłłów w pierwszej połowie XVI wieku," *PH*, IV (1907), 62-74 and 158-169.

25. "Przekładacie wielkie uciski, gwałty, najazdy, morderstwa, posiadanie gruntów waszych przez granice wielkiego xięstwa Litewskiego z strony Korony

Polskiey y xięstwa Mazowieckiego od sie ku darownym zaysciam między capituła Warszawskie a Lipcany y ynemi sobie przyleglemi, jako ich jest wielie w tych niedawnych czasiech zamordowano, z strony ziemie Podlaskiey wypisaliscie, prosząc o wyslanie na te roznice commisarzow.... Prosiliscie, aby jego kr. m. z ich mosciami pany radami o pokoju waszym z obywatelmi coronnemi obmyslawać a do uniey was z nim sposobić raczył, co jesliby nie bylo, tedy ziemie Podlaską Ukrainą rychlo rozumieiąc" (M. Dovnar-Zapol'skii, ed., *Dokumenty Moskovskogo Arkhiva Ministerstva Iustitsii*, 1, Moscow [1897], 185).

26. "...aby tym kgvaltam, naezdam, zaboistvam, i zabiran'iu zeml', i grabezhom, kotorye sia ot panov Poliakov vam deiut' byla spravedlivost' uchinena i konets slushnyi tomu postanovlen" (*AZR*, III [1848], 42).

27. "Nad to obyvatelei Koruny Polskoe oselykh, kotorie na granitsu y zemli ego Volynskogo imen'ia svoi i granitsy maiut', menechi vy sobe velikie krivdy, kgvalty, naezdy, zabran'ia kgruntov i liudei otchiznykh nechinene ot nikh zhadnoe spravedlivosti" (*Dokumenty Moskovskogo Arkhiva Ministerstva Iustitsii*, 488).

28. *Dokumenty Moskovskogo Arkhiva Ministerstva Iustitsii*, 173.

29. *AU*, 199-205, 303-306 and 314-317.

30. *AU*, 384.

31. *DD*, 68, 71.

32. *DD*, 77.

33. *DK*, 387-338; *DD*, 163. A similar assumption was extended to Bratslav and Vynnytsia (*DK*, 392).

34. "Przywilej aby Podlasianom i Wołyńcom byl dan, a nie dekretem nazwany, ale *privilegium restitutionis*" (italics mine, J.P.) (*DD*, 71).

35. Kutrzeba, "Unia Polski z Litwą," 607.

36. *AU*, 194. The historical claim to Podlachia and Volynia was spelled out simply and briefly in the *Uniwersal* of March 12, 1569 (*DK*, 189).

37. *DD*, 120. Cf. Kutrzeba, "Unia Polski z Litwą," 606.

38. For its dating, see Kutrzeba, "Unia Polski z Litwą," 611.

39. Since the restitution privileges have come down both in Latin and Polish versions, it is necessary to make a few remarks about these documents. All of them with the exception of the Polish text of the Podlachian restitution privilege were entered in the *Metryka Koronna* (XVIII, *legationum unionis 1569*), and thus automatically became official in nature (*AU*, XXVIII-XXIX). However, the Polish texts were of greater importance and therefore they became incorporated into contemporary and official collections of Polish laws, statutes and constitutions such as Jan Herburt, *Statuta i przywileje koronne* (Cracow, 1570); *Konstytucje, statuta i przywileje* (Cracow, 1579); Stanisław Sarnicki, *Statuta i metryka przywilejów koronnych* (Cracow, 1594); Jan Januszowski, *Statuta, prawa i konstytucje koronne* (Cracow, 1600); and finally into the *Volumina Legum*, I-II (Warsaw, 1732). In addition to being official publications, these works enjoyed fairly wide circulation among the elite and were used for legal and political purposes.

40. *AU*, 198-199. The corresponding Latin text coincides almost verbatim with the Polish (*AU*, 198-199).

41. *AU*, 301-303.

42. For a reliable summation of the facts on Podlachia in the context of Ruthenian-Polish and Polish-Lithuanian relations, see Hrushevs'kyi, *Istoriia Ukrainy-Rusy*, IV, 397-398, 236-237; II, 371, 388-389, 565-568; VI, 246-249.

43. *AU*, 80, 93, and 103-104.

44. For a factual discussion of the Volynian question in Polish-Lithuanian conflicts, see Halecki, *Ostatnie lata Świdrygiełły...*, especially 231-235.

45. *DK*, 392 and 393.

46. *DK*, 398. Cf. Hrushevs'kyi, *Istoriia Ukrainy-Rusy*, IV, 408.

47. "Podlasie, to już po zastawach od Wielkich książąt Litewskich u Mazowieckich bywało, czem się niemniejsza ale wieczna władza Książąt Wielkich Litewskich nad nimi znaczy, jakoż to zaś do tychże ręku, z kąd wyszło od dawnego czasu, się przywróciło" (*DD*, 133).

48. "...posse etenim id probari, quod istae terrae tempore Alexandri, qui ultimo uniones actu finivit, erant circa ducatum Lituaniae, quae sunt a majoribus nostris sanguine acquisitae, nec tempore Alexandri aliqua mentio de eis habita est" (*DK*, 395).

49. *DD*, 133.

50. For a good example of this generally accepted view, see J. Pajewski, "Zygmunt August and the Union of Lublin, 1548-1572," *The Cambridge History of Poland to 1696* (Cambridge, 1950), 364.

51. *DD*, 163.

52. *DK*, 387-388.

53. Hrushevs'kyi, *Istoriia Ukrainy-Rusy*, IV, 406-407.

54. The names of the four deputies were: Dobrogost Potworowski (the Kalisz land), Walenty Orzechowski (the Peremyshl' land), Marian Przelecki (Cracow), Jakub Ponętowski (the Łęczyca land) (*DK*, 400).

55. *DK*, 401.

56. *DK*, 404.

57. For a discussion of this campaign and the literature on the subject, see V. D. Koroliuk, *Zapadnye slaviane i Kievskaia Rus' v X-XI vv.* (Moscow, 1964), 233-268.

58. "...nam Ruthenorum principi per plures legationes eum interpellanti et pacem, modesto imposito tributo, restituit et singulos captivos liberaliter remisit" (J. Długosz, *Annales seu Cronicae incliti Regni Polaniae, Liber I-IV*, (Warsaw, 1964-1970, II, 282).

59. "...rex pacem dedit supplicibus, tributum, modicum imposuit: captivos omnes, quos vel hoc, vel superiori bello coeperat, vel obsidiu loco habuerat, liberaliter dimisit. Hoc bellum anno post Christum natum 1018 confectum est, ut vult Dlugossus" (M. Kromer, *De origine et rebus gestis Polonarum, Libri XXX*, in: J. Pistorius, *Polonicae historiae corpus*, 2 vols. [Basel, 1582], II, 444).

60. For an informative discussion of selected ancient, medieval, and early modern materials on conquest law in the West, see D. Sutherland, "Conquest and Law," *Studia Gratiana*, XV (1972), *Post Scripta*, 33-52.

61. *DK*, 401.

62. *DK*, 404.

63. The text of the oration was published in *DD*, 8-15.

64. *DD*, 15.

65. Koialovich, *DK*, 717; Hrushevs'kyi, *Istoriia Ukrainy-Rusy*, IV, 407. Cf. also I.I. Lappo, *Velikoe Kniazhestvo Litovskoe...*, 40.

66. The descriptions of the Kievan "conquests" in Długosz's *Annales* are so confusing that the present day scholars have been unable to solve their riddles and to clarify their chronology. According to Długosz, Kiev had been taken three times by Polish rulers (1008 ?/1018, 1070, 1075) (*Annales sue Cronicae...*, II, 259-263 and

280-282; III, 100-103 and 118-120). Kromer indiscriminately followed Długosz's narratives and made them even more confusing by his summaries and abbreviations. In reality, Kiev had been occupied twice by Polish rulers (1018 and 1069), and Iziaslav was able to take Kiev with Polish support in 1077.

67. For a discussion of the application of the Muscovite law of conquest to Kazan, see the author's *Russia and Kazan: Conquest and Imperial Ideology (1438-1560s)* (The Hague and Paris, 1973), Chpt. V.

68. *AU*, 309-310.

69. *AU*, 312-313.

70. The Polish claim to all of Rus' puzzled even the most astute historians. For example, Liubavskii repeated the Polish statement that "the Russian land belonged to Poland since antiquity"(?) and treated it as a curious misunderstanding (*Litovsko-russkii seim*, 835; *Ocherk istorii Litovsko-russkago gosudarstva do liublinskoi unii vkliuchitel'no* [Moscow, 1910], 290).

71. *AZR*, I (1846), 281; *Sbornik Imperatorskago russkago istoricheskago obshchestva* (cited hereafter as *SIRIO*), XXXV (1882), 460.

72. "...v korolevstve i pod korolevstvom est' bol'shaia chast' Rusi,..." (*AZR*, I, 1846, 347-348).

73. These claims were raised in 1517, 1542, 1549, 1553, 1561, 1562, 1563 (*SIRIO*, XXXV [1882], 509 and 512; LIX [1887], 184, 278, and 396; LXXI [1892], 43, 108, and 172).

74. The claim that Moscow was "the second Kiev" was most explicitly formulated in the famous ideological treatise, entitled *Kazanskaia istoriia*, the author or authors of which stated among others that "the capital and the most famous city of Moscow shines forth as a second Kiev..." (G.I. Moiseeva, ed., *Kazanskaia istoriia* [Moscow and Leningrad, 1954], 57). A relevant parallel to this statement is found in the last sentence of the *Otryvok russkoi letopisi*, which reads: "May we see as ruler in Kiev, the Orthodox tsar, Grand Prince Ivan Vasil'evich of all Russia" (*Polnoe sobranie russkikh letopisei*, VI [1853], 315). For additional comments and the literature on this problem, see the author's *Russia and Kazan...*, Chpt. VII.

75. *DK*, 401.

76. *DK*, 494.

77. The statement was made in the Discourse of the archbishop, forwarded to King Stefan Batory and published in M. Koialovich, ed., *Dnevnik poslednago pokhoda Stefana Batoriia na Rossiiu (osada Pskova) i Diplomaticheskaia perepiska togo vremeni, otnosiashchaiasia glavnym obrazom k zakliucheniiu Zapol'skago mira (1581-1582g.)* (St. Petersburg, 1867), 609-611, especially 610. The Discourse, which remained undated, was inserted in the diplomatic correspondence following a letter of December 28, 1581, and preceding a letter of November 16, 1581.

78. For some illuminating remarks on this problem, cf. M. Vladimirskii-Budanov, "Tserkovnyia imushchestva v iugo-zapadnoi Rossii XVI veka," *Arkhiv Iugo-Zapadnoi Rossii*, part VIII, vol. IV (1907), 3-224, especially, 41 and 223.

79. For an evaluation of the official treatment of the Orthodox upper classes in the fifteenth and sixteenth centuries, consult the studies of W. Czermak, "Sprawa równouprawnienia schizmatyków i katolików na Litwie (1432-1563r.)," *Rozprawy Wydziału Historyczno-Filozoficznego Akademii Umiejętności*, XLIV (1903), 348-405; M.K. Liubavskii, "K voprosu ob ogranichenii politicheskikh prav pravoslavnykh kniazei, panov i shlakhty v velikom kniazhestve Litovskom do Liublinskoi unii," *Sbornik statei, posviashchennykh V. O. Kliuchevskomu* (Moscow, 1909) ,1-17; W.

Kamieniecki, "Ograniczenia wyznaniowe w prawodawstwie litewskim w XV i XVI wieku," *PH*, XIII (1911), 268-282.

80. A. Lapiński, *Zygmunt Stary a Kościół prawosławny, Rozprawy Historyczne Towarzystwa Naukowego Warszawskiego*, XIX, 1 (Warsaw, 1937), 164-165.

81. For the best text editions of the Wilno privilege of 1563, see *AZR*, III, 32 (1848), 118-121 and *Monumenta Reformationis Polonicae et Lithuanicae* (Zbiór pomników reformacji kościóła polskiego i litewskiego, Zabytki z w. XVI), Staraniem Synodu Jednoty Ewangelicko-Reformowanej Litewskiej, ser. I, no. 1 (2nd ed., Wilno, 1925), no. 4.

82. The Grodno privilege was the last of the great land privileges for the Lithuanian state issued before the Union of Lublin. For the best editions of the text, see *Akty, otnosiashchiesia k istorii Iuzhnoi i Zapadnoi Rossii* (cited hereafter as *AIuZR*), II, 146 (1865/1970), 158-164, and *Monumenta Reformationis Polonicae et Lithuanicae*, no. 5. For a discussion of the land privileges, cf. the excellent article by I. Iakubowskii, "Zemskie privilei Velikago kniazhestva Litovskago," *Zhurnal Ministerstva Narodnago prosveshcheniia*, part I [April 1903], 239-278, especially 276 and part II [July 1903], 245-303.

83. "...a tak izh tot to narod Ruskii do takovogo spolnogo sluzhen'ia braterskago Unii khutlivi i gotovi sut', i odnako zo vsemi, to est' pospol' z bratieiu svoieiu Litvoiu, toho pozhadaiut' k tomu se maiut' i khochut' met'... " (*AIuZR*, II, 1865/1970, 163).

84. *Monumenta Confraternitatis Stauropigianae*, I, 53 and 57-62.

85. K. Chodynicki, "Geneza równouprawnienia schyzmatyków w Wielkim Ks. Litewskim. Stosunek Zygmunta Augusta do wyznania grecko-wschodniego," *PH*, XXII (1919-1920), 54-135, especially 113-131. Cf. also his *Kościół Prawosławny a Rzeczpospolita Polska* (Warsaw, 1934), 88-89. In his comments on the Union of Lublin, Bardach has attempted to fuse these two interpretations and to assign them equal significance (*Studia*, 49-52).

86. *Dokumenty Moskovskogo Arkhiva Ministerstva Iustitsii*, I, 186 and 492. Cf. Hrushevs'kyi, *Istoriia Ukrainy-Rusy*, VI, 248-249.

87. *DD*, 118.

88. Prince K. Vyshnevets'kyi, speaking for his compatriots and coreligionists, presented their common position with unmistakable clarity: "Przetoz prosimi, abismi [w] wolnoscziach swich bili zachowani, a tim wroczeniem y przistaniem, abi wolnosczi nasse niebili skazone, alie, jako liudziom utcziwem, chowane, y w tem sie wassei krolewskiei moszci opowiedami, iz przistajemi liudzie wolni, swobodni, abismi nie bili zacznosczciach swich slacheczkich unizeni, gdziesmi jest narod tak potczwi, jako zadnemu narodowi na swiecze naprzod nycz niedami, y czujemi sie w tim, zesmi kazdemu narodowi sa rowni sliacheczctwem. Czo wieczei, -- są u nas domy xiązeczie, ktorzi mają ossobne swe zawolania y zacznosczi s familiei swojej: nieradzibismi tego widzieli, abi zacznosczi ich mialo sie czo derogowacz, y owsem prosimy, abi w zacznoszczy w swei bili zachowane; tak tez, izesmi są roznei religiei, a zwlascza Graekowie, abismi tim nie bili ponizeni, -- abi nikt do inssej religiej niebil przicziągani" (*DK*, 381-382).

89. *AU*, 303, 305, 314, and 316.

90. "To też za prośbą wszech wołyńskiej (kijowskiej) Ziemie przerzeczonych stanow zostawujemy, iż we wszelakich sprawach ich sądowych, jako pozwy, wpisywanie do ksiąg, akta i wszelakie potrzeby ich, tak sądow naszych grodzkich i

ziemskich, jako z kancelarjej naszej koronnej, dekreta nasze i we wszytkich potrzebach naszych krolewskich i ziemskich koronnych do nich listy nie jakim inym, jeno ruskiem pismem pisane i odprawiane być mają czasy wiecznymi" (*AU*, 305 and 316).

91. *AU*, 346, 361, and 370.

92. Halecki, *Dzieje Unii Jagiellońskiej*, II, 341.

93. "Y juz Volijnczij podalij tego miedzy posłij, ze Kijow ij Brzecz ijm nalijczij, a zwłaszcza p. Bokij – wijwodzij po Narew y Jasołde, Pijnsk Cobrijn tez do Wolijnia zijcząc, czego Polaczij popijracz chczą" (letter of Jan Chodkiewicz to Mikołaj Radziwiłł of May 31, 1569). "Jakosz y teraz: instigatorow większych nie masz przeciwko Litwie, jako panowie Wolyńcy, chociasz snać nie wszyscy (bo y Brześć Litewski wszystek y Pińsk także aże po Jasiołdę rzeke odgraniczają od Corony), a zwłaszcza pan Bokiej, którego panowie Poliacy, dlia wielkiej wiadomości rzeczy, cronicą zową" (letter of Mikołaj Naruszewicz to Mikołaj Radziwiłł of June 11, 1569). Cf. *Arkheograficheskii Sbornik Dokumentov otnosiashchikhsia k istorii severozapadnoi Rusi*, VII (1870), 38 and 44. Havrylo Vasylovych Bokii, the judge of Lutsk, was one of the most vigorous Volynian politicians and a local exponent of incorporationist politics (Halecki, *PH*, XVIII, 1914, 335-336).

94. "Czo wieczej dossycz ma [z] sobą czo czynicz y s poddanemi swemi, ktorzy pewnie, bi wijechal s niemi w polie, zebi o garlo prziprawili, bo je pomordowal" (*DK*, 501). Cf. also *DD*, 204-205; *DK*, 499-501. I.I. Polosin's discussion of the controversies concerning the *oprichnina* at the Diet of Lublin in 1569 (as well as at other Polish Diets) represents a complete misunderstanding of the problems involved ("Spory ob 'oprichnine' na pol'skikh seimakh XVI veka [1569-1582]," *Sotsial'no-politicheskaia istoriia Rossii, XVI – nachala XVII veka* [Moscow, 1963], 156-181).

95. "Kniaź Konstanty kijowski także wojewoda, rad widział, by z Polaki była dobra zgoda" (Ponętowski, *Krótki Rzeczy Polskich Seymowych, pamięci godnych Commentarz...*, 21).

10

MUSCOVITE IMPERIAL CLAIMS TO THE KAZAN KHANATE [BASED ON THE MUSCOVITE THEORY OF SUCCESSION TO THE LANDS OF KIEVAN RUS']*

The final conquest of the Kazan Khanate by Muscovite armies occurred in 1552.[1] The periods immediately preceding and following this event – that is, the years between 1547 and the late 1560s – were of paramount importance to the history of Muscovite political thought, for they witnessed the appearance of a considerable number of significant historical and ideological works. Most of these works were written in one of two centers, the tsar's court or the metropolitan's chancery. The former produced official court chronicles, whereas the latter – particularly under the direction of Metropolitan Makarii – compiled interpretative works of a historical and religious character. Extant examples of the new court historiography are the *Letopisets nachala tsarstva tsaria i velikogo kniazia Ivana Vasil'evicha vseia Rusii* (the *Chronicle of the Beginnings of the Tsardom of the Tsar and Grand Prince Ivan Vasil'evich of All Russia*), which covers the period from 1533 to 1552,[2] its "Continuations" (based upon official documents and the "Draft Copies" [*Spiski chernye*] of the *Chronicle of New Years* [*Letopisets leta novye*])[3] and the *Tsarstvennaia kniga* (the *Imperial Book*) with its important interpolations.[4] The *Letopisets nachala tsarstva* and the "Continuations" were incorporated into the *Nikonovskaia letopis'* (the *Nikon Chronicle*) and the *L'vovskaia letopis'* (the *L'vov Chronicle*), which, together with the voluminous *Litsevoi letopisnyi svod* (the *Illuminated Chronicle*),[5] mark a high point in Muscovite imperial historiography.

In the metropolitan's chancery two important ecclesiastical works were compiled under Makarii's inspiration and guidance: the *Velikiie minei chetii* (the *Great Menology*), completed by 1552, and

---

* For illustrations pertaining to this chapter, see Plates 40, 41.

the *Kniga stepennaia* (the *Book of Degrees*), composed in the early 1560s (most probably between 1560 and 1563).[6] The first represented an attempt to compile a corpus of all literary texts known in Muscovy, and was intended as a reference work for high church and state dignitaries. The second provided the Muscovite ruling elite with a providential interpretation of history combined with a historical scheme of Russian national development.

The main factors in the emergence of these voluminous historical and religious treatises were the coronation of Ivan IV as the first "tsar" in 1547, which in contemporary eyes elevated Muscovy from the status of a grand principality to that of an empire, and the rapid acceleration of the process of Slavization or rather nationalization of the Russian Orthodox Church, as reflected in the work of the church councils of 1547 and 1549. Both contributed to the development of historical and national consciousness and to an attitude of religious exclusiveness and national superiority among the imperial elite.

The works of this period had as one of their aims the establishment of a clear-cut line of continuity from Kievan Rus' through (Rostovia)-Suzdalia-Vladimiria to Muscovy. This *translatio* theory was to serve as the primary historical basis for Muscovite political claims.[7] It was closely correlated with the notion of the unity of all the Rus' lands and the historical concept of Muscovy's role in "gathering them." The emphasis on the exclusive and uninterrupted dynastic succession from the rulers of Kievan Rus' to those of Muscovy served to extol the position of the Muscovite grand prince, and later the tsar. A similar approach can be observed in the interpretation of the history of the Russian Church. The authors and the editors of the compilations of the period in question aimed at the unification and "streamlining" of Russian history. The latter involved a retouching of the history of Kievan Rus', which was given the status of a tsardom by the compilers of the *Book of Degrees*.

It is against the background of these developments and tendencies in Russian political thought and historiography that we can begin to understand more clearly the evolution of Muscovite imperial claims to Kazan. Muscovite bookmen justified the conquest of the Kazan Khanate chiefly on the basis of five major claims. Before the conquest of 1552 only legal and religious claims to Kazan had been mentioned; the former can be found in chronicles and – more importantly – diplomatic correspondence, while the latter are attested in the epistles of Archbishop Feodosii of Novgorod and

Metropolitan Makarii written before the final Muscovite conquest. After the conquest, however, historical, dynastic, and national arguments also began to make their appearance in chronicles and ideological works, while religious justifications were integrated by Muscovite imperial ideologists into an overall providential interpretation of Russian history.[8] After 1552 a new type of legal relationship was developed between the central Muscovite government and the inhabitants of the former Kazan Khanate, and, for this reason, legal claims formulated before the conquest lost their political urgency and were seldom mentioned.

The legal claims dated from 1487, when Ivan III successfully intervened in a dynastic struggle in the Kazan Khanate on the side of the contestant, Muhammad-Amin. The phrase of the official Muscovite chronicles that "Grand Prince Ivan Vasil'evich invested Khan Muhammad-Amin with the tsardom [khanate] of Kazan,"[9] together with their interpretation of the events surrounding the new khan's ascension to the throne, became the foundation for the theory, developed by nineteenth-century Russian imperial historiography and reasserted by Soviet historians, that a Muscovite protectorate was established over Kazan as early as 1487 and that from that time on the khan was a vassal of the grand prince of Muscovy.[10]

This theory is in need of some qualification. It is true that Ivan III managed to impose a number of practical limitations on the sovereignty of the Kazan Khanate after 1487, particularly in the realm of foreign relations. On account of these limitations, Kazan became, to use a modern concept, a "satellite" country of the Grand Principality of Moscow. However, one can reach a better understanding of this problem by examining the use of legal titles in the diplomatic correspondence with the Crimea and the Nogais and in the letters exchanged by Ivan III and Muhammad-Amin, of which a few have been preserved.[11] For example, in 1489, the Nogai prince Ibak was informed that Ivan III "had invested in this *iurt* of Kazan his brother and son Muhammad-Amin."[12] A copy of this letter was sent to the khan of Kazan. In this copy, however, the word "son" is conspicuously absent.[13] It should be pointed out that the "father and brother" or "son and brother" relationship between Ivan III and Muhammad-Amin was recognized by the Nogai prince Musa and the khan's mother, Nur-Sultan, who was the wife of the Crimean khan Mengli Girei.[14] The terms "brother and son" and "father and brother" did reflect the real nature of the link between Muscovy and

Kazan. It was, however, used exclusively in the correspondence between Muscovy and the Nogais, or the Crimea. In direct exchanges Ivan III and Muhammad-Amin addressed each other as "brother" only, indicating a status of formal equality. This practice reveals Ivan's interest in maintaining correct relations with the khan of Kazan by recognizing his formal sovereignty and independence. At the same time the Muscovite ruler used all possible devices to strengthen his *de facto* and *de jure* position with regard to Kazan in his contacts with other interested powers.

One is justified, however, in speaking of the establishment of the Muscovite protectorate over the Kazan Khanate in the period between 1516 and 1519. In the year 1516, according to Muscovite chronicles, the seriously ill Muhammad-Amin and "the whole Kazan land" made a clear commitment (apparently for the first time) not to invite a khan or a prince to Kazan without the grand prince's knowledge.[15] Muhammad-Amin's death in December 1518 was exploited by Muscovite diplomacy to strengthen the Russian position in Kazan. The chronicles maintain that Kul-Derbish, a Kazanian envoy who arrived in Moscow to report the death of Muhammad Amin, delivered a document addressed by the princes, nobility, clergy, members of the council, and "all the people of Kazan" to the grand prince, containing the following declaration:

> The Kazan land belongs to God and to you, the Sovereign and Grand Prince, and we are servants (*kholopi*) of God and of you, the Sovereign, and you should bestow your favor upon us and think about the whole Kazan land, and grant us a sovereign, and consider what should become of us.[16]

While some may consider this to be a later interpolation, the subsequent agreements of the new Khan Shah-Ali and the representatives of the princes and the Muslim clergy, who apparently spoke for the Kazan state, indicate that the Tatar khanate had submitted to Muscovite sovereignty. Before his departure for Kazan in March 1519, Shah-Ali signed two agreements: first, a treaty of friendship and fraternity and, second, a personal oath of fealty.[17] Similar agreements were entered into by the princes, the nobility, and all the people of Kazan, who swore allegiance to the grand prince for themselves and for their children. Boris Nolde was the first to observe that the agreement concluded by Vasilii III and Shah-Ali in 1519 was tantamount to the establishment of a Muscovite protectorate over the Kazan Khanate.[18] Nolde's choosing of the year 1519 was a bit too literal, but it speaks for his precise legal thinking inasmuch as he had just grounds for rejecting the date of 1487. It seems more likely that Kazan did become a vassal state of Muscovy during the years 1516-1519.[19]

Moscow's legal claims to Kazan rested on the alleged prerogative of its grand princes to invest the khans with the throne of the khanate. This claim to a right of investiture dates back to 1487, but it was expanded into an elaborate theory and used in negotiations almost simultaneously with the events of 1516-1519, especially in the period between 1517 and 1521.[20] Although the Khanate of Kazan was completely independent of Muscovy between 1535 and 1551 (with the exception of a brief interlude in 1546), Muscovite diplomacy continued to emphasize its right of investiture.[21] In addition, beginning with the early 1520s, Muscovite spokesmen began to apply the term *votchina* (patrimony) when referring to Kazan in negotiations with other states.[22] Particularly in the years 1550-1552, the view that Kazan was an ancient patrimony of the Muscovite grand princes was vigorously advanced in contacts with Poland-Lithuania and the Nogais.[23]

The claim that the Russian rulers had an exclusive right to invest the khans of Kazan and the assertion that, on account of this, Kazan was a patrimony of the Russian grand princes were medieval and feudal in nature and the least ideological of all the arguments put forward by Muscovite statesmen and bookmen. The bond of personal fealty between the grand prince and the khan (later between the grand prince and the various groups comprising Kazan's population) was their most outstanding feature. This personal and contractual relationship was usually stressed in negotiations with foreign countries. In reviewing the history of these legal claims, one can observe that the Russian court had a profound understanding of the two elements which make such claims persuasive: antiquity and continuity.

As a corollary, a theory based upon the right of conquest was proposed. It was most probably first enunciated at the beginning of 1534.[24] This theory served not only to buttress historical claims, such as the alleged military conquest of 1487, but also to justify the annexation of the territory of the right-bank Cheremissians from the Kazan Khanate in 1551.[25] The sources indicate that this argument "by the sword" (*sableiu*) was applied primarily to intercourse with Muslim rulers and princes.[26] Religious explanations of the military conquest were reserved for contacts with Western countries whose representatives would be receptive to reminders of their common Christian heritage.[27]

Muscovite political thought of the crucial first decades of the second half of the sixteenth century was not satisfied with these relatively simple legalistic assertions. More ancient, famous, and durable justifications were needed to glorify the forward march of the new empire. For these justifications Muscovite bookmen turned to East Slavic antiquity. They advanced the thesis that Muscovite grand princes and the newly crowned tsar were entitled to the territory of the Kazan Khanate, since it had been for a variety of reasons a possession of the line of Riurik "from antiquity." The *Nikon Chronicle* and the *L'vov Chronicle*, in a brief separate history of the relations between Muscovy and Kazan inserted under the entry for 1555, stated that before the foundation of this Tatar khanate "Russian grand princes beginning with Riurik ruled and collected tribute as far as the Caspian Sea and the Kama River."[28] A modified version of this entry is to be found in the *Book of Degrees*, whose compilers contended that:

> the Kazan land, which was called the Bulgar land before, was ruled from antiquity by Russian sovereigns, beginning with Grand Prince Riurik, who collected tribute as far as the Volga River, and as far as the Caspian Sea, and the Kama River.[29]

Two questions arise with regard to these historical claims based on somewhat vague dynastic foundations: What were their sources? Who was their author? Regarding the first question, I would like to advance the hypothesis that the major sources were selected passages from the description of the East Slavic tribes and their neighbors and from the narrative concerning the activities of Riurik, the alleged founder of the Kievan dynasty, in the *Povest' vremennykh let* (the *Primary Chronicle*). That chronicle states, among other things, the following:

> The Volga...flows to the east and discharges through seventy mouths into the Caspian Sea.... Along the river Oka [which flows into the Volga] the Muroma, the Cheremissians, and the Mordva preserve their native languages.... The

following are other tribes which pay tribute to Rus': Chud', Meria, Ves', Muroma, Cheremis', Mordva.... After two years, Sineus and his brother Truvor died and Riurik assumed the sole authority. He assigned cities to his followers, Polotsk to one, Rostov to another, and to another Beloozero. In these cities there are thus Varangian colonists, but the first settlers were: in Novgorod, Slavs; in Polotsk, Krivichians; at Beloozero, Ves'; in Rostov, Merians; and in Murom, Muromians. Riurik had dominion over all these districts.[30]

These passages were quite skillfully adapted by the compilers of the Muscovite chronicles. At the same time certain modifications and simplifications were undertaken to make the claim more concise and comprehensive. The *Primary Chronicle* did indeed refer to the Cheremissians and the Mordvinians as paying tribute to Rus' and located them at the Oka River. Muscovite bookmen, however, readjusted the geographic boundaries of the tribute-paying areas from the Oka to the Kama River and expanded them along the Volga to the Caspian Sea without naming the individual tribes. They also extended the dominion of Riurik far beyond the territories indicated by the *Primary Chronicle*. It is quite probable that the reference to the Caspian Sea was included as an attempt to substantiate Muscovite imperial ambitions toward the Khanate of Astrakhan. In short, the historical claims to the territories of both Tatar khanates were arrived at on the basis of a successful amalgamation of the relevant elements from the *Primary Chronicle*.

To answer the question of authorship, it seems most likely that these claims originated either with Metropolitan Makarii himself or with his immediate circle. The brief history of Russian-Kazanian relations in the *Nikon Chronicle* and the *L'vov Chronicle* under 1555 was inserted into the account of a series of events in which Makarii had played an important role, namely, the decision to establish an archbishopric of Kazan, the investiture of Gurii as its archbishop, the decision to build a church dedicated to the Virgin Mary in gratitude for the Kazan victory (the Cathedral of Vasilii the Blessed), and, last, the consecration of the church on orders from Ivan IV.[31] This brief history of Russian-Kazanian relations, which includes the reference to the rule of the Russian princes over the territories of the later Kazan and Astrakhan khanates, is permeated with strong religious overtones and reflects the extremely intolerant anti-Tatar and anti-

Muslim spirit of their author. The commentary which immediately follows this passage reads:

> And with God's grace and because of the great faith of the Orthodox Tsar Ivan Vasil'evich, and on account of his heart's desire, God turned over to him the godless Kazan Tatars, and our pious Sovereign destroyed their Muslim faith, and he demolished and devastated their mosques, and he enlightened with his piety their dark places, and he erected God's churches there and introduced Orthodoxy, and he established there an archbishopric and many clergymen in the churches desiring God's love on account of his faith.[32]

The tone of this statement is reminiscent of Makarii's attested writings, and the crucial passage concerning the rule of Russian princes over the territories in question figures quite prominently in the *Book of Degrees*, which was undoubtedly inspired by him.

Closely correlated with the somewhat ambiguous historical contentions were the more clearly articulated dynastic claims, which appear to be an outgrowth of the Kievan-Muscovite theory of continuity. These dynastic claims rested on the assumption that the Bulgar land on the Volga River had been conquered by Volodimer I[33] and that, as a result, it had become a patrimony of the Russian grand princes. This in turn led to the argument that Ivan IV was simply reestablishing his rightful authority over the Bulgar-Kazan territories, an idea which was presented, apparently for the first time, in the *Otryvok russkoi letopisi* (the *Fragment of a Russian Chronicle*).[34] Three special chapters of this historical account deal specifically with the conquest of Kazan.[35] They were most probably written very soon after the conquest of the Tatar khanate (ca. 1553-1555).

The first of these chapters, entitled "The Succession of the Old, and in Addition the Recovery of [the Bulgar Land] by the Sovereign, Orthodox Tsar and Muscovite Grand Prince Ivan Vasil'evich of All Rus' in the Year 1552," provides a brief history of the Russian-Tatar conflict and states the reasons for Ivan's campaign against Kazan. Its author attempted to justify Muscovite claims to the Bulgar land by proving a dynastic continuity from Volodimer I to Ivan IV. He observed that Ivan, embarking upon the Kazan campaign, set out for the new city of Sviiazhsk, to seek there, with God's grace, the Bulgar land, the patrimony of his ancestors, the Russian Grand Princes Volodimer and the second Volodimer Monomakh, and Grand Prince Dmitrii Ivanovich Donskoi, who excelled in everything and who gained victory against his enemies and those who did not submit to him.[36]

The editors of the *Fragment*, and particularly the author of this passage, selected historical precedents which could support their case. Volodimer I had indeed defeated the Bulgars. Volodimer Monomakh invested his son Iurii with Rostov, and he in turn attacked the Bulgars in 1120, was victorious, and returned with many prisoners.[37] Since this event occurred in Monomakh's lifetime, his inclusion into the line of the Bulgar conquerors was easily accomplished. More appropriate was the reference to Dmitrii Ivanovich Donskoi. In 1376, some Russian princes succeeded in imposing their supremacy over the Bulgars for a brief period. A Russian expeditionary force, combining troops from the principality of Nizhnii Novgorod and Muscovy, attacked the Bulgars. The princes of the Bulgar state were defeated and forced to pay ransom and, in addition, to accept a Russian customs official, at least for a brief time.[38] It was not a lasting arrangement, however; Dmitrii Donskoi's position in the east was too weak to maintain it after 1382.

Metropolitan Makarii may have also been instrumental in fostering the idea that the Bulgar land had been an ancient patrimony of the Russian rulers since Volodimer I. A passage in the *Fragment* mentioned Makarii in connection with Ivan's plans and preparations for the Kazan campaign, and his activities received considerable attention in this fragment of a chronicle.[39] It is the only chronicle to include a copy of the metropolitan's letter to Ivan IV written in August or September 1552.[40] In this letter, when speaking of the Tsar's intentions concerning the Kazan Khanate, Makarii points out that the Russian ruler wanted "to seek the property of his ancestors, the Russian grand princes, his patrimony the Kazan land."[41] This phrase is almost identical with the corresponding remark in the *Fragment*, except that here the word Kazan is used instead of Bulgar.

The strongest argument in favor of crediting Metropolitan Makarii with the introduction of the claim that the Bulgar land was a patrimonial possession of the Russian dynasty is to be found in the *Book of Degrees*. In this work, the theory of the continuity of rights to the ancient Bulgar state from Volodimer I to Ivan IV and of the close identification of that state with the Kazan Khanate is strongly emphasized. It finds its clearest expression in the chapter, entitled *Pobeda na Bolgary Volzhskiia i noveishee odolenie tsaria i velikogo kniazia Ivana* (the *Victory against the Volga Bulgars and the Most Recent Triumph of the Tsar and Grand Prince Ivan*).[42] It must have been written after the creation of the archbishopric in Kazan and after the conquest of the Astrakhan Khanate, that is, between 1556 and the early 1560s.[43] There is some evidence suggesting that it was written on the expressed orders of Metropolitan Makarii,[44] who received respectful attention in this text. This chapter connected the political and religious activities of Volodimer I and Ivan IV directly. The Muscovite tsar had now taken up the tasks of his Kievan predecessor. In contrast to the *Fragment*, the corresponding chapter in the *Book of Degrees* eliminated all the rulers between Volodimer I and Ivan IV, probably in order to extol the personality of Ivan IV and to underline the direct continuity of claims and achievements from Volodimer I to the Muscovite present.

The historical and dynastic pretensions to the territories of the Kazan Khanate were supplemented with a national justification which embraced such notions as "Russian land" and "autochtonous Russians." Whereas the *Nikon Chronicle* and the *L'vov Chronicle* had rested their case on the sovereign rights of the line of Riurik in the Volga region, the *Book of Degrees* proclaimed that the areas inhabited by the Cheremissians and the Mordvinians, which for more than a century had comprised a considerable part of the territories of the Kazan Khanate, had been provinces of the "Russian tsardom," ruled by the Russian dynasty since Volodimer I.[45] More elaborate references to Kazan as a "Russian land" can be found in the *Kazanskaia istoriia* (the *History of Kazan*):[46]

> There was from the beginning the Russian land, as the Russians and the barbarians say, always one Russian land, where now the city of Kazan stands...on both sides of the great river Volga, down to the Bulgar [boundaries] and to the Kama River. All this was a Kievan and a Vladimirian state and province, and since then and until now [part of] the Muscovite [state]. Bulgar princes and barbarians lived beyond the Kama River in their part of the land, ruling the pagan Cheremissian nation, knowing no God, and having no law whatsoever. Both of them were serving and paying tribute to the Russian tsardom until [the time] of Batu.[47]

Having applied the term "Russian land" to the khanate's territories, the author of this work displayed remarkable consistency by maintaining that "peaceful [*smirennyia*] Russian people [had been] living in the neighborhood of Kazan"[48] until the legendary Sayin Bolgarskii[49] expelled them from their native land and settled the "Bulgar mob" and other pagans there. The *History of Kazan* referred to the expelled inhabitants of the area as "autochtonous Russians" (*Rus'-tozemtsa*).[50] This was, of course, the most "modern" claim of all, since it even used an ethnic argument. In this respect *History of Kazan* seems to have anticipated political concepts which are usually regarded as belonging to a much later period.

The notion of "Russian land" was also utilized by the Muscovite chronicles and the *Book of Degrees* to justify the conquest of the Astrakhan Khanate (1556) soon after that of Kazan. Astrakhan was declared to be the ancient Tmutorokan', although ancient Tmutorokan' was located on the Kerch Peninsula, that is, opposite the Crimea, whereas Astrakhan was in the area where the Volga flows into the Caspian Sea. While it is not impossible that the Russians of the mid-sixteenth century may have had a rather vague notion of the exact geographic location of the ancient Tmutorokan', the relevant passage in the *Nikon Chronicle* and the *L'vov Chronicle* clearly indicates that the identification of the cities was undertaken with the purpose of buttressing Muscovy's claim to an ancient "Russian land."[51]

All these propositions represent an extension of the "gathering of Russian lands," an argument which was now being applied to the former khanates of Kazan and Astrakhan. Once both came to be regarded as ancient "Russian lands," their recovery would easily be interpreted as the successful realization of the goal to unify all of Russia.

In conjunction with secular claims, Muscovite theorists promulgated a whole set of religious arguments in support of the Kazan conquest. To them the Russian advance against the khanate was but one phase in the protracted conflict of two antagonistic worlds in human history: Orthodox Christianity and Islam. Logically enough, the most determined exhortations to wage a relentless struggle against the dark forces of "heathenism" in its "lair" came from the leading representatives of the Muscovite clergy, particularly those of Josephan persuasion. Among them, Metropolitan Makarii played the most important role. He was, as a matter of fact, the chief ideologue of the Muscovite crusade against the Kazan Tatars. In 1552, on the eve of the conquest, Makarii, in a series of letters,[52] relying heavily on the arguments and stylistic devices of Vasiian Rylo's Epistle to Ivan III,[53] most dramatically drew the battle lines between the holy Orthodox faith and the forces of Mohammedanism or the "devil," as represented by the Crimean and Kazan Tatars. He portrayed the Ishmaelites, or sons of Hagar, as the great enemies of the Christian empire and eternal adversaries of the Russian people. Makarii did not fail to equate the sufferings of the Russian people, tormented by invasion, devastation, and servitude in Muslim captivity, with the universal struggle between the forces of good and evil. He indicated that these sacrifices would be avenged in the final encounter. In the epistles and statements included in the *Chronicle of the Beginnings of the Tsardom*, Makarii advocated the destruction of Islam in Kazan and the introduction of Christianity into the newly conquered land.

However, the emphasis on the religious motives for the struggle was not restricted to ecclesiastics. It can also be found in the works of laymen such as Ivan Peresvetov and Prince A.M. Kurbskii. These are not of much concern to us here since they reflect private, rather than official, views. Of greater importance are the attitudes expressed in the *Chronicle of the Beginnings* and the *Imperial Book*, since they represent works of official court historiography. They also use a providential interpretation of history in general and for the Russian-Tatar conflict in particular. The compilers of these works presented three major arguments to justify the struggle against Kazan: the notorious wickedness and perjury of the Kazan Tatars; the wrongs committed by Muslims against the Russian Christians; and the superiority of Christianity over Mohammedanism. Their message was simple and obvious: the Light (Russia or Christianity) must win in the end over the forces of Darkness (Mohammedanism or Kazan).

Abstract generalizations did not seem to satisfy the imperial apologists. More concrete revelations of divine support for the Orthodox cause were thought necessary, and Muscovite bookmen found them in prophecies and miracles which were a traditional part of Christian religious literature. The *Book of Degrees* became their major source. The compilers of this work wished to instill a belief in the inevitability of the final victory over the "pagan" khanate and the expansion of the Christian empire into its territories. In a special tale about the conquest of Kazan, entitled *O blagovedimom podvyze tsaria... (About the God-Inspired Achievement of the Tsar...)*, the author (most probably Andrei-Afanasii, chief compiler of the *Kniga stepennaia*, the tsar's confessor and metropolitan of Russia from 1564) enumerated a series of prophecies and miracles which foretold the final demise of the Kazan Khanate.[54] Some of these dealt with Tatars who made gloomy predictions regarding their future and foresaw their own destruction. For example, Princess Kovgorshad allegedly anticipated that Ivan IV would "conquer not only the Kazan tsardom, but also other countries."[55] Others were attributed to Russians – for example, the story of Ivan's hearing the ringing of bells in Muslim Kazan.[56] Most of these prophecies and omens were adopted by the *Imperial Book* and thus became integral elements of Muscovite state ideology.[57] Their extensive use in the *Tsarstvennaia kniga* suggests that by the 1560s Muscovite political thought had intensified its use of religious justifications for Russian foreign policy.

Speaking of divine revelations in support of Russian Orthodoxy in its confrontation with the forces of Islam, one might recall the role ascribed to the icon of Our Lady of Kazan and the legend attached to it. This legend is closely associated with the activities of Germogen, the first metropolitan of Kazan and Astrakhan, and later Patriarch of All Russia.[58] He should be considered the chief author and certainly the editor of the *Povest' (skazanie) o iavlenii i chudesakh ikony Kazanskoi Bogomateri* (the *Tale [Narration] about the Appearance and the Miracles of the Icon of the Mother of God of Kazan*) (in the manuscript it is entitled: *Mesiatsa iiulia v 8 den'. Povest' i chudesa prechistye Bogoroditsy chestnago i slavnago eia iavleniia obraza, izhe v Kazani. Spisano smirennim Ermogenom, mitropolitom Kazan'skim* [*On the Eighth Day of the Month of July. The Tale and the Miracles of the Virgin Mother of God (and) of the Honorable and Famous Appearance of Her Image (Icon) in Kazan. Written by the Humble Germogen, Metropolitan of Kazan*]),[59] which originated this famous legend. The final editing of the *Tale* was undertaken by Germogen in late 1594 or early 1595.[60]

According to the legend, a fire occurred in Kazan on June 23, 1579, which brought forth a miraculous appearance of the icon of the Virgin Mary. In the wording of the *Tale* the Muslims interpreted the outbreak of the fire as God's punishment of the Christians, who were committing idolatrous acts by venerating icons and other images. The Orthodox, on the other hand, were in need of evidence of divine assistance in their spiritual battle with the Muslims. The consequent providential interference was described in the *Tale* as follows:

> There were still many pagan peoples in the city, and they adhered to many religions. The true Orthodox faith represented to them foolishness and profanation, and there was no healing relic in the city at that time. The foreigners, their hearts possessed by unbelief, humiliated us, not knowing God's mercy and power.... God, loving mankind and seeing the sufferings of his people and their faith, and their profanation and abuse by the surrounding non-believers, could not bear the defamation and desecration of the holy icons...and so that their lips which spoke falsehood be closed, and that the Jewish and Muslim obstinacy and false defamation be ended and disappear, and that the pernicious heretical teaching be uprooted, and that the true Orthodox faith of the Greek law be asserted and glorified...God revealed upon earth the most illustrious icon...of Our Lady, the Virgin Mary.[61]

Although neither Judaism nor Christian "heretical teachings" were part of the religious struggle in Kazan, the author of the *Tale* used the attack against them to magnify the dangers which beset Orthodoxy and to show God's infinite mercy toward the true believers. The icon of Our Lady of Kazan became one of the most famous objects of religious veneration in Russian history. Whereas the miracles and legends of the *Book of Degrees* and the *Imperial Book* were reserved for the edification of the elite, the cult of the icon was meant to appeal to the masses, who were more easily impressed by a concrete and visible symbol. As late as 1912 the conservative historian S. Kedrov remarked that "from the time [of its appearance] until the present, this icon has symbolized the triumph not only of [Christian] Kazan but also of all Orthodox Russia over alien religions."[62]

With a few minor exceptions, the argument that the Kazanian wars were fought to liberate Christian captives appears quite late in Muscovite official sources, and only when the struggle reached its final stages did the problem of captives come to be part of the ideological program. It was given a great deal of prominence in the second part of the *Chronicle of the Beginnings of the Tsardom*, which deals exclusively with the last period of the Russian-Kazanian relations and the conquest of the khanate. The title of that part reads as follows:

> The Beginning of the Tale of How the All-Merciful God, Loving Mankind, Created the Most Famous Miracles in Our Nation through Our Orthodox, Pious Tsar, the Grand Prince Ivan Vasil'evich, the Sovereign and Autocrat of All of Rus' [by Liberating] the Orthodox Christians from Muslim Captivity and the Servitude of the Godless Kazan Tatars....[63]

One of the famous interpolations of the *Imperial Book* credited Ivan with being a liberator of Christians from the Muslim yoke.[64] Both the *Book of Degrees* and the *History of Kazan* consistently emphasized that concern for prisoners was a determining factor in Muscovy's struggle against the Tatar khanate.

The victory over Kazan was viewed by contemporary Muscovites as a triumph of Orthodoxy. Kazan was to be "enlightened" by their version of Orthodox Christianity; conversion came to be regarded as one of the great tasks which God had bestowed upon the Muscovite empire. Evidence both in the sources of the period and in official pronouncements suggests that the imperial government very soon embarked upon a conscious program to convert the various nationalities of the former Kazan Khanate. This program was formulated, almost immediately after the conquest, by Sil'vestr, the archpriest of the Annunciation Cathedral in the Kremlin, who was influential in state affairs between 1547 and 1553 and was also a leading publicist of his time. In his "Letter to Prince Aleksandr Gorbatyi" (the new governor of Kazan),[65] Sil'vestr asserted that it was one of the duties of Orthodox rulers "to convert pagans to the Orthodox faith even if they do not desire it...so that all the universe should be permeated with Orthodoxy."[66] On these grounds he concluded that all the "sons of Hagar [Tatars] and the Cheremissians who have been turned over to us by God [should] be enlightened with holy baptism."[67]

The establishment of the archbishopric of Kazan in 1555 and Ivan's instructions to Gurii in May 1555 and April 1557 are convincing evidence that the Muscovite government encouraged conversion of the population[68] by supporting it with funds and land grants to the Church. Christianization and, in consequence, Russification became integral elements of the official state policy in the newly conquered territory.[69]

The conquest of Kazan was hailed by Muscovite bookmen as a great national success for Russia. It served as a focus for the formulation of Muscovite Russia's mission in the world. Filofei of Pskov had already asserted that Russia was the one sanctuary of true Orthodoxy and the defender of pure faith chosen by God. Some thirty years later Makarii, Sil'vestr, and the compilers of the official chronicles were proclaiming that it was Muscovy's mission throughout the entire world to spread Orthodoxy among the "barbarian nations." Makarii had prayed during the coronation ceremonies in 1547 for their subjugation;[70] the conquest of Kazan had proved the efficacy of his prayers.

Muscovite diplomacy and historiography utilized the annexations of Kazan and Astrakhan to enhance the image of their country as a powerful and influential empire in international affairs.[71] Both the conquests themselves and the subsequent assumption of the titles "Tsar of Kazan" and "Tsar of Astrakhan" by the Russian ruler were used in diplomatic negotiations aimed at obtaining the recognition of the Tsar's imperial title by other powers.[72] The conquests also provided Muscovite theorists with an opportunity to define Russia's role in history and contributed to a growing awareness of this role in Russian political thought. Finally, they helped to make territorial expansion and annexation of populations a national virtue and political goal, an aim common to the majority of centralized national states.

Muscovite imperial claims to Kazan were not of a very sophisticated sort. However, the value of an ideology is not always determined by its level of sophistication. Muscovite bookmen may not have reached high intellectual standards from the theoretical point of view, but they certainly knew what they wanted – and this is, after all, one of the fundamental elements of success both in ideology and in politics.

NOTES

1. The historical background of this first major Muscovite expansion beyond Great Russian ethnic territories has been analyzed by M. Khudiakov, *Ocherki po istorii kazanskogo khanstva* (Kazan, 1923); Igor Smolitsch, "Zur Geschichte der russischen Ostpolitik des 15. und 16. Jahrhunderts (Die Eroberung des Kazaner Reiches)," *Jahrbücher für Geschichte Osteuropas*, VI (1941), 55-84; I.I. Smirnov, "Vostochnaia politika Vasiliia III," *Istoricheskie zapiski*, XXVII (1948), 18-66; Boris Nolde, *La Formation de l'Empire Russe*, vol. I (Paris, 1952); S.O. Shmidt, "Predposylki i pervye gody 'Kazanskoi voiny' (1545-1549)," *Trudy Gosudarstvennogo istoriko-arkhivnogo instituta*, VI (1954), 187-257; Edward L. Keenan, "Muscovy and Kazan: 1445-1552: A Study in Steppe Politics," doctoral dissertation (Harvard University, 1965). For a comprehensive treatment of the Russian-Tatar relations in the fifteenth and sixteenth centuries, see also V.V. Vel'iaminov-Zernov, *Izsledovanie o Kasimovskikh tsariakh i tsarevichakh*, vol. I (St. Petersburg, 1863); B. Spuler, *Die Goldene Horde (Die Mongolen in Russland: 1223-1502)* (Leipzig, 1943); B.D. Grekov and A.Iu. Iakubovskii, *Zolotaia Orda i ee padenie*, (Moscow and Leningrad, 1950); M.G. Safargaliev, *Raspad zolotoi Ordy* (Saransk, 1960; "Uchenye Zapiski Mordovskogo gosudarstvennogo universiteta," *Vypusk* XI).

2. The *Letopisets* was identified as a separate historical work and one of the sources of the *Nikon Chronicle* by A.A. Shakhmatov, in *Obozrenie letopisnykh svodov Rusi severovostochnoi I.A. Tikhomirova* (offprint from *Otchet o sorokovom prisuzhdenii nagrad grafa Uvarova*) (St. Petersburg, 1899), 73. For its components, dating, and probable authorship, consult N.F. Lavrov, "Zametki o Nikonovskoi letopisi," *Letopis' zaniatii Arkheograficheskoi komissii* (*LZAK*), *Vypusk* 1 (34) (Leningrad, 1927), 55-90; and A.A. Zimin, *I.S. Peresvetov i ego sovremenniki* (Moscow and Leningrad, 1958), 29-41. A critical edition of the text is to be found in the *Polnoe sobranie russkikh letopisei* (*PSRL*), XXIX (1965), 9-116. The *Letopisets* was most probably compiled between 1553 and 1555.

3. Lavrov has already suggested that the "Continuations" of the *Nikon Chronicle* for the years 1553-1556 constituted an independent text, the sources of which were the official documents of the Muscovite state archive and the "Draft Copies" of the *Chronicle of New Years* (p. 89). See also S.O. Shmidt, ed., *Opisi tsarskogo arkhiva XVI veka i arkhiva posol'skogo prikaza 1614 goda* (Moscow, 1960), 43. Zimin extended these observations to cover the "Continuations" for the period 1556-1558 in the *Nikon Chronicle* and for the years 1559-1560 in the *L'vov Chronicle* (*I.S. Peresvetov*, 29-31). For the text of the "Continuations" in the *Nikon Chronicle*, see *PSRL*, XIII, part 1 (1965; offset reproduction of the 1904 edition), 228-300; in the *L'vov Chronicle, PSRL*, XX, part 2 (1914), 538-621.

4. The text of the *Tsarstvennaia kniga* was published in *PSRL*, XIII, part 2 (1965; offset reproduction of the 1906 edition), 409-532. For an analysis and identification of the components of the text, see A.E. Presniakov, *Tsarstvennaia kniga, eia sostav i proiskhozhdenie* (St. Petersburg, 1893).

5. The *Illuminated Chronicle* represented an ambitious attempt to connect Russia's history with the universal historical developments of antiquity. Its coverage of Russian history embraced the period from 1114 to 1567. This huge compilation included 16,000 miniatures which illustrated the historical events of antiquity and of Russia's past. For an analysis of the components and the dating of this remarkable work, compare A.E. Presniakov, "Moskovskaia istoricheskaia entsiklopediia XVI

veka," *Izvestiia Otdeleniia russkogo iazyka i slovesnosti* (*IORIaS*), V, no. 3 (1900), 824-876, and separate reprint; N.P. Likhachev, *Paleograficheskoe znachenie bumazhnikh vodianykh znakov* (St. Petersburg, 1899), cliv-clxxxi and 300-315; O.I. Podobedova, *Miniatiury russkikh istoricheskikh rukopisei* (Moscow, 1965), 102-134.

6. A critical edition of the *Kniga stepennaia* was published in *PSRL*, XXI, part 1 (1908); part 2 (1913). The first comprehensive textual analysis of this work was provided by P.H. Vasenko, *"Kniga stepennaia tsarskogo rodoslaviia" i ee znachenie v drevnerusskoi istoricheskoi pis'mennosti*, I (St. Petersburg, 1904). For the discussion and the literature on this subject, see David Miller, "The Literary Activities of Metropolitan Macarius: A Study of Muscovite Political Ideology in the Time of Ivan IV," doctoral dissertation (Columbia University, 1967).

7. Russian historiography of the eighteenth and nineteenth centuries was profoundly influenced by the historical ideas and ideological propositions of the Muscovite chronicles of the fifteenth and sixteenth centuries. Russian historians of modern times, by reading these chronicles, were equipped with a ready-made conceptual framework for early Russian history. In particular, the idea of "continuity" from the Kievan state to Muscovy was accepted as a matter of fact. For some astute remarks on this problem, see P.N. Miliukov, *Glavnyia techeniia russkoi istoricheskoi mysli* (3rd ed., Moscow, 1913), 177; and A.E. Presniakov, *Obrazovanie velikorusskogo gosudarstva (Ocherki po istorii XIII-XV stoletii)* (Petrograd, 1920), 2-3, 7, and 19.

8. Muscovite sources quite naturally provide a biased view of the Slavic-Tatar relations. This view is predetermined by the propagandistic and ideological nature of the sources. Most regrettably, the lack of comparable sources from the Tatar side prevents us from drawing valid parallels. Thus, the very nature of sources in the realm of political thought and historiography makes a polycultural and pluralistic approach very difficult in this type of study.

9. *PSRL*, XXVII (1962), 288, 359; *PSRL*, VIII (1859), 217; *PSRL*, XII (1901/1965), 219.

10. Historians have used various legal terms to describe this "protectorate" more precisely. S.M. Solov'ev spoke of "subordination" (*Istoriia Rossii s drevneishikh vremen*, III [Moscow, 1960], 71; vol. III of this Soviet edition comprises the original vols. V and VI, which first appeared in 1855 and 1856). K.V. Basilevich stated that after 1487 Kazan came under Muscovite "protection" and Muhammad-Amin became a vassal of the Muscovite grand prince (*Vneshniaia politika russkogo tsentralizovannogo gosudarstva [Vtoraia polovina XV veka]* [Moscow, 1952], 205). George Vernadsky also described Muhammad-Amin as a "vassal" of Ivan III (*Russia at the Dawn of the Modern Age* [New Haven, 1959], 82). The idea of a "protectorate" was even used by Khudiakov (p. 43). J.L.I. Fennell certainly overstated the case for the vassalage theory by asserting that Muhammad-Amin "was as much Ivan's vassal as were the Tatar *tsarevichi* of Kasimov" (*Ivan the Great of Moscow* [London, 1961], 96). He also followed the propagandistic phraseology of the Muscovite chronicles a bit too closely when he spoke of "treacherous Kazanites." I.I. Smirnov attempted to buttress the theory of vassalage with a phrase from the *Ustiug Chronicle*, where the entry for 1486 contains the following reference: "This year Tsar [Khan] Muhammad-Amin fled from Kazan, from his brother Ali-Khan, and submitted to the grand prince [Ivan Vasil'evich]. And he called the grand prince his father, and he asked him for support against his brother Ali-Khan, the tsar [khan] of Kazan, and the grand prince promised him his support" (*Ustiuzhskii Letopisnyi Svod* [Moscow and Leningrad, 1950], 95-96). From this passage and some questionable evidence to be found in *Kazanskaia istoriia*, for example, the statement that the grand

prince installed in Kazan *sluzhashchego svoiego tsaria Mukhammed-Amina* (*PSRL*, XIX [1903], 22), Smirnov concluded that "*bit'e chelom* and recognition of someone as 'father' were concepts of Russian feudal law by which vassal dependence was expressed" (Smirnov, "Vostochnaia politika," 18, fn. 1).

11. *Sbornik Imperatorskogo russkogo istoricheskogo obshchestva* (*SIRIO*), XLI (1884), 85, 92, 96, 130, 131, 132, and 133.

12. *Ibid.*, 83.

13. *Ibid.*, 85.

14. The letter of Prince Musa to Ivan III includes the following statement: "You are father, brother, and friend of Muhammad-Amin.... If you should order [Musa] to give his daughter in marriage to Muhammad-Amin, he will do accordingly; if you should order him not to, he will not" (*SIRIO*, XLI, 90). A similar phrase is to be found in Nur Sultan's letter to Ivan III in 1491 (*ibid.*, 126).

15. *Ioasafovskaia letopis'* (*IL*), A.A. Zimin, ed. (Moscow, 1957), 167; *PSRL*, VIII, 260; *PSRL*, VIII, part 1, 25 ("...a Mukhammed-Emin tsar' da i vsia zemlia Kazanskaia dadut velikomu kniaziu pravdu, kakovu kniaz' pokhochet, chto im bez velikogo kniazia vedoma na Kazan' tsaria, ni tsarevicha [nikakova] ne vziat' ").

16. *IL*, 172; *PSRL*, VIII, 266; *PSRL*, XIII, part 1, 28.

17. *IL*, 176-177; *PSRL*, VIII, 266; *PSRL*, XIII, part 1, 32.

18. Nolde, I, 21.

19. The evidence for any hypothesis on this matter is fragmentary and incomplete. In Shmidt, ed., *Opisi tsarskogo arkhiva XVI veka* (p. 18), texts of agreements between the Muscovite rulers and Muhammad-Amin, Abdel-Letif, and"all the Kazan land" are mentioned which pertain to the period before 1516 ("Iashchik 13-i. A v nem gramota shertnaia Magmed'-Amineva tsareva s velikim kniazem Vasil'em o Abdelitefe tsare; i gramota shertnaia vsee zemli Kazanskie. Iashchik 14-i. A v nem gramoty shertnye Magemed'-Aminevy tsarevy i Abdeletifovy tsarevy s velikim kniazem Ivanom i s velikim kniazem Vasil'em -- vsekh gramot 11"). Unfortunately, the agreements dealing with the direct relations between Kazan and Muscovy are not available.

20. *Pamiatniki diplomaticheskikh snoshenii drevnei Rossii s derzhavami innostrannymi*, I (1851), 288-289; *SIRIO*, XXXV (1882), 531, and 559; *SIRIO*, LIII (1887), 218; *SIRIO*, XCV (1895), 685-696.

21. *SIRIO*, LIX (1887), 26, 40, 54, 116-117, 171-180, 227, and 320-321.

22. *SIRIO*, XXXV, 617 and 659.

23. *SIRIO*, LIX, 343; *Prodolzhenie Drevnei Rossiiskoi Vivliofiki* (*PDRV*), VIII (1793), 309.

24. To the best of my knowledge, the letter of the Muscovite court to Khan Sahib-Girei of the Crimea dated February 1534 has not been published. Excerpts from this important document have been utilized by Solov'ev (III, 418), Khudiakov (p. 94), and Shmidt, "Predposylki," 238), all of whom quoted as their source *Dela Krymskie*, Book 8, in Tsentral'nyi Gosudarstvennyi Arkhiv Drevnikh Aktov, fol. 123. There is some divergence between the versions offered by the three authors. All three contain the crucial allegation that Ivan III had conquered Kazan and, because of this, was the rightful sovereign of the khanate. The quotation in Shmidt reads as follows: "A chto esi pisal, nam, chto Kazanskaia zemlia iurt tvoi, to, posmotri v starye letopistsy, kotoryi gosudar pridet rat'iu da vozmet kotorogo gosudaria, da ego svedet, a zemliu ego dast komu vskhochet, ne togo li zemlia budet, khto ee vzial? I ty, Kazani pomogaiushche, molchal esi; tsari kotorye lishas' svoikh iurtov ordinskikh, prished na Kazanskii iurt, voinami i nepravdami, chto imali, i to ty pamiatuesh; a, chto ded nash

kniaz' velikii Ivan milostiiu Bozhiieiu Kazan' vzial i tsaria svel s mater'iu i s tsaritseiu
i s bratiieiu, togo ty ne pamiatuesh."
   25. *PSRL*, XXIX, 64; cf. Khudiakov, 129.
   26. *PSRL*, XXIX, 64, *PDRV*, VIII, 309; *PDRV*, IX (1793), 120.
   27. *SIRIO*, LIX, 103.
   28. *PSRL*, XIII, part 1, 251; *PSRL*, XX, part 2, 556-557. Equivalent wording
can be found in the *Letopisets russkii* (the *Lebedev Chronicle*) in the version published in *Chteniia v Obshchestve istorii i drevnostei rossiiskikh* (*ChOIDR*), 1895, book
3, sec. 1, 32. The relevant passage was not included in the most recent edition of the
Lebedev Chronicle (*PSRL*, XXIX, 235).
   29. *PSRL*, XXI, part 2, 653.
   30. *The Russian Primary Chronicle* (Laurentian Text), S.H. Cross and O.P.
Sherbowitz-Wetzor, eds. (Cambridge, MA, 1953), 53, 55, and 60.
   31. *PSRL*, XIII, part 1, 250-252; *PSRL*, XX, part 2, 555-557.
   32. *PSRL*, XIII, part 1, 251; *PSRL*, XX, part 2, 557.
   33. The problem of Volodimer's conquest of the Volga Bulgars represents
one of the most complicated issues of the history of Kievan Rus'. The *Primary
Chronicle*, under the entry for the year 985, reports: "Accompanied by his uncle
Dobrynia, Volodimer set out by boat to attack the Bulgars. He also brought Torks
overland on horseback, and defeated the Bulgars" (*Povest' vremennykh let*, D.S.
Likhachev, ed. [Moscow and Leningrad, 1950], I, 59). Russian historiography vacil-
lated for a long time over the issue whether this reference was made to the Bulgars on
the Volga River or to the Bulgarians on the Danube. For a discussion of the literature
on this problem, see *ibid.*, II, 328, and the *Russian Primary Chronicle*, Notes, 244, fn.
89. I accept the conclusions of those authors who maintain that the campaign was
directed against the Volga Bulgars because Iakov's *Pamiat' i pokhvala kniaziu
Vladimiru*, a work written relatively close to the event, corroborates their contention.
The best critical edition of this text, from a copy dated 1494, was published by V.I.
Sreznevskii, ed., "Pamiat' i pokhvala kniaziu Vladimiru i ego zhitie po sp. 1494 g.,"
Zapiski Imperatorskoi Akademii Nauk, Eighth Series, I, no. 6 (1897), 1-12. The
relevant passage reads as follows: "And wherever he went, he gained victory; he
defeated the Rademichians and the Viatichians and imposed tribute on both of them,
and he conquered the Iatviagians and he defeated the Silver Bulgars, and he went
against the Khazars and defeated them and imposed tribute on them" (p. 6).
Sixteenth-century Russian chronicles helped to clarify this issue by making unmistakable references to the Volga Bulgars. Whereas their compilers did not engage in any
outright tampering with the older sources, they apparently were not adverse to setting
the historical record straight (*PSRL*, VII [1856], 295 ["Victory against the Bulgars
who are on the Volga River"]; *PSRL*, IX [1862/1965], 42 ["Volodimer went against
the *Nizovzkie* Bulgars"]). Relying on the narrative of the *Primary Chronicle*, one is
justified in concluding that Volodimer failed to exploit his victory in political terms.
Vernadsky observed that the campaign of 985 "ended in victory but a rather indeci-
sive one" (*Kievan Russia* [4th printing; New Haven and London, 1963], 60). It is
only in the late fifteenth-century chronicles that one finds assertions concerning
Volodimer's imposition of tribute on the Bulgars (*PSRL*, XXVII, 23) or his subjugation of them (*PSRL*, XXVIII [1963], 17). Of particular importance for our purpose
are the references in the *Nikon Chronicle* to two additional campaigns against the
Bulgars (under the entries for 994 and 997), which are not attested in earlier sources
(*PSRL*, IX, 65, 66). A.P. Smirnov utilized the testimony of the *Nikon Chronicle* on
these campaigns without any critical evaluation ("Ocherki po istorii drevnikh

bulgar," *Trudy Gosudarstvennogo istoricheskogo muzeia, Vypusk* XI [1940], 86; and "Volzhskie Bulgary," *ibid.*, XIX [1951], 44). The entry under 997 reads as follows: "Volodimer went against the Volga and Kama Bulgars, and, having defeated them, he conquered them." A corresponding statement was included in the *Kniga stepennaia*, which contends that Volodimer "twice waged war against them [the Volga and the Kama Bulgars], and he triumphed, and defeated, and conquered them" (*PSRL*, XXI, part 1, 116). The *Nikon Chronicle* credited even the legendary Kii with having attacked and defeated the Volga and Kama Bulgars (*PSRL*, IX, 4).

   34. Published as a supplement to the *Second Sophia Chronicle* in *PSRL*, VI (1853), 277-315.
   35. *Ibid.*, 303-315.
   36. *Ibid.*, 304.
   37. *PSRL*, I (*Lavrent'evskaia letopis'*) (1962; offset reproduction of the 1926-1928 edition), 292; *Letopis' po Ipatskomu spisku* (St. Petersburg, 1871), 205. See also Solov'ev, *Istoriia Rossii*, I (1960), 408.
   38. *PSRL*, XVIII (1913), 117-118. See Solov'ev, *Istoriia Rossii*, II (1960), 282; M.N. Tikhomirov, *Rossiia v XVI stoletii* (Moscow, 1962), 21.
   39. *PSRL*, VI, 282; 284-285, 285-289, 289, 296, 297, and 299.
   40. *Ibid.*, 308-309.
   41. *Ibid.*, 308.
   42. *PSRL*, XXI, part 1, 115-116.
   43. Vasenko, 213 and 217.
   44. *PSRL*, XXI, part 1, 58.
   45. *Ibid.*, 63.
   46. The first scholarly founded dating of the *Kazanskaia istoriia*, that is 1564-1566, was provided by G.Z. Kuntsevich, *Istoriia o Kazanskom Tsarstve ili Kazanskii letopisets* (St. Petersburg, 1905), 176-179, subsequently narrowed down to 1564-1565 by G.N. Moiseeva, ed., *Kazanskaia istoriia* (Moscow and Leningrad, 1954), 20-21, fn. 5. In my opinion, the writing of the *Kazanskaia istoriia* took place in three stages. The bulk of the work (through chapter 67) was composed in the mid-1560s, additional writing and editing took place between 1584 and 1592/1594, and the third rewriting and editing was undertaken in the early seventeenth century. For a dissenting hypothesis, maintaining that version 1 of the text appeared most probably between 1626 and 1640, see E.L. Keenan, "Muscovy and Kazan, 1445-1552," 55-71. For reliable editions of the text of the *Kazanskaia istoriia*, see *PSRL*, XIX (1903) and G.N. Moiseeva, ed., *Kazanskaia istoriia*.
   47. *PSRL*, XIX, 2. Commentators on this passage compared its contents with the entry in the *Nikon Chronicle* (or the *Lebedev Chronicle*) under 1555, and Ivan IV's letter to the Nogai mirza Ismail of January 1553 in which the former observed "that the Kazan *iurt* [has been] our *iurt* from antiquity" (*PDRV*, IX, 63-64). Cf. Kuntsevich, 195; Moiseeva, ed., *Kazanskaia istoriia*, 177. The author of the passage in question also relied upon ideas and concepts in other works. Significant parallelisms can be detected in the seventh chapter of the first degree of the *Kniga stepennaia*, entitled "The Names of Russian Provinces" (*PSRL*, XXI, part 1, 63). This chapter represents an adaptation of the description of the old East Slavic tribes and their neighbors from the *Russian Primary Chronicle*, 55. Speaking of the Cheremissians and the Mordvinians, the author of the chapter asserted that they populated "countries of the Russian tsardom which were ruled over, and [from which] tribute was collected, by the blessed family of the Grand Prince Volodimer Sviatoslavich for generation after generation," and that their lands were integral parts of "one Russian

state." Another instructive parallelism is to be found in the *Russian Chronograph of 1512*. In this work, a chapter eulogizing the deeds of Vsevolod III Iur'evich of Vladimir (1176-1212) ended with the statement that he "ruled over all the Russian land along the Volga as far as the sea" (*PSRL*, XXII, part 1 [1911], 388). For many extensive borrowings from the *Russian Chronograph of 1512* by the *Kazanskaia istoriia*, compare A.S. Orlov, "Khronograf i 'Povest' o Kazanskom tsarstve," *Sbornik Otdeleniia russkogo iazyka i slovesnosti AN SSSR*, CI, no. 3 (1928), 188-193 (*Sbornik statei v chest' akademika Alekseia Ivanovicha Sobolevskogo*). The author of the passage in the *Kazanskaia istoriia* apparently integrated and adapted ideas from a variety of sources. He was quite certainly indebted to the *Kniga stepennaia* for the notion of Russian tsardom before Batu and the view of its unitary character. Furthermore, he may have depended on the *Russian Chronograph of 1512*, or its earlier version, for his own formulation of the additional national argument for the incorporation of Kazan.

48. *PSRL*, XIX, 12.

49. The story of Sayin Bolgarskii, the founder of the Kazan Khanate, is not historical (*PSRL*, XIX, 10-13; Moiseeva, ed., *Kazanskaia istoriia*, 47-48). It is a well-known fact that Sayin was an epithet for Khan Batu: "good" khan or "distinguished" khan (Spuler, 31-32; Kuntsevich, 229). The author of the story about Sayin Bolgarskii erroneously considered Batu and Sayin to be two different persons. In another context he stated that "after the death of Tsar Batu ...another tsar, by the name of Sayin, began to rule" (*PSRL*, XIX, 10; Moiseeva, ed., *Kazanskaia istoriia*, 46).

50. *PSRL*, XIX, 12.

51. *PSRL*, XIII, part 1, 235-236; and XX, part 2, 545. See also the *Lebedev Chronicle* on this point (*PSRL*, XXIX, 225).

52. "Poslanie Mitropolita Makariia v Sviiazhsk k tsarskomu voisku," *Akty istoricheskie* (*AI*), I (1841), no. 159, 287-290 (dated May 25, 1552); "Poslanie uchitel'no presviashchennogo Makariia Mitropolita vsei Rusii v Sviiazhskii grad," *PSRL*, XIII, part 1, 180-183; *PSRL*, XXIX, 75-78 (dated May 21, 1552). "Poslanie Mitropolita Makariia Tsariu Ioannu Vasil'evichu o ukreplenii na bran' s kazanskimi Tatarami," *AI*, I, no. 160, 290-296; *PSRL*, XIII, part 1, 192-197; *PSRL*, XXIX, 86-90. "Poslanie ot Mitropolita Makariia velikomu kniaziu," *PSRL*, VI, 308-309 (this letter, written in August or September 1552, must have reached Ivan IV before the fall of Kazan on October 2).

53. *PSRL*, VI, 225-230. Cf. I.M. Kudriavtsev, " 'Poslanie na Ugru' Vassiiana Rylo kak pamiatnik publitsistiki XV v.," *Trudy Otdela drevnerusskoi literatury*, VIII (1951), 182-183. Makarii lacked originality as a writer (Zimin, *I.S. Peresvetov*, 76); from a stylistic point of view, Makarii's letters were much weaker than Vasiian's epistle.

54. *PSRL*, XXI, part 2, 638-651.

55. *Ibid.*, 639.

56. *Ibid.*, 646.

57. For the first identification of the borrowings from the *Kniga stepennaia* in the *Tsarstvennaia kniga*, see Presniakov, *Tsarstvennaia kniga, eia sostav i proiskhozhdenie*, 12, fn. 19.

58. Germogen (ca. 1530 – Feb. 17, 1612) rose to ecclesiastical prominence during his service in Kazan. The first reference to his activity can be found under the year 1579, in connection with the discovery of the miraculous icon of the Virgin Mary. At that time he was a priest in Kazan. It is quite possible that he entered a

monastic order in 1587. Shortly after that he seems to have been appointed abbot, and later archimandrite, of the Spaso-Preobrazhenskii Monastery in Kazan, which had been founded in 1555. After the establishment of the patriarchate in 1589, Germogen became the metropolitan of Kazan with jurisdiction over the area of the former Astrakhan Khanate. He had been very active in proselytizing the local Tatar population. Particularly in the early 1590s, he distinguished himself in missionary work among the newly converted Tatars, who continued to cling to their old religious and national customs. Germogen was in office as metropolitan of Kazan for about seventeen years; he became Patriarch of All of Russia, probably in July 1606. For a factual account of Germogen's activities in Kazan, see S. Kedrov, *Zhizneopisanie Sv. Germogena, Patriarkha Moskovskogo i vseia Rossii* (Moscow, 1912), 13-31.

 59. The text of the *Tale* is published in *Tvoreniia sviateishago Germogena Patriarkha Moskovskogo i vseia Rossii* (Moscow, 1912), 1-16.

 60. A.I. Sobolevskii showed that the 36-page manuscript of the *Tale* was written by several people. One part of the manuscript (pp. 26-36) undoubtedly came from the pen of the metropolitan, according to Sobolevskii. Another part of the manuscript (pp. 1-25) represents a copy from an older draft which may have been composed by several authors, including Germogen. It is obvious that the latter edited the whole text, since it contains many of his remarks and additions, and for this reason he can be considered the chief author of the *Tale*. For an analysis of the components and the dating of the text, see Sobolevskii's foreword to "Skazanie o chudotvornoi ikonie presviatoi Bogoroditsy (Rukopis' Sv. Patriarkha Germogena)," *ibid.*, 3-8. On page 21 of the manuscript of the *Tale* Sobolevskii discovered a significant clause mentioning *tsarevichi* Ivan Ivanovich and Fedor Ivanovich and a comment in Germogen's hand that Fedor was "now" sovereign and tsar.

 From this he drew the conclusion that the manuscript had been partially compiled during Ivan IV's lifetime. Ivan IV died on March 18, 1584. The last date mentioned in the manuscript is October 27, 1594. Therefore, Sobolevskii dated the manuscript between 1584 and 1595. Since, however, Tsar Ivan's son Ivan Ivanovich is mentioned in the manuscript as, apparently, a living person, it would be more correct to speak of November 1581 as the earliest possible dating for one fragment of the *Tale*.

 61. *Tvoreniia sviateishago Germogena*, 4-5.

 62. Kedrov, 16.

 63. *PSRL*, XXIX, 59.

 64. *PSRL*, XIII, part 2, 515.

 65. The text of the letter was published by D.P. Golokhvastov and Leonid, "Blagoveshchenskii ierei Sil'vestr i ego pisaniia," *ChOIDR*, 1874, book 1, sec. 1, 88-100. According to V. Malinin, this letter was written in the early part of March 1553 (*Starets Eleazarova monastyria Filofei i ego poslaniia* [Kiev, 1901], 180). For an analysis of Sil'vestr's socio-political ideas, consult Zimin, *I.S. Peresvetov*, 41-70.

 66. Golokhvastov and Leonid, 89.

 67. *Ibid.*, 99.

 68. *Akty, sobrannye v bibliotekakh i arkhivakh Rossiiskoi imperii Arkheograficheskoiu Ekspeditsiieiu Akademii Nauk*, I (1836), no. 241 and 257-261; *PDRV*, V (1789), 241-244. Before the conquest the Muscovite government professed not to be interested in the Christianization of the Kazan Tatars. For example, the diplomatic instruction issued to the Muscovite envoy Vasilii Tretiak-Gubin in June 1521 for negotiations with Sultan Suleiman the Magnificent rejected Crimean accusations that the Russians were introducing Orthodoxy in the Kazan Khanate, emphasizing that

"our Sovereign did not order the mosques destroyed, and he did not order the churches built, and no bells were there, and their mosques stand there according to the old custom" (*SIRIO*, XCV, 696).

69. A.N. Grigor'ev, "Khristianizatsiia nerusskikh narodnostei, kak odin iz metodov natsional'no-kolonial'noi politiki tsarizma v Tatarii (S poloviny XVI v. do fevralia 1917 g.)," *Materialy po istorii Tatarii, Vypusk* I (Kazan, 1948), 226-229. For a conservative ecclesiastical interpretation of Muscovite policies with regard to the Tatar population of the former Kazan Khanate, see A.F. Mozharovskii, "Izlozhenie khoda missionerskogo dela po prosveshcheniiu kazanskikh inorodtsev, s 1552 po 1867 god," *ChOIDR*, 1880, book 1.

70. *PSRL*, XXIX, 50. It appears from an analysis of the ideological justifications for the Kazan conquest that the leadership of the Muscovite clergy influenced to a considerable degree their formulation. From this, however, it does not follow that the Church injected its ideological notions artificially into official Muscovite statements and that the political ideas of influential laymen were overshadowed by considerations of the clergy. Personalities like Makarii and Sil'vestr were not churchmen only. They played a considerable role in Muscovite politics. See I.I. Smirnov, *Ocherki politicheskoi istorii russkogo gosudarstva 30-50kh godov XVI veka* (Moscow and Leningrad, 1958), 194-202 and 231-257. A.A. Zimin expressed somewhat different opinions on the activities and contributions of these ecclesiastics, but he agreed that they were "prominent political figures" (*Reformy Ivana Groznogo* [Moscow, 1960], 320). It is justifiable to regard them as leading members of the Muscovite political establishment. When speaking of the attitudes of the Muscovite elite toward Tatars, one should remember that they were not necessarily shared by all segments of Muscovite society. Feodosii Kosoi may have expressed a view held by others as well, when he said that "all people are equal before God – the Tatars, the Germans, and other nations" (*vsi liudie edino sut' u Boga, i tatarove, i nemtsy, i prochii iazytsi*) ("Poslanie mnogoslovnoe: Sochinenie inoka Zinoviia," A. Popov, ed., *ChOIDR*, 1880, book 2, xv and 143). These words were attributed to him only after his defection to Poland-Lithuania (probably in 1555), where he apparently felt free to voice such radical opinions (Introduction, *ibid.*, i).

71. The best evidence is a passage from an interpolation in the *Tsarstvennaia kniga*: "...i khristiianskoe Rosiiskoe tsarstvo v'zvelichashesia i besermenskaia zhilishcha izsprazhniakhusia, Kazan' i Azstarakhan', i bezvernyia iazyty, Krym i Litva i Nemtsy, strakhova[sus]khusia, i ne be lukavomu terpeti, iako Khristovo imia proslavliaemo i velichaemo, a skvernaia ego zhilishcha razariaemy..." (*PSRL*, XIII, part 2, 522).

72. *SIRIO*, LIX, 437, 452. See also R.P. Dmitrieva, *Skazanie o kniaz'iakh Vladimirskikh* (Moscow and Leningrad, 1955), 144.

11

THE UKRAINIAN-RUSSIAN DEBATE OVER THE LEGACY OF KIEVAN RUS', 1840S-1860S

The debate between "Southerners" (*iuzhany*) and "Northerners" (*severiany*) – to use nineteenth century terminology[1] – was a debate about the Kievan legacy between Ukrainian and Russian scholars and intellectuals of various ideological and methodological orientations from the 1840s to the 1930s. The Ukrainian side was represented by M.O. Maksymovych (1804-1873), O.M. Bodians'kyi (1808-1877), M.I. Kostomarov (1817-1885), O.M. Ohonovs'kyi (1833-1894), V.B. Antonovych (1834-1908), O.O. Potebnia (1835-1891), P.H. Zhytets'kyi (1836-1911), M.F. Vladymyrs'kyi-Budanov (1838-1916), M.P. Dashkevych (1852-1908), I.Ia. Franko (1856-1916), M.S. Hrushevs'kyi (1866-1934), V.M. Peretts (1870-1935), and A.Iu. Kryms'kyi (1871-1941). On the Russian side, the leading scholars were M.P. Pogodin (1800-1875), I.I. Sreznevskii (1812-1880), P.A. Lavrovskii (1827-1886), A.N. Pypin (1833-1904), A.I. Sobolevskii (1857-1929), M.N. Speranskii (1863-1938), A.A. Shakhmatov (1864-1920), V.M. Istrin (1865-1937), and A.E. Presniakov (1870-1929). Also participating in the discussion was O.O. Kotliarevs'kyi (1837-1881), who was active both in Ukrainian and Russian scholarship. Though almost forgotten today, this debate had a tremendous influence on the development of Ukrainian and Russian scholarship and socio-political thought in the nineteenth and twentieth centuries.

I

To understand the Ukrainian-Russian debate, one must also understand the historical problem of the Kievan legacy and in particular the Ukrainian and Russian claims to this legacy.[2] The debate was a result, among other things, of the formulation, beginning in the second half of the eighteenth century, of modern Russian and Ukrainian national theories about the legacy of Kievan Rus'.

The Russian national theory of exclusive right to the legacy of Kievan Rus', formulated by Russian national historians like V.N. Tatishchev, M.N. Karamzin, M.P. Pogodin, and S.M. Solov'ev, rested on religious-ecclesiastical, historical-ideological, and juridical-political conceptions developed in Muscovite Russia over two centuries, that is, from the 1330s to the 1560s. The theory was based on arguments citing:

1. The transfer between the 1250s and 1300 of the Metropolitanate of Kiev from Kiev, first to Vladimir on the Kliaz'ma River and later, in 1326, to Moscow.
2. The dynastic continuity of the so-called Riurikides from Kievan Rus' through Suzdalia-Vladimiria to Muscovy, based on traditional patrimonial law.
3. The theory of uninterrupted succession (*translatio*) of states from Kievan Rus' through (Rostovia)-Suzdalia-Vladimiria and Muscovy to Russia, as reflected in religious-ecclesiastical, historical-political, literary, and iconographic traditions. As was evident in contemporary historical-political literature, the aim of the authors of this theory was to substantiate the claims of the Metropolitanate of Kiev and later of the Metropolitanate of Kiev and all of Rus' (which, in fact, was under the control of the Muscovite state, and specifically of its dynasty) to supremacy and sovereignty over all the lands and states of Rus'. In addition, they elevated the status of Kievan Rus' to the rank of "vol'noe i samoderzhavnoe tsarstvo" ("free and autocratic tsardom") allegedly partially inherited from the Byzantine Empire during the reign of Volodimer Monomakh at the beginning of the twelfth century, a rank that in reality was never achieved. And by connecting Kievan Rus' with ancient empires (even the Roman Empire) and the ancestry of the so-called Riurikides with Caesar Augustus, they elevated the status of the Muscovite rulers, both in their own state and in the international community of states in the sixteenth century. Despite its flaws and contradictions, this Muscovite theory of continuity had an extraordinary career, exerting a strong influence not only on Russian but also on Western scholarship.

The Ukrainian national theory of exclusive right to the legacy of Kievan Rus' was formulated by Ukrainian ideologists and historians from the end of the sixteenth to the nineteenth century and presented in its final form by Mykhailo Hrushevs'kyi in his multi-volumed works *Istoriia Ukrainy-Rusy* (*History of Ukraine-Rus'*) and *Istoriia ukrains'koi literatury* (*History of Ukrainian Literature*). In opposition to the Russian national theory, the Ukrainian national theory offered its own conception of continuity (from Kievan Rus' through Galicia-Volynia, Lithuania-Ruthenia, and Little Russia – Cossack Ukraine to modern Ukraine) and supported this with cultural, demographic, social, territorial, and institutional arguments.[3]

The Ukrainian continuity theory was based on arguments, derived from the *Hypatian Codex*,[4] citing the following:

1. The dynastic continuity of Galician-Volynian rulers from the Kievan legendary Askold and Dir to Danylo and his governor Dmytro, the last legitimate inheritors of Kiev prior to its conquest by the Mongol-Tatars in 1240.
2. The right to invest princes and governors.
3. The inclusion of the *Kievan Chronicle* in the *Hypatian Codex*, based on the assumption of the editors of that *Codex* that the entire Kievan Rus' legacy belonged to Galician-Volynian rulers. By contrast, the editors of the *Suzdalian-Vladimirian Chronicles* had included information about Kiev and Kievan Rus' only selectively and with appropriate ideological content.

After the fall of the Galician-Volynian state, the interest in the Kievan legacy in contemporary chronicle writing in the Ruthenian/Ukrainian lands declined. This can be explained by the lack of continuity in the Ruthenian/Ukrainian lands of independent or autonomous state institutions and by the complex and unstable development of metropolitanate centers in which chronicles and political treatises were written and edited. Yet from the late sixteenth century to the early eighteenth century, the tradition of a Kievan legacy was clearly part of Ukrainian culture. If the claims to the legacy were not substantiated systematically, it was because the native Ukrainians who inhabited the lands of Kievan Rus' regarded it as their natural property.

II

Because of the wide scope of a subject deserving more than one monograph, this study will be devoted to the initial phase of the Ukrainian-Russian debate. Specifically, I shall discuss the period from the late 1840s to the early 1860s, noting how the debate was brought to attention by the appearance of Iurii Venelin's essay "The Dispute Between the Southerners and the Northerners Concerning Their Russianism" in 1847,[5] how the subsequent discussion was opened in 1856, when M.P. Pogodin, a Russian participant of the debate, published his essay "About the Ancient Russian Language,"[6] and how it developed up to 1862, when the Ukrainian journal *Osnova* (*Foundation*), which played an important role in this debate, was terminated due to the pressures of the Russian authorities and because of financial difficulties.

Venelin, who adhered to the romantic Slavophile pro-Russian orientation and was critical of the Ukrainian national revival, was a Carpatho-Ruthenian amateur scholar with interests in history and philology. Nevertheless, his essay served as a point of departure for a more serious discussion of the Ukrainian-Russian debate, not only in its initial phase but also later on.[7]

The scholarly debate was actually started by Pogodin, who in his aforementioned essay advanced a hypothesis that Kiev and the Kievan land were Great Russian or Russian prior to the Mongol-Tatar conquest of Rus' in the thirteenth century and that they were inhabited by Little Russians or Ukrainians only after the alleged migration of the Great Russians to the North-East. He also argued that Little Russians were indigenous to the Carpathian Mountains and possibly even to Galicia, Volynia, and Podolia rather than to the Kievan land.

Pogodin's hypothesis was not based on his own research, but on the philological works of the Russian scholars I.I. Sreznevskii and P.A. Lavrovskii, who should be regarded as his precursors. Although Sreznevskii and Lavrovskii accepted a separate status for the Little Russian (Ukrainian) language, literature, and even nationality, they nonetheless developed a theory about the existence until the fourteenth century of the so-called "ancient Russian language." According to this theory Great Russian and Little Russian, that is, the Russian and Ukrainian languages, began to emerge only between the thirteenth and fourteenth centuries, thus substantiating the conception of unity of Kievan Rus' from the philological perspective. Sreznevskii advanced this theory in his work "Thoughts about the History of the Russian Language"[8] and in an article "About the Ancient Russian Language"[9] that preceded Pogodin's essay. Lavrovskii dealt with the subject parenthetically in his work *About the Language of the North Russian Chronicles*.[10]

Pogodin's hypothesis became the subject of a well-known polemic exchange between himself and M.O. Maksymovych, a Ukrainian participant of the debate. This appeared in the journal *Russkaia beseda* (*Russian Conversation*) and the newspaper *Den'* (*Day*) and was later picked up by the journal *Osnova*. In these Maksymovych disputed Pogodin's hypothesis in his articles: "The Philological Letters to M.P. Pogodin,"[11] "The Responding Letters to M.P. Pogodin,"[12] "About the Alleged Depopulation of Ukraine during the Batu Invasion and its Population by the Newly Arrived Inhabitants,"[13] and "About the Antiquity of the Little Russian Dialect."[14] Pogodin's responses came in the following articles: "The Response to the Philological Letters of M.O. Maksymovych"[15] and "The Response to the Last Two Letters of M.O. Maksymovych."[16]

An important role in the debate between Pogodin and Maksymovych was also played by P.A. Lavrovskii, another Russian participant of the debate. He contributed "The Description of the Seven Manuscripts of the Imperial St. Petersburg Public Library,"[17] "Survey of the Distinctive Features of the Little Russian Dialect as Compared to the Great Russian and Other Slavic Dialects,"[18] "The Response to the Letters of Mr. Maksymovych by Mr. Pogodin Concerning the Little Russian Dialect,"[19] and "About the Question of the South Russian Language."[20] In these articles, Lavrovskii came somewhat closer to Pogodin's views by asserting that from the tenth through the thirteenth century in "Southern Russia" there was neither a Little Russian nor a Great Russian language and that the latter language can be found only in Northern sources. He also argued that in Novgorod there was a separate Novgorodian dialect.

In addition, an article by O.O. Kotliarevs'kyi, "Were Little Russians the Native Inhabitants of the Polanian Land, or Did They Come from beyond the Carpathian Mountains in the Fourteenth Century,"[21] should be considered as part of the debate. And so should three influential treatises by M.I. Kostomarov (a Ukrainian participant of the debate) published in *Osnova*. These were "The Two Rus' Nationalities,"[22] "Thoughts about the Federal Origins in

Ancient Rus',"[23] and "The Characteristics of the National History of Southern Rus'."[24]

III

The mid-nineteenth century debate between Ukrainian and Russian scholars and intellectuals over the legacy of Kievan Rus' reflected an attempt on the part of a number of leading representatives of cultural elites on both sides to develop streamlined conceptions of national history and culture and root them, if possible, in the earliest antiquity. The debate also sheds light on the state of the humanities in the nineteenth century Russian Empire.

At that time, the humanities and the social sciences were not fully differentiated, and scholars like M.P. Pogodin and M.O. Maksymovych regarded themselves competent in various fields of scholarship, including, among others, philology, archeology, ethnography, history, the history of literature, philosophy, sociology, and political thought. At the same time, such scholars were also convinced that they were applying to the humanities and the social sciences the strict scientific approaches of mathematics and the natural sciences. Maksymovych even had a degree in botany, and Pogodin regarded himself as a representative of those who applied "mathematical" methodology to the study of history and literature. Similarly, Sreznevskii and Kostomarov treated related disciplines of learning as a single discipline, with Sreznevskii combining philology, literature, and ethnography, and Kostomarov doing the same for history, the history of literature, ethnography, philology, and political thought. Moreover, Kostomarov was of the opinion that the ethnographer should be a scholar of contemporary history, whereas the historian should promote recent ethnography in his works. Only P.A. Lavrovskii emphasized that he restricted himself basically to one discipline, namely philology.

All participants in the debate, with the exception of Kostomarov, emphasized the primary significance of fact in its positivistic nineteenth-century meaning. They also stressed the importance of what we consider critical antiquarianism – today an unappreciated methodology in the humanities and the social sciences. Such an antiquarian approach was most apparent in the debate between Pogodin and Maksymovych. In it both discussants attempted to prove, on the basis of examples borrowed from language, literature (particularly chronicles), and ethnographic materials, their arguments concerning the question of whether Kiev and the Kievan and Pereiaslav lands were Russian or Ukrainian prior to the Mongol-Tatar conquest of Rus' in the thirteenth century. Maksymovych, for example, argued, among other things, that prior to the Mongol-Tatar conquest of Rus' the Little Russian language was used in the Kievan, Chernihivian, and Galician lands, as well as in the *Povest' vremennykh let* (the *Tale of the Bygone Years*), and that the above mentioned lands were therefore inhabited by Little Russians. Pogodin, he said, had once conceded as much.

In this exchange, Maksymovych proved himself to be a better expert on the linguistic peculiarities of Old Rus' literature, and this allowed him to identify Kievan Rus' with Ukraine and the language of Kievan Rus' with that of Southern Rus', that is, Ukrainian. This opinion he presented in his *History of the Ancient Rus' Literature.*[25]

Maksymovych's approach can be regarded as analogous to the identification of Kievan Rus' with Russia in Russian national imperial historiography beginning with Tatishchev and Karamzin. Maksymovych argued:

> Just as Muscovite Russia or Great Russia, and just as Kievan Russia or Little Russia, or Ukraine...Polanians at first assumed the name of Rus'; their principal city, Kiev, became mother of the Rus' cities; from them spread the new life of Rus' at first throughout the Kievan Rus' land or Ukraine and later also throughout all Rus'. From that time that name became the generally accepted official name also for Novgorod, although until the early thirteenth century in Novgorod, as well as in Southern Rus', the name Rus' or the Rus' land in reality was applied to Kievan Rus' or Ukraine exclusively, and the name Rus' or the Rus' land belonged to the Kievan land or Ukraine.[26]

IV

The results of the first phase of the Ukrainian-Russian debate were several.

First, the debate helped to fortify the identification of Kievan Rus' with Ukraine, as postulated by Maksymovych and fully corroborated by Kostomarov.

Secondly, the debate solidified the conceptual foundations of the claim that the territories of Southern Rus' and Ukraine were the same. M.O. Maksymovych advanced the view that the area occupied by the native inhabitants of Southern Rus' corresponded to the territory of Ukraine and that in the tripartite classification of the East Slavic languages (Southern Rus', Great Russian, and Belorussian), the Southern Rus' language was the most ancient because of its territorial foundations. And M.I. Kostomarov, for his part, argued in his already mentioned treatise "The Characteristics of the National History of Southern Rus' " that Southern Rus' had been territorially unified and had comprised the Kievan, Pereiaslav (Poliany-Rus'), Polissian, Volynian and Podolian lands, as well as so-called Red Rus' (Galicia).

Thirdly, the Ukrainian-Russian debate confirmed the general parameters of the Ukrainian theory of continuity from Kievan Rus' through Red Rus' (Galicia) and Little Russia – Cossack Ukraine to Southern Russia as advanced by Maksymovych. In a sense, it recovered what the government and elites of tsarist Russia were trying to obscure by inventing and disseminating the term Southern Russia to denote Ukraine, as reflected, for example, in the subtitle of the journal *Osnova*, namely *Iuzhno-rossiiskii literaturno-uchenii vestnik* (*South Russian Literary-Scholarly Herald*). Subsequently, the tsarist government also began to eliminate even such historical terms as "Little Rus' " or "Little Russia." (At approximately the same time, the ethnic-national concept "Poland" gave way in tsarist nomenclature to the artificially constructed term, "Privislianskii krai" [the Vistula land].)

The formulation of the Ukrainian theory of "perpetual continuity" from Kievan Rus' through Red Rus' (Galicia) and Little Russia-Cossack Ukraine to Southern Russia has usually been attributed to Mykhailo Hrushevs'kyi. But actually, its construction was started with Maksymovych and continued with some help from Kostomarov and Antonovych. Maksymovych concentrated in his philological, literary, and historical works on the three phases of Southern Rus' history: first, Kievan Rus' with special consideration given to the history of the city of Kiev and the Kievan and Pereiaslav lands (making him the founder of the Ukrainian Kiev-centered school, although certain characteristics of the Kiev-centered approach were already present in the works of M.M. Berlyns'kyi [1764-1848] in the early nineteenth century);[27] second, the

Lithuanian-Ruthenian period; and third, the Cossack period. A similar approach was continued by Kostomarov, who supported the Kiev-centered outlook in his early works and concentrated on Cossack history in his later ones.

Hence, the basic parameters of the theory were already available to Hrushevs'kyi, who expanded and perfected it, apparently by using as models the tables of contents of the two-volumed, posthumously published works by Maksymovych, *Sobranie sochinenii* (tom 1 – *Istoriia*; tom 2 – *Tipografiia, arkheologiia, etnografiia*) (*Collected Works* [vol. 1 – *History*; vol. 2 – *Typography, Archeology, Ethnography*]).The two volumes were edited by V.B. Antonovych who provided for the first volume (Historical Section) the following chapter titles: "1. Articles Pertaining to the History of Rus' from the Earliest Times to the Middle of the Thirteenth Century"; "2. Articles Pertaining to the History of Lithuanian Rus'"; "3. Articles Pertaining to the History of Cossackdom."[28] Conceptually, Hrushevs'kyi followed already developed ideas, just as in his political thought, particularly his theories of autonomism, federalism, and constitutionalism, he did not go beyond the original theoretical thinking of M.P. Drahomanov.

Another outcome of the Ukrainian-Russian debate was confirmation of the Ukrainian theory about the legacy of Kievan Rus' through socio-political arguments. The view that the basic differences between Ukrainians and Russians rested more on socio-political factors than on ethnicity, language, or religion was formulated by Kostomarov in his already mentioned treatises "The Two Rus' Nationalities" and "Thoughts about the Federal Origins in Ancient Rus'," published in *Osnova* in the course of the Ukrainian-Russian debate. In the former work, in particular, Kostomarov dwelled upon the differences between the Russian and Ukrainian systems, not only in the realm of national customs, attitudes towards nature, relationships between an individual and the group, and attitudes towards property, but also and more importantly in respect to the socio-political systems characteristic of their historical development. In his view, these differences were already apparent in the period of Kievan Rus', particularly in the approach of the two peoples to the problem of organizing political power. The ancient Rus' organization of political power, which had been continued by the Ukrainians and Novgorodians, had rested on a so-called rule by the people expressed in the right of the popular council to invite and dismiss the prince and on the hypothetical federalism characteristic of the East Slavic Middle Ages. But the Great Russian, or Russian, organization of political power had been based on the centralism of the state and was closely related to the concept of centralized rule that had emerged in the twelfth century in the Suzdalian-Vladimirian Principality. That principality, according to Kostomarov, was the real nucleus of Great Russia.

For Kostomarov such a system of political rule was reflected in the Great Russian character. He argued that from the very beginning, the basic socio-political tendencies in Kievan and Southern Rus' were toward greater freedom, whereas in Vladimirian and Muscovite Rus' the ideas of collectivism, autocracy, and a powerful state prevailed. The Kievan and Southern Rus' societies were characterized by a spirit of tolerance toward the other confessions and nationalities who lived among them, whereas Great Russian society exhibited intolerance toward the other confessions and peoples who lived in the Muscovite state system. In Kiev and Southern Rus' hostility towards Catholicism was not common, but in Moscow the influence of Byzantium made it widespread. Southern Rus' Orthodoxy, according to Kostomarov, was devoid of the painful conflicts that were present in Great Russia, and even such deviations from Orthodoxy in Southern Rus' as the Union with Rome were attributable, in Kostomarov's opinion, to political and social factors. In Southern Rus' and subsequently during the Cossack and Hetmanate periods, society enjoyed autonomy in its relationship with the state. In Russia the state dominated society.

In his interpretation of Kievan Rus' and Ukrainian societies, Kostomarov approached the concept of society that in Western terminology is known as an "open society" or even "civil society." In this respect, Kostomarov not only laid the foundations for the Ukrainian-Russian political dialogue from the Ukrainian perspective, but he also initiated the modern analysis of the differences between the traditional socio-political systems of the two countries. In at least this one aspect, there was no crucial difference between the populist-autonomist and the state schools in Ukrainian political thinking.

Two examples will suffice to confirm this conclusion:

1. M.P. Drahomanov's well-known view:

> The preponderance of national differences between Ukraine and Muscovy can be explained by the fact that until the eighteenth century Ukraine was more closely bound to Western Europe and though with interruptions because of the Tatars its social and cultural processes developed similarly to those of Western Europe.[29]

2. A statement by V.K. Lypyns'kyi, the leading representative of the Ukrainian conservative state school:

> The basic difference between Ukraine and Muscovy is not the language, nor the tribe, nor the faith...but a different political system which had evolved over the centuries, a different...method of organizing the ruling elite, a different relationship between the upper and lower classes, between the state and society – between those who rule and those who are ruled.[30]

Other results of the Ukrainian-Russian debate were as follows:

1. The formulation of the Ukrainian populist concept of the basic developmental tendencies of the Ukrainian history, beginning with Kievan Rus';
2. The perception by the Ukrainian educated strata of the existence of separate Ukrainian and Russian national developments in the history of Eastern Slavs;
3. The capability of the Ukrainian cultural elite to create in a relatively brief period of time its own paradigm, not only in political ideology, but also in the general realm of critical thought;
4. The establishment of national and personal dignity for the emerging cultural-political elite. (It should be kept in mind that the Ukrainian side conducted the debate with influential scholars and politicians of the Russian imperial scholarly establishment);
5. A relatively tolerant attitude of the Russian scholarly and ideological establishment towards the Ukrainian side as a recognized partner.

The Ukrainian-Russian debate over the legacy of Kievan Rus' lasted until the early 1930s. It was terminated by well-known political developments. With the recent reestablishment of an independent Ukrainian state, its resumption will depend primarily on the Russians.

Philadelphia
1989-1991

NOTES

1. The terms "Southerners" and "Northerners," as applied in the nineteenth century to denote Ukrainian and Russian protagonists engaged in the debate over the claims to the Kievan Rus' heritage, were most probably first used by Iurii Venelin (real name Hutsa) (1802-1839) in his essay "O spore mezhdu iuzhanamy i severianamy na shchet ikh rossizma," written soon after 1832 and published in *Chteniia v Obshchestve istorii i drevnostei rossiiskikh* (hereafter *ChOIDR*), bk. 4 (1847): 1-16.

2. For a discussion of the origins of the contest for the Kievan Rus' legacy and the literature on the topic, see J. Pelenski, "The Origins of Official Muscovite Claims to the 'Kievan Inheritance'," *Harvard Ukrainian Studies* (hereafter *HUS*), 1, no. 1 (March 1977): 29-52 [see Chapter 5 of this volume]; *idem*, "The Sack of Kiev of 1482 in Contemporary Muscovite Chronicle Writing," *HUS*, 3-4 (1979-1980): 638-649 [see Chapter 6 of this volume]; *idem*, "The Emergence of the Muscovite Claims to the Byzantine-Kievan 'Imperial Inheritance'," *HUS*, 7 (1983): 520-531 [see Chapter 7 of this volume]; *idem*, "The Sack of Kiev of 1169: Its Significance for the Succession to Kievan Rus'," *HUS*, 11, no. 3-4 (December 1987): 303-316 [see Chapter 3 of this volume]; *idem*, "The Contest for the 'Kievan Succession' (1155-1175): The Religious-Ecclesiastical Dimension," *HUS*, 12-13 (1988-1989): 761-780 [see Chapter 2 of this volume]; *idem*, "The Origins of the Muscovite Ecclesiastical Claims to the Kievan Inheritance," *Nuovi Studia Storici*, 17 (1992): 213-226; a revised version "The Origins of the Muscovite Ecclesiastical Claims to the 'Kievan Inheritance'" was published in *Christianity and the Eastern Slavs*, vol. 1: *Slavic Cultures in the Middle Ages*, B. Gasparov and O. Raevsky Hughes, eds., *California Slavic Studies*, 16 (1993): 102-115 [see Chapter 4 of this volume]; *idem*, "The Contest for the Kievan Inheritance in Russian-Ukrainian Relations: Origins and Early Ramifications," in P.J. Potichnyj, M. Raeff, J. Pelenski, G.N. Zhekulin, eds., *Ukraine and Russia in Their Historical Encounter* (Edmonton, 1992), 3-19 [see Chapter 1 of this volume]; *idem*, "The Incorporation of the Ukrainian Lands of Old Rus' into Crown Poland (1569): Socio-Material Interest and Ideology – A Reexamination," *American Contributions to the Seventh International Congress of Slavists* (Warsaw, August 21-27, 1973), vol. 3: History (The Hague and Paris, 1973), 19-52 [see Chapter 9 of this volume]; *idem*, "The Contest between Lithuania-Rus' and the Golden Horde in the Fourteenth Century for Supremacy over Eastern Europe," *Archivum Eurasiae Medii Aevi*, vol. 2 (1982): 303-320 [see Chapter 8 of this volume].

3. For a good example of a seventeenth-century exposition of the Ukrainian continuity theory, see Feodosii Sofonovych, *Khronika z litopystsiv starodavnikh (Pidhotovka tekstu do druku, peredmova i komentari Iu.A. Mytsyka, V.M. Kravchenka)* (Kyiv, 1992). Feodosii Sofonovych, who died in 1677, was a leading

Kievan intellectual of his time. He taught at the Kievan Mohyla Academy in the 1640s and the early 1650s and from 1655 to 1677 was an abbott at the Mykhailivs'kyi Golden-domed Monastery. His compilatory codex consisted of three parts: 1) The Chronicle of Kievan Rus', followed by an account of the history of Galician-Volynian Rus'; 2) The Chronicle of the Lithuanian land (including the period of the Lithuanian-Ruthenian state); 3) The Chronicle of the Polish land (including the history of Cossack Ukraine). The original manuscript of the work has not been found as yet. However, several manuscript copies of parts of this work have been preserved. For a variety of reasons, the work could not be published until 1992.

The most complete edition, of M. Hrushevs'kyi's *History of Ukraine-Rus'* is the Ukrainian diaspora edition *Istoriia Ukrainy-Rusy*, 10 vols., 3rd rep. ed. (New York, 1954-1958). Another reprint edition of Hrushevs'kyi's multi-volumed *Istoriia Ukrainy-Rusy* has been started in Ukraine following the declaration of Ukrainian sovereignty in 1990. The second edition of M. Hrushevs'kyi's *Istoriia ukrains'koi literatury* was also published in the Ukrainian diaspora (5 vols. in 4 bks., 2nd rep. ed. [New York, 1959-1960]), and the third edition in Kiev, Ukraine in 1992. For a summary of M. Hrushevs'kyi's views and a convenient English translation of his seminal article on this subject, see "The Traditional Scheme of Russian History and the Problem of a Rational Organization of the History of Eastern Slavs, 1909," in *The Annals of the Ukrainian Academy of Arts and Sciences in the U.S.*, 2 (1952): 355-364.

4. For the text of the *Hypatian Codex*, see *Polnoe sobranie russkikh letopisei* (hereafter *PSRL*), vol. 2 (2nd rep. ed., 1908/1962). Its Ukrainian translation has been published under the title *Litopys rus'kyi* (translated by Leonid Makhnovets) (Kiev, 1989). Part three of the *Hypatian Codex*, namely the *Galician-Volynian Chronicle* has been translated into English by George A. Perfecky and published in the Harvard Series in Ukrainian Studies (Munich, 1973).

5. For Iurii Venelin's essay, see *supra*, fn. 1.

6. M.P. Pogodin's essay "O drevnem iazyke russkom," written in the form of a letter to I.I. Sreznevskii, was originally published in *Izvestiia Imperatorskoi Akademii Nauk* (hereafter *IIAN*), 5, issue 2 (5-8) (1856), cols. 70-92, and in *Moskvitianin*, 1 no. 2 (1856): 113-139.

7. See, for example, Aleksandr N. Pypin's *Istoriia russkoi etnografii*, vol. 3 (St. Petersburg, 1891), chapter 10, "Spor mezhdu iuzhanami i severianami" (301-338). For an ideologically tainted but factually useful summary of selected aspects of the debate from a Soviet Ukrainian perspective, particularly in reference to the study of Old Rus' literature, see N.K. Gudzii, "Literatura Kievskoi Rusi v istorii bratskikh literatur" (originally published in 1951), *Literatura Kievskoi Rusi i ukrainsko-russkoe literaturnoe edinenie XVII-XVIII vekov* (Kiev, 1989), 13-43.

8. I.I. Sreznevskii's "Mysli ob istorii russkogo iazyka" was originally published in *Godichnyi torzhestvennyi akt v Imperatorskom Sanktpeterburgskom Universitete* (St. Petersburg, 1849), 61-186 and in the journal *Biblioteka dlia chteniia*, 98 (1849): 1-55 and 117-138. Sreznevskii's work was published in 1850 and in 1959 as a separate book.

9. I.I. Sreznevskii, "O drevnem russkom iazyke," *IIAN*, 5, issue 2 (5-8) (1856), cols. 65-70.

10. P. Lavrovskii, *O iazyke severnykh russkikh letopisei* (St. Petersburg, 1852).

11. M. Maksimovich, "Filologicheskie pis'ma k M.P. Pogodinu," *Russkaia beseda* (hereafter *RB*), 3 (1856): 78-139; reprinted in *Sobranie sochinenii M.A. Maksimovicha* (hereafter *SSM*), vol. 3: 182-243.

12. M. Maksimovich, "Otvetnye pis'ma k M.P. Pogodinu," *RB*, 2 (1857): 80-104; reprinted in *SSM*, vol. 3 (1880): 244-272.

13. M. Maksimovich, "O mnimom zapustenii Ukrainy v nashestvie Batyevo i naselenii eia novopryshlim narodom," *RB*, 4 (1857): 22-35; reprinted in *SSM*, vol. 1 (1876): 131-145.

14. M. Maksimovich, "O starobytnosti malorosiiskogo narechiia," originally published in the newspaper *Den'*, 1863, nos. 8, 10, 15, 16 and separately; reprinted in *SSM*, vol. 3 (1880): 273-311.

15. M. Pogodin, "Otvet na filologicheskie pis'ma M.A. Maksimovicha," *RB*, 4 (1856): 124-141.

16. M. Pogodin, "Otvet na dva posledniia pis'ma M.A. Maksimovicha," *RB*, 3 (1857): 97-107. It should be mentioned that in Pogodin's available correspondence to Maksymovych during the period of their debate, there is practically no mention of their controversy.

17. P. Lavrovskii, "Opisanie semi rukopisei Imperatorskoi S.-Peterburgskoi publichnoi biblioteki," *ChOIDR*, 27, bk. 4 (1858): 1-90.

18. P. Lavrovskii, "Obzor zamechatel'nykh osobennostei narechiia malorusskogo sravnitel'no s velikorusskim i drugimi slovianskimi narechiiami," *Zhurnal Ministerstva narodnogo prosveshcheniia*, 102 (1859): 225-266.

19. P. Lavrovskii, "Otvet na pis'ma g. Maksimovicha k g. Pogodinu o narechii malorusskom," *Osnova*, no. 8 (1861): 14-40.

20. P. Lavrovskii, "Po voprosu o iuzhnorusskom iazyke," *Osnova*, nos. 11-12 (1861): 72-83.

21. O. Kotliarevs'kyi, "Byli li malorussy iskonnymi obitateliami polianskoi zemli, ili prishli iz-za Karpat v XIV veke," *Osnova*, no. 10 (1862): 1-12.

22. M. Kostomarov, "Dve russkie narodnosti," *Osnova*, no. 3 (1861): 33-80; reprinted in *Sobranie sochinenii N.I. Kostomarova* (hereafter *SSK*), bk. 1, vol. 1 (1903): 33-65.

23. M. Kostomarov, "Msyli o federativnom nachale v drevnei Rusi," *Osnova*, no. 1 (1861): 121-158; reprinted in *SSK*, bk. 1, vol. 1 (1903): 3-30.

24. M. Kostomarov, "Cherty narodnoi iuzhnorusskoi istorii," *Osnova*, no. 3 (1861): 114-165; reprinted in *SSK*, bk. 1, vol. 1 (1903): 69-158.

25. M. Maksimovich, *Istoriia drevnei russkoi slovesnosti* (Kiev, 1839); reprinted in *SSM*, vol. 3 (1880): 346-479.

26. M. Maksimovich, *Istoriia drevnei russkoi slovesnosti*; reprinted in *SSM*, vol. 3 (1880): 352, 365 and 370.

27. For M.M. Berlyns'kyi's works published in the early nineteenth century, see *Istoriia rossiiskaia dlia upotrebleniia iunoshestva* (1800) and *Kratkoe opisanie Kieva* (1820). His most important work, *Istoriia goroda Kieva ot osnovaniia ego do nastoiashchego vremeni*, written at the end of the eighteenth century, was ready for publication in 1800. However, it did not receive the censor's approval. Its first part was published only in 1972 (M. Berlyns'kyi, "Istoriia goroda Kieva," *Kyivs'ka starovyna* [1972], pp. 72-303 [Introduction and commentaries by M. Braichevs'kyi]). The entire text, including the second part "Topografiia goroda Kieva," was published with commentaries and introduction by M. Braichevs'kyi (*Istoriia mista Kyieva* [Kyiv, 1991]).

28. *SSM*, vol. 1 (1877): vii.

29. M.P. Drahomanov, "Avtobiograficheskaia zapiska," in *Literaturno-publitsystychni pratsi*, vol. 1 (Kiev, 1970): 58.

30. V. Lypyns'kyi, *Lysty do brativ-khliborobiv* (Vienna, 1926), xxv.

Appendix

STATE AND SOCIETY IN MUSCOVITE RUSSIA AND THE MONGOL-TURKIC SYSTEM IN THE SIXTEENTH CENTURY

A comparison of state-society relationships in Muscovite Russia and in the countries of the Mongol-Turkic system[1] has not yet been made, nor has any scholar attempted to determine whether there was any influence of one upon the other during the sixteenth century. General comparisons between Muscovy and the Golden Horde and some evaluations of the Mongol-Tatar impact on Muscovy had been undertaken by, among others, N. Karamzin, M. Kostomarov, B. Spuler, and G. Vernadsky, but their analyses did not extend beyond the first decade of the sixteenth century, i.e., the time of the final disintegration of the Golden Horde. With these notable exceptions, historians of Eastern Europe have tended to typologize the forms of government and the socio-political systems of Muscovy and the countries of the Mongol-Turkic system, and then to look to the West for similarities and differences. Some historians have attempted to develop broader frameworks into which the Muscovite system could be integrated in order to detect synchronic structural elements in the states and societies of both Eastern and Western Europe. One can discern three distinct phases in the development of scholarly views and theories which dealt with the definition of Muscovite socio-political system and the comparison of this system with other, primarily European, states during the period in question.

The first major phase in the development of these scholarly interests was dominated by historians of critical, positivist, philological, and juridical orientations, as well as of the social-institutional school, at the end of the nineteenth and in the early part of the twentieth century. After reevaluating the sources and rejecting many of the unfounded assumptions of traditional national historiography, they tried to define the form of government and the socio-political system of Muscovite Russia.

Of the theories pertaining to Muscovy, the most influential were those put forth by M.A. Diakonov, N.P. Pavlov-Sil'vanskii, and A.E. Presniakov. Diakonov maintained that the form of "theocratic absolutism" advocated by Iosif Volotskii combined with the notion of unlimited autocracy formulated in the official Muscovite pronouncements became the basis for the new concept of Muscovite ruler's authority and characterized best the political system of Muscovy.[2] The only limitation on the Muscovite ruler's authority was traditional religious morality (i.e., the Orthodox faith).[3]

Pavlov-Sil'vanskii came to another conclusion about the nature of the Muscovite political system. He characterized the Russian socio-economic system from the end of the twelfth century to the fifteen-sixties as "feudal,"[4] and regarded the last third of the fifteenth and the major part of the sixteenth century as the period of the formation of a Russian estate monarchy.[5] Pavlov-Sil'vanskii's book received the immediate recognition it deserved. The views of V. Latkin, who wrote an earlier book on the institutional foundations of a hypothetical Russian estate monarchy, attracted little attention.[6]

Presniakov advanced a thesis that, following the incorporation of a variety of Great Russian ethnic territories, and in particular after the annexation of Novgorod and the Grand Principality of Tver' in the 1470s and the 1480s, Muscovite Russia was transformed into a unitary national state, the political system of which represented a patrimonial autocracy (*votchinnoe samoderzhavie*).[7] The Russian state retained a patrimonial character until the later part of the six-teenth century, or, according to some authors, until the end of the seventeenth century, or even the end of the *ancien régime*.

The second major phase coincided chronologically with the 1950s, when the concept of a centralized national monarchy resting upon strong military foundations and a rapidly developing bureau-cracy became very popular. This particular system was considered as the most progressive among the existing socio-political systems of the late Middle Ages and the early modern period, and Muscovite Russia was regarded as having come very close to the ideal model, even when compared with Western monarchical states.[8]

Finally, since the mid-1960s, historians have placed less emphasis on the alleged superiority of the centralized, bureaucratic, and absolutistic monarchy and have attempted to establish institu-tional, as well as constitutional, parallels between Russia and the countries of Central and Western Europe. The theory that, from the late fifteenth century, Muscovite Russia, while retaining most of the typical features of a centralized national state, was moving in the direction of a representative and even limited estate monarchy, and indeed had become one by the mid-sixteenth century, is a striking example of this trend.[9]

It appears that most historians of Muscovite Russia have traditionally displayed a strong "Western" preference in their efforts to compare the Muscovite system with those of other countries, a tendency based on the assumption that, by the middle or the later part of the fifteenth century, alternative models had simply ceased to exist. Following rather uncritically the interpretations of Muscovite chroniclers and publicists, they have adopted the view that, after the fall of Constantinople in 1453 and the end of Mongol-Tatar supremacy in the late fifteenth century, Muscovy had extricated herself from traditional Byzantine and Mongol-Turkic dependence and influences and embarked upon a new and more dynamic course of socio-political development, similar to that of Western Europe. The evident neglect of Byzantine and Mongol-Turkic influences on the history of Muscovite Russia is probably the result of attempts to discover dynamic political transformation in Muscovy, despite the solid evidence for residual statism, stagnation, and even retardation. The latter revealed themselves in the continuous reception of traditional theoretical concepts and ideological justifications of rule from the cultural milieu of the bygone Byzantine Empire[10] and the belated acceptance and almost mechanical adaptation of institutional and societal models, as well as economic and political arrangements, from the Mongol-Turkic socio-political system (especially its Kazanian variant)[11] which was also departing from the historical scene.

The revival of the views of Latkin and Pavlov-Sil'vanskii on the institutional parallels between Muscovy and Western countries, and especially the classification of the Muscovite political system as a representative and limited monarchy, is indicative of the prevalence of "Western" preferences and also reflects the limitations of certain comparativist endeavors in contemporary studies of Muscovy. The view that reforms and institutional innovations in Muscovite Russia had resulted by the middle of the sixteenth century in her transformation into a new type of state on the Western model is not necessarily valid – it can be argued just as convincingly that Muscovite institutional changes and bureaucratic reforms from above were patterned on the Mongol-Turkic model and that they were instrumental in the evolution of the Muscovite system into a monarchical despotism based upon the service system of the *dvorianstvo* in Ivan IV's reign. It was precisely the establishment of this despotic form of government in the later part of the sixteenth century that prevented the formation of genuine estates and a limited, constitutional monarchy in Muscovite Russia.

Arguments in favor of the existence of a representative and limited estate monarchy in Muscovy have been based on the evaluation of the socio-political structure and the role of the *boiarskaia duma* (the Advisory Council of *Boiar*(s)) and the *zemskii sobor* (the Assembly of the Land). It has been maintained that the *boiarskaia duma* was an institution that represented the aristocracy and shared power and political decision-making with the ruler, that it actually participated in the exercise of administration with the grand prince and, later, the tsar, and that, more significantly, it limited his legislative authority.[12]

No conclusive answer can be given on the social composition of the *boiarskaia duma* until a comprehensive and methodologically updated study of this institution is undertaken.[13] Evidence that power and decision-making were shared by the grand prince or the tsar with the *boiarskaia duma* is derived from a few references in the chronicles to discussions of important state matters, i.e., the divorce of Grand Prince Vasilii III from his first wife Solomoniia and the preparation of his political testament.[14] These references may, however, simply mean that a distinction was made between "holding council" (receiving advice) and making decisions. The view that the *boiarskaia duma* placed legislative limitations on monarchical authority, is based on phrases in the Preamble to the *Law Code of 1497 (Sudebnik 1497 goda)* and the Preamble and Article 98 of the *Law Code of 1550 (Sudebnik 1550 goda)*,[15] but these provide insufficient evidence for upholding the assertions of the "neoconstitutionalists." In the Preambles of the Law Codes, not only the *boiar*(s) but also the "children" and the "brothers" of the rulers are mentioned: if we follow a "neoconstitutionalist" interpretation, this would suggest that members of a ruler's family could limit his legislative authority, which of course was not the case. These references more probably reflected a traditional patrimonial practice. Finally, the reference to the *boiar*(s) in Article 98 has to be regarded as an exception; in fact, Ivan IV more often than not disregarded the *boiars* when he enacted new legislation, and the wording of Article 98 was not invoked as a precedent in the history of Russian law. The conclusion that can be drawn is quite simple: the *boiarskaia duma* was an advisory council, the members of which, in addition to giving advice, performed a variety of undefined and often ambiguous administrative functions.

Of greater importance for our discussion is the assessment of the institutional character and the functional role of the *zemskii sobor*.[16] During the sixteenth century, seven safely attested *sobor*(s) were held (1549, 1550, 1566, 1575, 1580, 1584, 1598);[17] concrete data on the socio-political background of their members are available for the *sobor*(s) of 1566 and 1598, but the latter is of less importance to the present consideration. The *sobor* of 1566 was summoned to deal with problems arising from the Livonian War. Its membership was as follows:[18]

SOBOR of 1566

Participants	in numbers	in %
Osviashchennyi sobor (ecclesiastical hierarchy)	32	8.5
Boiarskaia duma	30	8.0
Dvoriane (predominantly service nobility)	204	54.7
Prikaznye liudi (bureaucrats)	33	8.8
Torgovye liudi (merchants)	75	20.0
Total	374	100.0

Since the *zemskii sobor* has been compared to such Western institutions as the *Etats généraux*, *Landtag*, *Cortes*, the Parliament, and *Sejm*, and its participants to the representatives of the estates, the first question that arises is whether one can justifiably speak of the existence of "estates" in sixteenth- and even seventeenth-century Russia.[19] The evidence is scanty. With the possible exception of the ecclesiastical "estate," all other Russian secular societal groups, members of which participated in the *sobor*(s), particularly in the sixteenth century, can hardly be classified as "estates" in the Western or East Central European sense of the term. First of all, they lacked that developed political and corporate organization so essential for the transformation of a relatively amorphous social group into an estate. Second, they had no concept of a contractual relationship with the ruler, either as a group or as individuals, and they failed to develop either noteworthy ideological justifications for their own significance or a legal substantiation of their status in the fabric of Muscovite society and in the structure of governmental hierarchy. Third, they did not act as a corporate group when called upon to take part in the proceedings of the *sobor*(s). Finally, the overwhelming majority of the participants was not elected by their peers to act as their representatives: the *sobor*(s) were summoned by the ruler to provide support in matters of crucial importance to the state. Furthermore, they had no prerogatives with regard to decision-making and no control over taxation.

What then was their model? Partly, it was the indigenous tradition of church councils, such as those of 1503, 1504, 1547, 1549, and the *Stoglav* of 1551. An even more influential model was the Mongol-Turkic *qurultai* (*xurultai, xuriltai*) (which had evolved from a family or tribal council into a more defined and structured "Assembly of the Land"), especially its Kazanian version.[20] The Kazanian *qurultai* is mentioned fourteen times in Russian sources: the first reference is dated 1496, the last, 1551. Interestingly enough, the terms used in Muscovite sources for the Kazanian *qurultai* and the Russian *sobor* are strikingly similar: *vsia zemlia kazanskaia, vse liudi kazanskoi zemli* were used for the former; and *vsia zemlia, vse liudi* for the latter. The function of the Kazanian *qurultai* and of its traditional Mongol-Turkic model was to deal with major problems of state.

The social composition of the Kazanian *qurultai* can be reconstructed from the sources. The *qurultai* of 1551, for example, was attended by high ranking ecclesiastics, the great *karaçi* (a Tatar council which bore some resemblance to the *boiarskaia duma*), princes and *mirza*(s), and the *oglan*(s), (i.e., landed aristocracy and military elite). Evidence exists that the social basis of the *qurultai* was broadened to include *tarkhan*(s) and *kazak*(s), as well. Thus, it is quite apparent that in structure the Kazanian *qurultai* closely corresponded to the Muscovite *sobor*. There is also little justification to view the *qurultai* and the *sobor* as representative bodies of estates or as parliaments. Both the *qurultai* and the *sobor* can be more justly regarded as servitorial assemblies, which were called occasionally by the Kazanian khans and Muscovite rulers to provide formal appearances of the socio-political support "of all the land" for their actions and policies.

The striking similarities between the institutions of the Muscovite *pomest'e* and the Kazanian *soyūrghǎl* and between the socio-political and military obligations of the Muscovite *dvoriane* (*pomeshchiki* and the Kazanian *tarkhan*(s) [and to some degree also *mirza*(s) and *oglan*(s)]) serve as further examples of the reception of Kazanian institutional models and societal arrangements in Muscovite Russia. In Muscovy the *pomest'e* represented conditional land-ownership contingent upon administrative and, especially, military service for the ruler. The term *pomest'e* appears in Muscovite chronicles for the first time under the year 1484.[21] The earliest legal definition of the status of *pomestnik* or *pomeshchik*, albeit pertaining only to land litigation, was made in the *Law Code of 1497*.[22] However, the development of the *pomest'e* into a specific type of conditional land-ownership contingent upon military service took place gradually during the last quarter of the fifteenth and the first half of the sixteenth century, and was institutionalized by the military service reform of 1555-1556,[23] a decade before the *sobor* of 1566. At the end of the sixteenth century, the distinction between *pomest'e* and *votchina* (patrimony)[24] became less pronounced, and the *Muscovite Law Code of 1649* (*Sobornoe ulozhenie 1649 goda*) was responsible for the further disappearance of legal differences between the institutions of the *votchina* and the *pomest'e*. The Decree of March 23, 1714 formalized the final fusion of the two forms of land-ownership and institutionalized their hereditary status.

The earliest historical parallel to the Muscovite *pomest'e* system was the Byzantine *pronoia*, a temporary, revocable grant of state-owned land, usually awarded for life in exchange for obligatory military service by the landholder and by the peasants tilling his land.[25] The origins of the *pronoia* institution can be dated back to the reign of Alexius I Comnenus (d. 1118) and the term itself can be documented by 1162. The *pronoia* became hereditary possession by the middle of the fourteenth century. Another Byzantine institution, the *topion* should also be mentioned because, according to some authors, it was used to designate military service grants.[26] *Topion* is derived from the word *topos* ("place," "locality," "piece of land"), meaning in Russian *mesto*. The Russian economic and socio-political term *pomest'e* was formed from the Russian translation of *topos*. Although the terminological borrowing is obvious, establishing a direct institutional adaptation from Byzantium is more tenuous, partly because the *pronoia* underwent changes over time, but more importantly because Byzantium had already been conquered by the Ottoman Empire by the time the *pomest'e* was introduced in

Muscovy. Furthermore, Muscovy tended more frequently to borrow its governmental practices and military models from those of the Mongol-Turkic system than from Byzantium.

It can be argued that the model for the Russian *pomest'e* service system, at least as it was defined by the military service reform of 1555-1556, was the Kazanian *soyūrghăl*.[27] Sh.F. Mukhamed'iarov, on the basis of evidence found in the *yarlik* (charter) of Khan Sahip Girey (1523), has advanced a convincing hypothesis for the existence of "a conditional military-feudal land-ownership in the form of *soyūrghăl* in the Kazan Khanate.[28] The term in Mongol meant "grant," or "bestowal" (*Lehen*)[29] and it was generally used to denote privileges, hereditary land grants and bestowal of offices in the Mongol, as well as Turkic, socio-political system beginning with the age of Chingiz Khan. The term *soyūrghăl* between the fifteenth and the seventeenth century included both grants awarded to the military, as well as to members of other social strata, and grants involving large territories. In Kazanian society during the latter part of the fifteenth and the sixteenth century the *soyūrghăl* was understood to mean land grants contingent on military service to the ruler. However, these lands were regarded as heredi-tary and were exempt from taxation. Since the Muscovite military service system based upon *pomest'e* received its final form in the mid-1550s, i.e., more than three decades following the granting of the *yarlik* of Sahip Girey of 1523, which attested to an already exist-ing system of *soyūrghăl*, it can be concluded that Muscovy had ample time and opportunity to borrow this institution from the Kazan Khanate.

The *tarkhan*(s)[30] were the principal social group which served in, and benefited from, the institution of the Kazanian *soyūrghăl* and which can be regarded as the closest societal prototype of the *dvoriane* (*pomeshchiki*). The original meanings of *tarkhan* in Mongol-Turkic social vocabulary were "smith," "master," or "crafts-man," but it could also designate a freeman. Already by the time of Chingiz Khan, *tarkhan*(s) were exempt from taxes and various economic services; they later became a privileged estate or class. In Kazanian society, the *tarkhan*(s) constituted a privileged, land-owning, and conditionally hereditary nobility which was exempted from taxes and most other obligations. The great majority of the Muscovite *dvoriane*, with their relatively clearly defined obligations for which they received conditional socio-economic rewards, were the obvious equivalents of the Kazanian *tarkhan*(s). Their participation in the *sobor* did not make them an estate, nor did it make the *sobor* a parliament.

The Muscovite service system received its tentative legal definition and rudimentary institutional structure during the reforms of the 1550s. It considerably strengthened the autocratic political regime. This system, which had survived in Russia for over two hundred years, had undergone some external organizational changes, but not substantial socio-political ones. It distinguished to a considerable extent Muscovite socio-political and institutional arrangements from those in East Central and Western Europe, and it represented the Muscovite version of the "Eastern" service model developed in Byzantium and in the Mongol-Turkic state system that had been transmitted to Muscovy by way of the Kazan Khanate with whom Muscovy had had an intimate relationship for over a century. This Muscovite service system also helped to prevent the formation of estates or other representative institutions and institutional barriers that could limit the authority of the ruler. Its implementation, along with other reforms of the 1550s, paved the way for the political and institutional legitimation of the despotic regime of Ivan IV in the period of the *oprichnina*,[31] which could not be resisted partly because of the new police forces which the ruler had at his disposal and partly because of the lack of limiting safeguards on the power of the ruler. Viewed against the background of institutional adjustments and bureaucratic reforms, the *oprichnina* can be regarded as a culmination rather than as a traumatic break with the past.

Finally, a few comparative comments on the concept of state authority. In the Mongol-Turkic system, the sovereignty of the state and political authority were vested in the office of the khan; he was, according to Mongol-Turkic political theory, an unlimited ruler. When the Mongol-Tatars established their supremacy over the lands of Rus', which were then incorporated into the Horde's imperial framework by the 1260s, the Russian sources began to translate – or substitute – the title of "khan" by "tsar," a Slavicized version of "caesar," "Kaiser," "emperor"; by analogy, "khanate" became the equivalent of "tsardom," "empire."[32] This usage and, more importantly, the political perception that the khan's authority was that of an emperor were perpetuated into the late fifteenth and sixteenth centuries, when Muscovite ideologists and political advocates of the grand prince's authority began to refer to him, at first in publicistic writings, as "tsar" and, simultaneously, to try to obtain formal recognition of this title from East Central European and Western powers.[33] The final assumption of the lofty title of "tsar" by the Russian ruler and his imperial coronation came in 1547,[34] an act meant to signify the transformation of the Muscovite grand princely territorial state into an empire. It was not a coincidence that this move was made in the last phase of the Kazanian wars and on the eve of the conquest of the Kazan Khanate (1552).

The immediate political and ideological consequences of the Kazan conquest were twofold. First, externally they can be seen in Ivan IV's assumption of the title of "Tsar of Kazan" and, somewhat later, "Tsar of Astrakhan," additions to the title of the Russian ruler which reflected a change in the character of the Muscovite state. Until 1552, it had primarily existed as a Great Russian state. By acquiring these new titles, Ivan IV acknowledged his succession to the thrones of the successor states to the Golden Horde and thus by implication to the Golden Horde herself. Subsequently Russia ceased to be regarded as a single homogeneous country and began to be viewed as an empire (state of states) composed of a diversity of tsardoms, lands, and cities.

The annexation of the two Tatar khanates and the subsequent assumption of the titles of "Tsar of Kazan" and "Tsar of Astrakhan" by the Russian ruler were used by the Muscovite government to enhance its ruler's monarchical status and exalt his position *vis-à-vis* other sovereigns. They were utilized in the diplomatic struggles for the recognition of the tsar's title by other powers, especially the Polish-Lithuanian state. In like manner, Ivan IV exploited the conquests of the Tatar khanates as an argument in favor of his request to the Greek patriarch to confirm his new title (1557). The patriarch granted the request in 1561 but used a different set of justifications, some of them based on Muscovite ideological claims resting in turn on Volodimer Monomakh's alleged acquisition of imperial regalia from Constantinople. It deserves to be noted that leading Muscovite writers of the seventeenth century, for example, Prince Ivan Katyrev-Rostovskii and Grigorii Kotoshikhin associated the foundation of the Muscovite tsardom with the conquests of Kazan and Astrakhan.[35]

Secondly, internally (and this is more important for our considerations) the reception of the Mongol-Turkic concepts of a ruler's power and authority over his subjects had profound and lasting implications for Russia's political and societal development. While speaking about the concepts of state power and authority, one should keep in mind that the Muscovite reception was characterized by the dichotomy (duality) of Byzantine and Mongol-Turkic influences. Whereas the Byzantine model and imagery were used for ideological justifications and theoretical substantiations, the Mongol-Turkic example was followed in practical matters (although, also, in some crucial instances, with regard to the definition of the ruler's authority). The notions of supreme sovereignty and unlimited authority were expressed in Russian sources by the term *vol'nyi* ("free"), a paradoxical definition for the contemporary reader. It was applied to the Kazan Tatar khan Mahmut in mid-fifteenth century by no other than Iona, the first autonomous metropolitan of Moscow.[36] Following the assumption of the title "Tsar" by Ivan IV, the term was used frequently by Muscovite bureaucrats and publicists.

The concept of a Muscovite "free" (i.e., unlimited) imperial autocracy had very concrete implications for the relationship between state authority and those segments of the society that participated in the political affairs of the country (peasants and plebeians were in general excluded from partaking in political affairs). The relationship between ruler and state, on the one hand, and the service aristocracy and service nobility, on the other, was characterized by extraordinary respect, obedience, and subordination of the latter to the former. The term used to denote members of elite groups in Muscovy can serve well to illustrate this relationship. In official Muscovite terminology, the highest official, or the servitor, was called, and referred to himself, as *kholop*, meaning "slave," at worst, and "servant," at best, at a time, when in neighboring Poland-Lithuania, for example, his Polish, Lithuanian or Ruthenian-Ukrainian counterpart was conceived of as *obywatel*, meaning "citizen" in the modern sense of the word.[37] If a member of the elite group was only a *kholop*, it is all too easy to surmise the status of the average member of society. The theoretical foundations being what they were, the Muscovite ruler could rely on extraordinary authority to a degree known in only a few other European states. He could easily dispose of his internal enemies, and his bureaucracy was never held in check by any effective countervailing socio-political force.

Thus, by studying the late medieval and early modern Muscovite notions and perceptions of the relationship between authority and societal elite groups, not to speak of the individual, at least some understanding of the longevity and extraordinary durability of Russian authoritarianism may be obtained. It is precisely this acceptance of state authority as the ultimate source of power, wisdom, and morality by the great majority of inhabitants of ethnic Russia that has decisively shaped the Russian political system, not only in the *ancien régime* but right up to the present day.

NOTES

1. The term Mongol-Turkic system refers to the socio-political organization and the state form or forms which were developed in the nomadic (and later mixed nomadic-sedentary) Mongol-(Tatar) Empire of the Golden Horde which existed in Eastern Europe roughly from the mid-thirteenth to the beginning of the sixteenth century. The socio-political organization and the state forms in question were perpetuated in modified form by the successor states of the Golden Horde, that is, the Khanates of Kazan, Astrakhan, Siberia, and Crimea, from the mid-fifteenth through the sixteenth century and, in case of the Crimea, until her annexation by the Russian Empire in the 1780s.

2. M. Diakonov, *Vlast' moskovskikh gosudarei (Ocherki iz istorii politicheskikh idei drevnei Rusi do kontsa XVI veka)* (St. Petersburg, 1889), especially chpts. IV and V; see also his *Ocherki obshchestvennogo stroia drevnei Rusi* (4th ed., Moscow and Leningrad, 1926), 314-348.

3. V. Val'denberg, *Drevnerusskiia ucheniia o predelakh tsarskoi vlasti (Ocherki russkoi politicheskoi literatury ot Vladimira Sviatogo do kontsa XVII veka)* (Petrograd, 1916), 351-352.

4. N.P. Pavlov-Sil'vanskii, *Feodal'nye otnosheniia v udel'noi Rusi* (St. Petersburg, 1901); *Feodalizm v drevnei Rusi* (2nd ed., Moscow and Petrograd, 1923); *Feodalizm v udel'noi Rusi (Sochineniia,* vol. III) (1916).

5. Pavlov-Sil'vanskii, *Feodalizm v drevnei Rusi,* 155.

6. V. Latkin, *Zemskie sobory drevnei Rusi, ikh istoriia i organizatsiia sravnitel'no s zapadno-evropeiskimi predstavitel'nymi uchrezhdeniiami* (St. Petersburg, 1885).

7. A.E. Presniakov, *Obrazovanie velikorusskago gosudarstva (Ocherki po istorii XII-XV stoletii)* (Petrograd, 1918), 457-458.

8. The most forceful presentation of this view is to be found in *Ocherki istorii SSSR (Period feodalizma IX-XV vv.)* (Moscow, 1953), part II, 144-166; *Ocherki istorii SSSR (Period feodalizma konets XV v. - nachalo XVII v.)* (Moscow, 1955), 101-147 and 321-349. The following are the major scholarly works in which this thesis has been advanced: L.V. Cherepnin, *Obrazovanie russkogo tsentralizovannogo gosudarstva v XIV-XV vekakh* (Moscow, 1960); Ia.S. Lur'e, *Ideologicheskaia bor'ba v russkoi publitsistike kontsa XV – nachala XVI veka* (Moscow and Leningrad, 1960); I.I. Smirnov, *Ocherki politicheskoi istorii russkogo gosudarstva 30-50kh godov XVI veka* (Moscow and Leningrad, 1958) and A.A. Zimin, *Reformy Ivana Groznogo* (Moscow, 1960).

9. For the origins of this reassessment, see S.V. Iushkov, "K voprosu o soslovno-predstavitel'noi monarkhii v Rossii," *Sovetskoe gosudarstvo i pravo*, 1950, no. 10, 39-51. However, more substantive statements on the problem of *soslovno-predstavitel'naia monarkhia* appeared in print beginning in 1964: G.B. Gal'perin, *Forma pravleniia russkogo tsentralizovannogo gosudarstva XV-XVI vv.* (Leningrad, 1964), and also his *Genezis i razvitie soslovnoi monarkhii v Rossii (XV-XVI vv.)*, Avtoreferat dissertatsii na soiskanie uchenoi stepeni doktora istoricheskikh nauk (Leningrad, 1968); N.E. Nosov, *Stanovlenie soslovno-predstavitel'nykh uchrezhdenii v Rossii; Izyskaniia o zemskoi reforme Ivana Groznogo* (Leningrad, 1969). The problem of the existence of a Russian representative estate monarchy during the period in question received renewed attention in the debates about the nature of Russian absolutism. In particular, see L.V. Cherepnin, "Zemskie sobory i utverzhdenie absoliutizma v Rossii," *Absoliutizm v Rossii (XVII-XVIII vv.) (Sbornik statei k semidesiatiletiiu so dnia rozhdeniia i sorokapiatiletiiu nauchnoi i pedagogicheskoi deiatel'nosti B.B. Kafengauza)* (Moscow, 1964), 92-106, and his "K voprosu o skladyvanii absoliutisticheskoi monarkhii v Rossii XVI-XVIII vv.," *Dokumenty sovetsko-ital'ianskoi konferentsii istorikov 8-10 aprelia 1968 g. Absoliutizm v Zapadnoi Evrope i Rossii, Russko-ital'ianskie sviazi vo vtoroi polovine XIX veka* (Moscow, 1970); A.Ia. Avrekh, "Russkii absoliutizm i ego rol' v utverzhdenii kapitalizma v Rossii," *Istoriia SSR*, 1968, no. 2, 82-104; M.P. Pavlova-Sil'vanskaia, "K voprosu ob osobennostiakh absoliutizma v Rossii," *Istoriia SSR*, 1968, no. 4, 71-85; cf. also A.A. Zimin "V. I. Lenin o moskovskom tsarstve' i cherty feodal'noi razdroblennosti v politicheskom stroe Rossii XVI veka," *Aktual'nye problemy istorii Rossii epokhi feodalizma (Sbornik statei)* (Moscow, 1970), 292-293. For a convenient summary of the debate on Russian absolutism, cf. H.J. Torke, "Die neuere Sowjethistoriographie zum Problem des russischen Absolutismus," *Forschungen zur osteuropäischen Geschichte* (cited hereafter as *FOG*), XX (1973), 113-133.

10. So far as Byzantine theoretical influences on Muscovite state ideology are concerned, the seminal study on the subject by I. Ševčenko has put to rest the lingering assumption that Iosif Volotskii may have been a Muscovite Machiavelli and that, beginning in the late fifteenth and especially in the sixteenth century, Muscovite political thought has reached new and original heights ("A Neglected Byzantine Source of Muscovite Political Ideology," *Harvard Slavic Studies*, II [1954] [Cambridge, Mass.], 141-180; for additional use of Byzantine materials in Muscovite political documents, see idem., "Muscovy's Conquest of Kazan: Two Views Reconciled," *Slavic Review* [cited hereafter as *SR*], XXVI, 4 [1967], 542-554 , fn. 1; and his study entitled "Agapetus East and West: Fate of a Byzantine 'Mirror of Princes'," published in J. Pelenski, ed., *State and Society in Europe from the Fifteenth to the Eighteenth Century [Proceedings of the First Conference of Polish and American Historians, Nieborów, Poland, May 27-29, 1974]* [Warsaw, 1985], 15-53). While acknowledging Ševčenko's contribution to the identification of Agapetus as a major source of Muscovite political ideology, a number of scholars still adhere to the notion of its relative originality in the late fifteenth and sixteenth centuries. For some examples of this attitude, see A.A. Zimin, *Rossiia na poroge novogo vremeni* (Moscow, 1972), especially chapter VII, "Zemnii Bog"; E. Donnert, *Russland an der Schwelle der Neuzeit (Der Moskauer Staat im 16. Jahrhundert)* (Berlin, 1972), 132-147.

11. For a discussion of Muscovy's annexation of the Kazan Khanate and in particular the relationship of ideology and the politics of conquest, as well as the literature on the subject, see J. Pelenski, *Russia and Kazan: Conquest and Imperial Ideology (1438-1560s)* (The Hague and Paris, 1974).

12. For a comprehensive statement of this view and the literature on the subject, cf. Gal'perin, *Forma pravleniia...*, 39-55. A. Wyczański, apparently by following this view, made an unwarranted comparison of the *boiarskaia duma* with the Polish *Sejm* (*Polska w Europie XVI wieku* [Warsaw, 1973], 156-157).

13. For some data on the problem, see V.O. Kliuchevskii, *Boiarskaia duma drevnei Rusi* (5th ed., Petrograd, 1919), 216-227; A.A. Zimin, "Sostav Boiarskoi dumy v XV-XVI vv.," *Arkheograficheskii Ezhegodnik za 1957 g.* (cited hereafter as *AE*), 1958; G. Alef, "Reflections on the Boyar Duma in the Reign of Ivan III," *The Slavonic and East European Review* (cited hereafter as *SEER*), XLV (1967), 76-123.

14. The relevant phrases are: "...i nachat dumati so svoimy boiary o svoei velikoi kniagine Solomonii chto nepladna est'... " and "I nacha zhe kniaz' velikii dumati s temi zhe boiary i prikazivati o svoem synu velikim kniaze Ivane, i o velikoi kniagine Elene, i o svoem synu kniazy Iuri Vasilevichi, i o svoei dukhovnoi gramote" (*Polnoe sobranie Russkikh letopisei* [cited hereafter as *PSRL*], VI [1853], 29, 270).

15. The phrase in the *Law Code of 1497* reads as follows: "...ulozhil kniaz' velikii Ivan Vasil'evich vseia Rusi s detmi svoimi i s bojari o sude..." (B.D. Grekov, ed., *Sudebniki XV-XVI vekov* [Moscow and Leningrad, 1952], 29); the relevant phrase in the *Law Code of 1550* states: "....tsar' i velikii kniaz' s svoieiu brat'eiu i boiary sei sudebnik ulozhil" (*ibid.*, 141); Article 98 reads as follows: "A kotorye budut dela novye, a v sem sudebnike ne napisani, i kak te dela s gosudareva dokladu i so vsekh boiar prigovoru vershaetsia, i te dela v sem sudebniki pripisyvati" (*ibid.*, 176). For the literature on the various interpretations of Article 98, cf. B.A. Romanov's Commentary (*Sudebniki XV-XVI vekov*, 334-337). A convenient English translation of the *Sudebniki* has been provided by H.W. Dewey, ed. and transl., *Muscovite Judicial texts, 1488-1556* (Michigan Slavic Materials, no. 7) (Ann Arbor, 1966).

16. The literature on the *zemskie sobory* is quite extensive. For the sixteenth century, the following selected studies ought to be mentioned: Latkin, *Zemskie sobory drevnei Rusi*; V.O. Kliuchevskii, "Sostav predstavitel'stva na zemskikh soborakh drevnei Rusi," *Sochineniia* (8 vols.; Moscow, 1956-1959), VIII, 5-112; S.A. Avaliani, *Zemskie sobory. Literaturnaia istoriia zemskikh soborov* (2nd ed., Odessa, 1916); M.N. Tikhomirov, "Soslovno-predstavitel'nye uchrezhdeniia (zemskie sobory) v Rossii XVI veka," in *Rossiiskoe gosudarstvo XV-XVI vekov* (Moscow, 1973), 42-69; V.I. Koretskii, "Zemskii sobor 1575 g. i postavlenie Simeona Bekbulatovicha velikim kniazem vseia Rusi," *Istoricheskii arkhiv*, 1959, no. 2; "Zemskii sobor 1575 g. i chastichnoe vozrozhdenie oprichniny," *Voprosy istorii* (cited hereafter as *VI*), 1967, no. 5; "Materialy po istorii Zemskogo sobora 1575 g. i o postavlenii Simeona Bekbulatovicha 'velikim kniazem vseia Rusi'," *AE za 1969* (1971); G. Stökl, "Der Moskauer Zemskij Sobor," *Jahrbücher für Geschichte Osteuropas* (cited hereafter as *JfGOE*), VIII, 2 (1960), 149-170; "Die Moskauer Landesversammlung – Forschungsproblem und politisches Leitbild," in K.E. Born, ed., *Historische Forschungen und Probleme (Festschrift für Peter Rassow)* (Wiesbaden, 1961), 66-87; A.A. Zimin, "Zemskii sobor 1566 g.," *Istoricheskie Zapiski* (cited hereafter as *IZ*), LXXI (1962), 196-236; S.O. Shmidt, "Stanovlenie zemskikh soborov," in *Stanovlenie rossiiskogo samoderzhavstva (Issledovanie sotsial'no-politicheskoi istorii vremeni Ivana Groznogo)* (Moscow, 1973), 120-261; L.V. Cherepnin, *Zemskie sobory russkogo gosudarstva v XVI-XVII vv.* (Moscow, 1978).

17. Shmidt has maintained that several additional *sobor(s)* had taken place in the late 1540s, the mid-1550s, one in 1560, and still another in 1564-1565. The last *sobor*, according to Shmidt, inaugurated the *oprichnina* (*Stanovlenie rossiiskogo samoderzhavstva*, 120-261). Serious reservations have been entertained as to this

extraordinary increase in the number of the *sobor*(s) held in the sixteenth century (cf.
N.I. Pavlenko, "K istorii zemskikh soborov XVI v.," VI, 1968, no. 5, 82-105).
    18. The *prigovornaia gramota* of the 1566 *sobor* dates from July 2, 1566,
and its text has been published in *Sobranie gosudarstvennykh gramot i dogovorov*, I
(1813), no. 192, 545-556. For the calculation of numbers and percentages, see Zimin,
IZ, LXXI (1962), 201. Zimin's categorization and his figures do not differ significantly from those offered by Kliuchevskii (*Sochineniia*, VIII, 26).
    19. The concept was applied to Russian conditions in a comprehensive but
vague manner by V.O. Kliuchevskii in a course he offered at Moscow University in
1886 (*Istoriia soslovii v Rossii* [3rd ed., Petrograd, 1918]). Its applicability to the
seventeenth century has been analyzed by G. Stökl, "Gab es im Moskauer Staat
Stände?" *JfGOE*, XI, 3 (1963), 321-342; cf. also J. Keep, "The Muscovite Elite and
the Approach to Pluralism," *SEER*, XLVIII, 3 (1970), 201-231. For comparativist
aspects of this problem, see D. Gerhard, "Regionalismus und ständisches Wesen als
ein Grundthema europäischer Geschichte," in: *Wege der Forschung*, II. *Herrschaft
und Staat im Mittelalter* (Darmstadt, 1956), 332-364; also D. Gerhard, ed., *Ständische
Vertretungen in Europa im 17. und 18. Jahrhundert (Veröffentlichungen des Max-
Planck-Institut*, XXVII) (Göttingen, 1969).
    20. M. Khudiakov was the first to raise the possibility of the influence of
qurultai on the *zemskii sobor* (*Ocherki po istorii Kazanskogo khanstva* [Kazan, 1923],
231). However, his comparison was restricted to the *qurultai* of 1551 and the Stoglav
of 1551. His response to his own inquiry was somewhat enigmatic ("Vopros etot
dolzhen byt' razreshen avtoritetnymi spetsialistami" [*ibid.*, 231]). Khudiakov's
analysis of the Kazanian *qurultai* is a good introduction to the problem (*ibid.*, 184-
188).
    The Mongol-Turkic *qurultai* dealt with important matters such as questions of
war and peace, trade and crucial policy decisions. The *qurultai* was attended by heads
of clans, prominent personalities, vassals, and service aristocracy or nobility (B.Ia.
Vladimirtsov, *Obshchestvennyi stroi mongolov* [Mongol'skii kochevoi feodalizm]
[Leningrad, 1934], 79, 99, and fn. 6, 115).
    21. *PSRL*, XXV (1949), 330; *PSRL*, XXVII (1962), 286. For the studies on
the *pomest'e* system and the literature on the subject, see Iu.G. Alekseev and A.I.
Kopanev, "Razvitie pomestnoi sistemy v XVI v.," *Dvorianstvo i krepostnoi stroi
Rossii XVI-XVIII vv.* (Moscow, 1975), 57-69, and the unpublished doctoral dissertation by G.V. Abramovich, "Pomestnaia sistema i pomestnoe khoziaistvo v Rossii v
poslednoi chetverti XV i XVI v.," *Avtoreferat dissertatsii na soiskanie uchenoi stepeni
doktora istoricheskikh nauk* (Leningrad, 1975).
    22. *Sudebniki XV-XVI vekov*, 28.
    23. A synopsis of the decree concerning the obligation of service is to be
found in the Continuations of the *Letopisets nachala tsarstva...*, (*PSRL*, XIII, part I
[1904/1965], 268-269).
    24. For a discussion of the meaning of the term *votchina* in the Old Russian
sources and the literature on the subject, see Pelenski, *Russia and Kazan ...*, 76-78, fn.
1.
    25. For the classical work on the subject of *pronoia*, see G. Ostrogorski,
Pronija, Prilog istoriji feudalizma u Vizantiji i u južnoslovenskim zemljama (Srpska
Akademija Nauka, Posebna izdanja, knjiga CLXXVI, Vizantološki Institut, knjiga I
[Beograd, 1951]), especially 22-23. Cf. also a review of this work by I. Ševčenko,
"An Important Contribution to the Social History of Late Byzantium," *The Annals of*

the Ukrainian Academy of Arts and Sciences in the U.S., II, 4(6) (Winter, 1952), 448-459.

26. G. Vernadsky, "On Some Parallel Trends in Russian and Turkish History," *Transactions of the Connecticut Academy of Arts and Sciences* (cited hereafter as *Transactions...*), XXXVI (July, 1945), 34.

27. For a discussion of the meaning of the term *soyūrghǎl* and the literature on the subject, see Pelenski, *Russia and Kazan...*, 57, fn. 112. Vernadsky mistakenly assumed that the Turkish *timar* was the closest parallel to the *pomest'e* (*Transactions...*, 33-34). It ought to be pointed out that it was the Golden Horde and her successor states and not the Ottoman Empire that provided governmental and social models for Muscovite Russia.

28. Sh.F. Mukhamed'iarov, "Tarkhannyi iarlyk kazanskogo khana Sakhib-Gireia 1523 g.," *Novoe o proshlom nashei strany* (Pamiati akademika M.N. Tikhomirowa) (Moscow, 1967), 106.

29. Vladimirtsov, *Obshchestvennyi stroi mongolov*, 115, fn. 2.

30. For a discussion of the meaning of the term *tarkhan* and the literature on the subject, see Pelenski, *Russia and Kazan...*, 56-57, fn. 109.

31. For the reevaluations and the literature on the subject, see A.A. Zimin, *Oprichnina Ivana Groznogo* (Moscow, 1964); R.G. Skrynnikov, *Nachalo oprichniny* (Leningrad, 1966), and *Oprichnyi terror* (Leningrad, 1969).

32. A.N. Nasonov, *Mongoly i Rus' (Istoriia tatarskoi politiki na Rusi)* (Moscow and Leningrad, 1940; 2nd ed., 1969) 30, fn. 2.

33. Muscovite diplomacy scored its first, albeit temporary, success by receiving the recognition of the title "tsar," or the Western "caesar" ("Kaiser") for its ruler from the real emperor, Maximilian I, in the anti-Polish offensive alliance treaty concluded by Muscovy and the Habsburg Empire in 1514. The best critical edition of the treaty, its German translation, and commentary were provided by G. Stökl, in L. Santifaller, ed., *1100 Jahre österreichische und europäische Geschichte* (Vienna, 1949), 53-56. For the historical background of the treaty and additional documents, cf. J. Fiedler, "Die Allianz zwischen Kaiser Maximilian I und Vasilij Ivanovič, Grossfürsten von Russland, von dem Jahre 1514," *Sitzungsberichte der Kaiserlichen Akademie der Wissenschaften, Philosophisch-Historische Classe*, XLIII, 2 (1863), 183-289, especially 196, 197-199 and fn. 1.

34. For an account of the coronation and the relevant literature, cf. D.B. Miller, "The Coronation of Ivan IV of Moscow," *JfGOE*, XV, 4 (1967), 559-574.

35. For a more extensive discussion of the external consequences of the Kazan conquest, see Pelenski, *Russia and Kazan...*, 299-301.

36. *Akty istoricheskie, sobrannye i izdannye Arkheograficheskoiu Kommissieiu*, I (1841), Nos. 67 and 266, 119-120 and 497.

37. For a more extensive discussion of these problems, see my study entitled "Muscovite Russia and Poland-Lithuania, 1450-1600: State and Society – Some Comparisons in Socio-political Developments" in J. Pelenski, ed., *State and Society in Europe from the Fifteenth to the Eighteenth Century (Proceedings of the First Conference of Polish and American Historians*, Nieborów, Poland, May 27-29, 1974) (Warsaw, 1985), 93-120.

Maps

MAP 1
Kievan Rus'
11th-12th centuries

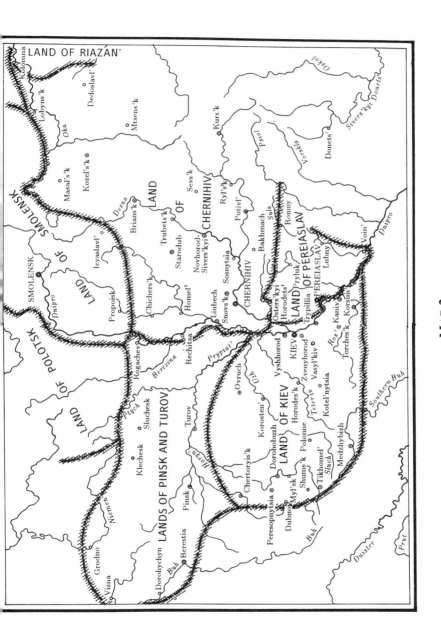

MAP 2
Corelands of Kievan Rus'
12th century

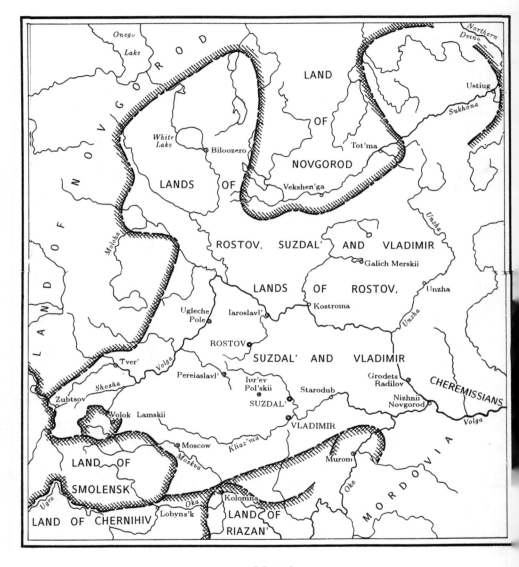

MAP 3
Rostov-Suzdal'-Vladimirian State
12th-13th centuries

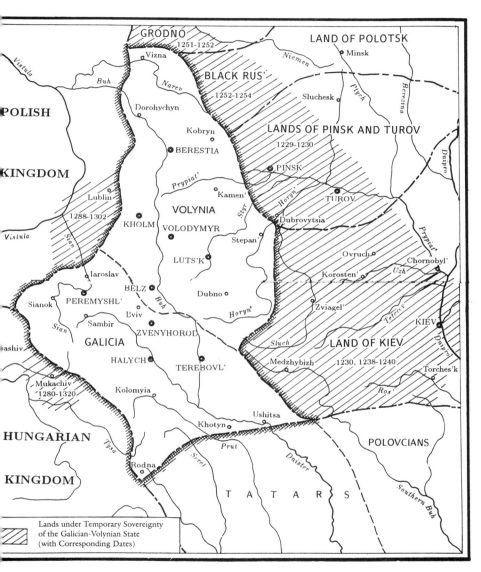

MAP 4
Galician-Volynian State
12th-13th centuries

MAP 5
Lithuanian-Ruthenian State
End of the 14th century

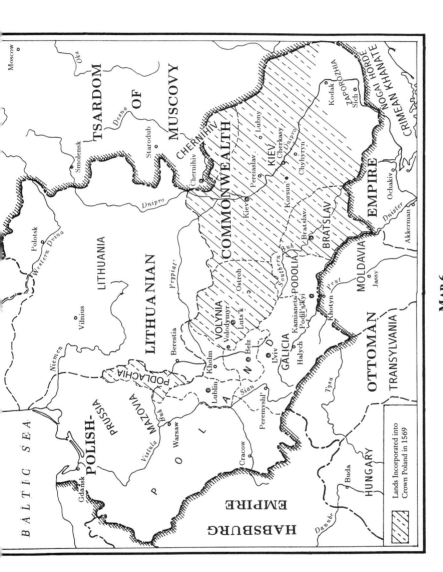

BALTIC SEA

Moscow

TSARDOM OF MUSCOVY

Oka
Desna
Starodub
Smolensk
Dnipro

Western Dvina
Polotsk

LITHUANIA

Niemen
Vilnius

POLISH-
PRUSSIA
Gdańsk

MAZOVIA

Vistula
Warsaw

Bub

PODLACHIA

P   O   L

Cracow

HABSBURG EMPIRE

Danube

Buda

HUNGARY

Prypiat

Berestia

Kholm
Lublin
Sian
Peremyshl'

VOLYNIA
Volodymyr
Luts'k
Ostroh

L   A   N   D

Belz
Lviv
GALICIA
Halych
Podil's'kyi

PODILLYA
Kamianets'

Tysa

TRANSYLVANIA

OTTOMAN

MOLDAVIA
Jassy

Prut
Khotyn

Southern Buh

CHERNIHIV
Chernihiv

COMMONWEALTH

LITHUANIAN

KIEV
Kiev
Pereiaslav'
Korsun'

Lubny
Cherkasy
Chyhyryn

BRATSLAV
Bratslav

Dnipro

ZAPOROZHIA
Kodak
Sich

NOGAI HORDE

CRIMEAN KHANATE

EMPIRE

Ochakiv
Dnister
Akkerman

Lands Incorporated into
Crown Poland in 1569

MAP 6
Polish-Lithuanian Commonwealth
After 1569

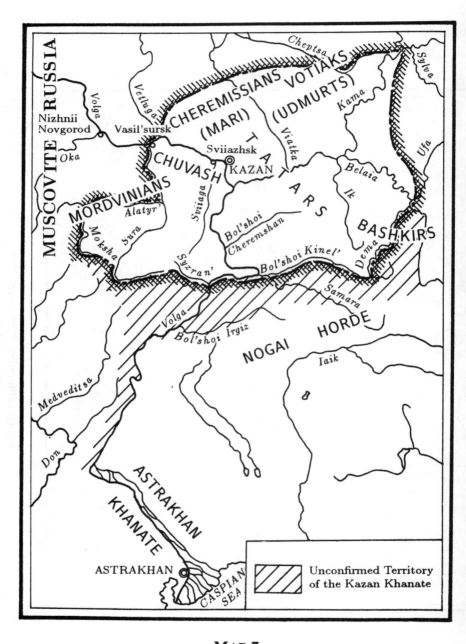

MAP 7
Kazan Khanate
End of the 15th – mid-16th centuries

Illustrations

Plate 1a   Silver coin of Prince Volodimer Sviatoslavich of Kiev (obv.). End of the 10th century. State Hermitage Museum, St. Petersburg.

Plate 1b   Silver coin of Prince Volodimer Sviatoslavich of Kiev (rev.). End of the 10th century. State Hermitage Museum, St. Petersburg.

Plate 2   Silver coin of Prince Volodimer Sviatoslavich of Kiev
               (obv.), c. 1000. State Hermitage Museum, St. Petersburg.

Plate 3   Silver coin of Prince Volodimer Sviatoslavich of Kiev
(rev.). End of the 10th century. State Hermitage
Museum, St. Petersburg.

Plate 4   Grand Princess Gertruda and her son Iaropolk Petr…
venerating Apostle Peter. Miniature from the *Egbert
Psalter* (*Codex Gertrudianus*), c. 1078-1086.

Plate 5   Prince Iaropolk Petr and his wife Kunigunda receiving from Christ the crown of life. Miniature from the *Egbert Psalter*, c. 1078-1086.

Plate 6   *Our Lady of Vladimir*. Icon. First half of the 12th century. Tretiakov Gallery, Moscow.

Plate 7   Andrei Bogoliubskii removing the icon of the Blessed
          Mother of God from Vyshhorod.... Miniature from
          the *Radziwiłł Chronicle* (*Radzivilovskaia letopis' RL*),
          end of the 15th century, entry 1155.

нъ же є андрѣи город и сь побѣдою · сиде погаиъ·чего
агарни зьнтъ · лѣ снои дрѣжнн бснѡ збраво · стон
хоу жи тѣшц нс стыю бцю ю напо лъицин по стати ·
итприѣ хад остъ ѣ бци · ид оптѣшец · ис прѣ ла гротвѣи со ·
гоур гемъ · сон з ас лаво · нѣ ро слабо · н со в сею дрѣжн
но
ю · ипоклониша прѣстою бцию · ипоч аша ц ѣ лов а
тнс тоубцию · срад остию вѣ ликою н сослезами · хвѣа
лъи пѣснн в ѣ з д ающе ѣи · нивъ шехаша грам с ла вны н ·
брах нмовъ · апрѣ дн г город ын по ятто ша · сиж е бъ
гонобое · стобѣци володнмерское · ю жи збраваше
ссобою · влго в ѣ рнъ н кнза андрѣн · нпрн нес съ сос ла
вою · инос тавни в ст ѣ бци · в володнмнри в бол о
ттобѣ рен · иддѣ жи стонтъ · ид о сего дни · ꙁ

Plate 8   Vladimirians expressing their gratitude to the icon of
          Our Lady of Vladimir.... Miniature from the *RL*,
          entry 1164.

дєвкнєвє · mo є aжєзнмы · послаискзьандрен · иссоу
нала спасвоємстислава · накнєвьскагокнзьмстні
слава · сростовцн · и володнмирьцн · исєб͠калцн · ни
ль͠ткнзєн · а͠ї · глъб͠ьтпє͠рєaславскни · романь смолєнь
скни · дьъвышєгородскни · володнмир͠зандриεвh
амитрокьгоргεвнчь · рoурнсь · собра͠тюмстнсла
вцє · флг͠тстославнчь собра͠тю · соигорε · мстнславь
жε нзаславнчь затворнся вкнεвε · н б͠ьляхоусакрoв

пкоснгорода · истогашεоугородл · г͠дни · н вгашлsн
євъ єго нєвымникогдатжε · амстнславьнн заславн вєна
сбра͠тю · исккнєва · кволоднмирю · смало мъ дроуны
акнагнниεгоизоймаша · нснаεго и д͠рокнлюvзаша ·
нвεськнεвь пограбнша · ицр͠кви и монастыирн заг·
дни · нисоллыпонмаша · икнагнирнзьl :

Plate 9   Capture of Prince Mstislav Iziaslavich's wife, his son,
and his retinue...following the sack of Kiev in 1169.
Miniature from the *RL*, entry 1169.

Plate 10   Mstislav Andreievich installing his uncle Gleb in
Kiev.... Miniature from the *RL*, entry 1169.

Plate 11   Mstislav Andreievich installing his son Gleb in Kiev....
Miniature from the *RL*, entry 1169.

Plate 12   Andrei Bogoliubskii installing Roman Rostislavich in
Kiev…. Miniature from the *RL*, entry 1171.

Plate 13   Vsevolod Iur'evich, Iaropolk Rostislavich, and their
           retinues taken prisoner by the Rostislavichi....
           Miniature from the *RL*, entry 1173.

Plate 14   Retreat of Andrei Bogoliubskii's army, following the
failed second major campaign against the Kievan land
and the siege of Vyshhorod in 1173. Miniature from
the *RL*, entry 1173.

Plate 15   Andrei Bogoliubskii's assassins breaking into the entrance hall of his castle. Miniature from the *RL*, entry 1175.

Plate 16   Assassination of Andrei Bogoliubskii in 1175. Miniature from the *RL*, entry 1175.

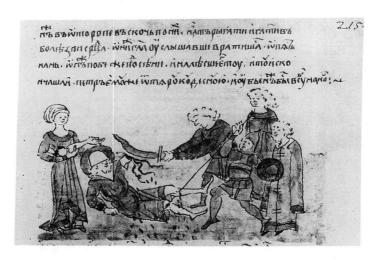

Plate 17   Assassins cutting off Andrei Bogoliubskii's arm….
Miniature from the *RL*, entry 1175.

ѡ свѣт сглоу тра мрть · внелю на пам̃ · ве апл̃
зоша апостѣ нь ми лежаща · н вземше на ковртѣ · ıсе
неѣ то любъскнн · внесоша въ вскнцю · пѣвшена
влонвнша въгрѣ камена · гороннивъто в любъскый
нераздравша докнцѣ · ıı дѣлатели ıı же ба хо прнш
ла · злато ıı срерро портын паволокнın мѣнне емоу

Plate 18   Andrei Bogoliubskii laid to rest…. Miniature from the
                RL, entry 1175.

МНОГОГЛАСО ТВОРЯ̈ВВОЛОСТИНЕГО · ПОСАДНИКЪЁ · И ТИ
ОӰНОВОДЕ · ДОМЫ ПОГРАБИША · А САМѢ̈НУЗБИША · ИДЕ ЦКЫЕ
ИМѢЧЕННИКЫИЗБИША · А ДОМЫИ ПОГРАБИША · НЕВЕДОЩЕГЛӒИ
МЛГО · ИДЕ ЖЕЗАКОНЪ ТОУ И Ѿ ВИ МНОГО · А ПАКНА ПӒК̈ ПА
ВЕЛѤ ГАТЬ · ВСАКА ДШАВЛАСТЕ ПОВИНОЁ ПТЬ · ЁСТВОӞЕ
МНЫ · ПОБѢГНѢ̈ ВСА КОМОӰЛКО ЦДЬ · ВЛАСТЬЮ ЖЕ САНА
ГӒСОВГ̈ · ВЕЩА ВЕЛИКИНЗ ЛА ОӰ СТПЕЦЬ · ТѢ МѤ̈ ПРОТИВӒ
ВОЛО СПН · ПРО ТИ ВИТЬ ЗАКОНӦ БЖҊ̈Ю · КНѤ ХЪБО НЕ ТӦ НЕ
МЕНѤСЩ̈ · БӜИЁ̈ БО СЛО ГАЁ̈ ТЬ ; ✦

Plate 19   Townspeople and servants of Andrei Bogoliubskii's
               court sacking the houses of his governor and adminis-
               trators, and killing them.... Miniature from the *RL*,
               entry 1175.

Plate 20   Feodul...the clergyman, the servants, and the Vladimirians transporting Andrei Bogoliubskii's body from Bogoliubovo to Vladimir. Miniature from the *RL*, entry 1175.

Plate 21   Grand Prince Vsevolod Iur'evich witnessing the miraculous appearance of the icon of the Blessed Mother of Vladimir.... Miniature from the *RL*, entry 1177.

Plate 22   Destruction of the city of Vladimir…by the great fire of 1185. Miniature from the *RL*, entry 1185.

Plate 23   Roman Mstyslavych of Halych entering Kiev....
Miniature from the *RL*, entry 1202.

о слано ѿ рюрикови · и ко ѡлгови че · и во дн рю́рика ·

и со крⷮⷪоу · и ѡлговнчн · а са книⷭртⷭ ц целовалъ · и по
стн рю́рика во вⷭрⷪ чии · а ѿлговн хадне́пръ кⷱчернигово ·
и по садн велнкн кн нⷭⷤ въ се воло · и романъ · и нⷤ гваⷬⷼ
гⷤро славнⷱⷶ · во кнⷭⷫневⷮⷣⷷ · ⁊

Plate 24   Ingvar Iaroslavych installed in Kiev.... Miniature
            from the *RL*, entry 1202.

Plate 25   Sack of Kiev in 1203.... Miniature from the *RL*, entry 1203.

соглтъ пррїскадъ · Бжепринишамазыцинадостоа
ннетвое · йискъвернишацрьбьстоутвои · положи
ша на росолима · гаковощиоехранилище · положи
шатроупиерабътвои · брашноптицамёны · плоть
пребобныйтвои · звбремъземыпролигашакробь
ихъ · акнводо · товсестасанакнебо · загрехнпаша ·
чернци йчерници · старыйисеисоша · ипопыстарые
йслепыйихромыим · йслоукыи · итродобатыи й · тавса
йсеисоша · ачточернноцб амть йчернць · амть йпопобъ
ипопаден · никыны · адщерки йсный товсевєдоша
иноплемениции ввєѣнисобтъ · тогаркиша йметии

СЛАВА · БОЛОДИМИРИЧА · РОСТИСЛАВЛА Д · роунагарослабла
иведеростиславысосновьсюе ксоки

Plate 26   Kievans taken into captivity, following the sack of
Kiev in 1203. Miniature from the *RL*, entry 1204.

Plate 27   Roman Mstyslavych of Halych advising Riurik
Rostislavich…. Miniature from the *RL*, entry 1204.

Plate 28   Roman Mstyslavych of Halych punishing Riurik Rostislavich of Kiev…. Miniature from the *RL*, entry 1205.

Plate 29   Dionisii, *St. Petr* (the Metropolitan of Moscow). Icon (detail). Late 15th century (?). The Cathedral of the Dormition, Moscow.

Plate 30   Dionisii, *St. Aleksei* (the Metropolitan of Moscow).
Icon (detail). Late 15th century. Tretiakov Gallery,
Moscow.

Plate 31   *St. Iona* (The Metropolitan of Moscow). Sculptural relief
on the wooden coffin panel (detail). 17th century. The
Church of the Repository of the Robe, Moscow Kremlin.

Plate 32   *Constantine and Helena*. Fresco. 1547-1551. The
Cathedral of the Annunciation, Moscow Kremlin.

Plate 33   *St. Volodimer and St. Olga.* Fresco. 1547-1551. The Cathedral of the Annunciation, Moscow Kremlin.

Plate 34   *Aleksandr Nevskii and Ivan Kalita*. Fresco. 1547-1551.
The Cathedral of the Annunciation, Moscow Kremlin.

Plate 35   *King Władysław Jagiełło*. Sculptural relief on the
tombstone (detail). After 1434. The Wawel Cathedral,
Cracow.

Plate 36   Wit Stwosz, *King Kazimierz Jagiellończyk*. Sculptural
             relief on the tombstone (detail). 1492. The Wawel
             Cathedral, Cracow.

Plate 37   Santi Gacci, *King Zygmunt II August*. Sculptural relief
on the tombstone (detail). 1574-1575. The Wawel
Cathedral, Cracow.

Plate 38   The Polish Parliament (*Sejm*). Woodcut from: Jan
Łaski, *Communes Regni Poloniae privilegium*
(Cracow, 1506).

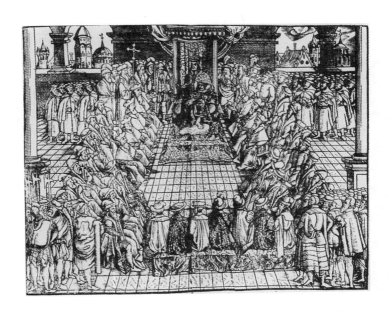

Plate 39   The Parliament (*Sejm*). Woodcut from: Jan Herburt, *Statuta* (Cracow, 1570).

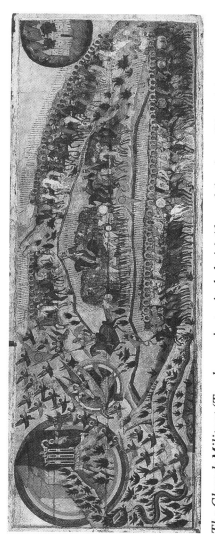

Plate 40   *The Church Militant (Tserkov voinstvuiushchaia)* (the celebration of Russia's conquest of Kazan in 1552). Icon. Second half of the 16th century. Tretiakov Gallery, Moscow.

Plate 41   *Our Lady of Kazan*. Icon. Mid-17th century. Russian State Museum, St. Petersburg.

NOTES ON LISTS OF RULERS AND HIERARCHS

For the chronological lists of (1) Kievan rulers to the Mongol conquest of Kiev in 1240, (2) rulers of the Suzdal'-Vladimir Grand Principality to its final merging with the Muscovite Grand Principality, (3) rulers of Muscovite Russia to the extinction of the "Riurikide" dynasty, (4) metropolitans of Moscow, and (5) khans of the Kazan Khanate, see J. Pelenski, *Russia and Kazan: Conquest and Imperial Ideology (1438-1560s)*(The Hague and Paris, 1974), pp. 328-334.

For the chronological lists of (1) princes of Halych and Halych-Volynia, (2) grand dukes of Lithuania, (3) kings of Poland, (4) metropolitans of Kiev, (5) metropolitans of Lithuania, see I. Ševčenko, *Ukraine between East and West: Essays on Cultural History of the Eighteenth Century* (Edmonton and Toronto, 1996), pp. 201-202, 203-205, 211-212, 213.

SUPPLEMENTARY SELECT BIBLIOGRAPHY

Alekseev, L.V. *Smolenskaia zemlia v IX-XIII vv.* (Moscow, 1980).

Alishev, S.Kh. *Istochniki po istorii Tatarstana (XVI-XVIII)* (Kazan, 1993-1994).

_____. *Istoricheskie sud'by narodov Srednego Povolzh'ia XVI – nachalo XIX v.* (Moscow, 1990).

_____. *Kazan i Moskva: mezhdugosudarstvennye otnosheniia v XV-XVI vv.* (Kazan, 1995).

_____. *Natsional'nyi vopros v Tatarii dooktiabrskogo perioda* (Kazan, 1990).

Al'shits, D.N. "Publitsisticheskie vystupleniia Sil'vestra v epokhu reform 'Izbrannoi rady'," *TODRL*, 42 (1989): 92-106.

Antonova, V.I., Mneva, N.E. *Katalog drevnerusskoi zhivopisi*, vol. 2 (Moscow, 1963).

Begunov, Iu.K., Kirpichnikov, A.N., eds. *Kniaz' Aleksandr Nevskii i ego epokha (Issledovaniia i materialy)* (St. Petersburg, 1995).

Blankoff, J. "Chernigov, rivale de Kiev? A propos de son dévelopment urbain," *Revue des études slaves*, 63 (1991): 146-155.

Bobrov, A.G. "Iz istorii letopisaniia pervoi poloviny XV v.," *TODRL*, 46 (1993): 3-20.

Borisov, N. *Ivan Kalita* (Moscow, 1995).

_____. "Moskovskie kniazia i russkie mitropolity XIV v.," *VI*, no. 2 (1986): 30-43.

Chernetsov, A.V. "K izucheniiu Radzivilovskoi letopisi," *TODRL*, 36 (1981): 274-288.

Chichurov, I.S., *Politicheskaia ideologiia srednovekov'ia: Vizantiia i Rus'* (Moscow, 1990).

Croskey, R.M. *Muscovite Diplomatic Practice in the Reign of Ivan III* (New York and London, 1987).

Dembkowski, H.E. *The Union of Lublin: Polish Federalism in the Golden Age* (Boulder and New York, 1982).

Demin, A.S. "Otgoloski 'Slova o polku Igoreve' v 'Kazanskoi istorii' (Gipoteza o promezhutochnim istochnike)," *TODRL*, 43 (1990): 124-130.

_____, "'The Testament' of Iaroslav 'The Wise': A Reexamination," *Canadian Slavonic Papers*, 29 (1987): 369-386.

Dimnik, M. *The Dynasty of Chernigov 1054-1146* (Toronto, Ontario, 1994).

Dmitriev, M.V., ed. *Ucrainica et Belorossica: Issledovaniia po istorii Ukrainy i Belorussii*, vyp. 1 (Moscow, 1995).

Dmitrieva, R.P. "Agiograficheskaia shkola mitropolita Makariia (na materiale nekotorykh zhitii)," *TODRL*, 48 (1993): 208-213.

Donnelli, A.S. *Zavoevanie Bashkirii Rossiei 1552-1740* (Ufa, 1995).

Drevneishie gosudarstva vostochnoi Evropy (Materialy i issledovaniia 1991 god) (Moscow, 1994), especially pp. 265-268, and *1992-1993 gody* (Moscow, 1995), especially pp. 209-216.

Dubrovina, L.A. *Istoriia o Kazanskom tsarstve (Kazanskii letopisets: Spiski i klassifikatsiia tekstov)* (Kiev, 1989).

Duzinkiewicz, J. *Fateful Transformations (The Four Years' Parliament and the Constitution of May 3, 1791)* (Boulder and New York, 1993).

Egorov, V.L. "Aleksandr Nevskii i Chingizidy," *Otechestvennaia istoriia*, no. 2 (1997): 48-58.

Ermolaev, I.P. *Kazanskii krai vo vtoroi polovine XVI-XVII v.* (Khronologicheskii perechen' dokumentov) (Kazan, 1980).

Ermolaev, I.P. *Srednee Povolzh'e vo vtoroi polovine XVI-XVII v.* (*Upravlenie Kazanskim kraem*) (Kazan, 1982).

Fennell, J. *A History of the Russian Church to 1448* (London and New York, 1995).

Filippovskii, G.Iu. " 'Slovo' Andreia Bogoliubskogo o prazdnike 1 avgusta," *Pamiatniki istorii i kul'tury*, vyp. 2 (1983): 75-84.

_____. *Stoletie derzanii (Vladimirskaia Rus' v literature XII v.)* (Moscow, 1991).

Floria, B.N. "Istoricheskaia traditsiia ob obshchestvennom stroe srednevekovogo Polotska," *OI*, no. 5 (1995): 110-116.

_____. *Otnosheniia gosudarstva i tserkvi u vostochnykh i zapadnykh slavian* (Moscow, 1992).

Franchuk, V.Iu. *Kievskaia letopis': Sostav i istochniki v lingvisticheskom osveshchenii* (Kiev, 1986).

Franklin, S., Shepard, J. *The Emergence of Rus' 750-1200* (London and New York, 1996).

Froianov, I.Ia. *Kievskaia Rus': Ocherki obshchestvennoi istoriografii* (Leningrad, 1990).

Golovko, A.B. *Drevnaia Rus' i Pol'sha v politicheskikh vzaimosviaziakh X – pervoi treti XIII vv.* (Kiev, 1988).

Goldberg, A.L. "Ideia 'Moskva – tretii Rim' v tsikle sochinenii pervoi poloviny XVI v.," *TODRL*, 37 (1983): 139-149.

Gorskii, A.A. "Politicheskaia bor'ba na Rusi v kontse XIII veka i otnosheniia s Ordoi," *OI*, no. 3 (1996): 74-92.

_____. "Politicheskie tsentry vostochnykh slavian i Kievskoi Rusi: Problemy evolutsii," *OI*, no. 6 (1993): 157-162.

_____. "Problemy izucheniia 'Slova o pogibeli Ruskyia zemli' (K 750-letiiu so vremeni napisaniia)," *TODRL*, 43 (1990): 18-38.

Halbach, U. *Der russische Fürstenhof vor dem 16. Jahrhundert: Eine vergleichende Verfassungsgeschichte der alten Rus'* (Stuttgart, 1985).

Hantsov, V.M. "Osobennosti iazyka Radzivilovskogo (Kenigsberg-skogo) spiska letopisi," *IORIaS*, 32 (1927): 177-242.

Hellmann, M. "Die Heiratspolitik Jaroslavs des Weisen," *FOG*, 8 (1962): 7-25.

Huttenbach, H.R. "Muscovy's Conquest of Muslim Kazan and Astrakhan, 1552-1556. The Conquest of the Volga: Prelude to Empire," in M. Rywkin, ed., *Russian Colonial Expansion to 1917* (London and New York, 1988), pp. 45-69.

Iakovenko, N.M. *Ukrains'ka shliakhta z kintsia XIV do seredyny XVII stolittia (Volyn' i tsentral'na Ukraina)* (Kiev, 1993).

"Issledovatel'skie materialy dlia 'Slovaria knizhnikov i knizhnosti drevnei Rusi'": *Letopistsi i istoriki XI-XVII vv.*, *TODRL*, 39 (1985): 18-277.

"Issledovatel'skie materialy dlia 'Slovaria knizhnikov i knizhnosti drevnei Rusi'": *Pisateli i knizhniki XI-XVII vv.*, *TODRL*, 40 (1985): 31-189.

"Issledovatel'skie materialy dlia 'Slovaria knizhnikov i knizhnosti drevnei Rusi'": *Drevnerusskie povesti i skazaniia, TODRL*, 41 (1988): 3-153; 477-478.

"Issledovatel'skie materialy dlia 'Slovaria knizhnikov i knizhnosti drevnei Rusi'": *Pisateli i poety XVII v.*, *TODRL*, 44 (1990): 3-160; *TODRL*, 45 (1992): 47-177.

Ivanov, A.B. *Tretii Rim: Rus' XIV-XVIII vv.* (Moscow, 1996).

Kachalova, I.Ia., Maiasova, N.A., Shchennikova, L.A. *Blagoveshchenskii Sobor Moskovskogo Kremlia* (Moscow, 1990).

Kappeler, A. *Russlands erste Nationalitäten: Das Zarenreich und die Völker der Mittleren Volga vom 16. bis 19. Jahrhundert* (Cologne and Vienna, 1982).

Kazakova, N.A. "Khozhdenie vo Florentsiiu 1437-1440 gg. (Spiski i redaktsii)," *TODRL*, 30 (1976): 73-94.

Khoroshkevich, A.L. *Russkoe gosudarstvo v sisteme mezhdunarodnykh otnoshenii kontsa XV – nachala XVI v.* (Moscow, 1980).

_____. "Tsarskii titul Ivana IV i boiarskii miatezh 1553 goda," *OI*, no. 3 (1994): 23-42.

Kirpichnikov, A.N. "Aleksandr Nevskii mezhdu Zapadom i Vostokom," *VI*, nos. 11-12 (1996): 115-118.

Kloss, B.M. "Nikonovskaia letopis' i Maksim Grek," *TODRL*, 30 (1976): 124-131.

Kloss, B.M., Nazarov, V.D. "Rasskazy o likvidatsii ordynskogo iga v letopisanii kontsa XV v.," in *Drevnerusskoe isskustvo XIV-XV vv.* (Moscow, 1984), pp. 283-313.

Kobrin, V.B. *Ivan Groznyi* (1989).

_____. *Vlast' i sobstvennost' v srednevekovoi Rossii (XV-XVI vv.)* (Moscow, 1985).

Kočetkov, I. "Die Ikone 'Die Kirche auf dem Kriegszug,' als Hauptwerk der russischen Ikonenmalerei der Zeit Ivans IV. Groznyj. Zur Frage der Interpretation," in Eva Haustein-Bartsch, ed., *Russische Ikonen: Neue Forschungen (Beiträge zur Kunst des christlichen Ostens, Band 10)*, (Recklinghausen, 1991), pp. 216-226.

_____. "K istolkovaniiu ikony 'Tserkov voinstvuiushchaia' ('Blagoslovenno voinstvo nebesnogo tsaria')," *TODRL*, 38 (1985): 185-209.

Koretskii, V.I. *Istoriia russkogo letopisaniia vtoroi poloviny XVI – nachala XVII v.* (Moscow, 1986).

Korinnyi, N.N. *Pereiaslavskaia zemlia: X – pervaia polovina XIII veka* (Kiev, 1992).

Krom, M.M. *Mezh Rus'iu i Litvoi. Zapadnorusskie zemli v sisteme russko-litovskikh otnoshenii kontsa XV – pervoi treti XVI v.* (Moscow, 1995).

Kuchkin, V.A. "Aleksandr Nevskii -- gosudarstvennyi deiatel' i polkovodets sredne-vekovoi Rusi," *OI*, no. 5 (1996): 18-33.

_____. *Formirovanie gosudarstvennoi territorii severo-vostochnoi Rusy v X – XIV vv.* (Moscow, 1984).

_____. "Itogi restavratsii dukhovnykh gramot Ivana Kality," *OI*, no. 6 (1992): 62-70.

_____. "Moskva v XII -- pervoi polovine XIII veka," *OI*, no. 1 (1996): 3-13.

_____. "Pervyi moskovskii kniaz' Daniil Aleksandrovich," *OI*, no. 1 (1995): 93-107.

Lenhoff, G.D. "Cannonization and Princely Power in Northeast Rus': The Cult of Leotnij Rostovskij," *Die Welt der Slawen*, N.F. 16 (1992): 359-380.

Letopisets Pereiaslavlia Suzdal'skogo (Letopisets russkikh tsarei), *PSRL*, vol. 41 (Moscow, 1995).

Likhachev, D.S., ed., *Slovar' knizhnikov i knizhnosti drevnei Rusi (XI – pervaia polovina XIV v.)* vyp. 1 (Leningrad, 1987); (*vtoraia polovina XIV-XVI v.*) vyp. 2, chast' 1 (A-K) (1988); (*vtoraia polovina XIV-XVI v.*) vyp. 2, chast' 2 (L-Ia) (1989).

Limonov, Iu.A. *Vladimiro-Suzdal'skaia Rus' (Ocherki sotsial'no-politicheskoi istorii)* (Leningrad, 1987).

Litopys rus'kyi za Ipats'kym spyskom [the Hypatian Codex], L.Ie. Makhnovets, Ukrainian transl., introduction, annotations, and indices, O.V. Myshanych, general editor.

Lur'e, Ia.S. "Eshche raz o svode 1448 g. i Novgorodskoi Karamzinskoi letopisi," *TODRL*, 32 (1977): 199-218.

_____. "Feodal'naia voina v Moskve i letopisanie pervoi poloviny XV v.," *TODRL*, 47 (1993): 82-94.

_____. "Genealogicheskaia skhema letopisei XI-XVI vv. vkliuchennykh v 'Slovar' knizhnikov i knizhnosti drevnei Rusi'," *TODRL*, 40 (1985): 190-205.

Lur'e, Ia.S. "Iz nabliudenii nad letopisaniem pervoi poloviny XV v.," *TODRL* (1985): 285-304.

_____. "K probleme svoda 1448 g.," *TODRL*, 24 (1969): 142-146.

_____. "'Lavrent'evskaia letopis' -- svod nachala XIV v.," *TODRL*, 29 (1974): 50-67.

_____. "Letopisi pervoi poloviny XV v. kak literaturnye i istoricheskie pamiatniki," *TODRL* (1990): 39-57.

_____. "Moskovskii svod 1479 g. i ego protograf," *TODRL*, 30 (1976): 95-113.

_____. "Nezavisimyj letopisnyi svod kontsa XV v -- istochnik Sofiiskoi II i L'vovskoi letopisei," *TODRL*, 27 (1972): 405-419.

_____. "Novgorodskaia Karamzinskaia letopis'," *TODRL*, 29 (1974): 207-213.

_____. "Obshcherusskii svod -- protograf Sofiiskoi I i Novgorodskoi IV letopisei," *TODRL*, 28 (1974): 114-139.

_____. "O proiskhozhdenii Radzivilovskoi letopisi," *VID*, 18 (1987): 64-83.

_____. "O vozmozhnosti i neobkhodimosti pri issledovanii letopisei," *TODRL*, 36 (1981): 13-36.

_____. "Rus' XV veka: Otrazheniia v rannem i nezavisimom letopisanii," *VI*, nos. 11-12 (1993): 3-17.

_____. "Skhema istorii letopisaniia A.A. Shakhmatova i M.D. Prisel'kova i zadachi dal'neishego issledovaniia letopisei," *TODRL*, 44 (1990): 185-195.

Martin, J. *Medieval Russia, 980-1584* (Cambridge, 1995).

Martyshin, O.V. *Vol'nyi Novgorod: Obshchestvenno-politicheskoi stroi i pravo feodal'noi respubliki* (Moscow, 1992).

Miller, D.B. "The Kievan Principality on the Eve of the Mongol Invasion: An Inquiry into Current Historical Research and Interpretation," *HUS*, 10, no. 1/2 (1986): 215-240.

_____. "The Many Frontiers of Pre-Mongol Rus'," *Russian Review*, 19 (1992): 231-260.

_____. "Monumental Building and its Patrons as Indicators and Political Trends in Rus', 900-1262," *JfGOE*, 38 (1990): 321-355.

_____. "Monumental Building as an Indicator of Economic Trends in Northern Rus' in the Late Kievan and Mongol Periods, 1138-1462," *American Historical Review*, 94 (1989): 360-390.

_____. "The Velikie Minei Chetii and the Stepennaia Kniga of Metropolitan Makarii and the Origins of Russian National Consciousness," *FOG*, 26 (1979): 263-382.

Mneva, N.E. "Stenopis' Blagoveshchenskogo Sobora Moskovskogo Kremlia 1508 goda," in O.I. Podobedova, ed., *Drevnerusskoe iskusstvo (Khudozhestvennaia kul'tura Moskvy i prilezhashchikh k nei kniazhestv XIV-XVI vv.)* (Moscow, 1970), pp. 174-206.

Morozov, V.V. "Ot Nikonovskoi letopisi k Litsevomu letopisnomu svodu (Razvitie zhanra i evoliutsiia kontseptsii)," *TODRL*, 44 (1990): 246-268.

Murav'eva, L.L. *Letopisanie severo-vostochnoi Rusi kontsa XIII – nachala XV veka* (Moscow, 1983).

_____. "Letopisi severo-vostochnoi Rusi," *VI*, no. 11 (1986): 88-101.

_____. "Literaturnye sochineniia kak istochnik severo-vostochnogo letopisaniia kontsa XIII – nachala XV v.," *Letopisi i khroniki*, 1984, pp. 147-166.

Nazarenko, A.V. "Neizvestnyi epizod iz zhizni Mstislava Velikogo," *OI*, no. 2 (1993): 65-78.

Nikolaeva, V.N., compl. *Mikhail Iaroslavich Velikii kniaz' Tver'skoi i Vladimirskoi* (Tver', 1995).

The Nikonian Chronicle, S.A. Zenkovsky, ed., introd. and annot.; S.A. and B.J. Zenkovsky, transl., 5 vols. (Princeton, NJ, 1984-1989).

Miliutenko, N.I. "Rasskaz o prozrenii Rostislavichei na Sniadyni (k istorii smolenskoi literatury XII v.)," *TODRL*, 48 (1993): 121-128.

Panchenko, A.M., Uspenskii, B.A. "Ivan Groznyi i Petr Velikii: kontseptsiia pervogo monarkha," *TODRL*, 37 (1983): 54-78.

Pashin, S.S. *Chervonorusskie akty XIV-XV vv. i gramoty L'va Danilovicha* (Tiumen, 1996).

Pashuto, V.T. *Aleksandr Nevskii* (Moscow, 1975).

Plugin, V.A. "Nereshennye voprosy russkogo letopisaniia XIV-XV vekov," *Istoriia SSSR*, no. 4 (1978): 73-93.

Pobol', L.O., et al., eds. *Kiev i zapadnye zemli Rusi v IX-XIII vv.* (Minsk, 1982).

Podobedova, O.I. *Moskovskaia shkola zhivopisi pri Ivane IV* (Moscow, 1972).

Poppe, A. *Państwo i Kościół na Rusi w XI wieku* (Warsaw, 1968).

Potichnyj, P.J., Raeff, M., Pelenski, J. Žekulin, G.N., eds., *Ukraine and Russia in Their Historical Encounter* (Edmonton, 1992).

Priselkov, M.D., ed. (until 1941), Likhacheva, O.P., Mavrodina, R.M., Piotrovskaia, E.K., eds.; Lur'e, Ia.S., introd., *Radzivilovskaia letopis'* [the Radziwiłł Chronicle] in *PSRL*, 38 (1989).

Prokhorov, G.M. "Kodikologicheskii analiz Lavrent'evskoi letopisi," *VID*, vol. 4 (1972), pp. 77-104.

_____. "Neponiatyi tekst i pis'mo k zakazchiku v 'Slove o zhit'i i o prestavlenii velikogo kniazia Dmitriia Ivanovicha, tsaria Ruskago'," *TODRL*, 40 (1985): 229-247.

_____. "Radzivillovskii spisok Vladimirskoi letopisi po 1206 god i etapy Vladimirskogo letopisaniia," *TODRL*, 42 (1989): 53-76.

Radzivilovskaia ili Keningsbergskaia letopis' [the Radziwiłł Chronicle]: I. Fotomekhanicheskoe vosproizvedenie rukopisi; II. Stat'i o tekste i miniaturakh rukopisi (Obshchestvo liubitelei drevnei pis'mennosti, vol. 118) (St. Petersburg, 1902).

Rogozhin, N.M. *Posol'skie knigi Rossii kontsa XV – nachala XVII v.* (Moscow, 1995).

Rusina, O. "Do pytannia pro kyivs'kykh kniaziv tatars'koi doby," *Zapysky naukovoho tovarystva imeni T. Shevchenka* (Pratsi istorychno-filosofs'koi sektsii), vol. 225 (L'viv, 1993): 194-203.

Rybakov, B.A. *Petr Borislavich: Poisk avtora 'Slova o polku Igoreve'* (Moscow, 1991).

Sakharov, A.N. "Politicheskoe nasledie Rima v ideologii drevnei Rusi," *Istoriia SSSR*, no. 3 (1990): 71-83.

Salmina, M.A. "Eshche raz o datirovke 'Letopisnoi povesti' o Kulikovskoi bitve," *TODRL*, 32 (1977): 3-39.

_____. "K voprosu o datirovke 'Skazaniia o Mamaevom poboishche'," *TODRL*, 29 (1974): 98-124.

Schwarcz, I.I. "Das Problem der Kontinuität von der Kiever Rus' zum Moskauer Staat in den Moskauer Chroniken des 14. bis zum Anfang des 16. Jahrhunderts," *Mitteilungen des Institutes für Österreichische Geschichtsforschung*, 99, no. 1-2 (1991): 69-81.

Sedova, R.A. "Sluzhba mitropolitu Petru," *TODRL*, 45 (1992): 231-248.

Semenchenko, G.V. "Drevneishie redaktsii zhitiia Leontiia Rostovskogo," *TODRL*, 42 (1989): 241-254.

Senyk, S. *A History of the Church in Ukraine*, vol. I: *To The End of the Thirteenth Century* (Rome, 1993).

Shchapov, Ia.N. *Gosudarstvo i tserkov Drevnei Rusi X-XIII vv.* (Moscow, 1989).

_____. "Ideia mira v russkom letopisanii XI-XIII vekov," *Istoriia SSSR*, no. 1 (1992): 172-178.

Shmidt, S.O. *Rossiiskoe gosudarstvo v seredine XVI stoletiia* (Moscow, 1984).

Sinitsyna, N.V. "Avtokefaliia russkoi tserkvi i uchrezhdenie Moskovskogo patriarkhata (1448-1589 gg.)," in *Tserkov, obshchestvo i gosudarstvo v feodal'noi Rossii* (Moscow, 1990).

Skrynnikov, R.G. *Gosudarstvo i tserkov na Rusi XIV-XVI vv. (Podvizhniki russkoi tserkvi)* (Novosibirsk, 1991).

_____. *Tragediia Novgoroda* (Moscow, 1994).

_____. *Tretii Rim* (St. Petersburg, 1991).

_____. *Tsarstvo terrora* (St. Petersburg, 1992).

_____. *Velikii gosudar Ivan Vasil'evich Groznyi*, 2 vols. (Smolensk, 1996).

Solodkin, Ia.G. "Po povodu atributsii Piskarevskogo letopistsa," *TODRL*, 44 (1990): 387-396.

Srednovekovaia Rus', Sbornik nauchnikh statei k 65-letiiu so dnia rozhdeniia R.G. Skrynnikova (St. Petersburg, 1995).

Stökl, G. "Das Fürstentum Galizien-Wolynien," in M. Hellmann, ed., *Handbuch der Geschichte Russlands*, I: *Von der Kiewer Reichsbildung bis zum Moskauer Zartum* (Stuttgart, 1981), pp. 484-533.

Sucheni-Grabowska, A. *Monarchia dwu ostatnich Jagiellonów a ruch egzekucyjny*, Part 1: *Geneza egzekucji dóbr* (Wrocław, 1974).

Ševčenko, I. *Ukraine between East and West: Essays on Cultural History to the Early Eighteenth Century* (Edmonton and Toronto, 1996).

Tolochko, A.P. *Kniaz' v drevnei Rusi: Vlast', sobstvennost', ideologiia* (Kiev, 1992).

Tolochko, P.P. *Drevniaia Rus': Ocherki sotsial'no-politicheskoi istorii* (Kiev, 1987).

_____. *Kiev i Kievskaia zemlia v epokhu feodal'noi rozdroblennosti* (Kiev, 1980).

Trudy Otdela drevnerusskoi literatury, vols. 26-50 (Leningrad–St. Petersburg, 1971-1996).

Tvorogov, O.V. *Drevnerusskie Khronografy* (Leningrad, 1975).

Volkova, T.F. "Kazanskaia istoriia," *Slovar' knizhnikov i knizhnosti drevnei Rusi (vtoraia polovina XIV-XVI v.)*, vyp. 2, chast' 1 (A-K) (Leningrad, 1988), pp. 450-458.

_____, ed. (and Russian transl.) "Kazanskaia istoriia," in *Pamiatniki literatury drevnei Rusi* (Seredina XVI veka) (Moscow, 1985), pp. 300-565, 601-624.

Voronin, N.N. "K kharakteristike Vladimirskogo letopisaniia 1158-1177 gg.," *Letopisi i khroniki*, 1976, pp. 26-53.

_____. "Sushchestvoval li 'Letopisets Andreia Bogoliubskogo'?" *Pamiatki istorii i kul'tury*, 1 (1976): 28-43.

Waugh, D.C., ed. *Essays in Honor of A.A. Zimin* ("Bibliography of the works by A.A. Zimin," pp. 59-88) (Columbus, 1985).

Zimin, A.A. *Rossiia na poroge novogo vremeni* (Moscow, 1972).

_____. *Rossiia na rubezhe XV-XVI stoletii: Ocherki sotsial'no-politicheskoi istorii* (Moscow, 1982).

_____. *Vitiaz' na rasput'e: Feodal'naia voina v Rossii XV v.* (Moscow, 1991).

Zimin, A.A., Khoroshkevich, A.L. *Rossiia vremeni Ivana Groznogo* (Moscow, 1982).

INDEX

– A –

About the God-Inspired Achievement of the Tsar: 201

About the Novgorodians and Vladyka Feofil: 89

About the Podolian Land: 136

Admonition of Metropolitan Petr: 63

Adrianova-Peretts, V.P.: 83

Advisory Council of *Boiar*(s): 231, 233

Agapetus, Byzantine author: 15

Ahmet, Khan of the Golden Horde: 108

Aleksander Jagiellończyk, King of Poland, Grand Prince of Lithuania: 92, 93

Aleksandr Gorbatyi, Governor of the Kazan Khanate: 203

Aleksandr Iaroslavich Nevskii, Prince of Suzdal'-Vladimir: 6, 7, 11, 14, 58, 62, 69

Aleksei, Metropolitan of Kiev: 67

Alexius I Comnenus, Emperor of Byzantium: 234

Algirdas (Olgierd, Olgerd), Grand Prince of Lithuania: 132-137, 139, 142

Andrei-Afanasii, Metropolitan of Russia: 201

Andrei Iur'evich Bogoliubskii, Prince of Suzdal'-Vladimir: 6, 8, 11, 21-39, 45-50, 53-57, 66

Andrii Iurievych, Prince of Galicia-Volynia: 12

Antonii, Bishop of Chernihiv: 48

Antonovych, V.B.: 134, 213, 221

Askold and Dir, legendary princes of Kiev (?): 8, 51, 215

Assembly of the Land: 231, 232, 233

Astrakhan Khanate: 105, 140, 145, 177, 195, 198, 199, 204, 237

Augustus, Emperor of Rome: 119, 121, 123, 125, 214

– B –

Battle beyond the Don River: 88

Batu, Khan of the Golden Horde: 8, 9, 51, 52, 104, 198, 217

Beloozero: 90, 195

Belorussia; Belorussian land (territory); Belorussians: 2, 3, 94, 105, 117, 133, 134, 144, 151, 174

Belorussko-litovskie letopisi: see the *Lithuanian-Ruthenian Chronicles*

Berendeis: 46, 48

Berlad': 38

Berlyns'kyi, M.M.: 220

Bielsk: 163, 175

Bilhorod: 37

Black Rus': 133

Black Sea: 15, 86, 138, 143

Blue Waters, river: 136
   – Battle of: 132, 136, 137, 143

Bodians'kyi, O.M.: 213

Bogoliubovo: 26, 38, 39, 56

Bogoliubskii Chronicle of 1177 (hypothetical): 23, 31, 52

Boiarskaia duma: see the Advisory Council of *Boiar*(s)

Bolesław the Valiant, King of Poland: 166

Bolesław of Mazovia, prince: 163

Book of Degrees: 25, 64, 67, 71, 80, 190, 194, 196-203

Boris Aleksandrovich, Grand Prince of Tver': 87

Boris and Gleb, Sts. of Rus': 7, 39, 56, 63, 82, 85

Boris Zhidislavich, prince: 46

Bratslav: 151, 156, 158, 160, 162, 164

Briansk: 91, 135, 175

Buh, river: 136, 143

Bulgar land; Bulgars on the Volga: 15, 27, 28, 29, 140, 141, 194, 196-199

Bulgar-Kazan continuity: 141

Byzantium: 62, 65, 66, 124-126, 142, 214, 222, 230, 234-236
   – Patriarchate of: 11, 28, 29, 67, 142
   – Second Rome: 125

311

– C –

Carpathian Mountains: 216, 217
Caspian Sea: 194, 195, 199
Chartoryis'kyi, Alexandr, Ruthenian
    prince: 175
Cheremis'; Cheremissians: 193-195,
    198, 203
Chernihiv; Chernihivia; Chernihivians:
    5, 8, 47, 48, 91, 135, 142
Chingiz Khan, Khan of the Mongol
    Horde: 235
Chodynicki, K.: 174
Chronicle of Iurii Dolgorukii
    (hypothetical): 52
Chronicle of New Years: 189
*Chronicle of the Beginnings of the
    Tsardom*: 189, 200, 202
Chronicle of 1212 (hypothetical): 52
Chud': 195
Church Council of 1547: 68
*Codex of Metropolitan Gerontii of
    1490*: 111
Codex of the 1480s: see the *Muscovite
    Codex of the 1480s*
Codex of 1448 (hypothetical): 82, 83,
    85
Codex of 1456 (hypothetical): 84, 85,
    88, 89
Codex of 1479: see the *Muscovite
    Codex of 1479*
Codex of 1497: 109, 110
Constantine II, Metropolitan of Kiev:
    28, 30-33, 49
Constantine IX Monomachus, Em-
    peror of Byzantium: 118, 120-
    123, 124, 125, 126
Constantinople: 11, 25, 26, 28, 55, 67,
    87, 120, 122, 123, 124, 237
    – Conquest of: 87, 125
    – Fall of: 87, 88, 94, 105, 117,
    230
    – Golden Gate of: 26
    – New Rome: 120
    – Patriarchate of: 11, 55, 80

Continuity (*translatio*; succession)
    theory:
    – Muscovite: 7, 57, 58, 68-72,
    89, 94, 105, 117, 118, 127,
    171, 190
    – Russian: 1-2, 45, 214
    – Soviet: 2-3
    – Ukrainian: 2, 45, 220
Cossack Ukraine: 2, 45, 78, 215, 220
Crimea; Crimean Khanate; Crimean
    Tatars: 7, 94, 103-105, 106, 108,
    109, 111, 118, 137, 140, 143,
    191, 192, 199, 200
Czarnkowski, Stanisław, Marshal of
    the Chamber of Deputies: 159,
    165, 167

– D –

Daniil, Metropolitan of Moscow: 110
Danylo Romanovych, Prince of Kiev
    and Volynia, King of Galicia: 8, 9,
    10, 12, 14, 52, 62, 133, 163, 215
Dashkevych, M.P.: 213
David Rostislavich, Prince of Vyshho-
    rod: 37, 38, 46, 47
Delektorskii, F.: 88
Diakonov, M.A.: 288
Długosz, Jan: 166, 167
Dmitrieva, R.P.: 119
Dmitrii Ivanovich Donskoi, Grand
    Prince of Vladimir and Muscovy:
    67, 81-89, 90, 119, 197
Dmitrii Shemiaka, Russian prince: 82
Dmytro, Governor of Kiev: 9, 52, 215
Dnieper, river: 15, 137, 143
Dniester, river: 143
Dorohozhych: 46
Dorohychyn: 163
    – Church of St. Kyrill: 46
Drahomanow, M.P.: 221, 223

– E –

Edigü, Emir of the Golden Horde: 82,
    104, 138, 144
Epifanii Premudryi, Russian author:
    83

Epifanii Slavenets'kyi, Ukrainian intel-
lectual and author: 67
Epistle of Spiridon-Savva: 118, 119,
120-122, 124, 125, 126
Epistle to Grand Prince Vasilii III: 126
Evfimii, Russian monk and author: 67

– F –

Feast of St. Feodor: 46
Feast of the Intercession (*Pokrov*): 27
Feast of the Savior: 7, 27, 28
Feast of the Veneration of the Virgin
Mary: 7
Fedor Biakont, father of Metropolitan
Aleksei: 67
Fedor Hol'shans'kyi, Lithuanian-
Ruthenian prince: 134
Feodor, ecclesiastic (vladyka?) of
Vladimir: 21, 28, 29, 32-34
Feodosii, Archbishop of Novgorod:
190
Ferapontov Monastery: 118
Filofei of Pskov, Russian author: 126,
204
Florence, Council of: 87, 94, 105,
117, 125
Fragment of a Russian Chronicle: 196,
197, 198
Franko, I.Ia.: 213

– G –

Galicia: 12, 64, 65, 216, 220
Galicia-Volynia; Galician-Volynian
Rus'; Galician-Volynian state: 2, 5,
8, 10, 11, 12, 13, 15, 16, 45, 64,
65, 70, 215, 216
Galician-Volynian Chronicle: 8, 9, 10,
16, 51, 57
Ğambek, Khan of the Golden Horde:
134
Gediminas (Gedymin), Grand Prince
of Lithuania: 133, 134, 141
Germogen, Metropolitan of Kazan and
Astrakhan, Patriarch of Russia:
201

Gerontii, Metropolitan of Moscow:
109
Girey, Ači [Ḥāǧǧi], Khan of the
Crimea: 106, 109
Girey, Mengli, Khan of the Crimea: 7,
94, 103, 106, 107, 108, 109, 111,
118, 191
Girey, Sahip, Khan of the Kazan
Khanate: 235
Gleb Iur'evich of Pereiaslav, prince: 9,
31, 34, 46, 47, 48, 52, 55, 56
Golden Horde: 11, 14, 15, 62, 66, 82,
103, 104, 108, 131-145, 228, 237
Gol'dberg, A.L.: 119
Great Menology: 64, 71, 189
Grekov, B.D.: 2
Grodno, Diet of: 157, 174
Gurii, Archbishop of Kazan: 195, 203

– H –

Halecki, O.: 152
Halych: 5, 9, 10
– Halych Metropolitanate of
"Little Rus'": 11
– Metropolitanate of: 5, 11, 65
– Second Kiev: 10
Halyts'ko-Volyns'kyi litopys: see the
Galician-Volynian Chronicle
History of Kazan: 198, 199, 203
Horodto, Union of: 173
Hrushevs'kyi, M.S.: 2, 3, 36, 45, 77,
134, 137, 140, 155, 165, 167,
213, 215, 220, 221
Hungary; Hungarians: 13, 15
Hypatian Codex: 8, 9, 11, 22, 50, 51,
52, 80, 215

– I –

Iam Zapol'skii, Truce of: 151
Iaropolk I Sviatoslavich, Prince of
Kiev: 8, 51
Iaropolk II Iziaslavich, Prince of Kiev:
8-9, 52
Iaroslav I Volodimerovich, Prince of
Kiev: 5, 7, 8, 51, 71, 126

Iaroslav III Vsevolodovich, Prince of Suzdal' and Vladimir: 7, 58, 71
Ibak, Nogai prince: 191
Igor', Prince of Kiev: 8, 51
Igor' Sviatoslavich, prince: 46, 47
Ilarion, Metropolitan of Kiev: 63, 86
Illuminated Chronicle: 189
Imperial Book: 189, 200, 201, 202, 203
Innocent IV, Pope: 14, 62, 133, 163
Ioasaf, Metropolitan of Moscow: 110
Iona, Metropolitan of Moscow: 67-68, 82, 238
Iosif Volotskii, Russian ecclesiastic and author: 229
Iov, Patriarch of Russia: 68
Ipat'evskaia letopis': see the *Hypatian Codex*
Islam: 199, 201
Istrin, V.M.: 213
Iurii Dolgorukii, Prince of Kiev: 22, 26, 27, 31, 53, 55, 57
Iurii I L'vovych, Prince of Galicia-Volynia, King of Galicia: 12, 62, 64, 65
Iurii II Boleslav, Prince of Galicia-Volynia: 12
Iuzhany: see the "Southerners"
Ivan Danilovich Kalita, Grand Prince of Moscow: 63, 85, 86
Ivan III Vasil'evich, Grand Prince of Moscow: 7, 90, 103, 104, 107-112, 118, 125, 171, 191, 192, 200
Ivan IV, Tsar of Russia: 141, 177, 190, 195, 196, 197, 198, 201, 230, 231, 236, 237, 238
Iziaslav I Iaroslavich, Prince of Kiev: 8, 51
Iziaslav II, Prince of Kiev: 9, 52
Iziaslav Mstislavich of Volynia, Prince of Volodymyr in Volynia: 53

– J –

Jagiełło (Władysław Jagiełło), Grand Prince of Lithuania, King of Poland: 144, 159, 161, 162, 163, 165, 168, 169, 170

Jazhelbitsy, Treaty of: 84
Jerusalem: 120, 123
John IV, Metropolitan of Kiev: 30

– K –

Kama, river: 194, 195, 198
Karamzin, M.N.: 1, 69, 136, 214, 219, 228
Karger, M.K.: 2
Karnkowski, Stanisław, Bishop of Cuiavia: 172
Katyrev-Rostovskii, Ivan, Muscovite author: 237
Kazan; Kazan Khanate; Kazan Tatars: 82, 105, 140, 145, 167, 177, 189-204, 235, 236, 237
– Icon of Our Lady of: 201, 202
– Russian land: 198
Kazanskaia istoriia: see the *History of Kazan*
Kazimierz Jagiellończyk, King of Poland, Grand Prince of Lithuania: 92, 108, 111, 118, 159-160, 161, 162, 163, 164, 168, 171, 173
Kazimierz the Great, King of Poland: 65, 153, 163
Kedrov, S.: 202
Kerch, peninsula: 199
Khodkevych, Ivan, Palatine of Kiev: 104, 106, 107, 108, 109
Kholm: 10
– Church of St. John: 10
Kiev: 1, 2, 4-11, 22-39, 45-58, 61-72, 77-94, 103-112, 118, 134, 136, 137, 138, 142, 156, 157, 165-172, 214, 215, 216, 219 220, 221, 222
– Campaign of 1154-1155: 22, 53
– Campaign of 1168-1169: 55
– Campaign of 1173: 21, 29, 34-39
– Church of St. Sophia: 7, 46, 48, 111
– Church of the Tithe: 46, 48
– Golden Gate of: 25-26, 39, 56

- Metropolitanate of Kiev; Metropolitanate of Kiev and all of Rus': 1, 5, 10, 11, 28, 30, 32, 55, 58, 61-68, 70-72, 80, 118, 132, 214
- Monastery of the Caves: 31, 47, 48, 49, 104, 106, 107, 109, 111
- Sack of 1169: 6, 21, 24, 28, 29, 31-32, 34, 37, 39, 45-58
- Sack of 1203: 6, 32, 49
- Sack of 1240: 104
- Sack of 1416: 104
- Sack of 1482: 7, 103-112, 118

Kievan Chronicle: 3, 10, 21-24, 32-39, 45-46, 48-52, 54-57, 69, 215

"Kievan Inheritance"; "Kievan succession":
- Contest for:
  - Chernihivian: 5
  - Galician-Volynian: 5, 7-9, 9-17
  - Muscovite: 21-39
  - Suzdalian-Vladimirian: 5, 6-7, 9-17
- Debate about: 213-224
- Claims to:
  - Golden Horde: 131-145
  - Lithuanian: 131-145
  - Muscovite: 61-72, 77-94, 103-112, 117-127, 151-177
  - Polish-Lithuanian: 151-177
  - Russian: 1-2, 213-224
  - Suzdalian-Vladimirian: 45-58
  - Ukrainian: 2, 213-224
- Theory of:
  - Muscovite: 61-72, 77-94
  - Russian: 1-2, 214
  - Soviet: 2-3
  - Ukrainian: 2, 215

Kievan land: 4, 7, 21, 24, 25, 27, 50, 52, 54, 70, 103, 104, 108, 120, 135, 137, 151, 154, 156, 158, 160, 162, 165-171, 175, 176, 216, 219

Kievan Rus': 1-7, 12-13, 34, 45, 50-53, 57, 58, 61, 62, 66, 69, 70, 71, 72, 81, 89, 94, 105, 117, 120, 127, 143, 151-152, 155, 158, 166, 171, 173, 190, 214, 215, 216, 218-224

Kievskaia letopis': see the *Kievan Chronicle*

Kipchak Horde: see the Golden Horde

Kiprian, Metropolitan of Kiev: 63, 64, 67, 69, 71, 79, 80

Kir Larius: see Michael I Kerularios

Kirill, Metropolitan of Kiev: 7, 10, 62

Kirill, Bishop of Turov: 34

Kliaz'ma, river: 1, 21, 53, 214

Kliuchevskii, V.O.: 1, 24

Kniga stepennaia: see the *Book of Degrees*

Konrad of Mazovia, prince: 163

Konstantyn Ostrozhs'kyi, Ruthenian prince: 174, 175, 177

Konstantyn Vyshnevets'kyi, Ruthenian prince: 175

Korets'kyi, Bohdan, Ruthenian prince: 175

Kostomarov, M.I.: 213, 217, 218, 219, 220, 221, 222, 228

Kotliarevs'kyi, O.O.: 213, 217

Kotoshikhin, Grigorii, Muscovite bureaucrat and author: 237

Kovgorshad, Tatar princess: 201

Krivichiian land; Krivichiians: 90, 195

Kromer, Marcin: 166, 167

Kryms'kyi, A.Iu.: 213

Kuczyński, S.M.: 136

Kul-Derbish, Kazanian envoy: 192

Kulikovo Field (*Pole*): 80
  - Battle of: 80-84, 132-133, 144-145

Kurbskii, A.M., Russian prince: 200

Kutuzov, Michail Vasil'evich, Muscovite envoy: 103

– L –

Latkin, V.: 229, 230
Laurentian Codex: 22, 28, 32, 50, 52, 69, 80
Lavrent'evskaia letopis': see the *Laurentian Codex*
Lavrovskii, P.A.: 213, 216, 217, 218
Law Code of 1497: see the *Muscovite Law Code of 1497*
Law Code of 1550: see the *Muscovite Law Code of 1550*
Leontii, Bishop of Rostov and Suzdal': 7, 30
Letopisets Bogoliubskogo 1177 goda: see the *Bogoliubskii Chronicle of 1177*
Letopisets leta novye: see the *Chronicle of New Years*
Letopisets nachala tsarstva: see the *Chronicle of the Beginnings of the Tsardom*
Letopisets Pereiaslavlia Suzdal'skogo: see the *Suzdal'-Pereiaslav Chronicle*
Letopisets velikii russki: see the *Russian Great Chronicle*
Lev Iurievych, Prince of Galicia-Volynia: 12
Life of Leontii of Rostov: 27
Likhachev, D.S.: 2, 61, 71, 78, 79
Lithuania; Lithuanian land; Grand Principality of Lithuania; Lithuanians: 2, 14, 45, 46, 49, 65, 69, 79, 89, 91, 92, 93, 106, 131-145, 151-157, 161-165, 170, 172, 173, 174, 176
– Diet of: 151, 154, 156
– Metropolitanate of: 65
Lithuania-Ruthenia; Lithuanian-Ruthenian State: 2, 45, 64, 65, 70, 78, 131-137, 143, 144, 153, 177, 215
Lithuanian-Ruthenian Chronicles: 134, 136, 140
Litovsko-russkie letopisi: see the *Lithuanian-Ruthenian Chronicles*

Litsevoi letopisnyi svod: see the *Illuminated Chronicle*
Little Rus'; Little Russia: 2, 12, 45, 215, 219, 220
Liubavskii, M.K.: 2
Livonian War: 172, 233
Lublin, Union (Diet) of 1569: 93, 151-159, 164, 165, 167, 172, 173, 175
Lukas Chrysoberges, Patriarch of Constantinople: 28, 29, 55
Lur'e Ia.S.: 84
Lutsk: 53, 134, 143
Lyko-Obolenskii, Ivan Volodimerovich, Muscovite prince: 104
Lypyns'kyi, V.K.: 223
L'viv: 143, 174
L'vov Chronicle: 80, 110, 111, 189, 194, 195, 198, 199
L'vovskaia letopis': see the *L'vov Chronicle*

– M –

Mahmut, Khan of the Kazan Khanate: 238
Makarii, Metropolitan of Moscow: 25, 67, 68, 189, 191, 195-200, 204
Maksim, Metropolitan of Kiev: 62
Maksymovych, M.O. (M.A.): 213, 217-221
Manuel I Comnenus, Emperor of Byzantium: 28
Maximilian I, Emperor of Rome: 127
Mazovia: 159-161, 163, 164
Meria; Merians: 13, 90, 195
Meyendorff, J.: 66
Michael I Kerularios, Patriarch of Constantinople: 120
Mielnik, Union of: 165
Mikhail Iur'evich, Prince of Kiev: 35, 37, 56
Mikhail of Chernihiv, Prince of Chernihiv, Grand Prince of Kiev: 14

Mikhail Olel'kovych, Ruthenian
    prince: 89
Miliukov, P.N.: 77, 78
Mindaugas (Mendovg), Grand Prince
    of Lithuania: 14, 133
Mongols: 7, 14, 58, 133, 135
Mordva; Mordvinians: 194, 195, 198
Moscow: 1, 5, 11, 12, 30, 61-68, 70,
    144, 192, 214
    – Cathedral of Vasilii the
      Blessed: 195
    – Patriarchate of: 67
    – Second Kiev: 172
    – Third Rome: 126
Mstislav I Volodimerovich Harold,
    Prince of Kiev: 5, 8, 51
Mstislav II Iziaslavich, Prince of Kiev:
    9, 46, 47, 48, 52
Mstislav Andreievich, Prince of
    Suzdal': 9, 46, 47, 48, 49
Mstislav of Volynia, prince: 35, 56
Mstislav Rostislavich, Prince of
    Bilhorod: 37, 38, 46, 47, 52
Muhammad-Amin, Khan of the Kazan
    Khanate: 191, 192
Mukhamed'iarov, Sh.F.: 235
Murom; Muroma; Muromians: 90,
    194, 195
Muscovite Codex of 1472: 85, 89, 105,
    117
Muscovite Codex of 1479: 84, 90, 108,
    110
Muscovite Codex of the 1480s: 110,
    111, 112
Muscovite Codex of 1518: 109
Muscovite Law Code of 1497: 231,
    234
Muscovite Law Code of 1550: 231
Muscovite Law Code of 1649: 234
Muscovite Russia; Muscovite Rus': 61,
    71, 77, 79, 112, 127, 131, 138,
    140, 141, 142, 145, 167, 177, 214
    – Expansion into the Kazan
      Khanate: 189-204
    – Contest for the Rus' lands: 51-
      154, 171-172
    – Political system of: 228-239

Muscovy, Grand Principality of
    Moscow: 1, 2, 7, 45, 57, 214, 223
    – Chronicle writing in: 68-72,
      79-94, 103-112
    – Contest for the Rus' lands:
      131-133, 139-145
    – Ecclesiastical claims to Kievan
      Rus': 61-72
    – Official claims to Kievan Rus':
      77-94, 117-127
Muslims: 112, 192, 194, 200-203
Myszkowski, Stanisław, Palatine of
    Cracow: 156

– N –

Narration about Mamai's Battle: 88,
    89
*Narration about the Grand Princes of
    Vladimir of Great Russia*: 118-
    119, 122-123, 124, 125
*Narration about the Miracles of the
    Vladimirian Icon of the Mother of
    God*: 24, 25, 26, 27
*Narration about the Victory against
    the Bulgars*: 27, 28, 29
Nerl', river: 26
    – Church of the Intercession
      (*Pokrov-na-Nerli*): 26, 27
Nestor, Bishop of Rostov: 28
Nicephoros II, Metropolitan of Kiev:
    33
Niemen, river: 133
Nikanor Chronicle: 81, 89
Nikanorovskaia letopis': see the
    Nikanor Chronicle
Nikon Chronicle: 71, 80, 139, 140,
    141, 189, 194, 195, 198, 199
Nikonovskaia letopis': see the *Nikon
    Chronicle*
Nizhnii Novgorod: 197
Nogais: 191, 192, 193
Nolde, B.: 192, 193
"Northerners": 1, 77, 213, 216
Novgorodskaia chetvertaia letopis': see
    the *Novgorodian Fourth Chronicle*

Novgorodskaia pervaia letopis': see the
   Novgorodian First Chronicle
Novgorod; Great Novgorod; Nov-
   gorodians: 69, 71, 79, 84, 89 90,
   91, 94, 105, 117, 195, 217, 219,
   221, 229
Novgorodian First Chronicle: 80
Novgorodian Fourth Chronicle: 81,
   82, 83, 84
Novhorod-Sivers'kyi: 91, 132
Nur-Sultan, mother of Muhammad-
   Amin: 191

– O –

O blagovedimom podvyze tsaria: see
   *About the God-Inspired Achieve-
   ment of the Tsar*
O novgorodtsekh i o vladytse Feofile:
   see *About the Novgorodians and
   Vladyka Feofil*
*O poboishche izhe na Donu, i o tom,
   kniaz' velikii kako bilsia s ordoiu*:
   81
O Podol'skoi zemli: see *About the
   Podolian Land*
*O prestavlenii velikago kniazia
   Dmitriia Ivanovicha*: 83
O velikom poboishche, izhe na Donu:
   81
*O zhitii i o prestavlenii velikogo
   kniazia Dmitriia Ivanovicha, tsaria
   rus'skago*: 82
Ohonovs'kyi, O.M.: 213
Oka, river: 194, 195
Oleg, Prince of Kiev: 8, 51, 120, 122
Oleg of Riazan', prince: 82
Oleg Sviatoslavich, prince: 46, 47
Olgerd: see Algirdas
Olgovichi, dynasty of Chernihiv: 35,
   56
Orthodox Christianity: 107, 109, 199-
   204
Osnova, Ukrainian journal: 216, 217,
   220, 221
Otryvok russkoi letopisi: see the *Frag-
   ment of a Russian Chronicle*

Ottoman Empire: 234
Özbeg, Khan of the Golden Horde:
   134

– P –

Padniewski, Filip, Archbishop of
   Cracow: 156
Pakhomii Logofet, Serbian author: 67,
   88
Patrimonial law: 117, 171, 214
Patrimony: 6, 27, 38, 81, 86, 90, 92,
   93, 171, 193, 196, 197, 234
Pavlov, A.: 88
Pavlov-Sil'vanskii, N.P.: 228, 229,
   230
Peace Treaty of 1494: 92
Pereiaslav: 11, 27, 48, 135, 219, 220
   – Treaty of: 3
Pereiaslavl'-Zalesskii: 62
Perekop Horde: 108
Peresvetov, Ivan, Muscovite author:
   200
Peretts, V.M.: 213
Perm: 67, 90, 107
Petr, Metropolitan of Kiev: 10, 62, 63,
   64, 67
Pitirim, Bishop of Perm: 67
Pobeda na Bolgary Volzhskiia: see the
   Victory against the Volga Bulgars
*Poboishche velikogo kniazia Dmitriia
   Ivanovicha na Donu s Mamaiem*:
   81
Podlachia: 133, 134, 151, 154, 156,
   157, 159-165, 174, 175
Podolia; Podolians: 103, 135, 136,
   137, 143, 157, 164, 168, 216
Pogodin, M.P.: 213, 214, 216, 217,
   218
Pokrov (Intercessory garment of the
   Virgin Mary), cult of: 27
Pokrovskii, F.P.: 83
Poland; Polish Kingdom; Crown
   Poland; Poles: 64, 65, 93, 140,
   151-177, 220

Poland-Lithuania; Polish-Lithuanian
Commonwealth: 65, 91, 92, 93,
103, 104, 105, 117, 126, 151,
152, 153, 167, 171, 177, 193, 237
Polissia: 133, 134, 176
Polikarp, Abbot of the Monastery of
the Caves: 31, 47, 49
Polotsk: 133, 195
– Conquest of: 172
Poltava, Battle of: 138
Pomest'e: 233-235
Poslanie k velikomu kniaziu Vasiliiu:
see the *Epistle to Grand Prince
Vasilii III*
Poslanie Spiridona-Savvy: see the
Epistle of Spiridon-Savva
Potebnia, O.O.: 213
Pouchenie Petra Mitropolita: see the
Admonition of Metropolitan Petr
*Povest' (Skazanie) o iavlenii i
chudesakh ikony Kazanskoi
Bogomateri*: see the *Tale
(Narration) about the Appearance
and the Miracles of the Icon of the
Mother of God of Kazan*
*Povest' ob ubienii Andreia
[Bogoliubskogo]*: see the *Tale
about the Slaying of Andrei
[Bogoliubskii]*
Povest' Simeona Suzdal'tsa: see the
Tale of Simeon of Suzdal'
Povest' vremennykh let: see the
Primary Chronicle
"Praise of Dmitrii Ivanovich
[Donskoi]": 84, 86
*Praise of Grand Prince Boris
Aleksandrovich*: 87
"Praise of Volodimer I": 63
Presniakov, A.E.: 2, 3, 57, 77, 213,
228, 229
Primary Chronicle: 50, 69, 79, 80,
194, 195, 219
Priselkov, M.D.: 69, 79, 81, 84
Privislianskii krai: see the *Vistula land*
Prokhorov, G.M.: 71
Prologue Life of Kirill: 34
Prologue Narration: 27

Prolozhnoe zhitie Kirilla: see the
Prologue Life of Kirill
Prolozhnoe skazanie: see the *Prologue
Narration*
Pronoia: 234
Prussia: 167
Pskovian Chronicle: 104
Pypin, A.N.: 2, 213

– Q –

Qurultai (Mongol-Turkic Assembly of
the Land): 233

– R –

Radzivilovskaia letopis': see the
Radziwiłł Chronicle
Radziwiłł Chronicle: 52, 69, 70
Radziwiłł, Mikolaj, Lithuanian prince:
154
Red Rus': see Galicia
Riazan': 67, 69, 79, 142
Riurik, legendary ruler in Rus' (?): 90,
120, 122, 194, 195, 198
Riurik of Ovruch, prince: 46, 47
Riurik Rostislavich, Prince of Kiev: 9,
35, 38, 52
Riurikides, dynasty: 4, 27, 30, 94,
117, 125, 171, 214
Rogozh Chronicle: 81, 135, 136
Rogozhskii letopisets: see the *Rogozh
Chronicle*
Roman Mstyslavych, Prince of
Galicia-Volynia: 8, 9, 52
Roman Rostislavich of Smolensk,
Prince of Kiev: 9, 35, 37, 46, 47,
52
Rome: 63, 120, 222
Rostislav I, Prince of Kiev: 9, 52
Rostislavichi, dynasty of Smolensk:
35, 37, 38, 56
Rostov; Rostovia; Rostovians: 24, 25,
27, 46, 47, 55, 195, 197
Rostov and Suzdal', Bishopric of: 30
Rostov Codex of 1489: 109, 110

Rostovia-Suzdalia-Vladimiria: 2, 7,
45, 57, 58, 68, 71, 94, 117, 127,
171, 190, 214
– Origins of: 21-39
Rostovian-Suzdalian-Vladimirian
Chronicles: see the *Suzdalian-*
Vladimirian Chronicles
Rus', Rus' lands: 1-8, 12-13, 21, 31,
33, 37, 45, 50, 51, 55, 57, 58, 79,
91-93, 103-105, 108, 117, 126,
190, 219
– Descendant of the Byzantine
and Roman Empires: 117-127
– Lithuanian expansion into:
131-145
– Metropolitanate of Kiev and
all of Rus': 10, 30, 61-72, 80,
118, 132, 214
– Mongol invasion of: 5, 15,
236
– Muscovy's ecclesiastical claims
to: 61-72
– Polish expansion into: 151-
177
– Political system of: 3-5, 13-17
Rus' Law: 3
Russia; Russians: 1, 2, 3, 12, 13, 15,
16, 17, 45, 122, 123, 124, 151,
200, 202, 213-224, 228, 229,
236, 237, 239
Russian Great Chronicle: 71, 81
Russkaia pravda: see the *Rus' Law*
Russkaia zemlia: 11, 12, 86
Rybakov, B.A.: 2

– S –

Salmina, M.A.: 81, 82, 83, 84
Sangushko, Roman, Ruthenian prince:
175, 176, 177
Sayin Bolgarskii, legendary Bulgar
ruler: 199
Selections from the Holy Writings: 87,
88
Sermon on Law and Grace: 3
Service Hymn: 27
Ševčenko, I.: 29

Severiany: see the "Northerners"
Shah-Ali, Khan of the Kazan Khanate:
192
Shakhmatov, A.A.: 69, 79, 80, 81, 83,
84, 213
Shakhovskoi, Semen Ivanovich,
Russian prince and author: 68
Shambinago, S.K.: 81
Sil'vestr, Archpriest of the
Annunciation Cathedral in the
Kremlin: 203, 204
Simeon of Suzdal', Russian author: 88
Simeonov Chronicle: 69, 79, 81, 83,
85, 90, 106, 108
Simeonovskaia letopis': see the
Simeonov Chronicle
Sineus, legendary ruler in Rus' (?):
195
Siniukha, river: 136
Siveria: 135, 142
Skazanie o chudesakh Vladimirskoi
Ikony Bozhiei Materi: see the
Narration about the Miracles of
the Vladimirian Icon of the Mother
of God
Skazanie o Mamaevom poboishche:
see the *Narration about Mamai's*
Battle
Skazanie o pobede nad Bolgarami: see
the *Narration about the Victory*
against the Bulgars
Skazanie o velikikh kniazekh
vladimerskikh velikia Russiia: see
the *Narration about the Grand*
Princes of Vladimir of Great
Russia
Slovo izbrano: see the *Selections from*
the Holy Writings
Slovo o zakone i blagodati: see the
Sermon on Law and Grace
Slovo o zhitii i o prestavlenii velikogo
kniazia Dmitriia Ivanovicha tsaria
rus'skago: 82

Slovo pokhval'noe o blagovernom velikom kniaze Borise Aleksandroviche: see the *Praise of Grand Prince Boris Aleksandrovich*
Sluzhba: see the *Service Hymn*
Smolensk; Smolenians: 5, 37, 38, 46, 47, 48, 56, 91, 92, 93, 142, 171
Snyvod', river: 136, 137
Sobolevskii, A.I.: 213
Sobornoe ulozhenie 1649 goda: see the *Muscovite Law Code of 1649*
Sofiiskaia pervaia letopis': see *Sophia First Chronicle*
Sofiiskaia vtoraia letopis': see *Sophia Second Chronicle*
Solov'ev, A.V.: 83
Solov'ev, S.M.: 1, 214
Sophia First Chronicle: 81, 82, 84
Sophia Palaeologue, wife of Grand Prince Ivan III of Moscow: 125
Sophia Second Chronicle: 110, 111
"Southerners": 1, 77, 213, 216
Speranskii, M.N.: 213
Spiridon-Savva, Russian cleric and author: 118, 119, 125, 126
Spuler, B.: 228
Sreznevskii, I.I.: 213, 216, 218
Starodub: 91
Stoglav of 1551: 233
"Stoianie na Ugre": see the "Vigil or the Ugra River"
Sudebnik 1497 goda: see the *Muscovite Law Code of 1497*
Sudebnik 1550 goda: see the *Muscovite Law Code of 1550*
Sushyts'kyi, T.: 136
Suzdalia-Vladimiria; Grand Principality of Suzdal'-Vladimir: 2, 5, 6, 7, 8, 11, 13, 16, 77, 85, 89, 105, 118
Suzdalian-Vladimirian Chronicles: 14, 22, 23, 31, 39, 45, 47-50, 52, 53, 54, 57, 58, 62, 69, 70, 215
Suzdal'; Suzdalian land; Suzdalians: 7, 8, 11, 12, 15, 21, 22, 23, 24, 25, 26, 30, 31, 45, 46, 47, 48, 49, 50, 53, 54, 55, 58, 63, 142
– Battle of: 81, 82
Suzdal'skaia letopis': see the *Suzdalian-Vladimirian Chronicles*
Suzdal'-Pereiaslav Chronicle: 52
Sviatopolk I Volodimerovich, Prince of Kiev: 8, 51, 82
Sviatopolk II Iziaslavich, Prince of Kiev: 8, 51
Sviatoslav I Igor'evich, Prince of Kiev: 8, 9, 51, 120, 124
Sviatoslav III of Chernihiv, Prince of Kiev: 9, 35
Sviiazhsk: 197
Świdrygiełło, Grand Prince of Lithuania: 164

– T –

Tale [Narration] about the Appearance and the Miracles of the Icon of the Mother of God of Kazan: 201, 202
Tale about the Battle on the Vorskla River: 140, 141
Tale about the Slaying of Andrei [Bogoliubskii]: 21, 24, 38-39, 56
Tale of Bygone Years: see the *Primary Chronicle*
Tale of Simeon of Suzdal': 87, 88
"Tatar Yoke": 132, 145
Tatars: 143, 223
– Crimean: 103-104, 108-109
– Kazanian: 82, 200, 201, 203
– Mongol: 9, 15, 62, 136, 138, 141-145, 236
Tatishchev, V.N.: 1, 214, 219
Temir Kutlu, Khan of the Golden Horde: 138
Tikhomirov, M.N.: 2
Tikhon, Archbishop of Rostov: 109, 110
Tipografskaia letopis': 109
Tmutorokan': 199
Tohtamış, Khan of the Golden Horde: 137-140, 144

Torks: 48
Trinity Chronicle: 68-72, 79-81, 83, 85
Troitse-Sergiev Monastery: 88
Troitskaia letopis': see the *Trinity Chronicle*
Truvor, legendary ruler in Rus' (?): 195
Tsar'grad; Tsesariagrad: 23, 54, 120, 123
Tsarstvennaia kniga: see the *Imperial Book*
Tver'; Grand Principality of Tver'; Tverians: 27, 62, 69, 91, 105, 117, 131, 141, 142, 229

– U –

"Ugorshchina": see the "Vigil on the Ugra River"
Ugro-Finnic tribes: 13, 15
Ukraine; *Ukraina*;Ukrainian Rus'; Ukrainian lands; Ukrainians: 1, 2, 3, 11, 13, 16, 17, 45, 67, 91, 94, 103-105, 117, 135-137, 143-144, 151-177, 213-224
Ulu Mehmet, Khan of the Kazan Khanate: 82, 139
Unova, river: 46

– V –

Varangians: 15, 90, 143
Vasiian Rylo, Muscovite ecclesiastic and author: 200
Vasilii I Dmitrievich, Grand Prince of Muscovy: 71
Vasilii II Vasil'evich, Grand Prince of Muscovy: 68, 82, 87, 88, 92
Vasilii III Ivanovich, Grand Prince of Muscovy: 117, 119, 122, 126, 141, 192, 231
Vazuza, river: 26
Velikie minei chetii: see the *Great Menology*
Venelin, Iu.: 216
Vernadsky, G.: 228
Ves': 90, 195

Viatichiians: 90
Victory against the Volga Bulgars: 198
"Vigil on the Ugra River": 108
Vistula land: 220
Vita (Zhitie) of Aleksandr Nevskii: 7, 58
Vita (Zhitie) of Dmitrii Ivanovich Donskoi: 82-89, 105, 117
Vita (Zhitie) of Metropolitan Aleksei:
– by Pitirim: 67
– by Pakhomii Logofet: 67
– by Evfimii: 67
Vita (Zhitie) of Metropolitan Petr: 63, 64, 67
Vitebsk: 134
Vladimir (on the Kliaz'ma River); Grand Principality of Vladimir; Vladimirians: 1, 6, 7, 12, 15, 21, 22, 23, 25, 26, 27, 29-33, 38, 39, 46, 47, 48, 53-55, 58, 62, 64, 70, 86,124, 126, 214
– Church of the Holy Mother of God (Dormition): 23, 26, 28, 33, 54
– Church of the Savior: 26
– Council of: 67
– Golden Gate of: 25-27, 39, 56
– Icon of Our Lady of: 6-7, 21, 22-25, 28, 54, 55; cult of: 27
– Metropolitanate of: 21, 28, 29, 32, 34, 55, 57-58, 62
Vladimirian Codex of 1177 (1178?) (hypothetical): 52
Vladimirian Codex of 1189 (hypothetical): 52
Vladimiro-Rostovskie letopisi: see the *Suzdalian-Vladimirian Chronicles*
Vladimiro-Suzdal'skaia letopis': see the *Suzdalian-Vladimirian Chronicles*
Vladymyrs'kyi-Budanov, M.F.: 213
Vodoff, W.: 29
Volga, river: 15, 194-196, 198
Volodimer I Sviatoslavich, St., Prince of Kiev: 5, 6, 8, 27, 51, 85, 86, 87, 90, 105, 117, 120, 122, 126, 196, 197, 198
– New Constantine: 85

Volodimer II Vsevolodovich Mono-
  makh, Prince of Kiev: 5, 8, 51,
  118, 120-124, 197, 214, 237
Volodimer III Mstislavich, Prince of
  Kiev: 9, 35, 52
Volodimer IV Riurikovich, Prince of
  Kiev: 9, 52
Volodimer Andreievich of
  Dorohobuzh, prince: 46, 47
Volodimer Glebovich of Pereiaslav,
  prince: 47
Volodymyr-Volyns'kyi: 10, 46, 47,
  134
Vologda: 107
Vologda-Perm Chronicle: 89, 106,
  107, 109
Vologodsko-Permskaia letopis': see the
  Vologda-Perm Chronicle
Volynia; Volynian land; Volynians:
  136, 143, 151-177, 216
Voronin, N.N.: 24, 29
Vorskla, river: 138
  –   Battle on: 132, 138-141
Voskresensk Chronicle: 71, 80
Voskresenskaia letopis': see the
  Voskresensk Chronicle
Votchina: see Patrimony
Vozha, river, Battle on: 132, 144
Vsevolod I Iaroslavich, Prince of
  Kiev: 8, 51, 120, 122, 124
Vsevolod II of Chernihiv, Prince of
  Kiev: 9, 52
Vsevolod III Iur'evich, Prince of
  Suzdal'-Vladimir: 6, 7, 8, 11, 32,
  46, 49, 58, 90
Vynnytsia: 164
Vyshhorod: 21-27, 37, 38, 46, 47, 53-
  56
  –   Icon of Our Lady of: 21-25,
    54, 55
Vytautas (Witold), Grand Prince of
  Lithuania-Ruthenia: 136-143, 163
Vytenis (Viten), Grand Prince of
  Lithuania: 133

– W –

Warsaw, Diet of 1563-1564: 164
  – Diet of 1570: 158
  – Diet of 1572: 174
Wilno, Diet of 1563: 174
  – Diet of 1566: 157
Władysław Jagielłończyk, King of
  Hungary: 92

– Z –

Zadonshchina: see the *Battle beyond
  the Don River*
Zagriazskii, Dmitrii Davidovich,
  Muscovite envoy: 91
Zapadno-russkie letopisi: see the
  Lithuanian-Ruthenian Chronicles
Zemskii sobor: see the *Assembly of the
  Land*
Zhdanov, I.N.: 119, 125
Zhitiie Leontiia Rostovskogo: see the
  Life of Leontii of Rostov
Zhytets'kyi, P.H.: 213
Zimin, A.A.: 119
Zygmunt I, King of Poland: 173
Zygmunt II August, King of Poland:
  93, 154, 173, 174, 175
Zygmunt Kiejstutowicz, Grand Prince
  of Lithuania: 159, 161, 163, 164

ABOUT THE AUTHOR

Jaroslaw Pelenski is Professor of Russian, Soviet, and East Central European history at the University of Iowa. He holds doctorates from Munich University (1957) and Columbia University (1968). He is the author of the book *Russia and Kazan: Conquest and Imperial Ideology, 1438-1560s* (1974) and over two hundred articles, essays, book chapters, and reviews on Russian, Ukrainian, Polish, and Mongol-Turkic topics. He is also the editor of *The American and European Revolutions, 1776-1848* (1980), *State and Society in Europe from the Fifteenth to the Eighteenth Century* (1985), *The Political and Social Ideas of Vjačeslav Lypyns'kyi* (1985/1987), *Viacheslav Lypyns'kyi: Historical-Political Legacy and Contemporary Ukraine* (in Ukrainian, 1994), and *Pavlo Skoropads'kyi, Memoirs* (in Russian, 1995); the general editor of the collected works of Viacheslav Lypyns'kyi and co-editor of six books, among them *Ukraine and Russia in Their Historical Encounter* (1992) and *Belarus, Lithuania, Poland, Ukraine: The Foundations of Historical and Cultural Traditions in East Central Europe* (1994). In addition, he has served as editor of the journal *Vidnova (Revival)* (1984-1987), is a member of the editorial board of several learned journals in Russia, Ukraine, and Poland, and has organized nine international historical and politological conferences. Since 1987 he has been president of the V.K. Lypyns'kyi East European Research Institute in Philadelphia, and since 1993 the director of the East European Research Institute of the National Academy of Science of Ukraine in Kiev. He is a foreign member (academician) of the National Academy of Science of Ukraine (since 1992); a member of the Polish-Ukrainian Historical Commission, sponsored jointly by the Polish Academy of Sciences and the National Academy of Sciences of Ukraine (appointed in 1993); and a member of the Bureau of the Division of History, Philosophy, and Law (Social Sciences), National Academy of Sciences of Ukraine (since 1994).